FFORUM

Essays on Theory
and Practice
in the
Teaching of Writing

FFORUM

Essays on Theory
and Practice
in the
Teaching of Writing

Edited by

PATRICIA L. STOCK

BOYNTON/COOK PUBLISHERS, INC.

Library of Congress Cataloging in Publication Data

Main entry under title:

Fforum—essays on theory and practice in the
    teaching of writing.

    Bibliography: p.
    1. English language—Rhetoric—Study and teaching—
Addresses, essays, lectures. I. Stock, Patricia L.
II. Fforum.
PE1404.F4 1983   808'.042'07   82-24490
ISBN 0-86709-089-8

For information address Boynton/Cook Publishers, Inc.
P.O. Box 860, 52 Upper Montclair Plaza,
Upper Montclair, New Jersey 07043

ISBN: 0-86709-089-8

Printed in the United States of America

    84   85   86   87   10   9   8   7   6   5   4   3   2

Preface

In June 1979 together with 125 other teachers from elementary and secondary schools, colleges, and universities throughout the state of Michigan, I attended the first in a series of annual workshops sponsored by The English Composition Board (ECB) of the University of Michigan. All of us who gathered in Ann Arbor that June shared both a common concern—we wanted to learn to teach writing more effectively—and a common experience: During the previous year, we had each participated in seminars on theory and practice in the teaching of writing conducted by the ECB at our individual schools. In the closing plenary session of our intense three days of talk and writing about the teaching of writing, one of the workshop leaders, Bernie Van't Hul, suggested that we continue our mutual discussion and instruction in a newsletter.

After accepting an invitation to become that newsletter's first editor, I envisioned its resemblance to the Roman forum and the Greek agora before it— marketplaces which fostered the practices of public business and open discussions in their respective societies. When Bernie Van't Hul recalled the practice of another age in which some scribes used double letters to serve as capital letters, the ECB's twentieth-century *fforum* was named both to remind those of us who would teach writing of the historical legacy of our profession and to lead us toward the promising future of a field of study coming to new understanding of itself.

As I set out to ask theorists, researchers, critics, and teachers to contribute essays for publication in the newsletter, I felt uncertain and insecure. But my anxieties were quickly dispelled. My first two calls were to Ken Macrorie and Ed Corbett, teachers who need no introduction to teachers of writing anywhere. Both were not only willing but pleased to address a small group of their colleagues in Michigan whose dialogue about the teaching of writing had begun with the ECB in 1978. And ever since its fortunate first issue in October 1979 *fforum* has continued to be nurtured by contributions from experts who have written informatively and concisely, as well as with clarity and grace. In just three years, their essays have attracted a readership of more than two thousand teachers from every state in the Union.

During the Spring of 1982, I asked the teachers who wrote the essays for *fforum* which especially bespoke my own convictions if they would permit me to collect their essays in this anthology, *fforum: Essays on Theory and Practice in the Teaching of Writing.* At the same time, I invited them to expand the necessarily brief essays they had originally written for *fforum* if they wished to do so. The varying lengths of the essays gathered here testify to the fact that some of the teachers decided to accept my invitation.

I believed in the Spring of 1982, and I believe now, that the chorus of voices in one setting could argue—as could no one voice alone—that writing is a complex and dynamic language act that can neither be taught by prescription nor learned quickly. I want to thank those teachers for making this book possible. And I want to recommend the approaches to the teaching of writing (and reading) they describe here to all teachers, in all disciplines, as they plan programs and practices for educating young people.

I also want to express my gratitude to a special group of people who have been extraordinarily helpful to me during the preparation of this book:

- to Bob Root for composing the annotated bibliography for this collection and for making it so rich a source of information for pre-service and in-service teachers;
- to Barbara Couture, Karen Wixson, Toby Fulwiler, and Steve Bernhardt for joining me in writing the essays which conclude each section of the book, for identifying common issues and themes in the collection, and for giving it character and integrity as they spoke their own minds about the teaching of writing;
- to Steve Bernhardt for reading every essay in this collection, for advising me about its shape at every stage of its composition, for giving the collection closure;
- to Ed Corbett for suggesting this book a long time ago;
- to Margaret Stephens for reading this manuscript and offering advice;
- to Teri Adams, Vicki Davinich, Dorothy La Barr, and Carol Thiry for transforming teachers' essays into the typed, bound, delivered newsletter that led the way to this book;
- to Teri Adams for her personal commitment to *fforum,* its readers, and this book, all along the way;
- to Dave Oliver for the look of *fforum* and this book;
- to Grace Rueter for all kinds of help given only as a friend can give help;
- to Bob Boynton for wisdom, courage, and service to our profession and for good advice to me;
- to Jay Robinson for his generosity and good counsel;
- and especially to Richard for encouraging me to *do fforum* in the first place, and to Heidi and Andrew for their interest, their pride, and their helping hands.

Contents

This book is for two teachers: Bernie Van't Hul, who is responsible for so much of what is good in it, and Dan Fader, who makes it possible for those who work with him to pursue their own best ideas.

Introduction

Historians of literacy agree that writing was invented to extend the limits of human memory and to enable people to communicate over distance and time; that it has contradictorily contributed to both the stratification of social groups and the democratization of societies, depending upon how individuals, once literate, practice their literacy; and that in spawning science, technology, and the proliferation of knowledge, it has divided people within cultures into specialized and separated communities. Critics of literacy might be expected to give it mixed reviews because it has provided not only the benefits for which it was originally invented, but also its share of human afflictions. However much expected, such mixed reviews do not exist, because literacy has become the most powerful technology of the intellect known to human kind.

As people write to record their experience, they compose their experience in language that can be contemplated, embellished, discarded, reorganized, and refined. To write is to shape thought in human speech and to suspend it in physical space so that it may be grasped. How effectively individuals use writing—this consummate human invention—depends both upon their diligence and the opportunities their society provides for its use.

The implications of these facts of literacy for those of us who teach are serious: to teach our students to write is not only to teach them the most powerful means of learning we know and to provide them occasions for its employment, but is also to provide them a means of communication based in human speech and realized in the capacity of the human mind. That is why I believe that all teachers of all subjects must be teachers of literacy, and that is why this book is shaped to invite teachers at all levels to reflect upon the nature and value of writing and reading (Chapter 1, "On Literacy "); upon the unique features and functions of writing as compared with the other language acts of speaking, listening, and reading (Chapters 2 and 3, "On Speaking and Writing" and "On Reading and Writing"); and upon the significance of writing as a heuristic for learning and a medium for communication (Chapters 4 and 5, "On Writing as a Way of Learning" and "On Writing and Rhetoric").

FFORUM

Essays on Theory and Practice in the Teaching of Writing

1.

On Literacy

In this chapter, teachers of the humanities, the social sciences, the natural sciences, medicine, and the law explore the social context within which we teachers of literacy meet our students and do our work. Furthermore, they provide us a context within which to read the essays collected in succeeding chapters.

In the first two essays, Robinson and Lakoff explore the myths and realities that define literacy in our time. Coles and Bailey follow, providing not only an overview of contemporary concern about teaching of literacy, but also critical commentary of contemporary practices for both the teaching of reading and writing and the evaluation of students' ability to read and write in Great Britain and the United States.

In the next three essays teachers recommend specific methods for teaching literacy. Rueter and Dunn encourage English teachers to teach a variety of literatures in their classes as a means of building bridges between disciplines traditionally isolated from one another by technical training and specialized uses of language. Siegel argues that physicians, like writers, must learn the uses of language and metaphor which structure and shape the consciousness of observant, sympathetic human beings. And White argues that instruction in specialized literacies such as the literacy of the law should be part of the general education of everyone who lives in a society such as ours where specialized discourse systems abound.

In a pair of essays, Clark and Barritt remind us that our practices as teachers of literacy must be firmly rooted in the purposes and settings of our work. Clark maintains that the methods and criteria we use to evaluate our students' literacy—specifically their writing—must grow out of the purposes for which we ask them to write as well as the contexts in which they write. Barritt urges us to join together to look at those problems of our practice which interest us as teachers of literacy and to let those problems define the research methods we use to study them.

Finally, in the last essay in this chapter, I reflect upon the other essays as I describe one faculty's efforts to develop a comprehensive program for teaching literacy to its students.

1 The Social Context of Literacy

Jay L. Robinson
Department of English, The University of Michigan

This essay, like most in the genre, has its roots in experiences—past, past continuous, and even future since anticipation works on one's mind. Past are seven years as an English Department Chairman; past and continuing is my work with the English Composition Board at The University of Michigan helping to develop a writing program for undergraduates; and in my future is a chairmanship of a Ph.D. program in English and Education. All of these, lumped together with reading that a sabbatical has allowed me to do, have provoked me to think about the topics addressed in these pages: how literacy functions (and does not function) in our society; how society influences what we do as learners and teachers of literacy.

It is important to discuss the social context of literacy for several reasons, some of them perfectly obvious. It is obvious, for example, that teaching—any teaching—takes place only in some one or another social context: We teach something to somebody some place at some particular time in some particular society. What we do is influenced not only by the *what,* but also by the *where, when,* and *to whom.* It is also obvious, when we think about it, that the teaching of literacy is especially sensitive to the pressures of social context. Language in all of its uses is an intimate part of human experience: Language is expressive of identity and personality, but it is also socially binding and expressive of collective values. Written language is peculiarly public, more so than speech, and as a consequence its forms are carefully scrutinized; reading and writing are highly valued activities and society monitors their acquisition—as we know from myriad articles in the public media about Johnnies and Janes who can't read or write. We teachers of literacy meet students in a charged atmosphere. We need to be sensitive to the prevailing currents, if for no other purpose than to avoid electrocution.

A compelling reason for talking about the social context for literacy is that our profession has usually avoided the subject in spite of its importance, leaving it to sociologists, sociolinguists, and social historians. Let me cite just one example, borrowed from an essay by Frank D'Angelo (*Literacy for Life,* forthcoming). Richard Ohmann, when he was Editor of *College English,* requested manuscripts for a special issue on the publicly proclaimed literacy crisis. This was his challenge to his colleagues:

> Is there a decline in literacy? in writing ability? If so, what are its causes? To what extent is it accountable to changes in schooling? To changes in American society? What can—or should—college English teachers be doing about it? Are there college programs that successfully make up deficits in verbal skills? Is "bonehead English" an idea whose time has come again? Do competency requirements for graduation help? Should this be a problem of the English department, or the whole college or university? Can we distinguish between the traditional basics—spelling, usage, etc.—and some others that have more to do with intellectual competence? Can English teachers usefully shape the

national concern with verbal competence, rather than simply respond to
needs expressed by pundits, legislators, regents, and businessmen?

If, on the other hand, there has been no significant decline in reading or
writing ability among college students, what explains the outcry? What can
English teachers do to correct public misconceptions? Is our responsibility
confined to the classroom, or does it include social and political action?
(1976, p. 819).

Ohmann asked us to look at the social dimensions of the literacy crisis and at
the social meaning of the public's concern; to decide whether or not a crisis
existed and to discover its causes; and only then to reach decisions about how to
deal with it. But when the special issue of *College English* appeared, Ohmann
published his disappointment with the contributions:

A large proportion merely reiterated the public concerns and in terms very
similar to those employed by the media. Others devoted most of their energy
to suggesting better ways to teach writing. We might infer from these facts
that the profession accepts not only the public assessment of the literacy
"crisis" but also the blame for it. Our original call queries whether in fact
there has been a significant decline in reading and writing ability among students. Yet not one contribution reviewed and analyzed in any detail the
assumptions, methods, and statistics of the testing on which so much of the
public outcry seems to be based. Are these assumptions, methods, and
statistics as invulnerable to criticism as our professional silence suggests?
(1977, p. 44).

Nastier questions than Ohmann's last can be put: Does our profession's silence
on such topics suggest that we are willing to let others tell us what to do and
then develop methods for getting it done better or more efficiently? Does our
silence imply contentment with the status quo? The world may well need a
better rat trap, but does it really need a better sentence combiner?

A fact of life in our world is that the possession of literacy correlates almost
perfectly with the possession of power and wealth. And in general, the more
literacy one has or can control, the more power one can exercise—real power,
not something metaphorical like the power of self-expression. Now I intend no
causative implication in the statement; to achieve literacy does not necessarily
earn one power, as we well know. But the powerful are usually themselves
literate, or if not, they can purchase the services of those who are.

Another fact of life in our world is that the *profession* of literacy, as contrasted with its possession, correlates not with power and wealth but with
relative powerlessness and relative poverty. English teachers do not exert much
influence in the world of raw power, even though they live and work in it. The
humanities, when compared with the sciences, the social sciences, or professional
schools, are under-funded both within their own institutions and nationally, and
humanists are under-represented both in academic governance and in government.

These facts of our own social existence are more than unpleasant, they are
dangerous. The danger is not to our persons, yours and mine, nor even to our

sense of personal worth. The danger is rather to our profession—to our collective sense of endeavor and to the ethics we apply in the teaching of literacy. We have or can claim to have two things useful to those who possess power—namely, the ability to make students literate and squatting rights in classrooms where literacy is assumed to be taught. But as poor cousins, we are particularly vulnerable both to the temptations of utility (we call it service), and to the temptations of the money that pays for our services. Methods can be endlessly adjusted to ends and aims, to the aims and ends of others as easily as to our own. And what if our academic discipline does not enjoy intellectual prestige? We can always try to achieve status by borrowing prestigious theory and adapting it to the demand for new methods. But when we do, does the right brain always know what the left brain is doing?

I am oversimplifying and being facetious, and with issues that are neither simple nor funny. We do have a responsibility to the society that sustains us, and at least equal responsibility to students whose pragmatic needs must be met. But we can meet these responsibilities only if we understand at least something of the social context in which literacy presently functions.

What kinds of things constitute the social context of literacy in our time? More than I can mention, of course, but I will touch on these four: First, on inherited conceptions of literacy and the values we attach to them; second, on real and socially perceived needs for literacy; third, on ideal and ethnically conceived needs for literacy; and fourth, on some few of our institutions for the fostering of literacy.

Inherited Concepts and Values

Practice is always rooted in concepts even when the concepts are unstated or even unstatable; and what we practice most energetically is that which we value most highly. The *concept* of literacy is highly valued in our own as in other Western and Westernized industrial societies. Historians, recognizing this special phenomenon, are now writing about a "literacy myth"—a configuration of generally held and privileged notions about literacy and its functions in modern society. Harvey J. Graff, for example:

> The rise of literacy and its dissemination to the popular classes is associated with the triumph of light over darkness, of liberalism, democracy, and of universal unbridled progress. In social thought, therefore, these elements relate to ideas of linear evolution and progression; literacy here takes its place among the other successes of modernity and rationality. In theory and in empirical investigation, literacy is conceptualized—often in stark and simple fashion—as an important part of the larger parcel of factors that account for the evolution of modern societies and states (p. xv).

With its wide acceptance, the literacy myth benefits us poor cousins, of course. Foundations fund our programs, deans find money for English departments, enlightened school boards reduce loads for writing teachers (though rarely), and in general our public and professional stock rises. In the short run, we prosper;

but we might be better off in the longer run if we try to find out how much truth the myth contains and then act on that. What we inherit is not always to our good.

Robert Disch, in his introduction to *The Future of Literacy* writes that:

the twentieth century inherited a mystique of literacy born out of . . . two tendencies. One, essentially utilitarian, was committed to the functional uses of literacy as a medium for the spread of practical information that could lead to individual and social progress; the other, essentially aesthetic and spiritual, was committed to the uses of literacy for salvaging the drooping spirit of Western man from the death of religion and the ravages of progress (p. 3).

The utilitarian benefits of literacy, so goes the myth, are economic, social, and intellectual. Economic benefits include enhanced access to employment and to information leading to a better life (for example, information about birth control or about sanitation). Social benefits include a broadening of personal perspective beyond the tribal or local; acquisition of societal norms and values leading to public spiritedness; participation in democratic means of governance. Claims for the intellectual benefits of literacy have gone beyond the obvious ones of access to stored knowledge to stronger ones asserting a causal relation between literacy and general learning as well as between literacy and full cognitive development.[1] How many of these claims correspond to established fact?

In fact, we do not know, but in some few cases we are beginning to find out. And what we are discovering, when the myth is tested, is that it proves to be mythical. For only one example, consider the following results of historical research into the correlations of literacy with liberalized social attitudes and with expanded economic opportunity. In a study of literacy in Colonial New England, Kenneth A. Lockridge (1974) found that Protestantism was a stronger impetus to literacy than secular school laws; that schools were dominated by conservative, not progressive, educational impulses; and that when literacy became nearly universal in New England near the end of the 18th century, attitudes toward society and the larger world were not discernibly modified. In another study, treating some 19th century Canadian cities, Harvey Graff found that:

. . . literacy—a phenomenon suggestive of equality—contributed regularly as an element of the structure of inequality, reinforcing the steep ridges of stratification, and also as a force for order and integration. It also served as a symbolic focus of other forces of inequality: ethnicity, class, sex, and age. Literacy, then, did not universally serve to benefit all who had attained it, but neither did it disadvantage all those who had not (p. 19).

Graff does not claim that literacy holds no potential for liberalization; rather he demonstrates that powerful, deeply embedded social forces can override its potential. Literacy can be an effective means of social control, when educational institutions use it for this purpose; or it can be a means of social liberation, when individuals are encouraged to think, read and write for themselves. Ohmann presses the pertinent question: Where do we stand as teachers when we emphasize means over ends or methods over purposes? In answering the question, we do well to be mindful that ours is a society that has sanctioned a back-to-basics movement, that is enamored with competency testing, and that presently values vocational over liberal education. Few vocations in our society encourage an exercise of literacy that is liberalizing and liberating.

Even if all of our students were to achieve literacy, not all would benefit unless allowed and encouraged by society to put their competencies to use. Our aims and especially our methods have to accommodate to this brute fact of social reality. We need to know much more than we now do about the forces and institutions in our society that constrain literacy, both those that inhibit its exercise and those that make it serve as an instrument of unconscious socialization to mores and values we would not endorse. Without such knowledge, we could well help create a reality more malignant than that figured in the literacy myth.

Real and Socially Perceived Needs for Literacy

So far I have been talking about literacy as a "buzz word"—as a concept or a symbol incorporating notions of aspiration and value. Now I want to define the term, or at least to limit its reference. Let *literacy* mean *functional literacy;* and let *functional literacy,* for the moment, mean only this: the ability to read and write well enough to compete for economic sufficiency. Such literacy is essential for all students and for all citizens, and insofar as we are able and insofar as social circumstances will allow, we must help provide it. I quote some experts on the demographics of literacy:

Ralph W. Tyler: In 1800, the unskilled in all categories [of employment] comprised more than 80 percent of the labor force; in 1900 they made up 60 percent and in 1980, about 6 percent. The rapid development of employment in the various services . . . has largely taken place since 1948. Now, jobs requiring no schooling are few in number while tasks requiring at least a high school education make up nearly two thirds of employment opportunities (*Literacy for Life,* forthcoming).

Paul A. Stassman: Since the 1950's our country has become predominantly occupied with the creation, distribution, and administration of information. By 1990 about fifty percent of the workforce will not be producing food or manufacturing objects; instead the workforce will occupy most of its time just communicating (*Literacy for Life,* forthcoming).

Arthur M. Cohen and Florence B. Brawer: Literacy is certainly related to success in nearly all community college programs: transfer courses demand proficiency in reading, writing and/or mathematics, and licensure examinations admitting students to practice after completing a technological program are closed to students who cannot pass an entrance examination that is based on literacy (*Literacy for Life,* forthcoming).

Robben W. Fleming: Meanwhile, it is estimated that there may be as many as 57 million adult illiterates in the United States (*Literacy for Life,* forthcoming).

John Oxenham: In 1971, some 780 million people over the age of fifteen all over the world were classed as illiterate. . . . by 1980 they will total perhaps 820 million (p. 2).

Functional illiteracy does correlate with poverty and powerlessness; the problem of illiteracy is as urgent as any in our society.

But ironically, the needs of the poor could well be forgotten because recently we have discovered other needs among the better-off and the more influential. We have discovered that middle-class students don't write very well, not even those who enroll in prestigious schools; that businessmen don't write very well, or at least don't think that they do; that bureaucrats and lawyers write even worse; that the new information-society requires a new kind of literacy—in software, rather than in ordinary printed language. The *influential* public is now more often asking "Why can't Johnny write?" than it is "Why can't Johnny read?" Yet as Edward Corbett so accurately points out, reading is far more important for economic sufficiency (even for survival) than is writing:

> . . . writing will never be as crucial a skill for surviving or thriving in our society as reading is. Functional illiterates who cannot even write their names may suffer embarrassment because of their deficiency but they somehow manage to subsist in our technological society. But those functional illiterates who cannot even read street signs and simple directions are so severely handicapped that it is questionable whether they can survive, much less thrive, in our society. Thirdly, only a minuscule portion of the total population will regularly have to compose important, influential documents. The majority of literate people have to do some writing occasionally—letters, notes, fill-in-the blanks forms—but only a minority have to write regularly and seriously in connection with their jobs (1981, p. 47).

The present emphasis upon writing over reading doubtless reflects a bias in favor of the upper of our social classes, where needs take precedence. If not restrained or balanced against the need for reading, the bias could well contribute to a widening of the gulf between rich and poor that now seems so permanent a feature of our national topography. As Richard Hendrix writes:

> The emphasis on writing clarifies the gap between a commitment in principle to universal opportunity and the fact of unequal opportunity. Writing ability is unevenly distributed in our society along class lines. Indeed, writing and access to writing improvement is as good an indicator of the difference between, say, white collar and blue collar career tracks as we are likely to find (p. 53).

Our problems are made more difficult to solve because just when we begin to recognize the number and complexity of them, the public develops an aversion to taxation and politicians a preference for bombs over books. How, then, are we to react to the perfectly legitimate demands placed upon us in our social role as teachers of literacy when we know that resources will be limited—perhaps severely?

We could, of course, take battlefield medicine as our model and practice triage on some principle of social utility, fitting our teaching to present social realities and comforting ourselves with some resigned but basically optimistic notion of social inevitability. Maybe only a minority do need to learn to write; maybe the masses need only to learn to read, and then only marginally; and maybe, because of technology, the masses don't even need to read. And maybe the socially disintegrating effects of such specialization could be avoided if some such vision of social interdependence as John Oxenham's is an accurate one:

> [F] or the masses to enjoy literature without literacy, a minority would need to be highly literate. The paradox evokes two reflections on technological change. One is that, as science and technology introduce new changes in production and services, a growing majority with decreasing skills seems to become increasing: dependent on a highly skilled but shrinking minority. The trend appears to lead to a dictatorship of technocrats. On the other hand, while a necessary consequence of the extension of specialization may well be the dependence of majorities upon minorities, oppressive technology is not the necessary end. The reason is simply that the proliferation of specializations generates a net of interdependence and a homeostatic distribution of power (p. 131).

Perhaps a stable and healthy interdependence can result from a planned distribution of the assets of literacy. Perhaps we can focus our attention and concentrate our resources upon training a fully literate elite without oppressing the masses. Perhaps that is what we are doing anyway, without much thought for the masses.

There is nothing of the conditional in these two assertions: Resources will be limited as we seek to meet needs for literacy; priorities will be set—either by us or by others, either by intention or through thoughtless inertia. Policy should be at least as well-planned as good writing. Right now we need good policy more than better lesson plans.

Ideals and Ethics

In June 1980 the English Composition Board of the University of Michigan sponsored a conference on "Literacy in the 1980's." Experts from various occupations and professions were invited to the conference and asked to respond to this question: "What will be the needs for literacy in your field as we look from now toward the end of the century?" As I review the conference, two presentations stand out: one by a lawyer and professor of law; another by a scientist who is also Manager of the Central Research Division of the Mobil Research and Development Corporation. These two impressed me because they called not for more emphasis upon utilitarian writing (and reading), but for a more expansive and humane literacy.

James White, Professor of Law at the University of Chicago and the author of a distinguished book on lawyers' use of language, described what he calls "the invisible discourse of the law":

> unstated conventions by which the language [of law] operates . . . expectations that do not find explicit expression anywhere but are part of the legal culture that the surface language simply assumes (this volume, pp. 48-49).

But White did more than describe. First, he enriched existing definitions of (functional) literacy:

I start with the idea that literacy is not merely the capacity to understand the conceptual content of writings and utterances, but the ability to participate fully in a set of social and intellectual practices. It is not passive but active; not imitative but creative, for participation in the speaking and writing of language includes participation in the activities it makes possible (this volume, p.56).

Then he described a course in writing and reading that he teaches in The University of Chicago, which invites such participation. White helps his students to perceive how rule and procedure constitute social organization and govern social cooperation; how language is the means of such constitution; and how law is related to everyday social behavior. In so doing he demystifies the law, making it more subject both to lay understanding and to personal control. According to White:

All this [can] be done with materials from the students' own life, without the use of legal terms or technicalities. It need not even be done in Standard English: the students' writing . . . should indeed reflect the way people actually speak in their own world. And one important lesson for us all might be the discovery that it is not only in the law, or only in the language of the white middle class, that community is constituted or that argument about justice proceeds (this volume, p. 58).

Paul Weisz, a scientist and businessman, called for clarity and broad comprehensibility in scientific language: for the development and use in science of a common language enabling more citizens "to benefit from the knowledge which abounds around us," a language that would also serve to combat the socially and intellectually fragmenting effects of specialization. He sees the need as essential:

The relationship between division of knowledge in our society and presence of social tension is clear. As knowledge and activity become more sophisticated, the bridges of understanding and interaction grow weaker and weaker. Now, more than ever before, such bridges are needed for both social and psychological survival (*Literacy for Life,* forthcoming).

Weisz's concern echoes that expressed in the recent report of the Rockefeller Commission on the Humanities:

Our citizens need to become literate in a multiple sense. We all need to understand the characteristics of scientific inquiry and the repercussions of scientific research. We must all learn something about the use of the media and of new technologies for storing, transmitting, and expanding knowledge. Without this sort of literacy, our society as a whole will be less able to apply science and technology to humanistic needs, less able to measure the human effects of scientific achievements, less able to judge the information we produce and receive (*The Humanities,* 1980, pp. 18-19).

Our profession has begun to recognize that its own notions about needs for literacy do not always match day-to-day needs outside the classroom. But most who have argued for adjustment to the real world have addressed only economic needs. White and Weisz, both practitioners in the world of work, suggest other ways: White by linking language use with social behavior and to intellectual activity rooted in social practices; Weisz by linking the aims of writing with a democracy's needs for information and knowledge essential for the solution of human problems. Both programs are *ethical* in conception.

Caesar exacts his due, but we need not pay the tax-master so unthinkingly as to leave in his control all decisions about what social reality ought to be. Societies exist in the mind as well as in fact, in ethical standards for behavior as well as in behavior patterns. It is our particular obligation as teachers of literacy to recognize this, and with our students' help to frame ideals constructive of a world we would willingly inhabit. Ideals and ethics find their most permanent expression in public language.

Institutions: Who Teaches the What to Whom?

Existing institutions, like inherited concepts and values, are part of the social context for literacy. As things are now established, we English teachers are the ones customarily assumed to be responsible for teaching literacy (along with elementary school teachers, who can do anything). But given existing and shifting needs for literacy, it is not at all clear that we will continue to be held responsible or considered responsible enough to be so held.

In an article in a volume containing the proceedings of a conference sponsored by the National Institute of Education, Richard Hendrix—who is associated with the Fund for the Improvement of Postsecondary Education—asks this question: "Who is responsible for improving writing?" He says this about English departments:

> Writing instruction was for years a stepchild of English departments, who have always dominated it. As recently as fifteen years ago many colleges dropped composition altogether—partly on the basis that the high schools were handling the job, and mainly to give still greater emphasis to literary study. That development should make us hesitate about trusting that English departments, as they are presently constituted, will solve the problem.
>
> Now there has been a resurgence of active involvement by English faculty along with others. Writing instruction could be a boon for underemployed humanists, a large and influential group. But teachers trained in literature may not necessarily be well situated to work with beginning students, nor to prepare students for the kinds of writing tasks they will likely face after school. English professors are not even necessarily good writers themselves, and their commitment to specialization has been at least as strong as any other discipline's (p. 56).

There are grounds for Hendrix's suspicion. They exist in the prevailing attitudes of most college and many high school English teachers toward the teaching of writing; in the way composition teachers are treated in their own departments;

and in the way composition programs are funded, staffed, and managed. And in the meantime societal needs are not being met, neither by instructional programs that address vocational needs nor by research programs that address the need for better understanding of the relations of literacy to society, to learning, and to the determination of value. Can and will English departments change enough to meet such needs? My own experiences as a teacher of writing, as a program planner, and as an English department chairman, give me grounds for doubt at least as strong as that expressed by Hendrix.

The trouble with literacy is that it enters all aspects of human life in literate societies. The trouble with questions about literacy is that the important ones are general in their application to human discourse and its functions. The trouble with our answers, when we are English teachers, is that we are all specialists. And it is possible—at the least arguable—that a specialization in literature is less adaptable than many to a broad understanding of literacy.

Raymond Williams, in a challenging critique of dominant trends in literary study, reminds us that the term *literature* once applied more broadly than to imaginative works of a certain kind and quality. In one of its earlier usages, "it was often close to the sense of modern *literacy*"; its reference was to "a condition of reading: of being able to read and of having read" (pp. 45–54). Histories, biographies, works of philosophy, political and scientific treatises were once all works of literature. In his argument, Williams traces the specialization of the term to the domain of "creative" or "imaginative" works, and the development of literature departments in academies as units concerned exclusively with this narrowed domain and with the practice of criticism.

The problem arising from this development is that it invites us, as inheritors of the tradition, to equate "literacy" with knowledge of a special kind of literature, without recognizing that such an equation is a socially privileged and economically self-serving one: more a matter of status and value than of fact. The study of imaginative literature may well contribute to the complex of abilities, capacities, and attitudes that function in good reading and good writing; but to claim that it necessarily and sufficiently does is patently absurd.

If departments of English continue to define themselves as departments of literature and mean by that term imaginative works only, and if English teachers restrict themselves to reading only such works and commentaries on them, then there is need for new kinds of departments just as there is for differently prepared teachers. Harvey Graff gets to the heart of the problem:

> Discussions of literacy are confused and ambiguous—an ironic, and even startling, phenomenon, which contrasts sharply with the high value we assign to the skills of reading and writing. Vagueness pervades virtually all efforts to discern the meaning of literacy; moreover, there is surprisingly little agreement on or special evidence for the benefits of literacy, whether socially or individually, economically or culturally. Rather, assumptions preempt criticism and investigation, and agencies and specialists whose business it is to promote literacy shrink from asking fundamental questions in their campaigns to disseminate skills (p. 3).

Certain questions cannot be avoided any longer. Serious research is needed into literacy and its place in our present social context, and such research should take precedence over concern with method. There is little profit in trying to do better what cannot or should not be done.

Notes

[1] These last claims are now much in the literature, especially the literature justifying writing programs. Before believing them completely, teachers and administrators should read the very important book by Sylvia Scribner and Michael Cole, *The Psychology of Literacy* (Cambridge, Mass.: Harvard University Press, 1981).

2   Literacy in a Non-literate Age

Robin Tolmach Lakoff
Department of Linguistics, University of California at Berkeley

Writing skills, like most other academic skills, tend to be taught locally: they are taught in terms of sentence structure—or at a slightly more abstract level—in terms of cohesive devices and narrative strategies. While teaching these skills is necessary, it can be argued that by concentrating on teaching them, one loses a sense of the issues that underlie the real problem for teachers of writing: Why has writing (and reading, for that matter) become so hard to learn? Perhaps it is time to take a global, more abstract, look at the problem, to ask broader questions such as: What is it like to write—as opposed to talking? What is the purpose of communicating in writing? What function does literate communication play in our lives and in our cultural consciousness today? What are the benefits of literacy?

It is worthwhile to point out that, just as the human race has not been literate from its beginnings, neither has it been in agreement about the virtues of the written medium since the advent of literacy. Indeed, it is often noted that Plato, only a couple of centuries after literacy had been introduced into Greece, wrote into the voice of Socrates words about literacy that sound remarkably like the words of contemporary commentators about non-literate communication:

> The fact is that this invention [writing] will produce forgetfulness in the souls of those who have learned it. They will not need to exercise their memories, being able to rely on what is written, calling things to mind no longer from within themselves by their own unaided powers but under the stimulus of external marks that are alien to themselves. . . . And as for wisdom, you're equipping your pupils with only a semblance of it, not with truth.
> (*Phaedrus*, 275).

Plato's dour view soon gave way to another, which prevails into the present day. More often implicitly than explicitly, we feel that literature and literacy are unequivocally good, that literacy is an essential skill, valuable for its own sake, a mark of a person's—or a culture's—entry into true civilization. This view was expressed long ago by Cicero:

But these pursuits [literature] nurture youth, give pleasure to old age. They are an embellishment in good fortune, and in adversity a refuge and comfort. They entertain us at home, are no inconvenience in public; they pass nights with us, they travel with us, they go to the country with us. (*Pro Archia Poeta Oratio,* 7)

In fact, today we view the ideal human being as a literate person. Hence, the preferable channel of communication is the written one, and the ideal way to represent discourse—whether it originates in the written medium or not—is as it appears in writing. As we see, this attitude, dating back a couple of millennia, was strengthened by the invention of movable type 500 years ago. The printing press made literacy and its products generally accessible, so that reading and writing were no longer reserved for the few. At the same time the gulf between written and oral communication widened because they produced different emotive effects. Talk, produced by speakers for hearers in face-to-face contexts, is immediate and personal; written manuscripts, produced by scribes, in some sense still remain personal documents, one-to-one communication between writer/copier and reader; printed works, produced in huge impersonal numbers, fail to communicate the personal transmission of meaning from writer to reader. The printing press simultaneously increased our expectations for universal literacy and intensified our different attitudes toward the written and oral media and their effects upon us.

Consider an example of what I suggest: There is a preference, even in the recording of oral discourse, for doing so in a style more appropriate to the written medium. For example, Boswell represented Samuel Johnson's talk—those wonderfully orotund, periodic sentences—as if it were literate discourse. Granting that Johnson was probably unusually fluent, even for his time, a time when the most articulate conversationalist was one who adhered most closely to literate forms of expression, and granting further that the rhetorical style of Johnson's time encouraged the development of a more convoluted oral style than one usually encounters today, it is hard to believe that anyone could have spontaneously produced the utterances attributed to Johnson. It is equally hard to imagine someone intending to memorialize a great person today who would choose to do so by exemplifying the person's "wit and wisdom" in Johnsonian style. Something has changed.

Still, even in the works of most contemporary writers, the representation of oral conversation is "cleaned up" in ways seldom obvious to the reader. An unretouched transcript of authentic ordinary conversation is almost impenetrable to us because we are so accustomed (1) to the conventions of "idealized" conversation as represented in writing and (2) to the oral, non-spontaneous dialogue of the movies or television. We do not find false starts, interruptions, overlaps, and hesitations used in these forms as we do in truly spontaneous discourse. In real conversation, inadvertencies are profuse, and tend to have a pragmatic rather than a semantic function: They give us organizational "space" in conversation, but they do not have real "meaning." We do not assume that a *vocalized pause* means: "I am nervous"; or a *hesitation* means: "I have something to hide." In the constructed dialogue of film or television such devices are utilized specifically for these semantic purposes; in such dialogue, we do not adhere to the conventions of ordinary spontaneous conversation, in spite of the fact that we are at pains to represent our constructed dialogue as spontaneous conversation.

There is another reason for our preference for writing over speaking. Writing is cool, dignified, controlled; while ordinary talk is warm and responsive, but not quite trustworthy. In part this attitude is due to the fact that, until very recently, oral discourse could not be reproduced: Once uttered, it was gone, so that it really could not be taken very seriously.

Now, with the advent of audio- and video-tape, oral productions are as permanent as written ones, and this is causing us to change our attitudes toward the two media once again. In addition to new technology, re-evaluation of the preferred "character-style" of people has added to renewed appreciation for the spoken medium. In the past the good person was one who was reticent, private, and logical rather than emotional; controlled rather than spontaneous. Today's ideal person is quite the reverse. If we begin to look at the differences between talk and writing from this newer global perspective, talking begins to be seen as preferable to writing.

We have some suggestive evidence that this is happening. For one thing, non-spontaneous speech style has changed from a form intended to recall the written medium (think of the Churchill era) to one structured to evoke a sense of spontaneity, a conversational responsiveness to an audience (a style which Ronald Reagan uses superlatively). In formal and sophisticated writing, too, we find reflections of a change. Consider someone whom many have called one of the foremost stylists of our time—Tom Wolfe: His most salient characteristic as a stylist is his incorporation of the conventions or ordinary conversation—exclamations, italics, false starts, and so forth—into expository prose.

> The thing was, he said, the Mercury system was completely automated. Once they put in the capsule, that was the last you got to say about the subject.
>   whuh!
>   "Well," said Yaeger, "a monkey's gonna make the first flight."
>   *A monkey?*
>   The reporters were shocked . . . Was this national heresy? What the hell was it . . .
>   But f'r chrissake . . . (*The Right Stuff,* pp. 105–6).

We see further evidence of this trend in the proliferation of italics and quotation marks in written prose where formerly they would never have appeared. They are found in numerous forms of expository prose, as if to signal, "This is only meaningful if you can hear a human voice literally speaking behind this print." Although the italicized style abounds in such genres as *Cosmopolitan* magazine, examples are everywhere. Quotation marks, enclosing everything that is not an aspect of a formal, "voiceless" style of written discourse is often found in student papers, but can be seen elsewhere too; for example, a sign held up in Wiesbaden, Germany, to greet the returning American hostages from Iran, read, "WELCOME!" (with quotation marks in the original).

In our society we indeed note evidence of a shift from the primacy of the literate medium to its secondary place as non-print media assume the primary place. It can no longer be asserted with confidence that literacy is an essential part of the equipment of a cultured and sophisticated person. Since this is true, we must—if we are to inculcate literacy at all—reassess the way in which it is presented. To tell students, overtly or convertly, that they *must* achieve literacy to survive, if they are to have respect, is rapidly becoming a dangerous strategy: It will backfire once it becomes clear that this is no longer really true. Rather, perhaps it is time for us to think of literacy as a skill akin to, say, quilting: Once a survival skill, part of one's ordinary set of skills to protect one's self from the cold, but now something learned as a special aesthetic ability, yielding a special and unique kind of pleasure to its possessor. It isn't that literacy makes us better—just that it makes us happier.

3 The Literacy Crisis: A Challenge How?*

William E. Coles, Jr.
Department of English, University of Pittsburgh

When Robert Benchley, some years back, was doing "Talk of the Town" for *The New Yorker,* he happened, as will happen, to fill in a glancing reference he was making to Mozart's musical precosity by saying that the composer had written his first music at the age of three. To judge from the outraged letter of rebuke that the president of The New York Mozart Society sent Benchley, it was the sort of chance the man had spent most of his life waiting for. He marshalled his evidence as though he were moving a phalanx. First, of course, came the Authorities, the hallowed and hyphenated names, then the rumble of quotations in several languages, followed by the clattering clean-up of supplementary bibliographical references—the whole of which proved unequivocally, undeniably, and absolutely that Mozart's first musical composition had not been written until he was five. The tone of the president's valediction in the letter, delivered as though from a knoll, was predictable. One would have thought that at *least* with *The New Yorker,* at *least* with a man of Benchley's prestige and pretentions to sophistication, and on and on. In his next column Benchley printed the letter and then he himself began the scholarship game: the citations of authenticating correspondence, transcripts of conversations, holograph musical scores offered in evidence, unimpeachable personal testimony—all documenting beyond question that Mozart had indeed written music at the age of three just as Benchley had originally claimed—that is *his* Mozart had, one Sam Mozart of 196th Street, New York City. The only possible explanation of the confusion here so far as *he* could see, Benchley concluded by saying, was that the president of the Mozart

*Portions of this article appeared in another form in *The AAUP Bulletin,* Autumn, 1963, and also in *Issues in English,* May, 1978.

Society must have had some other Mozart in mind. And how was he, Benchley, to have known there were two.

For a Mozart which had been bled of life and music, a name become a label, made the instrument of meanness, Benchley returned a Mozart transcendent, the composer recomposed as the composer plus. Much of the talk of the literacy crisis confronting teachers of writing, I would argue, is analogous to what Benchley found himself facing with that president's letter. And, I want to suggest, I think we, as he did, can do better in the face of the prevailing criticism than feeling obliged to come up with an apology, a hand grenade, or a small traveling bag.

There's not much question that there's an issue, though the problem, or rather the problems, are another thing again. The *Newsweek* article published in 1976, "Why Johnny Can't Write," certainly the most highly publicized instance of the current consumer revolt, is a case in point. The argument is familiar; the details may be filled in: the decline of verbal aptitudes across the board across the nation, inadequate grounding in something called the basics, the creeping cancer of television, reading comprehension plummeting, standards acrumble, bad news from Berkeley, things gone to hell in Georgia, at Michigan State, Temple frantic, even Harvard gravely concerned—in the face of which of course, the sacred cows—namely the professional societies, the Universities, the public school systems—are said to be monumentally indifferent. Sacred cows with crumpled horns who in their placid, cud-chewing way—the follow-up pieces have been legion—simply refuse to kick the dog into worrying the cat to kill the rat that's eating the malt that lies in the house that Westing built. Nothing less than the culture, or more pregnantly, in *Newsweekese,* "a culture's ideas, values, and goals," is said to be at stake. Which is to say that IBM are not amused. Hence, "literacy crisis"—the label was as inevitable as it is ironically appropriate—on the analogy of "energy crisis" or the sort of thing that seems to happen periodically with rivers or in the Middle East, that which calls for sandbags, or guns, or Quick Henry the Flit Kissinger, or more money for the oil companies: a clear emergency for which the remedy is no less clear. Graveyard talk really. What D. H. Lawrence would have called a vast post-mortem effect. Indeed, the huzzerai that has been raised over the issue has obscured the way in which approaches like that of the *Newsweek* article to what it calls "the literacy crisis" are themselves an example of illiteracy, displaying as they do a blindness to the implications of certain ways of using language that are rooted in either an ignorance of or an indifference to what language is, how it functions, why it is important. The *Newsweek* analysis, self-styled, of the problem, from another point of view is part of it—a generalization I would extend, by the way, to a great many of the countercharges against the *Newsweek* piece that make the mistake of accepting *Newsweek*'s definitions—which is how Richard Ohmann among others at what I would call rock bottom can argue as he did in *The Chronicle of Higher Education* that we really don't have a problem, a suggestion not that the emperor has no clothes, but that there isn't any emperor. There's a confusion here I think, but it's precisely in this confusion that I see the challenge for us as teachers. The challenge and the chance.

The real trouble with the *Newsweek* piece, the reason I began by sketching some of the meaner implications of it as a way of talking, is that though the article is not concerned with literacy as a concept, not really—does not in fact deal with the issue of literacy at all—it raises the issue in such a way as to create the illusion that it *is* dealing with literacy, *and* as a problem, *and* as a problem to which the solution is easy because it is so mechanically simple. What *Newsweek* means by literacy is mechanical correctness, knowing the four rules for the comma and how to apply them, being able to spell acceptably, and so forth. What it means by writing is communication, a matter of product rather than process, the simple mechanical transfer of information, which students can be trained to manage in the same way they can be taught to use adding machines or learn to pour concrete. Hence the activity of writing is totally covered by the use of a term like skill. Writing itself is a tool. Or just a tool.

Given such definitions, of course the solution to the problem is simple. The kind of illiteracy being referred to by *Newsweek,* an inability to manipulate what the NCTE has called the conventions of edited American English, exists in high schools and at universities because it is tolerated, indeed because it is countenanced. Not for some other reason. Or reasons. We do not, after all, certify accountants who are unable to add or subtract. Failure to understand this, by the way, I think is the main reason that so many of the standard solutions to even the most simplistic definitions of illiteracy—making it synonymous with incorrectness—have worked so badly. A heightened emphasis on what are called "basics" (by which is meant drill in the diagramming of sentences, improving vocabulary, etc.), the use of teaching machines, even requiring students to take more and still more composition courses—all of these are solutions mentioned by *Newsweek* and all of them are seemingly reasonable—particularly when they receive the explicit endorsement of organizations such as the MLA. "Whereas college students throughout the country," intones that hoary old mother in her *Newsletter* of spring a year ago, "exhibit a marked lack of competence in writing, be it resolved that the Modern Language Association recommend the reinstatement of the freshman composition requirement in colleges and universities that have dropped the requirement." Etcetera. Etcetera. But at the level of practice such solutions have the effect of perpetuating precisely the sort of slovenliness they are designed to eliminate, because they all depend upon making literacy—even the simple-minded form of it—the responsibility of a *Department,* an English Department, a Humanities Department, a Speech Department, some single Department—which is to place the problem in just the kind of academic vacuum that will free a faculty at large, an administration at large, the students at large, and the public at large from having themselves to behave as though they believed correctness were important enough to be worth standing for. For everybody, the problem of correctness, like the hell of Ezra Pound, conveniently becomes someone else's. Hence graduate schools blame the universities, who in turn blame the high schools, who point back to the grammar schools from which we then move to the home, the culture, the *zeitgeist*—and then what? Fallout? Sunspots? Thus *Newsweek's* solutions even to the problem of what it is calling the problem of literacy—the same snaky circularity is at the bottom of most of them—buy a sense of Virtue in much the same way the White power structure sought to imagine it was opening the world to Blacks by building Stuyvesant Village. Most of the time a sense of virtue is the most that such solutions buy.

Still, I would maintain that the solution to the problem of correctness is simple. My standard response to someone who is objecting, say, to bad spelling, with the question of why we don't teach 'em how to write over there in the English Department is: "Why do you make our job so much more difficult than it would have to be by accepting or tolerating what you have a responsibility to refuse to accept, to refuse to tolerate?" I do not say, I said to the Board of Trustees of the University of Pittsburgh in explaining why there is no required course in composition at the university, I do not say that a Professor of Sociology or a member of the faculty of the Law School must him or her*self* know how to teach a student to improve her ability to write. That *is* the province of the English Department. But at the level of what is conventionally acceptable, a person does not have to be a carpenter to know a shaky table or to find fault with it for not being stable; and such teachers—the generalization might easily be opened to include the public at large—can put students in a position to recognize the importance of courses in composition to their development, in any event by refusing to read what is not correct, and by penalizing, I mean by failing if they have to, students who will not deal with a deficiency it has to be up to them to remove in the first place. Of course, the solution to the problem of correctness would be simple—if anyone gave much of a damn about it—*Newsweek*'s crisis cant notwithstanding. The solution would be as simple as it is in fact impossible.

Thus far I have taken some care, you will notice, to distinguish between what *Newsweek* calls literacy and what I would call literacy, between what the general public seems to understand by the term and what we understand by it—or what I think we should understand by it. What is this other literacy (our Mozart vs. theirs), the quality I see the *Newsweek* piece ironically so deficient in, the quality that I think a certain attention to correctness can retard if not make impossible the growth of, the quality I have referred to negatively as involving an ignorance of or indifference to what language is, how it functions, why it is important? For I do believe there is a problem with literacy in the United States, a problem far deeper and more complicated than the rhetoric of "crisis" would have us understand. I think I can describe this problem best by means of an example, a negative example, but one that suggests a positive direction for us as teachers.

Not so long ago, close to ten thousand students elected to take the Advanced Placement Test in English, a test devised by the Educational Testing Service to provide an opportunity for those students already admitted to college to demonstrate a particular competence in certain subjects, to show, that is, not simply ability, but excellence. One section of this three hour test, a section designed to examine the students' ability to analyze a prose passage, had the following as its center.

"Who is James K. Polk?" The Whigs promptly began campaigning on that derision, and there were Democrats who repeated it with a sick concern. The question eventually got an unequivocal answer. Polk had come up the ladder, he was an orthdox party Democrat. He had been Jackson's mouthpiece and floor leader in the House of Representatives, had managed the anti-Bank legislation, had risen to the Speakership, had been governor of Tennessee. But sometimes the belt line shapes an instrument of use and precision. Polk's mind was rigid, narrow, obstinate, far from first-rate. He sincerely believed that only Democrats were truly American, Whigs being either the dupes or the pensioners of England—more, that not only wisdom and patriotism were Democratic monopolies but honor and breeding as well. "Although a Whig he seems a gentleman" is a not uncommon characterization in his diary. He was pompous, suspicious, and secretive; he had no humor; he could be vindictive; and he saw spooks and villains. He was a representative Southern politician of the second or intermediate period (which expired with his Presidency), when the decline but not the disintegration had begun.

But if his mind was narrow it was also powerful and he had guts. If he was orthodox, his integrity was absolute and he could not be scared, manipulated, or brought to heel. No one bluffed him, no one moved him with direct or oblique pressure. Furthermore, he knew how to get things done, which is the first necessity of government, and he knew what he wanted done, which is the second. He came into office with clear ideas and a fixed determination and he was to stand by them through as strenuous an administration as any before Lincoln's. Congress had governed the United States for eight years before him. But Polk was to govern the United States from 1845 to 1849. He was to be the only "strong" President between Jackson and Lincoln. He was to fix the mold for the future in America down to 1860, and therefore for a long time afterward. That is who James K. Polk was.

That passage is from an essay by Bernard De Voto. It is out of context, and as an example of De Voto's ability as a writer or of his assumptions about government, misrepresentative. But this does not exonerate the passage from an essential dishonesty, from the charge of pretending to an impartiality and objectivity that never amounts to anything more than a gesture. In fact, for all of its journalistic skill, the passage is a good working definition of what I would call illiteracy, the failure of a writer to be responsible to the implications of his language—whether consciously or unconsciously is irrelevant.

The voice which speaks in the passage, for example, is not a voice which is positive so much as it is one trying to sound positive. Note its aggressive, self-defensive tone. This is particularly obvious in the staccato punching of the last few sentences, so notably lacking in any examples of just exactly what James K. Polk's accomplishments were, and in the belligerence of the final, "That is who James K. Polk was." What does one do with those uneasy quotation marks around "strong"; and how explain the jarringly self-conscious introduction of such honorific slang as "he had guts," and "no one bluffed him"; or the Babbitt-like praise of "powerful," "his integrity was absolute," "he could not be scared," and so forth? The grassroots America language is a good indication of what De Voto's sentences are appealing to and on what level, and cannot be explained away simply as racy popularization. The passage is playing upon the most unsophisticated of American prejudices: that energy, strength, and forcefulness are good in themselves because they are ends in themselves. That a man knows "how to get things done" and what he wants done (called the first and second necessities of government!) here overrides the question of the value of what gets done and smothers the possibility that the means may not always justify the ends. That a man "has guts" neutralizes, even discounts, the narrowness of his mind—and this in a sentence the form of which suggests a distinction is being made. A similar bit of smuggling goes on in: "If he was orthodox, his integrity was absolute and he could not be scared, manipulated, or brought to heel," whereby a moral vocabulary is given the appearance of having a moral syntax. Is "integrity" the equivalent of not being "scared"? "Integrity" in that sentence is a trick, a word not that the subject demands but that the writer wants in order to play upon the common notion that integrity automatically means Virtue, is a Good Thing. Finally, the image of Polk's wresting control from Congress and governing the United States alone for four years (seen cozily in the company of Jackson and Lincoln), together with the implication that it was not only in spite of but because of his "limitations" that Polk succeeded as President, points up the entire first paragraph as mere rhetoric, in the worst sense of the word, a smoke screen, the language of someone more concerned with appearing than being fair. Prune the passage of its proper nouns and what sort of person is defined by it? How much of the passage would have to be changed to have it apply to Adolf Hitler?

Since the De Voto passage was chosen for the purpose of testing students' ability to analyze prose, the questions asked about it did not depend on how much the students knew about James K. Polk and were not concerned with whether or not they agreed with De Voto's estimation of him. Of the several questions asked about the passage, in other words, not one was clearly designed to take the students into the propagandistic nature of De Voto's prose, let alone into the way language shapes the world of experience—another instance of what I would call illiteracy.

However, an ambiguity in one of the test questions ("Is the passage generally favorable or unfavorable to James K. Polk?") led well above 80% of the students to comment on what they thought of the conception of a United States president offered by the passage, and 94% of this 80% read the passage as being generally favorable to Polk in the sense of approving of the conception of a president offered by it. The following examples of student responses are representative, the illiteracy of which, even at this remove, still has the power to make the blood run cold:

1. Because Polk took over Congress and cut through the red tape of legislation which had hamstrung the presidents before him, he was a great man. It takes a strong man to be a great one, and Polk was strong enough to know how to get what he wanted.
2. When it comes to government, it's not a man's personality that counts but what he does. Polk got things done any way he could. In spite of his faults, he was strong and efficient, a fine President.

3. Polk was prejudiced yes, but he was "sincerely" prejudiced and believed what he was doing was right. That's what America needed in a president and that's what it got.
4. Anyone who can "fix the mold of the future in America" is certainly presented favorably. Polk had his faults yes, but he made a name for himself. The faults don't matter when you think of what he accomplished.

There are several things to be noted about such responses, the most obvious of which is the utter unconsciousness on the parts of the writers of them of the implications of De Voto's point of view. Not for any of the students is there anything strange or objectionable in someone's conceiving of a totalitarian leader as a hero, or in the open admiration of this conception as an ideal. Indeed, the majority of students went even beyond De Voto, the substance of whose praise of Polk is mainly a matter of drift and innuendo. Second, I want to be sure to emphasize that the examples I have given are by no means the utterances of a crackpot few. They are absolutely representative and they became for those of us who were reading the examinations absolutely predictable. The answers were not all so pointed, of course, but with unfailing regularity the bland equations of strength with goodness, of force with greatness, of the efficient with the benign appeared on paper after paper. In fact so unusual was it for a student to recognize that what De Voto is saying amounts to praising authoritarianism, to recognize that any exception might be taken to the values exhibited by the passage (the best the students could do with De Voto's language was to object to some of his phraseology as "slangy" or "in bad taste" without giving any indication of what might be wrong with either or what this wrongness could lead to, and frighteningly enough the closest equivalent to the term "propaganda" was the word "clever")—so unusual was it for a student to take exception to the values of the passage, that when such a paper was discovered by the readers of the examination it was read aloud. I do not remember more than ten papers being read—this out of almost ten thousand examinations. And finally, I think it important to point out that however morally illiterate such remarks may appear, they are not the remarks of stupid or uneducated people. The students who wrote them know how to put sentences together; they come close to knowing how to read—particularly in *Newsweek's* terms. What they don't know is how to evaluate what they read, how to see it in terms of who they are and other things they know, how to test on their pulses the real assumptions beneath the ostensible ones. Most of the students, I suppose, would have been ready to condemn totalitarianism if they had seen it. The problem is to get them to recognize it when they see it.

It is true that the students were under pressure and said not what they thought, but what they thought they ought to say, what they thought their examiners wanted to hear. But is this not even worse?—not simply because it implies that one of the reasons the good student is a good student is that he has learned to feed back "right" answers, but because in this case the "good" student assumes that the "right" answer, the one wanted by his or her teachers, is one that splits public and private life, condones power as an end in itself, supports the doctrine that might is right, endorses efficiency as the *ne plus ultra* of

government, and represents the politically expedient as not only morally justi-
fiable, but necessary. The "right" answer here, in short, on the part of over three-
quarters of the best students our high schools and preparatory schools are
producing—is authoritarianism.

Such an analysis I have no doubt would horrify the writers of the majority
responses enumerated above. "But this is an English test" one can imagine their
saying, or "I'm talking about language not politics." And of course that is just
the trouble. The responses were partial, written in a vacuum by people who
never imagined that language involved more than getting commas in the right
places or building a strong vocabulary. The responses are divorced from history,
divorced from government, divorced most of all from the students themselves.
Because they make no attempt to connect various areas of their experience, to
see Spinoza, the sound of the typewriter, and the smell of cooking as having anything to do with each other (of which their blind and appalling faith in the
printed word is one symptom), the students have not in any significant way
involved themselves as human beings in what they have read or written. In writing for someone else the way they have, they become less than who they are.

One further thing to be noted about the phenomenology of the student responses I have quoted, perhaps the greatest of the illiteracies here, is that all
four of them, and all responses like them, were judged by the examiners—that is,
the officials of the Educational Testing Service in conjunction with the actual
readers of the examinations, educators drawn from a number of colleges and
high schools throughout the country—all such responses were judged as worthy
of the top score awarded on the test. Our concern as readers of the examination,
we were told, and told rightly I think, was to be neither political nor moral. But
we were also told that in spite of its ambiguity, the question we were working
with we were to consider as designed solely to test the students' awareness of
matters technical and rhetorical. Since the scoring of the responses to the question could be evaluated on that basis, they were therefore going to be evaluated
on that basis, and on that basis alone—as though language meant no more than it
said, as though the matter of style were no more than a matter of taste.
Newsweekese.

Finally, as a way of addressing the question of whether or not there is a "literacy crisis" in the United States, in the sense of there being some brand new fall
from some traditional state of Grace, I would like to point out that the situation
I have just described occurred in 1962. It would not be particularly difficult to
find examples of the same thing a hundred years before that, or to move back
from the 1860's to Jonathan Swift's excoriation of madness, to Pope on dull-
ness in the *Dunciad.*

The situation of the AP examination epitomizes what for me is the real literacy problem in the United States and why to conceive of literacy as involving no
more than an awareness of conventions, in terms of correctness only, merely
perpetuates it. What I would call true literacy, the ability to make sense of what
one reads and with what one writes, is really the ability to conceptualize, to
build structures, to draw inferences, to see implications, to generalize intelli-
gently—in short to make connections, to make relationships between words and

other words, sentences and other sentences, this idea and that idea, language and experience, what is being said and who one is. But concern with only the *appearance* of this conceptualizing process, far from being a step on the way to an involvement with it, is really a step in another direction, leads *away* from involvement in much the same way that sex manuals can lead the loveless even further from love—as the situation of the AP examination demonstrates. What's really appalling about that situation is not that the students should have condemned De Voto's prose and didn't; I'm much less interested in students being liberal or conservative than I am in their being aware of themselves as liberal or conservative, of what it means for them to be liberal or conservative. What's appalling is that the majority of students had no idea of what they *were* doing with De Voto—not any more than did the examiners who made the exam. It's what comes of concern with convention that has no reference to what the convention is about or for.

I want to make very clear—you see how careful one learns to become in trying to forestall ignorant criticism—I want to make very clear that I am not for a moment suggesting that I think we ought to forget about what *Newsweek* calls literacy and concern ourselves as teachers of reading and writing with something else instead: social issues, consciousness-razing, entertainment with films or art prints—the fluff of the late 60's. What I am suggesting is the necessity of providing a context for correctness that will make it possible to insist on in the name of something. This is why I think that language understood in its broadest sense, the means by which we run orders through chaos, shape whatever worlds we live in, and as a consequence give ourselves the identities we have, ought to be the focus of all courses designed to enable students to become literate. For to see writing and reading both as forms of language-using is to be able to suggest that the processes involved in writing and reading—those of selecting, arranging, putting together—are relevant to all disciplines and to any life, whether one's language is chemical symbols or mathematical notation, gestures, colors, notes, or words. It is to be able to suggest to a future physicist, say, that a better understanding of the workings of the English language can enable her to become more conscious of what she is doing as a user of the language of physics—and *vice versa*. The same goes for a future historian, mathematician, musician, or anthropologist. And it is to be able to insist that facility with the processes of reading and writing, more than being a requirement for a student to fulfill is the *sine qua non* of his education. To become alive to the implications of language-using is not, of course, to become free, but it is to have choices that one cannot have without such an awareness. This is what I see the hullabaloo over correctness giving us a chance to shoot for as teachers. There is no reason we cannot use the concern with what are called "mechanics" to introduce our students to an idea of them as much more than that. There is no reason we cannot use concern with the way sentences look to talk with our students about what sentences are, and about what it can mean to read and to write them. There is no reason we can't use their Mozart to talk about ours—pretending, whenever we need to, like Benchley, that neither did we understand there were two.

4 # Writing Across the Curriculum: The British Approach

Richard W. Bailey
Department of English, The University of Michigan

Educational programs in Great Britain differ in significant ways from those in the United States. Universal primary schooling was not mandated until 1870—at that time more than half the school-age children in Britain did not attend school at all—and only after 1945 did schools begin a slow and still incomplete progress toward equality of opportunity. Differing curricula still shape programs for "early school-leavers" and potential university students, and very different types of schools provide (or inhibit) education that is reflective of a more candidly class-stratified social structure than North Americans are willing to acknowledge here.

While schools are governed by local authorities in Britain, many features of publicly-supported education there distinguish the schools from those in North America. The role of the Ministry of Education and Science is far more influential than the corresponding federal agencies in the United States and Canada. Centralized decision-making and uniform national examinations limit the scope for educational innovation by teachers and local schools, and the historic recognition of ethnic and cultural diversity found in our schools is only beginning to emerge as British educators recognize the special traditions and cultures of minority groups. (See Edwards, 1979, listed in the bibliography.) These and many other differences in both the system of education and in the presumptions about who will be educated for what purpose need to be frankly acknowledged as North American teachers examine the innovations now underway in Great Britain.

Despite these differences, the British example has much to offer us. Since educational reforms are national in scope, new approaches are likely to involve the simultaneous efforts of many teachers working together on a common agenda. Innovations in the United States and Canada, needless to say, depend much more on the initiative of individuals; the recent steep decline in enrollments and in the number of newly trained teachers—a major source of fresh ideas in past decades—will doubtless lead to a stultification of our curricula unless we are willing to make greater investments in the in-service training of teachers now employed. The same demographic decline in school population has begun to occur in Britain, and the economic recession has likewise reduced investment in educational programs there. Some of the trends that make change difficult here, in short, also afflict the introduction of new ideas in Britain.

Of particular interest to readers of this volume are efforts now underway there to improve the teaching of writing at all educational levels, particularly in the secondary schools. While "writing across the curriculum" has emerged as an attractive new idea here in the last half dozen years, the theme was popularized in works by James Britton and Douglas Barnes in the late 1960's. In 1972, responding to indications that reading skills were declining among British school children, Margaret Thatcher, then Secretary of State for Education and Science, appointed a Committee of Inquiry to explore possible reforms in the teaching of

English.[1] The Committee conceived its mandate broadly and set out to investigate the entire range of "language in education" across the curriculum. Following hearings and extensive surveys of established practices, the "Bullock Report"—named for the Chair of the Committee, Sir Alan Bullock—was submitted to the government at the end of 1974 and published in 1975 under the title *A Language for Life*. The report contains more than three hundred recommendations, each carefully argued, for action organized around varying constituencies in education—young children, secondary students, adult illiterates, and teachers themselves.[2] The recommendations then became the focus of widespread public discussion, by no means all of it favorable, and occupied the attention of school authorities and teachers who, as the report stated, are most responsible for the "quality of learning."

Two of the recommendations are of particular interest to those who wish to explore the rationale and implications of "writing across the curriculum":

In the secondary school, all subject teachers need to be aware of:

- the linguistic processes by which their pupils acquire information and understanding, and the implications for the teacher's own use of language;
- the reading demands of their own subjects, and ways in which the pupils can be helped to meet them.

To bring about this understanding every secondary school should develop a policy for language across the curriculum. The responsibility for this policy should be embodied in the organisational structure of the school (Bullock, p. 529).

Naturally enough, the "language policies" developed by various schools differed in significant ways, and the *process* by which teachers of different subjects achieved consensus on the role of language in learning was almost certainly as useful and invigorating as the written policies that were eventually developed. Not all schools undertook the exercise with enthusiasm (and some ignored the matter altogether), but large numbers did engage the issues formulated in the Bullock Report in a careful and productive way.

Since the whole matter of a "language policy" is virtually unknown in North America—except for schools offering bilingual programs—it will be helpful to quote a portion of one of them:

The Language in the Curriculum policy has these purposes:

1. to make teaching staff more aware of the language demands made on pupils;
2. to propose that staff should teach the particular language skills required by their subject;
3. to suggest the place of language in the curriculum;
4. to improve the quality of teaching;
5. to implement the recommendation in the Bullock Report (quoted in Marland, p. 279).

In elaborating these recommendations, the staff of the Abbey Wood School in London provided detailed guidelines for making writing, reading, and oral uses of language more effective as vehicles for instruction and learning. While the policies that have been published are doubtless some of the most highly elaborated documents (Torbe, 1976), the one devised at Abbey Wood seems representative of efforts to engage all teachers in the concern for language (not merely English teachers); it both recognizes that each subject makes distinctive uses of language in the conventions of its discourse and asserts the centrality of language in all aspects of intellectual inquiry.

Naturally, the idea of a school-wide language policy was not greeted with universal enthusiasm. Jeanette Williams, a former English teacher now affiliated with the University of London Institute of Education, argued that "writing across the curriculum" was an ill-understood slogan based on merely "a few metaphysical statements about what is likely to happen if the project's hunches about language are taken up in practice" (Williams, 1977). Even one of the participants in the Schools Council's effort to promote the idea found, on returning to a full-time teaching position, that the heavy demands of a typical class load and the "lack of real contact between members of staff in my school outside their own department" made it extraordinarily difficult to design a language policy and to work through its implications for practice (D'Arcy, 1977). What is surprising, however, is not the dissent but the widespread support for the idea from influential groups. The National Union of Teachers, for instance, did not qualify its support of the basic notion: "*All teachers* must accept responsibility for improving standards of reading and language" (*A Language for Life,* 1976, p. 30; my emphasis).[3]

Three closely related assumptions underlie the recommendations elaborated in the Bullock Report, all of them deriving from, among other sources, the work of L. S. Vygotsky as interpreted by Britton, particularly in *Language and Learning* (1970). In the Report, they are stated in this way:

> In the Committee's view there are certain important inferences to be drawn from a study of the relationship between language and learning:
>
> - all genuine learning involves discovery, and it is as ridiculous to suppose that teaching begins and ends with 'instruction' as it is to suppose that 'learning by discovery' means leaving children to their own resources;
> - language has a heuristic function; that is to say a child can learn by talking and writing as certainly as he can by listening and reading;
> - to exploit the process of discovery through language in all its uses is the surest means of enabling a child to master his mother tongue (Bullock, p. 50).

Though the Committee does not make this clear, these are truly radical (though not novel) assumptions to make about the process of education. Conventionally organized classrooms, particularly those commonly encountered in higher levels of education are founded on quite different principles. A lecture directed to several score of passive students does not presume that "discovery" is the essence of "genuine learning," or at least it assumes that "genuine learning" must take place elsewhere, perhaps in laboratories or in some quite place of study. Examinations that assign a high value to the accurate recapitulation of ideas previously discussed or read are likewise inimical to the "genuine learning" of which the Committee speaks. In short, the basic assumptions of the Report that encouraged a national transformation of education have more in common with Rudolf Steiner, Maria Montessori, and Paulo Freire than they do with John Locke or with the immemorial and unanalyzed tradition that usually shapes the schedule of a school day, the arrangement of furniture in a classroom, and the foundations of testing and certification.

The role of language in the Committee's conception of learning is likewise radical and follows from the first principle, the principle of discovery. If thought is construed as "inner speech" (to use Vygotsky's notion), the most direct access to that thought is through *articulation,* the formation of sensory impressions and inchoate ideas into linguistic form. Discovery is an active, not a passive, process, and so is articulation. Hence the notion that "talking and writing" are of enormous importance—at least as significant as "listening and reading"—implies, too, a different kind of classroom and a different kind of teacher from the conventional one. As a consequence of the recommendations made by the Bullock Committee, the Abbey Wood School (among many others) determined in its language policy that

> staff should give time in a variety of ways for pupils to talk about the material that is presented to them, whether in small groups in a structured situation or the more formal class discussion (Marland, p. 278).

If articulation is indeed the basis for discovery and learning, teachers need to find ways to manage the expressive opportunities they provide for their students. There are, of course, immense practical difficulties. As Pat D'Arcy discovered:

> the children who most need to use talking for learning are just the ones in a class group of 30 whose talk is nearly always disruptive and disturbing for the rest. Given time and patience, such children may learn to use talk for constructive purposes—it is certainly important to give them the chance—but the wear and tear over weeks, even months, is bound to be considerable.

Of all the factors that inhibit the use of talk as a form of articulating and refining "inner speech," perhaps the most resistant to change is the students' own low estimation of it. Schools, and to a great extent contemporary English-speaking society, tend to undervalue speech as a vehicle for serious and enduring expression, and children are right in suspecting that "just talking" is a form of recreation rather than central to learning. (One need not turn to pre-literate cultures to see different assumptions about serious talking; the recent broadcasting of debates in Parliament has jarred members of the British public who reasonably imagined that Margaret Thatcher and Michael Foot engaged in political oratory at the same level of formality employed by Gladstone and Disraeli a century ago.) Effective uses of talk in school settings can be organized, but only with considerable imagination and daring (Barnes, 1973).[4]

As a consequence of its three basic principles, the Bullock Committee also

made a rich set of recommendations for revising the teaching and role of reading
in school programs. Once again they presumed that *every* teacher should be concerned with assessing and improving students' reading skills, and the Abbey Wood
School incorporated this view in its own language policy with a series of recommendations on reading:

> In presenting reading material, teachers should ensure that the material is ap-
> propriate to the reading abilities of their pupils and, where anyone is unable
> to meet the demands, it is the responsibility of *subject specialists* to help
> improve reading skills (Marland, p. 277; my emphasis).

While the policy does mention that such "specialists" might invoke the help of a
reading consultant in particularly difficult cases, those who formulated it presume
that all teachers are able to distinguish reading difficulties from other obstacles
to learning and to make an accurate evaluation of the reading matter used in
their classes. Such a presumption is not unreasonable, but many teachers must
feel ill-prepared to perform the sort of analysis of materials and students imposed upon them by the policy.

Of the four language skills involved in learning—listening, talking, reading, and
writing—the Committee placed greatest emphasis on writing, although it is already a primary mode of expression in British classrooms. Most secondary students in North America write extended essays only occasionally, and what
extended writing they do is mainly assigned in classes in English. In Britain, on
the other hand, extended essay writing is commonly assigned in all subject areas,
and organized instruction in composition as a subject in its own right is virtually
unknown in secondary and higher education. Hence, the idea of writing across
the curriculum did not face the obstacles typically encountered by teachers in
American settings nor did it strike most subject teachers as an unreasonable
imposition of new duties.

Nevertheless, the Bullock Committee was not satisfied with existing practices.
School prose, they argued, was virtually restricted to a single kind: the marshal-
ing of facts and observations into an organized exposition of an idea. Product
rather than process and the results of discovery rather than the unfolding of
inquiry were emphasized. If language in school has its primary role in a "heuristic function," the emphasis on the outcome of study is clearly misplaced. As
a consequence of this view, then, British teachers were plunged into the sort of
preoccupation with invention—and its consequence, "pre-writing" and "free
writing"—that was then exciting American educators and altering the role of
written expression in schools and colleges here.

British linguists in this century have generally been concerned with the function of language in social settings (following the tradition of Malinowski and
Firth) rather than with a focus on linguistic structure itself (following the example of Saussure and Chomsky). That intellectual background is evident in
Britton's work and in the assumptions accepted by the Bullock Committee. Thus
the Committee and many of the language policies that resulted from its recommendations drew attention to three main functions of linguistic behavior: the
expressive, the *poetic,* and the *transactional.*[5] What was wrong with nearly all

writing done in schools, they believed, was its almost exclusive emphasis on the transactional function—the use of language to inform, advise, persuade, or instruct. The other two functions, however, are much more central to the idea of language as a heuristic. The poetic function—language used as "an art medium" provides opportunities for "a child to master his mother tongue," but more consequential for writing across the curriculum is the expressive function—the use of language for "thinking out loud on paper." Once more the Abbey Wood School provides a succinct statement of the idea: "expressive language is a matrix from which other language functions develop" (Marland, p. 277). Thus, writing activities which devote primary attention to the expressive function are important as students evolve as writers through the school years and as they grow in mastery of a subject or discipline. At least some writing assignments should therefore be devised, in this view, to capture the process of learning—the false starts and wrong inferences developed in a scientific experiment, for instance, rather than the exposition of the "right answer" eventually achieved.

However radical a departure from existing practices, the notion of the three functions of language and their presumed position in learning seems to have stimulated imaginative new approaches to teaching. In *Language and Learning,* Britton carefully distinguished two roles that teachers might take in their interaction with students—the *participant* and the *spectator.* Spectators merely observe; participants are engaged in the social activity of which language is a part. In principle, both roles can be adopted in the teacher's engagement with writing in any of its three functions, but the spectator role is normally associated with the progression from the expressive to the poetic function and the participant role with the movement from expressive to transactional discourse. Hence teachers—*all* teachers—are encouraged to vary the classroom setting to promote both a variety of functions in the articulation of learning and in its reception by others. In encouraging such variety, the Committee asserted the belief "that progress in writing throughout the school years should be marked by an increasing differentiation in the kinds of writing a pupil can successfully tackle" (Bullock, p. 166). Such a notion of "progress" as a main object of schooling is evidently quite different from the conventional practice of gradually perfecting a single kind of writing.

Throughout the Bullock Report and in the publications related to it, one finds almost universal agreement that the best learning is active learning, that articulation in all its forms is the basis for understanding, and that writing, in particular, occupies a privileged place in all disciplines as the preferred vehicle for expressing the process by which understanding is achieved. How widely accepted these ideas are is difficult to evaluate from a distance, but it is significant that the Association of Teachers of Mathematics endorsed the idea that language is important in the learning of that subject shortly after the Bullock Report was issued (Marland, p. 250). As already noted, however, the regular use of extended writing activities in all school subjects has long been an established practice in British schools, thus making the strategy of "writing across the curriculum" a matter of revising and refining rather than of revolution.

In the course of collecting evidence, the Bullock Committee conducted a thorough and extensive survey to establish a profile of schools, teachers, and educational practices. Regrettably, this survey did not measure the nature of language activities in all disciplines; it did, however, determine the distribution of time spent in English classes. In an average school week, 14-year-old students spent time on the four uses of language in the following proportions: 22.5% in oral activities, 29.6% in writing, 22.0% in language study, and 25.9% in reading. (These proportions include students from all ability groupings and do not take account of work done outside of class.) Types of writing varied according to the educational streams in which children had been placed, and remedial pupils spent more time writing about personal experiences while those preparing for national examinations were more likely to engage in argument and exposition. All groups, however, spent about one hour per week in writing activities during English classes. A popular and important writing task, according to the survey, involves "reproductive" work, "writing in the pupil's own words of material derived from printed or oral sources." Students in every ability grouping devoted considerable time to this activity (36 minutes per week) which ranges from interpretation to the writing of a précis or summary. In addition, students were often engaged in copying printed materials verbatim, a particularly popular activity with remedial groups (Bullock, pp. 434–43).

While there is no entirely comparable survey for schools in the United States, what information is available suggests quite a different role for writing in schools. In a study of secondary schools conducted in 1979–80, Arthur N. Applebee found that "writing activities occupied a major proportion of class time in all of the subject areas observed" (p. 30). Yet these activities hardly ever resulted in organized and continuous prose: "only 3 percent asked for writing of at least paragraph length" (p. 30). Only in English classes do teachers commonly ask for writings longer than a paragraph, and of the 82.4% of English teachers who make such assignments, the majority "typically" require exercises not longer than 250 words. Most school writing activities in the United States thus involve note-taking, short answers to test questions, and fill-in-the-blank responses to prepared exercises. From Applebee's results, it would appear that *more* time in English classes is devoted to writing in American schools (41.1%) than in schools in Great Britain (29.6%)[6]; the types of writing actually done by students, however, vary greatly in the two systems.

Brief written answers of the kind typical of American classrooms cannot capture the process by which learning has taken place. Even those teachers who value personal engagement with a topic do not construct examinations in which its quality is a significant measure of achievement (Applebee, p. 63). Though American teachers may value the kind of active learning praised by the Bullock Report, they seldom use writing as a means of achieving it or as a vehicle for expressing it. As Applebee reports:

> the teacher takes over all of the difficulties inherent in using language appropriate to a subject area—including much of the specialized vocabulary and rules of procedure which are embedded in the text—and leaves the student only the task of mechanically "slotting-in" the missing information (p. 99).

Even when more extended writing is assigned, only 29% of American teachers provide models for the kind of discourse they seek (and most of these are foreign-language teachers); most teachers (70%) did not ask for more than a single draft of a piece of writing; and

> in a typical writing situation, just over three minutes elapsed from the time the teacher began to pass out or discuss the assignment until students began to write (p. 90).

Hence the emphasis on writing as a tool for inquiry, a stage in the articulation of knowledge, seems so rare in American schools that it plays a negligible role in the educational system, at least at the secondary level.

As North Americans view the Bullock Report, they need to keep in mind that it was conceived as a plan of action rather than an account of accomplishments already achieved. Nonetheless, it is clear that its recommendations were closely related to practices already in place, at least as far as the role of writing in learning is concerned. Yet for its purpose to be fulfilled, significant new expenditures for in-service training, resource centers, and curricular materials were required; even as it was accepted by the government, the Secretary of State noted tersely that "recommendations with financial implications must be subject to current constraints; for the time being action on those which would involve additional resources must be postponed" (Bullock, p. iii). Since 1974, educational expenditures in Britain have steadily declined, and as early as 1977, James Britton reflected that

> the Bullock Report begins to look like a beacon that shines brighter and brighter as the skies around it darken. Amid all the talk of "literacy" and "evaluation," both very narrowly conceived, can it survive to keep before us a more enlightened view of language and learning? (Foreword to Davis and Parker, p. xiii).

Nonetheless, writing across the curriculum remains as an important priority for educational reform and renewal. Britton's image is entirely appropriate: the Bullock Report *is* a beacon, dimly seen from North American shores; it is a light that can illumine our work as educators.

Notes

[1] After careful study, the Bullock Committee could not detect a statistically significant change in *average* reading test scores since 1948. However, the distribution of reading ability may have changed. "The indications are that there may now be a growing proportion of poor readers among the children of unskilled and semi-skilled workers" (Bullock, p. 25).

[2] A great variety of related publications appeared during the time that the Bullock Committee deliberated or immediately after it was submitted to Mrs. Thatcher's successor as Secretary, Reg Prentice, M.P. Several of these are listed in the bibliography: Britton *et al.*, 1975; Davis and Parker, 1978; Hargreaves, 1980; Harpin, 1976; Marland, 1977; Martin *et al.*, 1976; Rosen, 1975.

In addition, American teachers had the opportunity to learn about the developments taking place: see Brunetti 1977 and "The Teaching of Writing in Great Britain." The remarkable harmony between these publications and the Bullock Report is no accident; James Britton, himself a member of the Committee, was apparently persuasive in gaining assent for ideas he and his colleagues had been developing at the Institute of Education at the University of London. The London Association for the Teaching of English, closely affiliated with Britton's group, was another influential source of ideas.

[3] Proponents of these recommendations of the Bullock Report have been remarkably candid in documenting the success, failure, and half-successful attempts in engaging all teachers in a school in implementing them; see especially "Initiating and Implementing a Policy" (Marland 1977, pp. 231–60).

[4] British linguists have devoted particular attention to spoken interaction in various settings, particularly in schools. For the theoretical background of such work, see Coulthard and Montgomery (1981).

[5] These are by no means the only functions of language that have been proposed. Halliday divides language functions into interpersonal, ideational, and textual; Fawcett (1980) has recently argued for eight functions. There is probably no limit to the number of functions that might be specified: for instance, the *archival* function might be designated for documents that are virtually never read (e.g., insurance policies) or the *lapidary* function for texts to be inscribed on structures (e.g., tombstones or monumental buildings).

[6] Applebee's results are expressed as percentages of class time but the total time devoted to each class is ambiguously expressed. Assuming 55-minute class periods and a five-day school week, American ninth graders spent 80 minutes in English classes engaged in writing activities compared to 57.3 minutes for British 14-year-olds in a week of school However, some of the activities counted as writing in Applebee's study (e.g., note-taking) may have been classified as an oral activity (e.g., "class discussion on topics chosen by teacher") in the Bullock survey. As American students progress through high school, more time is devoted to writing activities; thus Applebee found that nearly half of the time in English classes was spent in writing activities in the eleventh grade (or about 138 minutes each week). Most British school children will have completed (or are about to complete) school at the same age.

5 Science Writing and Literacy

Grace Rueter
English Composition Board, The University of Michigan

Thomas M. Dunn
Department of Chemistry, The University of Michigan

One of the most important developments in education in the last decade—perhaps the most important—has been the enormous growth in the cultural and ethnic diversity of the student body and, indeed, of the programs offered in schools. This growth, accompanied by decreased homogeneity in all student groups, has been reflected in the broader base upon which many of the subjects, particularly those of an anthropological and cultural nature, have been considered. As might be expected, the concept of literacy itself has been broadened; but in most classes where reading and writing are taught, it has not been broadened to include science and its literature as part of the definition. It is not, perhaps, surprising that this should have happened since, traditionally, teaching functional literacy has been regarded as the province of the teachers of English and of English literature, and knowledge of science and its literature has not been one of their high priorities. If, however, students are to become fully literate, they must become familiar with the literature of science as well as the imaginative prose and poetry traditionally taught as literature. English teachers who want to help their students become literate today can and should introduce them to the literature of science.

As Jay Robinson suggests earlier in this chapter, teaching imaginative literature exclusively is different from teaching literacy. Since literacy implies a capacity to understand ethics and culture in their broadest sense, the teaching of literacy requires the teaching of a plurality of literatures. Interestingly enough, this plurality was once encompassed by the word *literature* in its singular form, and it included writings in all areas of what are now classified as the humanities and sciences. Today, as the 21st century approaches, and as an understanding of scientific thought becomes increasingly important, English teachers who teach literatures have it in their power to lead students to a broadened appreciation of human experience in which the sciences and the humanities are reunited. We urge English teachers to begin the process of reintegrating the two traditions by including selections from the literature of science in their curricula.

Our purposes are to call attention to the neglected area of science literature and also, through examples which are not only good science but excellent writing, to begin to introduce non-scientists to the ideas and procedures of science itself. We believe the second objective is just as important as the first, and that it provides a way into modern science for those who have felt intimidated by its apparently formidable structures and technology. A large part of the intimidation has arisen from confusion in the public mind of what are, in fact, two distinct kinds of writings within the literature of science. We call them *scientific writing* and *science writing,* and they are clearly distinguished by the purposes, uses of language and by the different audiences for which they are intended. *Scientific writing,* the writing which appears in scientific journals, is written by scientists for an audience of peers to acquaint them with advances in their fields, and it bristles with the formalisms and abstract symbolisms on which the progress of many sciences depends. *Science writing,* on the other hand, appears in widely available books and essays and is written by scientists for general audiences to make the concepts and methods of diverse areas of science accessible in everyday language. It is not *scientific writing* but *science writing* that can, and should, be included in English curricula.

There are, of course, important differences between science writing and imaginative literature. Perhaps the most important difference lies in the kinds of human experiences they treat. In an aesthetically pleasing essay which introduces readers to science, Aldous Huxley explores this difference:

> All our experiences are strictly private; but some experiences are less private than others. They are less private in the sense that, under similar conditions, most normal people will have similar experiences and, having had them, can be relied upon to interpret the spoken or written reports of such experiences in much the same way.

About the more private of our experiences no such statements can be made. For example, the visual, auditory and olfactory experiences of a group of people watching the burning of a house are likely to be similar. Similar, too, are the intellectual experiences of those members of the group who make the effort to think logically about the causes of this particular fire and, in the light of current knowledge, of combustion in general. In other words, sense impressions and the processes of rational thought are experiences whose privacy is not too extreme to make them unsharable. But now let us consider the emotional experiences of our fire watchers. One member of the group may feel sexual excitement, another aesthetic pleasure, another horror and yet others human sympathy or inhuman and malicious glee. Such experiences, it is obvious, are radically unlike one another. In this sense they are more private than sense experiences and the intellectual experiences of logical thought.

In the present context, science may be defined as a device for investigating, ordering and communicating the more public of human experiences. Less systematically, literature also deals with such public experiences. Its main concern, however, is with man's more private experiences, and with the interactions between the private worlds of sentient, self-conscious individuals and the public universes of "objective reality," logic, social conventions and the accumulated information currently available (pp. 4–5).

This passage immediately distinguishes for us in clear, beautifully structured prose, those things we might legitimately call science from those we might define in other terms, the most private of which we sometimes express in poetry. Aldous Huxley was a man of letters with the ideal scientific background to appreciate the private as well as the public experiences and to write about them with equal fervor and conviction. The quotation is the second of thirty-eight contributions in a small volume entitled *Literature and Science,* and Huxley's analytical treatment of the subject is scientific, perceptive, and literate.

Recognizing that science and imaginative literature are grounded in different domains of experience, we must learn to understand and appreciate both. Studying science writing can facilitate the process for, as scientists have continued to publish books and essays for the public, the vast area of human experiences explored by science has become increasingly accessible to people whose primary interests are literary. As we all know, the realm of experience which imaginative literature treats, the realm of private experiences, is largely concerned with human interactions. In most of this literature, the environment, both animate and inanimate, if not simply taken for granted, either reflects those interactions in some way or is used as a backdrop for occasional sensual or colorful description. In the real world, there is no doubt that human relationships are powerful determinants of both our courses of actions and our life styles, but the environment which surrounds and impinges on those relationships has a major effect on our behavior, our values, and our aesthetics. To be truly literate, we and our students must have total access, through reading and writing, to the physical and biological environments as well as the human relationships that shape our culture, our ethics, and the quality of our lives.

One of the problems faced by non-scientists who wish to extend their understanding of ethics and culture is where to begin, how to find a bridge from imaginative literature into science. The best science writing offers that bridge, since it shares much with imaginative literature. As Ann E. Berthoff points out later in this book, the study of literature is not so much what one reads as how one reads it. Teachers and students who read and enjoy imaginative literature can also read and enjoy science writing. Many of us have long marveled and often been exhilarated at the sense of beauty invoked by majestic phenomena such as waterfalls, mountains, clouds, sunrises and sunsets; this sense of marvel and exhilaration is deeply embedded in our cultural heritage and our imaginative literature. The intricate constructs of nuclear physics, chemistry, or molecular biology, not perceivable to the naked eye, have the same capacity to thrill and to awe those who seek to "see" them.

Just as Huxley's elegant discussion of science and literature offers an introduction to the domain of science, so other science writings provide non-scientists with clearly-written, substantive expositions of the way science works. In the following piece, for example, from *Science and Society*—a collection of essays by authors as well known as Jacob Bronowski, James B. Conant, Erwin C. Schrödinger, Michael Polanyi and John Z. Young—Norman Campbell offers a strikingly lucid discussion of theories and laws in science. Campbell's essay "The Explanation of Laws," speaks even more specifically than Huxley's to the distinctions between science and non-science and does so in a way which makes us feel the presence not only of a powerful intellect but also of a humane scientist:

> Explanation in general is the expression of an assertion in a more acceptable and satisfactory form. Thus if somebody speaks to us in a language we do not understand, either a foreign language or the technical language of some study or craft with which we are not familiar, we may ask him to *explain* his statement. And we shall receive the explanation for which we ask if he merely alters the form of his statement, so as to express it in terms with which we are familiar. The statement in its new form is more acceptable and more satisfactory, because now it evokes a definite response in our minds which we describe by saying that we understand the statement. Again we sometimes ask a man to *explain* his conduct; when we make such a demand we are ignorant, or pretending to be ignorant, of the motives which inspired his action. We shall feel that he has offered a complete explanation if he can show that his motives are such as habitually inspire our own actions, or, in other words, that his motives are familiar to us (p. 41).

From this brief introduction, Campbell, a physicist, develops for non-scientists what is probably one of the clearest and most literate statements about theories and laws ever written. In only a few pages, he condenses for those who wish to read and seek new experiences what might have been expected to fill at least a volume devoted to critical thinking and symbolic logic. The ideas as well as the clarity and the economy of the language lure the reader to read on and on, further and further into what is normally regarded as an abstruse and academic topic, with understanding and pleasure.

Since science writing, like imaginative literature, is an attempt to make sense of human experience, it is not surprising that some of the familiar themes of great literature also run through science writing. These themes provide a context which helps non-scientists integrate unfamiliar ideas into familiar ones. The concept of "oneness," for example, of the inter-relatedness of everything, a pervasive theme in imaginative literature, is also evident in science writing. The idea of *relativity* as developed by Einstein is an expression of this theme in terms of scientific events and metaphors. This theme recurs in the writing of many other scientists as well. It is, in fact, the thread that binds together the twenty-nine essays of Lewis Thomas' *The Lives of a Cell.* In these essays, Thomas, a biologist, draws on many of the familiar devices of imaginative literature while he explores and makes sense of the unfamiliar, as the introduction to the title piece shows:

> We are told that the trouble with Modern Man is that he has been trying to detach himself from nature. He sits in the topmost tiers of polymer, glass, and steel, dangling his pulsing legs, surveying at a distance the writhing life of the planet. In this scenario, Man comes on as a stupendous lethal force, and the earth is pictured as something delicate, like rising bubbles at the surface of a country pond, or flights of fragile birds.
>
> But it is illusion to think that there is anything fragile about the life of the earth; surely this is the toughest membrane imaginable in the universe, opaque to probability, impermeable to death. We are the delicate part, transient and vulnerable as cilia. Nor is it a new thing for man to invent an existence that he imagines to be above the rest of life; this has been his most consistent intellectual exertion down the millennia. As illusion, it has never worked out to his satisfaction in the past, any more than it does today. Man is embedded in nature (p. 3).

In this essay, Thomas expresses, almost as a conclusion to an argument not presented, the affirmation of the "oneness" of man and nature, an affirmation which seems to have almost the same ring and the same conviction as Beethoven's 9th Symphony. Through a myriad of unifying metaphors, Thomas makes significant scientific and social statements which encapsulate much of what we regard as important in the contemporary world; and these statements seem less didactic than beguiling because of the graciousness of their form.

As Thomas's essay suggests, much of the world of science is as metaphorical as the world of imaginative literature and, by necessity, writers must use the same language to express the great truths of both the public and the private domains. All of this is summed up very succinctly by Aldous Huxley in the final essay of *Literature and Science:*

> Words are few and can only be arranged in certain conventionally fixed ways; the counterpoint of unique events is infinitely wide and their succession indefinitely long. That the purified language of science, or even the richer purified language of literature should ever be adequate to the givenness of the world and of our experience is, in the very nature of things, impossible.

Cheerfully accepting the fact, let us advance together, men of letters and men of science, further and further into the ever-expanding regions of the unknown . . . (p. 118).

And, we might add, into the expanding literacy of the 21st century.

In the foregoing discussion we have cited only three of the many writers whose works we believe invite non-scientists into science, but we hope that teachers will be sufficiently intrigued by them to consider doing further reading on their own. We conclude with a short annotated bibliography of selected science writings, those we have cited, along with a half-dozen others, which teachers and their students in English classes will find a useful bridge from imaginative literature into science. We have kept the list short because we felt it should be manageable and also because we wanted to focus attention on books and essays which are reasonably accessible in school and city libraries. Furthermore, consciously drawing on materials written by active scientists, we have included selections which cover a wide scientific experience ranging from theories of scientific education through medicine and biology to physics because we hope to suggest at least some readings that will appeal to all tastes and interests. Finally, we would like to emphasize that this list is only a beginning. We see it as an appetizing *hors d'oeuvre* which may tempt teachers and students and sharpen their appetites for science writing in the quest for literacy.

Bibliography

Bernstein, Jeremy. *Science Observed: Essays Out of My Mind.* NY: Basic Books, 1982.
    Seventeen essays. Particularly recommended: "Nuclear Research," "Shooting the Pussycat," and "Furth's Reactor and Fusion." An intelligent introduction through well-written essays to the advantages and problems of nuclear reactors and to their mythology. Also recommended: "Can TV Really Teach Science?"

Campbell, Norman. "The Explanation of Laws," *Science and Society.* Eds. Alexander Vavoulis and A. Wayne Colver. San Francisco: Holden-Day, 1966, pp. 41–48.
    A short, strikingly lucid introduction to the concepts of theories and laws in science.

Dyson, Freeman. *Disturbing the Universe.* NY: Harper & Row, 1979.
    The story of a scientifically creative life told by a humane scientist in a form easily readable by non-scientists. Particularly recommended: Chapters 1, 5, 8 and 9.

Eiseley, Loren. *The Firmament of Time.* NY; Atheneum, 1967.
    Six lectures. These beautifully written essays direct one's thoughts toward nature and the mystery of human emergence while clarifying the role of the evolution of science in society. Particularly recommended: "How the World Became Natural."

Huxley, Aldous. *Literature and Science.* NY: Harper & Row, 1963.
    Thirty-eight numbered essays. Probably the most literate account ever written of the relationship between science and literature and their similarities and distinctions. Particularly recommended: 1, 2, 3, 4 and 38.

Huxley, Julian. *New Bottles for New Wine*. NY: Harper & Row, 1957.
    Thirteen essays on biologically-oriented science. Particularly recommended:
"New Bottles for New Wine." A scientific yet all-embracing view of Western
scientific philosophy. Somewhat scholarly, but its subject matter is as valid now
as when it was published.

Huxley, Thomas H. *Science and Education: Essays*. NY: D. Appleton and
    Company, 1910. Reprinted, Norwood Editions.
    Seventeen essays. Particularly recommended: "On Science and Art in
Relation to Education." Engagingly written by the "father of scientific education," this essay reminds us that relations between science and art have long
been uneasy and that thoughtful people have long seen the value of bringing the
two traditions together through education.

The Mystery of Matter. Ed. Louise B. Young. NY: Oxford University Press,
    1965.
    Particularly recommended: Part 11, "Is Science Destroyer or Creator?"
Through a varied collection of writings from science and imaginative literature,
this serves as a highly readable introduction to the philosophy of science and
society and to the study of relationships between them.

Science and Society: Selected Essays. Eds. Alexander Vavoulis and A. Wayne
    Colver. San Francisco: Holden-Day, 1966.
    Fifteen essays. A treasure trove of science writing by such superb and authori-
tative authors as Jacob Bronowski, John Z. Young, Erwin C. Schrödinger,
Werner Heisenberg, and Ernst Cassirer. Particularly recommended: Norman
Campbell's "The Explanation of Laws," Banesh Hoffmann's "Wave or Particle?"
and Michael Polanyi's "Passion and Controversy in Science."

Thomas, Lewis. *The Lives of a Cell: Notes of a Biology Watcher*. NY: Viking
    Press, 1974.
    Twenty-nine essays, all informative and delightful. As Joyce Carol Oates
wrote in her review, "*The Lives of a Cell* anticipates the kind of writing that will
appear more and more frequently as scientists take on the language of poetry in
order to communicate human truth too mysterious for old fashioned common
sense."

_____. *The Medusa and the Snail: More Notes of a Biology Watcher*. NY:
    Viking Press, 1979.
    Twenty-nine essays. An engaging exposition, through short essays, on the
beauties and surprises of the biological universe and its interrelationship with
human beings.

6 Language, Literature, and the Humanistic Tradition: Necessities in the Education of the Physician

John H. Siegel, M.D.
Deputy Director of The Maryland Institute for Emergency Medical Services Systems (MIEMSS), Director of the MIEMSS Clinical Center and Professor of Surgery at The University of Maryland

Medicine is an art and a science. And, it is ultimately the most humanistic of all of the disciplines, for it seeks to heal the body and the mind. The humble roots of medicine are grounded in the classic literature of antiquity and the lofty branches are high in the brilliant atmosphere of science. But, as with many tall trees, when the nourishing source of life is far from the germinating buds, the fruit can be misshapen and unpleasant to taste.

We realize how far we have come away from our roots when we read or know of physicians whose greed for personal gratification or glory has led them to sacrifice the humanism on which their profession is based. We celebrate in our hearts those doctors who show by their conduct that they truly understand the first aphorism of Hippocrates that, "Life is short, and the art long; the occasion fleeting; experience fallacious, and judgment difficult. The physician must not only be prepared to do what is right himself, but also to make the patient, the attendants and the externals cooperate" (from "Writings of Hippocrates," in Ralph H. Major, *Classic Descriptions of Disease, With Biographical Sketches of the Authors.* Baltimore, Maryland: C. C. Thomas, 1939, p. 3).

For Hippocrates, observation of the sick person and synthesis of observations into a pattern of the disease process becomes the key to understanding the nature of the affliction besetting the patient. This knowledge also has its pragmatic usefulness to the physician. Since by cultivating the ability to prognosticate, the physician will be esteemed to be good, "for he will be better able to treat those aright who can be saved, from having anticipated everything; and by seeing and announcing beforehand those who will live and those who will die, he will thus escape censure" (p. 4).

Observation and description of events with a sense of their relationship over time underlie the physician's narration of a clinical history. However, to communicate these patterns to others one must develop the skills of language and learn how to concatenate mere words into metaphors which organize our consciousness of the world around us. Hippocrates described the countenance of the patient in whom death is impending as one having, "a sharp nose, hollow eyes, collapsed temples; the ears cold, contracted, and their lobes turned out; the skin around the forehead being rough, distended, and parched; the color of the whole face being, green, black, livid, or lead colored" (p. 5). This is known the world over as the "Hippocratic facies," and this term in itself has become a universal metaphor for the appearance of the patient in whom certain death is at hand.

I emphasize the value of observation and description of complex life processes, and the ability to use language to extract the essence of this experience in order to communicate it to others as an analog of experience, to make a point. To function well, the physician must act as a parallel processor, a pattern recognition device who tempers observation and action with the qualities of compassion and empathy to fulfil the dual role of scientist and humanist. Unfortunately, the present approach to the education of the future physician and scientist is failing to develop these qualities essential to communication and humanism. Current premedical and medical teaching deliver education in a format which is too rigorously scientific, in a linear rather than integrative way, and in a way which de-emphasizes the interaction with human experience. As a result, we all too often read physician's notes which are dry, uninformative catalogues of events with the flesh, blood and emotion wrung out of them. More disturbingly, we hear a patient referred to in a dehumanizing fashion as an anatomic abnormality, "the fractured femur in bed two," or as the living manifestation of a biochemical process gone wrong, "the little glycogen storage disease in the nursery."

While there are many reasons for the humanistic educational failures that we produce as graduates of our colleges and universities, part of the problem may lie in our failure to find ways to compensate for the early-childhood acquisition of a disproportionate amount of information from the 2-dimensional medium of television rather than the 4-dimensional medium of life. "TV" minimizes two-way communication and more important, it is not structured to emphasize the conscious creation of an awareness of the events seen, nor does it impart a realistic sense of time or process. The viewer-student is not forced to create a metaphoric description of what has been seen. As a result, he develops a poor structure of conscious awareness, which may lead to an acting out rather than to an internalization of the process experienced. For example, we often see in children a mimicking of the perceived acts of violence seen on the screen, rather than an understanding of the pain and suffering incurred by the victims of such violence.

I believe that there is a great deal of evidence to support Julian Jayne's contention, in his book on the bicameral mind, *The Origins of Consciousness in the Breakdown of the Bicameral Mind* (Boston: Houghton Mifflin, 1976), that metaphor and analog are the means by which we create a structure to our consciousness that enables us to view the present and the future with a sense of self. Without a sense of self involvement, it is not possible to develop those qualities of empathy and compassion which are the hallmarks of the good doctor, and without a comfortable use of language as a means of structuring our feelings it is not possible to communicate them to others. It is often said that the physician treats the disease, but the *doctor* treats the patient. We train lots of physicians, but educate few doctors.

The doctor, like the writer, needs to develop skills in metaphor generation and in the use of language for communication which accurately describe events and processes in a humanistic manner. Below are two passages presented as examples of the similarity in approach to compassionate description fitting the needs of the doctor and the writer; each passage fits the needs of its author. The first is by Aretaeus, the Cappadocian, a physician of the second century AD, describing acute suppurative tonsilitis. The second, written by Giovanni Boccaccio, is from the introduction to the *Decameron* describing the epidemic of bubonic plague in Florence that occurred in 1348.

Aretaeus by his metaphor of fire or carbuncle, meaning a live coal, conveys the sense of a soul in the torments of a Hell in life, brought to surcease only by death itself, but his description of the disease process is also an accurate and complete narrative of the clinical course:

> The manner of death is most piteous; pain sharp and hot as from carbuncle; respiration bad, for their breath smells strongly of putrefaction, as they constantly inhale the same again into their chest; they are in so loathesome a state that they cannot endure the smell of themselves; countenance pale or livid; fever acute, thirst as if from fire, and yet they do not desire drink for fear of the pains it would occasion; for they become sick if it compress the tonsils, or if it return by the nostrils; and if they lie down they rise up again as not being able to endure the recumbent position, and if they rise up, they are forced in their distress to lie down again; they mostly walk about erect, for in their inability to obtain relief they flee from rest, as if wishing to dispel one pain by another. Inspiration large, as desiring cold air for the purpose of refrigeration, but expiration small, for the ulceration, as if produced by burning, is inflammed by the heat of the respiration. Hoarseness, loss of speech supervene; and these symptoms hurry on from bad to worse, until suddenly falling to the ground they expire (*The Extant Work of Aretaeus, the Cappadocian.* Ed. and Trans. Francis Adamis. London: Sydenham Society, Francis, 1856, p. 253).

Boccaccio also conveys the inevitability of a horrible spreading death but adds the artist's license of attributing causation to the divine wrath of a just God.

> I say, then, that the years (of the era) of the fruitful incarnation of the Son of God had attained to the number of one thousand three hundred and forty-eight, when into the notable city of Florence, fair over every other of Italy, there came the death dealing pestilence, which, through the operation of the heavenly bodies or of our own iniquitous dealings, being sent down upon mankind for our correction by the just wrath of God, had some years before appeared in the parts of the East and after having bereft these later of an innumerable number of inhabitants, extending without cease from one place to another, and now unhappily spread toward the West. And thereagainst no wisdom availing nor human foresight (whereby the city was purged of many impurities by officers deputed to that end and it was forbidden unto any sick person to enter therein and many were the counsels given for the preservation of health) nor yet humble supplications, not once but many times both in ordered processions and in otherwise made unto God by devout persons—about the coming in of the Spring of the aforesaid year, it began in horrible and miraculous wise to show forth its dolorous effects, yet not as it had done in the East, where, if any bled at the nose, it was a manifest sign of inevitable death! Nay, but in men and women alike there appeared at the beginning of the malady, certain swellings, either on the groin or under the armpits, whereof some waxed of the bigness of a common apple, others like unto an egg, some more and some less, and these the vulgar named plague-boils. From these two parts the aforesaid death-bearing plague-

boils proceeded, in brief space, to appear and come indifferently in every part of the body; wherefrom, after awhile, the fashion of the contagion began to change into black or livid blotches, which showed themselves in many (first on the arms and on the thighs) and after spread to every other part of the person, in some large and sparse and in others small and thick-sown, and like as the plague-boils had been first (and yet were) a very certain token of coming death, even so were these for every one to whom they came.

To the cure of these maladies nor counsel of physicians nor virtue of any medicine appeared to avail or profit aught.

Because the writer needs to have a broader view of disease than does the physician, Boccaccio provides the sense of the historical tragedy occasioned by the outbreak of plague.

Alas, how many great palaces, how many goodly houses, how many noble mansions once full of families, of lords and of ladies, abode empty even to the meanest servant. How many memorable families, how many ample heritages, how many famous fortunes were seen to remain without lawful heir. How many valiant men, how many fair ladies, how many sprightly youths, whom, not others only but Galen, Hippocrates or Easculapius themselves, would have judged most hale, breakfasted in the morning with their kindsfolk, comrades and friends and that same night supped with their ancestors in the other world.

In contrast, the physician is constrained by experience and training to choose a metaphoric structure to his descriptive language that develops a structure of consciousness allowing for further investigation from the same group of observations. This language structure also projects the imperative for therapeutic action, if and when the real, not the theologic, cause of the malady becomes known. Consider, for instance the description, again by Aretaeus the Cappadocian, of the disease we now know as *diabetes mellitus:*

Diabetes is a wonderful affection, not very frequent among men, being a melting down of the flesh and limbs into urine. Its cause is of a cold and humid nature, as in dropsy. The course is the common one, namely, the kidneys and bladder; for the patients never stop making water, but the flow is incessant, as if from the opening of aqueducts. The nature of the disease, then, is chronic, and it takes a long period to form; but the patient is short-lived, if the constitution of the disease be completely established; for the melting is rapid, the death speedy. Moreover, life is disgusting and painful; thirst unquenchable; excessive drinking, which, however, is disproportionate to the large quantity of urine, for more urine is passed; and one cannot stop them either from drinking or making water. Or if for a time they abstain from drinking, their mouth becomes parched and their body dry; the viscera seem as if scored up; they are affected with nausea, restlessness, and a burning thirst; and at no distant term they expire. Thirst, as if scorched up with fire. But by what method could they be restrained from making water? Or how can shame become more potent than pain? And even if they were to restrain themselves for a short time, they become swelled in the loins, scrotum, and hips, and when they give vent, they discharge the collected urine, and the swellings subside for the overflow passes to the bladder (*The Extant,* p. 338).

Written in the second century after Christ, this is indeed a remarkably accurate portrayal of this disease, made even more impressive in the preciseness of its organizing metaphor that diabetes is " . . . a melting down of the flesh and the limbs into urine." Its accuracy is especially impressive since seventeen hundred years later we have just come to understand that the biochemistry of this disease is a pathophysiologic conversion of muscle protein and body fat stores into excess production of glucose, which cannot be metabolized in the absence of the hormone insulin. The glucose produced by this gluconeogenic process is therefore excreted by the kidney, osmotically carrying with it large quantities of body water as urine. Indeed, it was the discovery in the 18th century by Willis (courageous fellow) that the large quantity of urine described by Aretaeus, "as if from the opening of aqueducts," was sweet, "as if imbued with sugar or honey," that opened the modern era of biochemical investigation of disease.

The fascination that both writers and physicians have for each other's thought processes and powers of observation has produced some interesting and powerful literary works, and I believe that it is more than random chance that so many modern writers have first trained as physicians—A. Conan Doyle, A. J. Cronin, Somerset Maugham, and Chekov, to name but a few. What is often forgotten, however, is that the early premedical education of these men was in the classic tradition, where language and metaphor structured their consciousness along humanistic lines.

It is also no accident that the most famous detective of fiction, Sherlock Holmes, was modeled after the leading physical diagnostician and surgeon of his day, Joseph Bell, a teacher of A. Conan Doyle, Holmes' creator. Bell uniquely combined the scientific and humanistic traditions. He saw individual men and women in the context of their social subcultures, adapting to or suffering from their disease processes. Nowhere are the physician's powers of observation and deductive logic better synthesized with realistic descriptive writing and a sense of the classic educational tradition than in the Holmes stories, as shown in this brief excerpt from "The Red-headed League":

The portly client puffed out his chest with an appearance of some little pride and pulled a dirty and wrinkled newspaper from the inside pocket of his greatcoat. As he glanced down the advertisement column, with his head thrust forward and the paper flattened out upon his knee, I took a good look at the man and endeavoured, after the fashion of my companion, to read the indications which might be presented by his dress or appearance.

I did not gain very much, however, by my inspection. Our visitor bore every mark of being an average commonplace British tradesman, obese, pompous, and slow. He wore rather baggy gray shepherd's check trousers, a not over-clean black frock-coat, unbuttoned in the front, and a drab waist-coat with a heavy brassy Albert chain, and a square pierced bit of metal dangling down as an ornament. A frayed top-hat and a faded brown overcoat with a wrinkled velvet collar lay upon a chair beside him. Altogether, look as I would, there was nothing remarkable about the man save his blazing red head, and the expression of extreme chagrin and discontent upon his features.

Sherlock Holmes's quick eye took in my occupation, and he shook his head with a smile as he noticed my questioning blances. "Beyond the obvious facts that he has at some time done manual labour, that he takes snuff, that he is a Freemason, that he has been in China, and that he has done a considerable amount of writing lately, I can deduce nothing else."

Mr. Jabez Wilson started up in his chair, with his forefinger upon the paper, but his eyes upon my companion.

"How, in the name of good-fortune, did you know all that, Mr. Holmes?" he asked. "How did you know, for example, that I did manual labour? It's as true as gospel, for I began as a ship's carpenter."

"Your hands, my dear sir. Your right hand is quite a size larger than your left. You have worked with it, and the muscles are more developed."

"Well, the snuff, then, and the Freemasonry?"

"I won't insult your intelligence by telling you how I read that, especially as, rather against the strict rules of your order, you use an arc-and-compass breastpin."

"Ah, of course, I forgot that. But the writing?"

"What else can be indicated by that right cuff so very shiny for five inches, and the left one with the smooth patch near the elbow where you rest it upon the desk?"

"Well, but China?"

"The fish that you have tattooed immediately above your right wrist could only have been done in China. I have made a small study of tattoo marks and have even contributed to the literature of the subject. That trick of staining the fishes' scales of a delicate pink is quite peculiar to China. When, in addition, I see a Chinese coin hanging from your watch-chain, the matter becomes even more simple."

Mr. Jabez Wilson laughed heavily. "Well, I never!" he said. "I thought at first that you had done something clever, but I see that there was nothing in it, after all."

"I began to think, Watson," said Holmes, "that I make a mistake in explaining. *Omne ignotum pro magnifico,* you know, and my poor little reputation, such as it is, will suffer shipwreck if I am so candid."

Finally, and most importantly, a sensitive appreciation of humanistic tradition makes it possible to develop a consciousness that permits the physician to feel and to give voice to his own feelings of frustration, anguish and loss, as a means of learning to empathize with his patients and their families in times of need. Familiarity with the metaphors and images of great literature can sensitize the consciousness to respond anamnestically and can show that such conduct is not only permissible but virtuous and laudatory. Such a use is well illustrated in the following passage from *The Plague,* by Camus, in which the doctor, Rieux, distraughtly attends and then mourns the death of his friend, Tarrou.

At noon the fever reached its climax. A visceral cough racked the sick man's body and he now was spitting blood. The ganglia had ceased swelling, but they were still there, like lumps of iron embedded in the joints. Rieux decided that lancing them was impracticable. Now and then, in the intervals between bouts of fever and coughing fits, Tarrou still gazed at his friends. But soon his eyes opened less and less often and the glow that shone out from the ravaged face in the brief moments of recognition grew steadily fainter. The storm, lashing his body into convulsive moment, lit it up with ever rarer flashes, and in the heart of the tempest he was slowly drifting, derelict. And now Rieux had before him only a masklike face, inert, from which the smile had gone forever. This human form, his friend's, lacerated by the spear-thrusts of the plague, consumed by searing, superhuman fires, buffeted by all the raging winds of heaven, was foundering under his eyes in the dark flood of the pestilence, and he could do nothing to avert the wreck. He could only stand, unavailing, on the shore, empty-handed and sick at heart, unarmed and helpless yet again under the onset of calamity. And thus, when the end came, the tears that blinded Rieux's eyes were tears of impotence; and he did not see Tarrou roll over, face to the wall, and die with a short, hollow groan as if somewhere within him an essential chord had snapped.

The next night was not one of struggle but of silence. In the tranquil death-chamber, beside the dead body now in everyday clothing—here, too, Rieux felt it brooding, that elemental peace which, when he was sitting many nights before on the terrace high above the plague, had followed the brief foray at the gates. Then, already, it had brought to his mind the silence brooding over the beds in which he had let men die. There as here it was the same solemn pause, the lull that follows battle; it was the silence of defeat. But the silence now enveloping his dead friend, so dense, so much akin to the nocturnal silence of the streets and of the town set free at last, made Rieux cruelly aware that this defeat was final, the last disastrous battle that ends a war and makes peace itself an ill beyond all remedy. The doctor could not tell if Tarrou had found peace, now that all was over, but for himself he had a feeling that no peace was possible to him henceforth, any more than there can be an armistice for a mother bereaved of her son or for a man who buries his friend.

The point in this brief essay is not that some doctors make good writers, nor is it that good narrative writing is a common feature of a good story and of a classic description of disease. Rather, it is to emphasize that the physician serves his patients and his art best when he functions in the humanist tradition. Training in the skills of observation and description, and in the use of metaphor as a means of structuring a common consciousness, is an important feature of pre-medical and medical education.

Most important, it is through the development of a humanistic consciousness that we can imbue best a sense of the patient as a person (like the doctor believes himself to be) whose psychological and emotional needs must be attended to along with his disease process. The seamless web of *persona* and *physiologica* is not derived from the scientific tradition, although modern medical science has reluctantly come around to that view, but is rather a product of our culture and our literary heritage and is embedded in our metaphors of life, growth, reproduction and death.

To know, to understand, and to teach the lessons of the past are the joint responsibility of both the medical and humanistic faculties of our colleges and universities. But, in a time when values are in question and there are conflicting winds of opinion, there is need for the re-establishment of the humanistic tradition of Western civilization as the core program in primary, secondary, and university education. For this program, an emphasis on the relationship between our language and *all* of our cultural roots would seem to offer a way to create anew the important aspects of a common consciousness on which our society is based. The true reconciliation between science and humanism can occur only in the mind of each man or woman who *is* a scientist or physician, not in some ill-defined aspect of the non-conscious society around them. The use of language and metaphor to structure and shape that consciousness is too important a task to leave to the teachers of English alone. It must be developed as a clinical tool common to all disciplines, to be handled with the same care and under the same kind of peer review as we believe necessary for those who use the scalpel to cure or who administer any dangerous therapeutic medicine.

7 The Invisible Discourse of the Law: Reflections on Legal Literacy and General Education*

James Boyd White
The Law School, The University of Chicago

My subject today is "legal literacy," but to put it that way requires immediate clarification, for that phrase has a wide range of possible meanings, with many of which we shall have nothing to do. At one end of its spectrum of significance, for example, "legal literacy" means full competence in legal discourse, both as reader and as writer. This kind of literacy is the object of a professional education, and it requires not only a period of formal schooling but years of practice as well. Indeed, as is also the case with other real languages, the ideal of perfect competence in legal language can never be attained; the practitioner is always learning about his language and about the world, he is in a sense always remaking both,

*This essay is based upon a talk delivered at the conference on "Literacy in the 1980's," sponsored by the English Composition Board at The University of Michigan from 24–27 June, 1981. It is reprinted here as it appears in the *Michigan Quarterly Review.* vol. 21, no. 3 (Summer, 1982), and as it will appear in *Literacy for Life: The Demand for Reading and Writing.* Eds. Richard W. Bailey and Robin Melanie Fosheim (New York: The Modern Language Association of America forthcoming), by permission of James B. White, the *Michigan Quarterly Review,* and Richard Bailey and Robin Fosheim.

and these processes never come to an end. What this sort of professional literacy entails, and how it is to be talked about, are matters of interest to lawyers and law teachers, but are not our subject here. The other end of the spectrum of "legal literacy" would mean the capacity to recognize legal words and locutions as foreign to oneself, as part of the world of the Law. A person literate in this sense would know that there was a world of language and action called "law," but little more about it: certainly not enough to have any real access to it.

Between these extremes is another possible meaning of "legal literacy": that degree of competence in legal discourse required for meaningful and active life in our increasingly legalistic and litigious culture. The citizen who was ideally literate in this sense would not be expected to know how to draft deeds and wills or to try cases or to manage the bureaucratic maze, but he would know when and how to call upon the specialists who can do these things. More important, in the rest of life he would be able to protect and advance his own interests: for example in dealing with a landlord or a tenant, or in his interactions with the police, with the zoning commission, or with the Social Security Administration. He or she would be able not only to follow but to evaluate news reports and periodical literature dealing with legal matters, from Supreme Court decisions to House Committee Reports; to function effectively in positions of responsibility and leadership (say as an elected member of a school board, or as chairman of a neighborhood association, or as a member of a zoning board or police commission). The ideal is that of a fully competent and engaged citizen, and it is a wholly proper one to keep before us.

But this ideal is for our purposes far too inclusive, for however one defines "legal literacy," such a figure possesses a great deal in addition to that: he has a complete set of social, intellectual, and political relations and capacities. But perhaps we can meaningfully ask: what is the "legal literacy" that such an ideal figure would have? How could this sort of competence be taught? What seem to be the natural barriers to its acquisition? In the first part of this paper I deal with these questions, but in reverse order: I begin by identifying those features that make it peculiarly difficult for the nonlawyer to understand and to speak legal discourse; I then suggest some ways in which those features might be made comprehensible and manageable, and their value and function appreciated. This in turn will constitute my answer to the first question, i.e., what kind of legal literacy an ordinary citizen ought to have, and how it can contribute not only to the development of social competence but to a true education of the mind and self.

The Invisible Discourse of the Law

It is a common experience for a nonlawyer to feel that legal language is in a deep sense foreign: not only are its terms incomprehensible, its speakers seem to have available to them a repertoire of moves that are denied the rest of us. We neither understand the force of their arguments nor know how to answer them. But the language is, if possible, worse than merely foreign: it is an unpredictable, exasperating, and shifting mixture of the foreign and the familiar. Much of what lawyers say and write is after all intelligible to the nonlawyer, and he can sometimes speak in legally competent ways. But at any moment things can change without notice: the language slides into the incomprehensible, and the nonlawyer has no idea how or why the shift occurred. This is powerfully frustrating, to say the least.

But is is more than frustrating, for it entails an increasingly important disability, almost a disenfranchisement. At one time in our history it could apparently have been assumed that a citizen did not need to have any specialized knowledge of law, for our law was a common law that reflected the customs and expectations of the people to such a degree that ordinary social competence was normally enough for effectiveness in the enterprises of life. No special legal training was required. But in our increasingly bureaucratic and legalistic world, this seems less and less the case: the frustrated citizen is likely to feel that his life is governed by language—in a lease, in a form contract, or in a federal or state regulation—that he cannot understand. Who, for example, can read and understand an insurance contract, or a pension plan? An OSHA or IRS regulation? Yet these govern our lives, and are even said in some sense to have the standing of our own acts: either directly, as in the case of the contracts we sign, or indirectly, as in the case of laws promulgated by officials who represent us. In a democracy this unintelligibility is doubly intolerable, for the people are supposed to be competent both as voters to elect the lawmakers, and as jurors to apply the laws, and they cannot do these things if they cannot understand the law.

What can explain this flickering pattern of intelligibility and unintelligibility, the stroboscopic alternation of the familiar with the strange? The most visible and frequently denounced culprits are the arcane vocabulary of the law, and the complicated structure of its sentences and paragraphs. This leads some to ask: why can the lawyers not be made to speak in words we recognize, and in sentences we can understand? This would enable the ordinary citizen to become competent as a reader of law, and even as a legal speaker. Our political method of democracy, and its moral premise of equality, demand no less. It may be, indeed, that the only actual effect of this obfuscating legal jargon is to maintain the mystique of the legal profession and if that mystique is destroyed so much the better.

Impulses such as these have given rise to what is known as the Plain English Movement, which aims at a translation of legal language into comprehensible English. This movement has had practical effects: at the federal level, for example, one of President Carter's first actions was to order that all regulations be cast in language intelligible to the ordinary citizen, and New York and other states have passed laws requiring that state regulations and form contracts meet a similar standard.

If such directives were seriously regarded, they might indeed reduce needless verbosity and obscurity, and streamline unwieldy legal sentences. But even if they succeeded in these desirable goals, they would not solve the general problem they address, for, as I will try to show, the most serious obstacles to comprehensibility are not the vocabulary and sentence structure employed in the law, but the unstated conventions by which the language operates: what I call the "invisible discourse" of the law. Behind the words, that is, are expectations about the ways in which they will be used, expectations that do not find explicit expression anywhere but are part of the legal culture that the surface language simply assumes. These expectations are constantly at work, directing argument, shaping responses, determining the next move, and so on; their effects are everywhere but they themselves are invisible. It is these conventions, not the diction, that primarily determine the mysterious character of legal speech and literature: not the "vocabulary" of the law, but what might be called its "cultural syntax."

In what follows I will identify those features of what I call the "cultural syntax" of legal language that seem most radically to differentiate it from ordinary speech. I will then outline some methods by which I think students can be taught to become at least somewhat literate in a language that works in these ways. Finally I will suggest that this kind of literacy not only entails an important increase in social competence, but itself contributes to that development of mind and attitude which is the object of a general education.

The Language of Rules

Many of the special difficulties of legal language derive from the fact that at the center of most legal conversations will be found a form we call the legal rule. Not so general as to be a mere maxim or platitude (though we have those in the law, too), nor so specific as to be a mere order or command (though there are legal versions of these), the legal rule is a directive of intermediate generality. It establishes relations among classes of objects, persons, and events: "All A are [or: shall be] B"; or, "If A, then B." Examples would include the following:

1. "Burglary consists of breaking and entering a dwelling house in the nighttime with intent to commit a felony therein. A person convicted of burglary shall be punished by imprisonment not to exceed 5 years."
2. "Unless otherwise ordered by the court or agreed by the parties, the former husband's obligation to pay alimony terminates upon the remarriage of his former wife."

Legal conversations about rules such as these have three major characteristics that tend to mystify and confuse the nonlawyer.

The Invisible Shift from a Language of Description to a Language of Judgment

The first of these is that the form of the legal rule misleads the ordinary reader into expecting that once it is understood its application will be very simple. The rules presented above, for example, have a plain and authoritative air and seem to contemplate no difficulty in their application whatever. (Notice that with the possible exception of the word "felony," there is nothing legalistic in their diction.) One will simply look to the facts and determine whether or not the specified conditions exist; if so, the consequence declared by the rule will follow; if not, it will not. "Did she remarry? Then the alimony stops." Nothing to it, the rule seems to say; just look at the world and do what we tell you. It calls for nothing more than a glance to check the name against the reality, and obedience to a plain directive.

In practice of course the rule does not work so simply, or not always. Is it "breaking and entering" if the person pushes open a screen door but has not yet entered the premises? Is a garage with a loft used as an apartment a "dwelling house"? Is dusk "nighttime"? Is a remarriage that is later annulled a "remarriage" for the purpose of terminating prior alimony? Or what if there is no formal remarriage but the ex-wife has a live-in boyfriend? These questions do not answer themselves but require thought and conversation of a complex kind, of which no hint is expressed in the rule itself.

Of course there will be some cases so clear that no one could reasonably argue about the meaning of the words, and in these cases the rule will work in a fairly simple and direct fashion. This is in fact our experience of making most rules work: we can find out what to do to get a passport or a driver's license, we know what the rules of the road require, we can figure out when we need a building permit, and so on. But these are occasions of rules-obedience in which no special social or intellectual competence is involved.

One way to identify what is misleading about the form of a legal rule might be to say that it appears to be a language of description, which works by a simple process of comparison, but in cases of any difficulty it is actually a language of judgment, which works in ways that find no expression in the rule itself. In such cases the meaning of its terms is not obvious, as the rule seems to assume, but must be determined by a process of interpretation and judgment to which the rule gives no guidance whatever. The discourse by which it works is in this sense invisible.

The False Appearance of Deductive Rationality

Even if one recognizes that there may be difficulties in understanding and applying a rule, one may still be misled by its form into thinking that the kind of reasoning it requires (and makes possible) is deductive in character. A legal rule looks rather like a rule of geometry, and we naturally expect it to work like one. For example, when the meaning of a term in a rule is unclear—say "dwelling house" or "nighttime" in the burglary statute—we expect to find a stipulative definition somewhere else (perhaps in a special section of the statute) that will define it for us, just as Euclid tells us the meaning of his essential terms. Or if there is no explicit definition, we expect there to be some other rule, general in form, which when considered in connection with our rule will tell us what it must mean. But we look for such definitions and such rules often in vain, and when we find them they often prove to be of little help.

Suppose for example the question is whether a person who is caught breaking into a garage that has a small apartment in the loft can be convicted of burglary: does a statutory definition of "dwelling house" as "any residential premises" solve the problem? Or suppose one finds in the law dealing with mortgages a definition of "dwelling house" that plainly does (or does not) cover the garage with the loft: does that help? Upon reflection about the purpose of the burglary statute, which is to punish a certain kind of wrongdoing, perhaps "dwelling house" will suddenly be seen to have a subjective or moral dimension, and properly mean: "place where the actor knows that people are living" or, if that be thought too lenient, "place where he has reason to believe that people are living."

Or consider the annulment example. Suppose one finds a statutory statement that "an annulled marriage is a nullity at law." Does that mean that the alimony payment revives upon the annulment of the wife's second marriage? Even if the annulment takes place fifteen years after the marriage? Or suppose that there is another statute, providing that "alimony may be awarded in an annulment proceeding to the same extent as in a divorce proceeding"? This would mean that the wife could get alimony from her second husband, and if the question is seen in terms of fairness among the parties, this opportunity would be highly relevant to whether or not her earlier right to alimony has expired.

The typical form of the legal rule thus seems to invite us to think that in reading it our main concern will be with the relations among propositions, as one rule is related to others by the logical rules of noncontradiction and the like; and that the end result of every intellectual operation will be determined by the rules of deduction.

In fact the situation could hardly be more different. Instead of each term having a meaning of the sort necessary for deductive operations to go on in the first place, each term in a legal rule has a range of possible meanings, among which choices will have to be made. There is no one right answer to the question whether this structure is a "dwelling house," or that relationship a "remarriage"; there are several linguistically and logically tolerable possibilities and the intellectual process of law is one of arguing and reasoning about which of them is to be preferred. Of course the desirability of internal consistency is a factor (though we shall soon see that the law tolerates a remarkable degree of internal contradiction), and of course in some cases some issues will be too plain for argument. But the operations that lawyers and judges engage in with respect to legal rules are very different from what we might expect from the form of the rule itself: they derive their substance and their shape from the whole world of legal culture, and draw upon the most diverse materials, ranging from general maxims to particular cases and regulations. The discourse of the law is far less technical, far more purposive and sensible, than the nonlawyer is likely to think. Argument about the meaning of words in the burglary statute, for example, would include argument about the reasons for having such a statute, about the kind of harm it is meant to prevent or redress, and about the degree and kind of blameworthiness it should therefore require. Legal discourse is continuous at some points with moral or philosophic discourse, at others with history or anthropology or sociology; and in its tension between the particular and the general, in its essentially metaphorical character, it has much in common with poetry itself. The substantive constitution of legal discourse is of course too complex a subject for us at present; what is important now is to see that this discourse is invisible to the ordinary reader of the legal rule.

These characteristics of legal language convert what looks like a discourse connected with the world by the easy process of naming, and rendered internally coherent by the process of deduction, into a much more complex linguistic and cultural system. The legal rule seems to foreclose certain questions of fact and value, and of course in the clear cases it does so. But in the uncertain cases, which are those that cause trouble, it can better be said to open than to close a set of questions: it gives them definition, connection with other questions, and a place in a rhetorical universe, and this permits their elaboration and resolution in a far more rich and complex way than could otherwise be the case. Except in the plainest cases the function of the ordinary meanings of the terms used in legal rules is not to determine a necessary result but to establish the uncertain boundaries of permissible decision; the function of logic is not to require a particular result by deductive force, but to limit the range of possibilities by prohibiting (or making difficult) contradictory uses of the same terms in the same sentences.

But you have perhaps noticed an odd evasion in that last sentence, and may be wondering: does not the law prohibit inconsistent uses of the same terms in the same rules? Indeed it does not, or not always, and this is the last of the three mystifying features of legal discourse about which I wish to speak.

The Systematic Character of Legal Discourse and the Dilemma of Consistency.

I have thus far suggested that while the legal rule appears to operate by a very simple process of looking at the world to see whether a named object can be found (the "dwelling house," or the "remarriage"), this appearance is highly misleading, for in fact the world often does not present events in packages that are plainly within the meaning of a legal label. Behind the application of the label is a complex world of reasoning which is in fact the real life of the law, but to which the rule makes no overt allusion, and for which it gives no guidance. To the extent that the form of the rule suggests that the controlling mode of reason will be deductive, it gives rise to expectations that are seriously misleading. The real discourse of the law is invisible.

This may seem bad enough, but in practice things are even worse, and for two reasons. First, however sophisticated and complex one's reasoning may in fact be, at the end of the process the legal speaker is required after all to express his or her judgment in the most simple binary terms: either the label in the rule fits or it does not. No third possibility is admitted. All the richness and complexity of legal life seems to be denied by the kind of act in which the law requires it to be expressed. For example, while we do not know precisely how the "dwelling house" or "remarriage" questions would in fact be argued out, we can see that the process would be complex and challenging, with room both for uncertainty and for invention. But at the end of the process the judge or jury will have to make a choice between two alternatives, and express it by the application (or nonapplication) of the label in question: this is, or is not, a "dwelling house." In this way the legal actors are required to act as if the legal world really were as simple as the rule misleadingly pretends it is. Everything is reduced to a binary choice after all.

Second, it seems that the force of this extreme reductionism cannot be evaded by giving the terms of legal rules slightly different meanings in different contexts, for the rudiments of logic and fairness alike require that the term be given the same meaning each time it is used, or the system collapses into incoherence and injustice. The most basic rule of logic (the rule of noncontradiction) and the most basic rule of justice (like results in like cases) both require consistency of meaning.

A familiar example demonstrating the requirement of internal consistency in systematic talk about the world is this: "However you define 'raining' the term must be used for the purposes of your system such that it is always true that it either is or is not 'raining.'" Any other principle would lead to internal incoherence, and would destroy the regularity of the discourse as a way of talking about the world. To put the principle in terms of the legal example we have been using: however one defines "dwelling house" for purposes of the burglary statute it must be used in such a manner that everything in the world either is or is not a "dwelling house"; and because the law is a system for organizing experience coherently across time and space, it must be given the same meaning every time it is used. Logic and fairness alike require no less.

The trouble is that these principles of discourse are very different from those employed in ordinary conversations. Who in real life would ever take the view that it must be the case that it either is or is not "raining"? Suppose it is just foggy and wet? If someone in ordinary life asked you whether it was raining out, you would not expect that person to insist upon an answer cast in categorical terms, let alone in categorical terms that were consistent over a set of conversations. The answer to the question would depend upon the reason it was asked: does your questioner want to know whether to wear his raincoat? Whether to water the garden? To call off a picnic? To take a sunbath? In each case the answer will be different, and the speaker will in no case feel required to limit his response to an affirmation or negation of the condition "raining." One will speak to the situation as a whole, employing all of one's resources. And one will not worry much about how the word "raining" has been used in other conversations, on other occasions, for the convention of ordinary speech is that critical terms are defined anew each time for the purposes of a particular conversation, not as part of a larger system.

What is distinctive about conversations about the meaning of rules is their systematic character: terms are defined not for the purposes of a particular conversation, but for a class of conversations, and the principle of consistency applies across the class. And this class of conversations has a peculiar form: in the operation of the rule all experience is reduced to a single set of questions—say whether the elements of burglary exist in this case—each of which must be answered "yes" or "no." We are denied what would be the most common response in our ordinary life, which would be to say that the label fits in this way and not in that, or that it depends on why you ask. The complex process of argument and judgment that is involved in understanding a legal rule and relating it to the facts of a particular case is at the end forced into a simple statement of "application" or "nonapplication" of a label.

But there is another layer to the difficulty. We may talk about the requirement of consistency as a matter of logic or justice, but how is it to be achieved?

Can we for example ensure that "dwelling house" will be used exactly the same way in every burglary case? Obviously we cannot, for a number of reasons. First, different triers of fact will resolve conflicts of testimony in different ways— one judge or jury would believe one side, a second the other—and this builds inconsistency into the process at the most basic level, that of descriptive fact. Second, while the judge may be required to give the same instruction to the jury in every case, the statement of that instruction will to some extent be cast in general terms and admit a fair variation of interpretation, even where the historical facts are settled. (E.g., a definition of "dwelling house" as "premises employed as a regular residence by those entitled to possession thereof.") Third, if the instruction includes, as well it might, a subjective element (such as something to the effect that the important question is whether the defendant *knew* he was breaking into a place where people were living), there will be an even larger variation in the application of what is on the surface the same language.

In short, the very generality of legal language, which constitutes for us an important part of its character as rational and as fair, means that some real variation in application must be tolerated. As the language becomes more general, the delegation of authority to the applier of the language, and hence the toleration of inconsistency in result, becomes greater. As the language becomes more specific, this delegation is reduced, and with it the potential inconsistency. But increasing specificity has its costs, and they too can be stated in terms of consistency. Consider a sentencing statute, for example, that authorizes the punishment of burglars by sentences ranging from probation to five years in prison. This delegation of sentencing authority (usually to a judge) seems to be a toleration of wide variation in result. But it all depends upon how the variation is measured. For to insist that all burglars receive the same sentence, say three years in jail, is to treat the hardened repeater and the inexperienced novice as if they were identical. That treatment is "consistent" on one measure (burglars treated alike) "inconsistent" on another (an obvious difference among offenders not recognized).

For our purposes the point is this: the requirements (1) that terms be defined not for a single conversation, but for the class of conversation established by the rule in question, and (2) that the meaning given words be consistent through the system, are seriously undercut in practice by a wide toleration of inconsistency in result and in meaning. I do not mean to suggest, however, that either the requirement of consistency or its qualifications are inappropriate. Quite the reverse: it seems to me that we have here a dilemma central to the life of any discourse that purports to be systematic, rational, and just. My purpose has simply been to identify a structural tension in legal discourse that differentiates it sharply from most ordinary speech.

In addition to the foregoing I wish to mention one other quality of legal literature, which radically distinguishes it from ordinary language: its procedural character.

The Procedural Character of Legal Speech

In working with a rule one must not only articulate the substantive questions that it is the purpose of a legal rule to define—is dusk "nighttime"? Is a bicycle a "vehicle"?, etc.—one must also ask a set of related procedural questions, of which very little recognition is usually to be found in the rule itself. For every question of interpretation involves these related questions: who shall decide what this language means? Under what conditions or circumstances, and subject to what limits or controls? Why? And in what body of discourse are these questions to be thought about, argued out, and decided?

Suppose for example the question is what the word "nighttime" should mean in the burglary statute; or, to begin not with a rule but with a difficulty in ordinary life, whether the development of a shopping center should be permitted on Brown's farm. It is the professional habit of the lawyer to think not only about the substantive merits of the question, and how he would argue it, but also about (a) the person or agency who ought to decide it, and (b) the procedure by which it ought to be decided. Is the shopping center question a proper one for the zoning commission, for the neighbors, for the city as a whole, or for the county court? Is the "nighttime" question one for the judge to decide, for the jury, or—if you think what matters is the defendant's intent in that respect—in part for the defendant himself? Every legal rule, however purely substantive in form, is also by implication a procedural and institutional statement as well, and the lawyers who read it will realize this and start to argue about its meaning in this dimension too. The function of the rule is thus to define not only substantive topics but procedures of argument and debate, questions about the definition and allocation of competencies to act; the rule does this either expressly or by implication, but in either event it calls upon discourse that is largely invisible to the reader not legally trained.

To sum up my point in a phrase, what characterizes legal discourse is that it is in a double sense (both substantively and procedurally) constitutive in nature: it creates a set of questions that define a world of thought and action, a set of roles and voices by which experience will be ordered and meanings established and shared; a set of occasions and methods for public speech that constitute us as a community and as a polity. In all of this it has its own ways of working, which are to be found not in the rules that are at the center of the structure, but in the culture which determines how these rules are to be read and talked about.

I have identified some of the special ways of thinking and talking that characterize legal discourse. Far more than any technical vocabulary, it is these conventions that are responsible for the foreignness of legal speech. To put it slightly differently, there is a sense in which one creates technical vocabulary whenever one creates a rule of the legal kind, for the operation of the rule in a procedural system itself necessarily involves an artificial way of giving meaning both to words and to events. These characteristics of legal discourse mean that the success of any movement to translate legal speech into Plain English will be severely limited. For if one replaces a Legal Word with an Ordinary English Word, the sense of increased normalcy will be momentary at best: the legal culture will go immediately to work, and the Ordinary Word will begin to lose its shape, its resiliency, and its familiarity, and become, despite the efforts of the draftsman, a Legal Word after all. The reason for this is that the word will work as part of the legal language, and it is the way this language works that determines the meaning of its terms. This is what I meant when I said that it is not the vocabulary of the legal language that is responsible for its obscurity and mysteriousness, but its "cultural syntax," the invisible expectations governing the way the words are to be used.

Teaching Legal Literacy: The Method of a Possible Course

Thus far I have been speaking to you as a lawyer to nonlawyers, describing those features of legal discourse that most mark it off from ordinary speech and make it difficult to understand. Now I wish to speak to you differently, as one teacher to another, and ask what kind of knowledge of this language can best be the object of an advanced high school or college writing course. What kind of legal literacy is it possible to help a nonprofessional attain? How can this best be done?

As I have made clear above, I start with the idea that literacy is not merely the capacity to understand the conceptual content of writings and utterances, but the ability to participate fully in a set of social and intellectual practices. It is not passive but active; not imitative but creative, for participation in the speaking and writing of language is participation in the activities it makes possible. Indeed it involves a perpetual remaking both of language and of practice.

To attain full legal literacy would accordingly require that one master both the resources by which topics are argued in the law and the set of procedural possibilities for argument that are established by the law, from the administrative agency to the jury, from the motion to strike to the writ of mandamus. Literacy of this sort is the object of a professional education and requires full-time immersion in the legal culture. It obviously cannot be attained in a high school or college course.

But this does not mean that nothing can be done to reduce the gap between the specialized language of the law and the ordinarily literate person. While one cannot make nonlawyers legally literate in the sense of full and active competence at law, one can do much to teach them about the kind of language law is and the kind of literature it produces. I think a student can come to understand, that is, something of what it means to speak a discourse that is constitutive and procedural in character and founded upon the form we call the rule. The successful student will not be able to practice law, nor even follow the lawyer in all of his moves, but he will have some knowledge, both tacit and explicit, of the kind of expectations the lawyer brings to a conversation, the kinds of needs and resources he has, and the kinds of moves he is likely to make. If what is at first invisible can be seen and understood, legal discourse will lose some of its power to frighten and to mystify. One will of course still experience a lack of comprehension, but these experiences will more often occur at expected moments and be of expected kinds. This means that one will be more confident about what one does comprehend, more certain about the moments at which one is entitled to insist upon clarification, or upon being heard. All this can come from an understanding of the legal system as a constitutive rhetoric based upon the rule.

But how is such an understanding to be created? An explicit analysis of the sort I have sketched above will be of little assistance to most students, for it proceeds largely at the conceptual level and literacy involves knowledge of a very different kind. (A student could learn to repeat sentences describing the rhetoric of the law, for example, without ever having any real sense of what these sentences mean.) Of almost equally limited value for our purposes are most courses in the structure and nature of our government, for once again the student often learns to repeat what he hears without any sense of what it means (think of the clichés about "checks and balances," for example, or the "imperial presidency"). Courses that attempt to teach students legal substance are often not much better, for knowledge of the rules does little good unless the student understands something of what it means to read and write a discourse based on rules. Besides, it frequently happens that the topics chosen are those of current popular interest, like abortion or the death penalty, where legal discourse (at least at the Supreme Court level) is not very sharply distinguished from ordinary political and journalistic talk.

More promising than the foregoing, or useful perhaps as a possible supplement to them, would be a course that asked students to write not about the law, but about analogues to the law in their own lives. The idea would be that they would become more competent not at law itself, but at law-like writing, and that this would teach them much not only about the law, but about themselves and their world.

What I have in mind is something like the following. Suppose students were asked to write a series of assignments about an aspect of their own lives that was regulated by rules—say their athletic team, or the school itself, or their apartment house, or their part-time jobs. These rules could be examined from several different perspectives. First, for example, students might be asked simply to reproduce the rules governing parts of their lives. Without overtly burdening the students with the knowledge, this assignment would raise very sophisticated and interesting questions about the nature of rules in their social context (for example about the relation between written and unwritten rules). One might ask the students: "In what form do these rules appear in the world? Are they written and published, and if so where? How do you know that these rules apply to you? Are they all the rules that do apply, and if so how do you know that? If the rules are not written and published, how do you even know what the rules are? Why do you suppose they are not written and published?" Or: "What exceptions are there to these rules, and how do you know?" And so on. Similar questions could be raised about the relationship between rules and authority: "Who promulgated these rules, and upon what authority? How do you know? What does it mean to have authority to promulgate rules of this kind?" And so on.

The students could then be asked to talk about the ways in which questions arising under their rules should be resolved. What problems of meaning do these rules present? How should they be resolved, and by whom, acting under what procedures? Perhaps here a teacher could reproduce one or two sets of rules the students had provided, and think up imagined situations where the application of the rules would be problematic. (After one or two such assignments, the students could be asked to do it themselves.) This would present the students with the difficulty of thinking in terms of a system meant to operate with constant or consistent—or at least apparently consistent—definitions over time, for they can be led to see that the way they resolve the meaning of the rules in one case will have consequences for others. This involves an extension both of imaginative and sympathetic capacities, and a complication of the idea of fairness. It might also begin to teach them that in difficult cases the meaning of the rules cannot be seen in the rules themselves but must be found elsewhere: in the resources and equipment one brings to thought and argument about the questions. What is more, since these resources are partly of our own invention, it is right to ask how they can be improved. Finally, depending on the particular system of rules, this method may lead the students to think in terms of procedures and competences: why the judgment whether a particular player is "trying hard" (as required by a rule) is a matter for the coach, not for the players (or vice versa); why the umpire's decision that a pitch is a strike or a ball must (or must not) be final, and so on. Or one might consider rules governing life in a cooperative apartment, and the procedures by which decisions should be made when there are real differences of opinion about the necessity of roof repair, the costs of heating, and so on.

Finally, students could be asked to draft rules of their own devising, whether regulations or contractual provisions, and submit them to collective criticism. This could be a real lesson in the limits both of language and of the mind, as the student realizes how little power he actually has to determine how his words will be given meaning by others, and how little he can imagine the future that his rules are intended to regulate.

All of this could be done with materials from the student's own life, without the use of legal terms or technicalities. It need not even be done in Standard English: the student's writing (or talking, if these assignments were done orally) should indeed reflect the way people actually speak in their own world. One important lesson for us all might be the discovery that it is not only in the law, or only in the language of the white middle class, that community is constituted, or that argument about justice proceeds.

To do this with material from the students' own lives would tend to make the process seem natural and immediate, within their ordinary competence. But in the process they should be introduced to questions of extraordinary depth and sophistication: about the construction of social reality through language (as they define roles, voices, and characters in the dramas they report); about the definition of value (as they find themselves talking about privacy or integrity or truthfulness or cooperation); about the nature of reasoning (as they put forward one or another argument with the expectation that it cannot be answered, as they try to meet the argument of another, and so on); and about the necessarily cooperative nature of society (as they realize that whatever rules they promulgate can work only with the assistance of others and must work equally for all people and all cases); and so on. They might learn something of what it means that the law seeks always to limit the authority it creates. They might even come to see that the question, "what is fair?" should often include the qualifications "under this set of rules, under these procedures, and under these particular circumstances." It might be a good thing at this stage to read as well some actual legal materials: a statute, a judicial opinion, a piece of a brief. If I am right in my expectations, after working on rules in their own lives the students would find this material more complex, more interesting, and more comprehensible—also perhaps more difficult—than before. This would itself be an important demonstration of legal literacy, and a direct manifestation of the student's increasing competence as an educated citizen.

The law itself can be seen as a method of individual and collective self-education, as a discipline in the acknowledgement of limits, in the recognition of others, and in the necessity of cooperation. It is a way in which we teach ourselves, over and over again, how little we can foresee, how much we depend upon others, how sound and wise are the practices we have inherited from the past. It is a way of creating a world in part by imagining what can be said on the other side. In these ways it is a lesson in humility. Of course a professional training is no guarantee of such an education—far from it—but it is not a prerequisite either. What I mean to suggest in this paper is that a training in the analogues of law that are found in ordinary life, if done in the right way, can be a stage in such a development: that this kind of legal literacy may be a true part of general education.

8 Evaluating Writing in an Academic Setting

Michael Clark
Department of English, The University of Michigan

The current debate about the decline of literacy will probably have no more influence over the use and evolution of language than such debates have had in the past, but it has produced significant changes in the institutional programs responsible for the perpetuation and dissemination of literacy in our culture. Among these changes is the move away from ancient prescriptivisms and mechanistic drills on sentence patterns and towards a more utilitarian or functionalist presentation of reading and writing as useful skills. This shift in pedagogical goals and techniques has resulted in a number of curricular changes, and within the past five years it has also begun to alter both the character of textbooks designed for college students and, to a lesser degree, those designed for elementary and secondary school students as well. Most of the changes involve the incorporation of a much broader range of reading and writing into the "English" curriculum than has been customary, with the aim of introducing students to the many forms of language they will encounter outside the classroom. From a practical perspective, such reforms are eminently sensible, and when the greater variety of texts spans racial, sexual, and class differences, these changes also perform important cultural functions.

It is unlikely that these concrete changes will have much effect on the debate that inspired them, since opinions about the state of literacy in our society are usually motivated by broader political concerns rather than specific evidence or systematic research. Neither teachers nor linguists have been able to identify features of written English that can serve as reliable and consistent measures of quality, and even if they could, the increasing heterogeneity of the student population in the United States renders historical comparisons between the writing occurring in today's classrooms and that from fifty or even twenty years ago meaningless and misleading.

The growing uncertainty about the possibility of absolute qualitative judgments across a wide range of writing has, however, generated a healthy skepticism about tests that are used to make such comparisons, such as the standardized tests designed by the Educational Testing Service and other organizations. Much of the current concern about the demise of reading and writing has been inspired by the decline in SAT scores in the last ten years (even though ETS has repeatedly warned against drawing such broad conclusions from the scores), and those who propose these tests as evidence for the degeneration of literacy usually cite the accuracy with which the scores can predict a student's grades in college. But teachers interested in a wide variety of writing situations and in equipping students to deal with specific tasks and strategies in their writing have become suspicious about the validity of measuring writing ability according to the abstract, generalized form in which written texts are usually presented in these tests, and that suspicion has led to a number of efforts to design writing tests and develop criteria that reflect the new attitudes towards writing that have emerged in the classroom. Unlike the standardized tests, these locally developed measures of writing skill deliberately reflect the specific programs from which they emerge and focus on the specific interests and needs of the teachers who design them and the students who take them. They usually predict students' success in these programs as well as or better than standardized tests do, but more importantly they constitute an explicit public commitment to evaluate students according to the same principles by which they are taught. As such, these tests serve an important ideological function as well as meeting the bureaucratic needs of assessment, diagnosis, and placement. By connecting the evaluation of written texts to the material conditions in which they are produced and read, these local tests reinforce the truth that real literacy is always a specific response to a concrete situation and never a generalized touchstone for personal development, social respectability, or pedagogical success.

The necessarily decentralized character of efforts to develop these local tests has precluded the formation of a systematic paradigm for their construction. Among the more useful attempts to get beyond the trial-and-error stage of these efforts are the descriptive *Guide to Published Tests of Writing Proficiency* and *A Directory of Writing Assessment Consultants,* both published by the Clearinghouse of Applied Performance Testing, and the formation of a National Testing Network in Writing at the City University of New York, which plans a number of forums for the exchange and publication of information regarding the design of different kinds of writing tests.[1] A number of large universities have also combined private and government funds with extensive research facilities to conduct large-scale experiments with testing procedures and curricular designs, and these programs have begun to yield instructive if not conclusive results.

The Writing Assessment Examination developed at the University of Michigan makes an interesting case study of one such effort. Recent changes in the program of Introductory Composition at the University of Michigan reflect the general movement towards a more eclectic, functionalist approach towards the teaching of writing. However, rather than trying to incorporate a full range of writing tasks like many writing programs in secondary schools and community colleges quite rightly do, the program at Michigan focuses almost exclusively on the sophisticated modes of academic inquiry and expository forms characteristic of reading and writing tasks that the students encounter in their other classes at the university. The program thus resembles more traditional composition programs that focus on academic writing, yet at Michigan that focus is motivated and informed by an emphasis on the connection between the written text and the institutional structure of the functions it must serve. The test used to place students in that program and the criteria used to evaluate that test therefore make a useful illustration of the similarities and differences between tests and criteria proposed to measure writing against a disembodied, generalized standard and those that assess writing as a concrete act within a specific setting.

All students enrolling in the University of Michigan for the first time must visit the campus for an orientation session before they register for classes. During that visit, they take a number of tests to determine their placement in several subjects; among those tests is the Writing Assessment Examination administered by the English Composition Board. This examination lasts one hour and students are required to write about a given topic that changes daily. The examination specifies the audience to whom the students are to address the essay, the purpose for which the essay is to be used, and, through the sentences that the students must adopt as the beginning of their essay, the tone, level of diction, and language-conventions to be used. The following assessment examination is one of the many which are used to elicit student writing:

> Write a letter to the parents of a young child advocating a particular policy of television watching for their child. Explain to them why you advocate such a policy.
>
> Begin your letter with the following sentence (which you should copy into your bluebook):
>
> By the time the average person in North America graduates from high school, she or he will have seen 18,000 hours of television.
>
> Now select *one* of the following as your second sentence and copy it into your bluebook:

- The present generation of preschoolers watches an average of 42 hours of television a week.
- Since real experience is the primary source of learning, children are growing up addicted to television and ignorant of life.
- According to a well-known critic, television is giving the present generation "an extraordinary exposure to standard adult English and opportunities to see many things."

Now complete your letter developing the argument that follows from the first two sentences. Do your best to make your argument convincing to the parents who are your readers.

Each sample of student writing is then evaluated holistically and scored by at least two trained readers, and students are assigned to one of three categories on the basis of that score. Some students are exempted from Introductory Composition, but, like all other students, in their junior or senior years they must enroll in an upper-class composition course taught by faculty members in their areas of concentration. Most incoming students are assigned to Introductory Composition; others are required to enroll in special tutorial classes where they receive individualized instruction to meet their special needs. These tutorials last seven weeks; students who successfully complete the tutorial course may then enroll in Introductory Composition the following semester. In some cases, students are required to take a second tutorial course before going on to Introductory Composition, and, occasionally, a student progresses so rapidly in the tutorial that he or she takes the assessment again and is exempted from the introductory course. All students, however, may appeal their assignment if they feel they have been misjudged and if their work early in the first semester indicates that they have already mastered the writing skills they will need in their future classes.

The readers who evaluate the writing samples are all experienced teachers of composition. Before they begin evaluating the samples written by the new students, they participate in training sessions in which they read a selection of samples from previous examinations, compare the scores they give with scores given by other readers, and discuss their reasons for scoring each essay as they do. Among those experienced teachers, significant disagreement about the visible characteristics of a specific essay is rare. There is, however, legitimate debate about the relative importance of these characteristics; when disagreements do arise in the training sessions, they usually center on this issue. Although complete agreement about the absolute value of any aspect of the composing process is unlikely, readers must agree on the relative importance of certain characteristics in order to standardize their scores. Therefore, a list of guidelines or criteria has been developed to assign specific weight to those features of the text which best predict students' potential to perform the composing tasks they will confront in their future classes. Training sessions continue until all readers have incorporated these criteria into their responses to the essays and correlated their scores as closely as possible.

Pairs of readers then begin reading essays of new students who take the examination on orientation days throughout the summer; as part of the reading routine, the two people reading together each day compare their scores for the first few essays in order to insure a continuing correlation among the responses of the whole group. If readers disagree about an essay, they review it with reference to the criteria, and if disagreement persists a third reader scores the essay. Such problems are rare, however, and the correlation among the scores of these trained readers usually remains consistently high over the months of reading, even though the combination of readers changes daily.

The criteria used to train these readers take into account two major sources of information about student writing in the university: (1) actual student essays obtained during preliminary administrations of the assessment examination, and (2) a survey of faculty members' attitudes toward student writing as they see it in their classes. As a result, the criteria reflect both what students do when they try to write well and what their teachers expect them to do to write well in class and in other assignments. This balance of student performance with faculty expectation results in criteria that exempt from Introductory Composition only those students who can already meet the expectations of their future teachers, and that require special work only of those students whose needs are unlike those of most incoming students.

Since these criteria were compiled by professional teachers of composition with years of experience at all levels of the undergraduate curriculum and with the help of an interdisciplinary committee composed of departmental chairman and writing specialists from most of these disciplines in which the students will major, the readers' evaluations should be good predictions of students' ability to perform the writing tasks they will encounter in their classes. Nevertheless, the accuracy of these predictions is limited by the nature of the skill that is being tested and by the undeterminable relations of that skill to the other factors influencing students' performance in college. This latter problem imposes a formidable obstacle to the reliability of predictions based on any test that focuses on a specific skill. The Educational Testing Service has found that students' success in college is better predicted by their high school grades and counselors' recommendations than by the "raw" ability measured by conventional IQ or aptitude tests. And, while some important factors such as emotional stability, the ability to perceive and adapt to the demands of a specific task, and general psychological traits can be measured by combining the results of several different kinds of tests, there is yet no way to assess accurately the whole complex of forces and influences that determine a student's success or failure in college. As a result, even experienced educators using assessments of psychological health, general aptitude or intelligence, or writing ability at times dismiss the results as hopelessly inadequate predictors of performance.

The skepticism behind this attitude has long been prevalent among educators, counselors, and testers alike. This recognition of fallibility has, however, performed a valuable function in the design and use of such examinations because it requires testers to identify functional limits that specify and measure discrete abilities without having to determine their absolute value.

When a student is asked to explain a chemical reaction, for example, or to solve a mathematical equation or standardize the grammar and syntax of a sentence, the assigned task isolates and tests the discrete ability to remember or recognize an abstract formula or process and then to use that process to manipulate the specific elements of the problem. In such cases when the skill to be assessed can be so isolated and narrowly defined, criteria can be designed that assess with great accuracy a student's ability to solve such problems. In simpler versions of this kind of examination, the criterion determining the ability to solve the problem is quite simple: the students' solution corresponds to the correct answer. When there are no variables allowed in the solution, such as in arithmetic problems, that correspondence can be measured with absolute accuracy. Moreover, the assessment of ability that results from this criterion is also highly accurate since the solution itself can be identified with the *process* of solution because only one process will produce the correct answer. Thus, if the ability to be measured is defined within such narrow parameters and if the variables in the solution are held to a minimum, criteria can be designed that will accurately measure that ability and, consequently, reliably predict a student's success in situations that are of comparable complexity.

The key to the accuracy of such assessments is the identification of the process of solution with the product, the solution itself. As soon as a solution may be produced by more than one process, however, or as that process entails more than one or two simple steps, the reliability of evaluations based on the identification of the product with the process begins to decrease. If, for example, the answer to a question can be guessed, the correct answer is not necessarily a criterion for mastery of the process of solution; similarly, if the process involves a number of steps, the last of which is a simple arithmetical calculation, a student may master the entire process, make a mistake on the last step, and still get the wrong answer. In both cases, the evaluation of the product will not be a reliable measure of the student's ability to perform the task. This dilemma can be resolved to some extent by increasing the variables in the solution so that the failure to complete one aspect of the process does not render the solution totally incorrect; but, just as the accuracy of the criteria decreases when the complexity of the process increases, when the complexity of the solution increases, the correspondence between student answers and the acceptable range of answers can no longer be measured exactly. When the process is as various and ill-defined as the process of writing an essay, and when the product has as many variables as a piece of writing, the number and obscurity of the variables render the identification of the product with the process totally intractable. As a result, if assessments of the composing process are to claim any accuracy at all, that accuracy cannot be based on the same principles that determine the criteria for other kinds of tests. Those who use the assessments as unconditional statements about students' ability would imbue the results with a precision that is not only impossible to obtain but different *in kind* from the use for which the examinations were originally designed.

The simplest solution to this problem would be to measure the quality of the finished product. But, since the assessment is used to predict a student's future ability to write very different kinds of essays under very different circumstances and constraints, the quality of the specific essay a student writes for the assessment is largely irrelevant to the purpose of the examination if it does not in some way point beyond the limits of the text. Measuring the process of composition itself is equally untenable, for even if the practices of every student could be observed while they wrote their essays, the actual stages in the composing process are virtually impossible to document and judge. It is possible, however, to justify criteria based on those features of the writing sample that are least restricted to the particularity of the finished text, under the assumption that such features—because they are not determined by the specificity of the product—indicate the ability to produce different texts with similar features. In the following passage, for example, ideas are arranged in no apparent order other than their linear association on the page, an order inherent in the medium and therefore unrelated to the student's own organizational ability.

Example One

[1] By the time the average person in North America graduates from high school, she or he will have seen 18,000 hours of television.
[2] The present generation of preschoolers watches an average of 54 hours of television a week.
[3] Instead of children actively participating in sports and strenuous exercise, so vastly needed for their newly developing bodies, they are now being drawn indoors to watch the television.
[4] Kids from the very start are being indoctrinated. [5] They are not having to communicate or somehow express themselves to anyone.
[6] Parents later can't seem to comprehend why their children cannot play with others in a normal fashion and why they can't learn at school. [7] The kids after watching the boob-tube, having been constantly entertained, grow bored with school and therefor learning stops.
[8] Practical experience is the key source to learning and this is not being presented to the kids. [9] Parents have a moral obligation to converse with their children and not stick them in front of the television, because they're busy. [10] It's easy to keep kids quiet and keep them from bothering you, if one chooses to do so; and thereby neglecting one's kids. . . .

Even if this specific arrangement possessed a rhetorical or affective power of its own, there is nothing to indicate that this student could reproduce the effect with other ideas or subjects. In the next example, though, separate ideas are arranged according to a cause-effect sequence that is emphasized by references to this abstract principle itself in the structural markers that introduce most of the sentences.

The average home in North America has a television set on for more than six hours a day. Since all experience contributes to learning, children in North American homes learn a great deal from television. The quality of daytime programming, as well as that which is termed "prime time" does not, however, contribute to a necessarily positive experience. It is important, therefore, when parents are considering whether to permit television viewing to analyse the programs their children want to watch. As television substitutes visual experience for real experience, those television shows which simplify and falsify reality should be deleted from the schedule. In this way, parents play a role in discouraging the dillusion which such programs as the "bionic man" support.

As the statistics show, many hours a day are spent watching television. This means that a considerable amount of play hours, when children are not in school, are spent before the television screen. It is my opinion and that of many other scientists, that children should be encouraged to seek activities which challenge them physically as well as mentally, rather than such idle entertainment as television viewing. Furthermore, it is an easy route to leisure time for parents to plant their child before the 'set.' The television acts as an unpaid babysitter in many homes. While parents who are critical of what their children should be able to watch, allow their children to be babysat by the t.v., they are still allowing inactivity, however "educational" or "beneficial" to fill their children's time.

It is important for children to gather their experiences through means other than television. Television, too often, serves as a substitute for other, more worth while experience as a time filler. Parents, if they allow television to be viewed at all, should be very careful what shows the family sees and furthermore, what shows *they,* themselves, watch and express interest in. Because, as children will believe the television, even more than the television will they believe their parents.

This manifest attention to the cause-effect relationship itself suggests that the writer knows and can use an organizational principle that is not constituted by the specific subject of his essay. This student could presumably organize a variety of subjects in this way. Thus, even though the second example may be no more acceptable than the first to a reader looking for polished texts—indeed, in some ways the first is more interesting—the second indicates a grasp of the principles by which other organized texts may be produced and so would receive a better score by the readers in the assessment program. (In this case, the author of the first essay was required to do tutorial work before enrolling in Introductory Composition, whereas the author of the second was allowed to enroll directly into the introductory course.) To be considered for exemption, a writer must be able to integrate such indicators of organizational ability more smoothly with the specific content of the essay than this writer did. So even in the evaluation of the more accomplished essays, criteria are used that measure those features of the text that indicate such an effort rather than measuring the complete success of the attempt to polish the final product. Consequently, these criteria should be reasonably accurate measures of the writer's ability to produce a number of different texts in different situations as well as direct evidence of the ability to complete the specific task of the assessment examination. Evaluations based on these criteria should be judgments of the writers' potential rather than of a product written under the artificial and unique constraints of the examination.

In addition to this theoretical framework, development of criteria used to evaluate the writing samples was influenced by a more practical consideration. At any large university, completely individualized instruction in composition cannot be offered to all students. If, however, the needs of most incoming students can be determined and are made the basis for the central program in composition, then instruction in that program can be particularized if not individualized. This particularization in turn allows for a more thorough treatment of the problem shared by most students than would be possible in a class designed to meet the needs of all the students. Because the curriculum of Introductory Composition has been designed with this goal in mind, the course is limited to those students who have already mastered three composing skills that are basic to writing in the university: (1) they can organize their essays to fulfil simple argumentative or rhetorical purposes; (2) they can write sentences that present a specific idea and recognize the place of that idea in the structure of the whole essay; and (3) they can maintain consistent patterns of case endings and punctuation marks. Since the purpose of the assessment is to place students where they can receive instruction suited to their needs, the criteria must reflect this purely pragmatic division of skills and distinguish the features that indicate their mastery. In the rare cases when students are unable to perform one of these three kinds of tasks but are able to perform the other two quite easily, they may be allowed into Introductory Composition and advised to attend voluntary individual counseling sessions in the Writing Workshop to bring their weakest skill up to the level of the others. Should a student's essay indicate not only mastery of all three skills but also demonstrate the ability to adjust these skills precisely to the specific task of the assessment, then that student may be exempted from Introductory Composition.

Because the criteria used in the assessment procedure must respond not only to the nature of the examination but also to the role that examination plays in the entire composition program at the University of Michigan, the features described by those criteria are distinguished by their usefulness to the evaluative procedure rather than by any value or function they may have in a specific text. Thus, the examples used below to help characterize those features are not in themselves necessarily examples of good or bad writing. Their exemplary function exists only within the parameters established by the purpose of evaluation, and that purpose is, in turn, a product of the specific theoretical and practical constraints described above.

Description of the Criteria Used to Evaluate the Writing Samples

I. *Organizational Features:*

These features indicate the students' knowledge of simple organizational principles and their ability to adjust them to the specific constraints of the examination.

A. The specific topic of the examination appears as the central focus of all parts of the essay. The topic must be presented in a form general enough to comprehend all subjects in the essay and yet not exceed the boundaries of the topic as it is presented in the examination and limited by the combination of sentences that the student chooses from the given options. The essay, in turn, must explore a range of subjects encompassed by the central topic while recognizing the limits it imposes.

The range of subjects treated by each of the better essays usually reflects the breadth of possibilities encompassed by the topic given in the examination as well as its limits. Thus, the following example deals only with the relation of TV to a child's other experiences, but it explores several aspects of that relation.

Example Two

[1] By the time the average person in North America graduates from high school, she or he will have seen 18,000 hours of television. [2] Dr. Edward Palmer, head of research at *Sesame Street,* writes: "I think that watching television is a rather remarkable act in itself. All the while kids are watching they're . . . actively relating what they're seeing to their own lives." [3] Because early childhood is a crucial developmental stage in which the individual forms the skills of comprehending reality and living in the real world, it is consequently crucial that the television programs viewed by the young, impressionable mind give it the kind of experiences which are *wholesomely* relevant to its own real life experiences.

[4] This is particularly true because recent experimental work has shown that young children cannot distinguish between the commercial and the program, nor do most regard the characters seen on the television screen as electronic reproductions of fictional characters. [5] Rather, most young children actually percieve even cartoon characters as living beings who exist within the television. [6] The very young apparently cannot distinguish between the fantasy world and the real world. [7] It can thus be seen that virtually anything viewed on the television could be interpreted by children to be something very real.

[8] Additionally, it has long been observed that children seem to have a need for role models. [9] That is, children have a need to emulate people and their actions for the purposes of forming their own identity. [10] For those unfamiliar with psychological theories, most people in the field agree that human beings have a need to define themselves in terms of other people and other experiences. [11] This process of forming an identity, for example, "I am a boy," and then later in life "I am a Catholic," or "I am a doctor," begins very early in childhood.

[12] In the past, parents and close relatives served as almost exclusive as the role models. [13] Today, parents as well as relatives are often absent, so that television characters become surrogate role models for the children. [14] Since children percieve television characters as real, and since children will emulate whatever is available, it is crucial that children view proper television material, particularly during their early childhood.

[15] Caution and vigilance must be exercised by the parents in view of all the violence and sexually inclined actions on the air. [16] For example, sexually oriented actions occur at the rate of two per hour on television, mostly between unmarried persons. [17] Unless parents are present to give at least equal time for a counter-example, the child is in danger of forming his values and concepts around the fantasy-type world of television programming which only the adults can percieve as fantasy, fiction, or entertainment.

[18] Although children can profit immensely from television, they can do so

only if society is willing to insure that the content of these programs is positive and relevant. [19] The child's programs should be oriented towards reality as it is, but should also directly and indirectly emphasize values other than instant gratification of one's own need for excitement and pleasure. [20] Values such as concern for others, honesty, diligence, etc., are present in some television programming. [21] Parents should consequently view a television series before the child does, or at least with him, so that positive things can be reinforced while negative aspects can be interpreted to the child so that he does not develop inaccurate concepts or emulate values which are contrary or undesireable to his parents and society at large. [22] It is essential to realize that the adults of tomorrow's world may very well be practicing the values which they have derived from the childhood experiences. [23] If that experience contains only the assertions of violence, sex, and self-gratification seen on so much of television today, many people will be living lives devoid of those values which distinguish man as an intelligent, moral being.

Most of the essays lack the sharply defined limits of Example Two, and they also fail to recognize adequately the range of subjects relevant to their topic. In the following example, the topic of a child learning from TV is restricted without justification to the topic of televised information about birth control.

Example Three

[1] The average home in North America has a television set on for more than 6 hours a day. [2] Since all experience contributes to learning, children in North American homes learn a great deal from television. [3] The topic of birth control and the use of contraceptives is one important subject that should be expressed in television.

[4] In today's complex society, little is done to teach young children of the vital issues dealing with birth control. [5] On the other hand, television allows it's viewers to watch commercials publicizing the consumption of alcoholic beverages and other such invaluable products. [6] North American children should approach sexual activities in a mature manner. [7] Since most parents explain very little to their children about this topic, it is up to the television networks to use their control with the utmost concern.

[8] A program in this form would eliminate many problems between the young adults of America. [9] It could decrease the percentage of unwed mothers, abortions, forced marriages, and other social disorders. [10] Problems such as these, are only a menace to society and should be treated with great care. [11] Publicizing birth control and the use of contraceptives could only help children, as well as the parents.

[12] Television in America can be a tool used to support American youth throughout society. [13] Birth control is one of many topics that should be accepted in a civilization of the future. [14] The use of this topic through television will give all Americans a better understanding of the proper care in their future lives.

Here, even though the essay is clearly focused on something the child can learn from TV, the writer's failure to broaden the focus to the full range of the topic described by the first two sentences of the essay suggests that she or he would have difficulty adapting this skill to other tasks and subjects.

In the poorer essays, the range of subjects usually is similarly limited, but here even the restricted range is poorly focused and at times ignores the limits of the topic.

In the following example, the writer begins by ostensibly limiting the essay to the waste of time involved in watching TV, but then addresses the problems of value vs. entertainment, irresponsible procedures, commercialism, and exploitive sex:

Example Four

[1] The average home in North America has a television set on for more than 6 hours at a time. [2] Every member of the average North American family watches at least 3 hours of T.V. a day. [3] It's very important that the programs viewed are of worth and value, as 3 hours is a long time to waste on useless trash. [4] If a child is left alone, with his eyeballs staring motionless into a T.V. he/she will surely pick the most entertaining programs. [5] These, however, are not necessarily the most beneficial to the child, yet it is difficult to constantly police the T.V. set. [6] So the root of the problem lies in the lack of concern of T.V. producers with the quality of T.V. [7] They're just trying to attract attention for their sponsors, and they do so by kramming their 1/2 situation comedies with sex. [8] But for the time being, parents, just keep an eye on what your kids watch, and try not to act like the culprits on T.V. themselves.

B. The essay consists of several discrete units distinguished by their subjects and/or functions. One of the units must clearly function as an introduction, another as a conclusion. Intermediate sections should perform a variety of clearly distinguished functions such as definition, exemplification, qualification, restriction, or elaboration, and the boundaries between sections should be distinct and firm. Where the boundaries are unclear, markers such as "in conclusion" or "for example" should reinforce divisions in the text (see II.D, below).

In the better essays, subjects are clearly grouped according to their function, and that function is usually described implicitly by sentence modifiers when it is not obvious. A wide variety of functions is demonstrated, and the subjects are appropriate to the function they perform. Thus, in Example Two, the subjects of the introductory paragraph are broad enough to include all of the specific subjects of the essay: the introduction enumerates a "developmental stage," "skills of comprehending reality and living in the real world," "the kind of experiences which are *wholesomely* relevant" to "real life experiences." All of the general subjects are then made more specific and concrete in a section devoted exclusively to that function (sentences 4–7). Following this section, another specific subject of the topic appears (role models), its function in relation to the preceding subjects is described ("Additionally"), and the subject is then defined (sentence 9), its relevance to a developmental stage explained (sentence 10), and concrete examples are offered (sentence 11). After several other sections, which demonstrate other functions, the essay concludes with a section that moves back to more general subjects (sentences 18 ff.) by referring to the specific subjects of the essay in terms that give them the broadest scope possible within the limits of the topic (see especially sentence 22). Within each section, the subjects can easily perform their function; in sentence 11, for instance, the examples offered to explain the process of forming an identity are concrete enough to serve as clear examples and specific enough to identify stages in that process as the nature of that identity moves from the general ("I am a boy") to the more particular ("I am a Catholic").

Most of the essays differ from Example Two in that they demonstrate fewer functions, the differences between sections are not as clear, and the boundaries between sections are less sharply defined. In the poorest essays, such as Example Four, only a few simple functions are present, they are not confined to discrete units, and their connections to one another are ambiguous. In Example Four, the central topic is difficult to identify because most of the subjects exist at the same level of generality; hence the difficulty of finding a clearly introductory unit (though sentence 8 provides a clear conclusion). There are no examples offered as such, little explanation, and no elaboration of the absolute and apparently arbitrary statements. Consequently, this essay offers little to indicate even an awareness of these basic principles of exposition.

C. The essay recognizes and responds to the extratextual constraints of audience and purpose as defined by the examination. The explicit references to these constraints should be appropriate, and the diction of the essay and the extent of elaboration and definition should fulfill the specific demands of the purpose and the specific needs and expectations of the given audience. Thus, whereas the writer of Example Two has chosen an objective, declarative voice, she or he also explicitly recognizes the breadth of the given audience and responds to it (sentence 10). Furthermore, since the specific subject chosen to elaborate role models is especially appropriate to an audience of parents, the central topic of the relation of TV to a child's life is brought to bear directly on the concerns of the audience. In the conclusion, the application of the topic to its ultimate purpose is made explicit (sentence 21) without completely changing the focus of the essay to describe the details of the policy, a gesture that indicates the author's full incorporation of the precise task described in the exam.

This precise adjustment of broad organizational features to the constraints of a given audience and purpose characterizes only the better samples. The majority of the essays do not incorporate the demands of the audience and purpose into the text so thoroughly, although many address the audience directly and explicitly explain a policy for controlling a child's viewing habits. In the poorer essays, these features are often internally inconsistent as well as isolated from the extratextual constraints. For instance, in Example Four the formal syntax and careful diction of the first clause in sentence 3 is quite different from the strident, colloquial phrases that end the sentence, and sentence 4 reflects a similar contrast between the formal features of the last clause ("he/she," "surely," "the most entertaining") and the informal phrasing of the interjected prepositional phrase "with his eyeballs staring." Similar inconsistencies characterize the rest of the essay, such as the abrupt shift from the indicative to the imperative mood and the shift into the informal phrasing and diction of sentences 7 and 8. When they are controlled, such contrasts can be very effective and can indicate exceptional skills. Here, however, there is no context in which the shifts can function, so they suggest that the writer is both unsure of the expectations of the audience and unable to control diction and syntax. Furthermore, the recognition of the assigned purpose in sentence 8 is irrelevant to the rest of the essay, and its connection to the essay through the introductory phrase implies some sort of long-range plan that is not mentioned in the preceding sentences. Not only is this writer unable to identify and manipulate those features of the text that would enable a response to extratextual constraints, she or he is also unable to control them to meet the purely textual demands of consistency and internal coherence within the essay itself.

II. Local Features:

These features indicate the student's ability to portray words, phrases, sentences, and even groups of sentences as part of larger units up to and including the essay. These features are not, of course, independent of the organizational features; indeed, those global features emerge only from the local features, and the propriety of the local features, in turn, is determined by the global characteristics of the essay they constitute. Consequently, distinctions between these two groups of features cannot reflect separate stages of composition or even clearly discernible levels of the text. These distinctions, like the features they categorize, are only articulations of the evaluative process, and the skills they indicate are similarly only convenient predictors of a student's ability to meet the demands of future teachers, not characterizations of the composing process.

A. The semantic information conveyed by the unit (i.e., a phrase, clause, group of sentences, etc.) is appropriate to the local boundaries of the unit.

Semantic information is simply the meaning of the text, its propositional content. In an essay about the debilitating effects of watching TV, for example, all comments should in some way convey information about that problem, and in a section of the essay devoted to explaining how TV stifles the imagination, all the statements should convey information about that specific debilitating process. The importance of this feature as a unifying device and its consequent relation to I.A is obvious enough; its properties, however, are not always easy to identify. Generally, the semantic range in any unit must be wide enough to elaborate the relationships that the writer wishes to convey and narrow enough to remain within the boundaries of the unit. Thus, the semantic information of a unit can indicate a student's ability to recognize the limits of that unit and explore the range they delimit. This feature thus indicates the same skills indicated by the features in I.A and differs from the global features it resembles only in its extension down to units smaller than the essay. Semantic information thus furnishes a criterion for identifying those students whose difficulty in organizing their essays stems from their inability to decide how much and what kind of information to put in their sentences rather than from an inability to handle larger units.

In the poorer essays, the semantic information of sentences and divisions within paragraphs tends to be completely restricted to the boundaries of the unit itself. Thus, in Example One, the semantic information conveyed by sentence 3 is unrelated to that conveyed by sentence 4, and the information conveyed by sentence 5 bears little relevance to the information in sentences 4 and 6. At other times, the limits of the unit are ignored, and totally unrelated kinds of information are enclosed by a single unit. In sentence 6 of Example One, the children's isolation and their inability to learn in school are both confined by the same part of the same sentence, though the following sentence makes no effort to connect them. Occasionally, as in Example Four, the poorer essays will organize semantic information into larger units, e.g., the pair (sentences 6 and 7), but those units are then relatively isolated from surrounding units. In the better essays, on the other hand, the semantic information of one unit often appears as a subordinate part of the surrounding units, creating a coherent passage that develops an idea by gradually increasing the range of semantic information used to express it. In the following example, the semantic information of one sentence appears in a slightly varied form in the next sentence, which in turn goes on to focus on the variation, and so on. In this case, by systematically repeating this technique the author is able to develop the purely statistical information given by the examination into a powerful rhetorical force that justifies the purpose of the essay.

Example Five

[1] The average home in North America has a television set on for more than 6 hours a day. [2] Every member of the average North American family watches at least 3 hours of television a day. [3] This means that 21 hours a week are spent in front of a television by an average family member. [4] When viewed in such short time spans, the hours are not necessarily seen as many. [5] When you consider that this also means 84 hours a month and 1008 hours a year, the statistics become a bit more frightening. [6] If you consider that your child is spending 42 days out of one year in front of a television set, you might begin to feel strongly about establishing a policy for television watching.

B. The grammatical relationships among elements of a proposition accurately reflect the logical or affective relationships determined by other features of the essay.

The grammatical information conveyed by a unit enables us to determine causal, circumstantial, or other relations between the pieces of semantic information it conveys. For example, in the sentence "The police arrested my roommate yesterday," the action of the event is done by "the police" and done to "my roommate." The surface subject of the sentence is "police" and the surface object is "roommate." In the following sentence, the surface roles have been reversed but the grammatical information is unchanged: "My roommate was arrested by the police." Here, the action is still performed by "the police" and still done to "my roommate." Thus, if a student is discussing the ways that TV affects a child's relationship to his parents and then without explanation writes a sentence in which the familial relationships affect the child's viewing habits, that grammatical information would contradict the information given by the surrounding sentences even though the semantic information would remain with the boundaries of the unit. (If such boundary violations are frequent, then the problem may be organizational rather than grammatical; i.e., the sentence may correctly represent the student's idea but simply be in the wrong place in the essay.) Without specific diagnostic testing, the exact nature of the problem can only be assumed to stem from a generally tenuous grasp of the information being conveyed by the sentence and so always indicates potential problems.

The basic relationships conveyed by the grammatical information are quite simple, and only the poorest essays contain serious inconsistencies in this feature. Perhaps the most common problem occurs when a student is unsure of the technique by which modifying clauses and phrases may be related to the independent clause of a sentence and so tends to use dangling modifiers ("Flying over the city, my house looked great") or to confuse the agent role in passive constructions ("My roommate was arrested by not being able to run fast enough"). Such problems are usually accompanied by many others. The assessment process penalizes no student for occasional slips if the context of the unit clearly compensates for the error.

C. The thematic information determining relative importance of elements within a unit is clear and consistent, and it is appropriate to the role of the elements in the context of the unit and the essay.

This feature, which is sometimes called "foregrounding" or "weighting," indicates the ability to manipulate the grammatical and syntactical roles of elements in the sentence so that the sentence emphasizes certain pieces of information and therefore reflects priorities determined by such extratextual factors as the purpose of the essay and the expectations of the audience as well as by the function of a sentence in the context of the essay. Information about the relative importance of these pieces is carried by syntactic structures and by the order of words in clauses and phrases, as well as by explicit description such as "And now for the most important factor in TV programming: commercials." For example, in the noun phrase "A white powdery snow" the most important word is the substantive, "snow"; in the following phrase, however, departure from conventional word order gives special emphasis to the adjectives: "A snow, white and powdery." Moreover, a number of other syntactical constructions can reverse the usual dominance of subject over modifiers: "The snow was white and powdery." More complex relationships can be further described by subordination and coordination. The relative importance of the elements in the sentence "The white powdery snow blew against the house" changes when the semantic information is rearranged: "The snow was white and powdery, and it blew against the house." Depending on the specific connectors that are introduced, both the relative importance of the pieces and their relationship to one another can change: The causal connection in "The snow blew because it was white and powdery" is different from that in "The snow blew although it was white and powdery," and so forth.

The criteria for determining a student's grasp of these principles are the number of different kinds of constructions that appear in the essay and the correspondence of those constructions to the context in which they appear. In Example One, sentence 6, two different grammatical relationships are contained in the same sentence and joined by the coordinating conjunction "and." Their relationship is therefore merely additive, and they are roughly of equal importance. Since the sentence is serving as the topic sentence of a paragraph about the latter relationship, it should indicate that the latter relationship is the true focus of the unit. The function of the sentence would have been more precise and its relationship to the sentences that surround it would have been clearer had the student changed the grammatical information to emphasize the true actor in the group and subordinated the first action to the second: "Not only can children not play with others in a normal fashion after they have watched a lot of TV, they can't even learn at school." This rewrite assumes, of course, that the parents' comprehension is not the true subject of the unit and that the paragraph's real subject is the child's learning difficulties. As the student has written the passage, these assumptions are tenuous at best, based on an independent interpretation of the semantic information rather than a reading of the essay. While the semantic information carried by the words of the unit is not contradicted by other information, the context of the unit does contradict both the grammatical information concerning the role of the parents and the thematic information concerning the relative importance of the two clauses about the children's difficulties. Naturally, when two or more such sentences are strung together, the degree to which each sentence is vague cannot be determined because the context created by the sentences is vague too. In the following passage, the grammatical relationships between the participants in the proposition are unclear, and no focus emerges because emphases determined by the thematic information are inconsistent.

Example Six

[1] The human imagination, which is so necessary to achievement, becomes worsened after exposure to television. [2] Television shows everything in detail, leaving little to the imagination. [3] Problems are almost always solved correctly, making only one solution to a problem seem possible. [4] The element of uncertainty rarely becomes visible. [5] Although it shows bright, imaginative people as winners, children who watch television are assumed to be dull and unimaginative by television programmers.

When the grammatical and thematic information is made more consistent, however, a focus emerges and the relationships among the participants are clarified:

TV worsens the human imagination, which is so necessary to achievement, by showing everything in detail and leaving little for the imagination to do. Because problems are almost always solved correctly, TV suggests that only one solution to a problem is possible so the element of uncertainty rarely becomes visible. Although TV shows bright, imaginative people as winners, TV programmers assume that children who watch television are dull and unimaginative.

The difference between these two passages indicates the difference between the way these features appear in the poorer essays and the level of proficiency that a student must demonstrate before enrolling in Introductory Composition. The essays of those exempted from the introductory course seldom contain evidence of difficulty with the grammatical and thematic properties of text.

D. The function of discrete units, their boundaries, and the relationships between the units are clearly marked where necessary.

This purely structural information is usually carried by adverbs and sentence modifiers such as "consequently," "thus," "secondly," and so on, though occasionally a sample will contain transitional sentences or even paragraphs that explain the relationship of two sections of the essay. In general, because structural information is simply predictive in nature and signals that a particular unit of the discourse is to follow or has just ended, a structural division can be marked by almost any change in the syntax, mood, or person of the text. In the better essays, such as Example One, these markers are unobtrusive and appear only when the structural function they mark might otherwise be unclear. In the poorer essays, the markers might be absent altogether or they might not correspond to the textual property they ostensibly mark. For instance, in Example Four, sentence 8, the introductory phrase alludes to an antecedent plan that is not in the text, and more obvious discrepencies occur when a student uses logical markers such as "thus" and "consequently" without arranging the essay to reflect the logical sequence they suggest.

These markers are present in most essays, but if students are unsure of their writing or unaware of the techniques by which the markers can be incorporated into the rest of the text, the markers may be redundant and obtrusive:

Example Seven

[1] The average home in North America has a television set on for more than six hours a day. [2] Every member of the average North American family watches at least three hours of television a day.

[3] What does this mean? [4] Well, on an average it means that every member of the average North American family spends one-fifth of their time awake watching television. [5] Assuming then that that person either works or goes to school for approximately eight hours, he then spends about one-third of his 'spare time' watching television.

[6] Is this then good or bad? [7] First of all it depends upon what type of programs are watched, and secondly, what is done in their 'spare time' while they are not watching television. [8] We first of all have to ask ourselves, or the other person, "Why am I, or you, watching television?" [9] Are we watching television because we enjoy it, because we hope to get something out of it, or are we just watching television for lack of something better to do. [10] This is where I feel television can be harmful, when someone turns on the television and watches whatever is on for lack of something better to do. . . .

The better essays, therefore, will be marked neither less nor more than is needed to indicate the movement of the argument. Most essays are marked excessively, but this redundance is not in itself a serious problem unless the lack of confidence it suggests becomes troublesome. Only if the markers are totally absent, or if they do not correspond to the text, does the essay indicate serious problems that usually require work in addition to that available in the introductory course.

III. Graphemic Features:

These features, which include spelling, capitalization, paragraph indentation, grammatical case endings, and punctuation marks, indicate two very different kinds of skills. A consistent marking of the grammatical and syntactical properties of a text, regardless of the markers themselves, is considered an indication of the writer's recognition of those properties. Thus, if the inflection of the verbs in an essay is consistent though non-standard, such as with the unorthodox person-number concord of certain present indicatives resembling "I does," or "he do," the regularity of the marking suggests that the student recognizes the person-number distinction despite the non-standard nature of the actual marker used. Similarly, if an essay contains a number of sentence fragments, all of which are relative clauses following a sentence ending with a substantive, then the consistency of the fragment suggests that the writer knows what a relative clause is and how to use it (though she or he may not, of course, know what the name is) and is simply marking it with a period and capital letter instead of a comma. Since in both cases the graphemic features indicate a thorough understanding of the priorities of the sentence, no student is prevented from enrolling in Introductory Composition by the use of non-standard marking alone.

The criteria for exempting a student from the introductory course do, however, recognize a priority of standard over non-standard systems of graphemic features. To be exempted, students must submit a sample that indicates they will be able to successfully complete writing tasks assigned in a wide variety of classes, and the survey of the faculty's attitudes towards their students' writing indicated that most features of non-standard graphemic systems were associated with poor writing even by those faculty members who theoretically relegated such features to a trivial status. Also, since the standard systems of grammar and punctuation were determined by the sentences of the examination that began the students' essays, failure to continue using them indicates the students' inability to perceive and adjust to the specific graphemic systems required by the examination and favored by the faculty. Consequently, no students are exempted if their essays do not exhibit the graphemic features considered standard for written English.

The application of criteria such as these is not, of course, a guarantee of consistent and accurate evaluation. The complex social context in which writing always functions complicates its evaluation, and that evaluation, in turn, must take into account the very special configuration of the testing situation itself. Examples Two and Three are eloquent comments on the effects of the examination situation on the writing that it produces. The text of Example Two is followed by this note: "please forgive the handwriting as I have a slight physical disability." Long before the last page, this essay exhibits all of the features necessary to exempt the author from Introductory Composition, but this direct address to the actual readers makes the author's precise response to the given tasks even more exceptional. This student clearly understood that the essay, as part of the assessment procedure, was to be written for two different audiences and for two purposes: the ostensible audience and purpose prescribed by the examination, and the actual audience and purpose of the assessment. As a result of conscious separation of the two kinds of constraints, the author was able to distinguish between the necessary specific response to the given tasks and a more comprehensive but unfocused demonstration of isolated, technical skills. Writers who fail to make the distinction between the two kinds of contexts in which their writing functions tend either to treat the examination simply as an occasion to display every technical skill they have or to limit their essay cautiously to the one or two tasks they know they can perform. Such efforts to perform for the assessment readers cannot, of course, bear much relevance to the purposeful essay that the examination asks for, and often these efforts to use the essay as a showcase result in texts that are internally inconsistent as well.

Example Three exhibits another feature peculiar to the situation of the examination. Because the assessment examination is offered as one of a battery of tests facing the student during a visit to the campus, most of the tests conforming to the first type of examination described above, it is perhaps inevitable for students to assume that their writing will be evaluated according to the kind of criteria usually associated with more objective examinations. This assumption, in turn, leads them to prepare for the assessment just as they might for the other examinations. By the middle of the summer many students have thoroughly researched the topics used in earlier examinations described by their friends, and they are often determined to display their knowledge regardless of the topic they are given. (The author of Example Three apparently had prepared to write about the questions of making contraceptives available to teenagers without their parents' consent, one of the topics assigned earlier in the summer.) A similar and even more common case is the essays of students eager not only to write a good essay but to give the "right" answer. They try to incorporate into their essays all three of the statements offered in the examination as choices, even when the attitudes and perspectives of the statements are completely different. Fortunately, many of these students are able to create enough coherent units within the essay to demonstrate at least a rudimentary grasp of several basic skills, but it is virtually impossible for them to create the unified, precisely focused essay necessary for exemption from such a congeries of purposes, audiences, and topics.

Both kinds of problems are endemic to any examination which calls for a response as complicated as a written essay, and they are especially troublesome in examinations which propose to assess the students' potential to respond to tasks in situations quite different from that of the examination itself. Since in this instance, however, the problems generated by the unusual situation of the examination can be identified and distinguished from those features which are more indicative of the potential quality of students' writing, they do not pose a substantial obstacle to the accurate evaluation of that potential.

Yet the absurdity that results from the students' misguided efforts is often so obvious that the confusion it connotes about the nature and function of writing must have serious implications for the students' university careers. Most of the samples suggest that the writers are simply unsure of what is being asked of them by an examination that requires them to use their own experience and ideas to communicate a point of view, attitude, or idea. In part, their indecision reflects their limited but genuine difficulty in distinguishing between criteria used to evaluate more simple skills associated with objective tests and those used to evaluate their essays. If this description of those criteria serves only to alleviate some of that perplexity, it will be an important step toward helping students adjust to the new tasks they will encounter at the university.

Because the criteria also testify to a general conformity among the beliefs of faculty from a wide range of disciplines about the nature of writing and its importance to all careers, this description should also provide a clearer idea of those properties of communication that are esteemed in the university as a whole and so form part of the ground on which the separate disciplines meet and share their common values. For as long as the pedagogical convenience of the traditional separation of hard sciences from the humanities stands as a justification for relegating the teaching and even existence of writing exclusively to the latter—and often to only one area, English—higher education will be merely a collection of curricular fragments rather than a unifying and liberating experience, and the humane growth generated by the exchange of ideas among the various disciplines will remain an elusive and abstract ideal.

Note

[1] The Clearinghouse for Applied Performance Testing is part of the Northwest Regional Educational Laboratory, 300 S.W. Sixth Avenue, Portland, Oregon 97204. The address of the National Testing Network in Writing is CUNY, 535 East 80th Street, New York, NY, 10021.

9 Practicing Research by Researching Practice

Loren S. Barritt
School of Education, The University of Michigan

At the June 1981 Conference on "Literacy in the 1980's" sponsored by The University of Michigan's English Composition Board, a group of us, all teachers, spent three afternoons together doing research about our practice. On the first afternoon after preliminary discussion, we decided to study students' experience of "coming to class unprepared." Using ourselves as informants for the study, each of us thought back to a time when he or she had been an unprepared student, and we each wrote a description of what had happened. We reflected upon what we had done and how we had felt. Then together we analyzed these descriptions by looking for common themes among them. We found some important ones: feeling uncertain and nervous; wanting to avoid going to class; avoiding eye contact with the teacher; waiting for time to pass, ever so slowly; and experiencing relief at escaping detection if, indeed, we "escaped" detection; or suffering embarrassment if, in fact, we were "caught." There were also interesting and significant variations in our individual descriptions. After we had identified these variations, we focused our attention upon what could be done to help students in our classes profit from a lesson even when they were unprepared for it.

Our discussion immediately led to disagreement about whether fear, embarrassment, and avoidance in such cases are counterproductive or whether these reactions in students could be used to motivate their performance. Our differing interpretations of the impact of fear, embarrassment, and avoidance upon learning arose from our different teaching philosophies. I recall one participant saying, "Education isn't therapy," in the midst of a discussion that took for granted that it was. Our differing interpretations also arose from our personal experiences of being unprepared. Some of us had grown thick skins, others thin ones.

The group effort in which we teachers were engaging is educational research. We were studying an educational experience from the point of view of individuals who lived through it. And whatever else education is, it is most importantly individuals' experiences. It was experience we found easy to reflect upon because we were examining something all but one of us* had lived through, and furthermore it was experience in which we all had an interest.

The word research comes from the French *rechercher,* to look again, carefully; to examine things closely. How one does research is always a matter for choosing. The choice is influenced—or should be—by what is being studied. It is not surprising that different academic disciplines have become associated with different research traditions, for the research which scholars within the different disciplines choose to do is defined itself by the subjects they research. For example, astronomers and ethologists choose to observe the subjects of their research while physicists and chemists experiment with the subjects of their research and biologists classify the subjects of their research. If we accept this lesson from the natural sciences, which demonstrates that the method of research is determined by the subject being studied, then we accept the premise that for every research question the important prior question is: What should we be studying? What is important enough *to us* that we would take the trouble to examine it more closely? Because we cannot study all that occurs, we must make choices. If we are to be effective researchers, we will choose methods designed to help us discover more about the events or problems of the subjects we choose to study. Our methods follow from our problems. Problems will not follow from methods—at least they should not.

One way to choose what is important enough to study is to do as my colleagues and I did in June 1982 to discuss a number of puzzling things that happen in classrooms and choose one to examine—one that intrigues *us.* Research which begins with a problem researchers choose is unlikely to be dull or irrele-

---

*The one person who had herself no memory of ever coming to class unprepared wrote a description of two students who were chronically unprepared in her class. Her account of her students' behavior shared a great deal with the recollections from the rest of us and served to strengthen our understanding of the analysis we had done.

vant; interesting research flows from researchers' choice of a real problem.

It is a sad paradox that topics of concern to teachers are often believed by those same teachers to be of little importance because the problems cannot be studied "scientifically"—where scientifically is taken to mean according to scientific method. This belief that scientific method is the arbiter of what is significant is as pervasive as the myths which surround literacy that Jay Robinson writes about in the first essay of this volume. The myth of the primacy of scientific method should not inhibit practitioners from going ahead with research. There is no such thing as *the* scientific method. We come to believe in the unfortunate fairy tale of the scientific method in elementary and secondary school when we study "science." We begin to revere the illusion when we learn just enough about research design and statistics in college to know that we don't understand them. Then that realm, the scientific one, becomes the mystical province of experts, and those experts seem to be the only ones who know those topics important enough to be the subjects of research.

Science is, in fact, a great variety of traditions to which we are able to give a single name, but to which we are unable to give a single definition. I think of science as the body of knowledge that results when critical minds attempt to understand important, puzzling problems. My view of science has much in common with my view of rhetoric: The task of both is to explore and understand something well enough to describe it accurately to others. If scientists' or rhetoricians' audiences remain unconvinced of the claims made to them, they can use the scientific or rhetorical accounts of those claims to check up on the evidence or arguments presented in them and see for themselves. True scientific methods are the methods used to reduce puzzlement.

This view of science is not universally accepted. One need only look at the methodologically complex but uninteresting articles which fill the educational research journals. These are studies whose importance lies more in their methodological sophistication than in the practical significance of their results. I believe the studies are like this because too many social scientists are absolutely convinced that there is *a* scientific method; that they know what it is; and that they have an obligation to impose it on the rest of us. These same social scientists often control editorial boards of educational research journals. However, their power to dictate one vision of science does not change the fact that science is a human enterprise which means that individuals always choose problems to study and methods to study them—and these choices, even in the most rigorous of the sciences, are not themselves scientific. This focus on method has allowed a gulf to develop between research and practice. However, it is not a necessary gulf. It can be overcome if practitioners assert their right to choose problems of practice as legitimate problems and—for education—necessary problems in the scientific enterprise. It can be overcome if practitioners and researchers would recognize each other as legitimate partners and—for education—necessary partners in the scientific enterprise.

By researching and writing about practice, researchers and practitioners can focus attention upon the practice studied, and thereby those practices become important. If teachers ever wish to get their agenda of problems before a wider audience, they must start studying what intrigues them. That is how science works. The scientific enterprise is very much a human enterprise, a social enterprise. Paired associate learning and serial position effects become important after they were studied, not before. Why shouldn't practitioners be able to turn their real concerns into interesting problems for study and discussion?

This vision of a practical social science or what I prefer to call a human science approach differs in important ways from the stereotypical viewpoint about scientific study which pervades the so-called social sciences. I shall briefly describe some of the differences here. First, from the viewpoint of social science, all research must strive to be objective, which means that researchers must try to disappear behind the methods used. Every study done in this way should be, in the ideal, like every other one. The result is that social science appears to be impersonal, almost automatic. From the human science viewpoint, investigators strive to be fair and honest about what is done, why and what the results of research mean, but they do not attempt to vanish behind methods. They acknowledge that science is always done by individuals with personal interests, that science is not the result of an anonymous process, and that it is, therefore, all right to say "I"—and a silly charade to hide behind the "the researcher"—in reporting the results.

Second, in the social sciences, researchers always try to measure treatments and outcomes in numerical values. In the human sciences, ordinary language is the preferred mode of communication. Third, in the social sciences prediction is the goal. In the human sciences, the goal is understanding and appreciation of individuals' situations. Fourth, in the social sciences results are supposed to be generalizable; they should apply beyond the situation studied. Many of the elaborate procedures used in research—sampling, control, measurement—are specifically chosen to make this generalization possible. In the human sciences since understanding and not generalization is the goal, there is no need to construct procedures to amplify the importance of findings. Readers must decide for themselves whether results are likely to apply beyond the situation studied.

Fifth, in the social sciences the outcome sought is a clear, certain "yes" or "no" answer to a particular issue. Hypotheses are framed and procedures developed to give a single response to a carefully framed question. Research design and statistics training can be viewed as enculturation to a world which constructs simple research questions, designed to give solutions once and forever to complex issues of everyday life. This practice is a radical rejection of the ever-changing nature of human experience. In the human sciences instead of simple results and clear answers, researchers usually emerge from their studies with a complex understanding of what is going on. The more they learn about situations, the more complicated those situations tend to become. Results are always tentative; there is always more to be learned. Although such research can be frustrating, it is seldom boring or irrelevant.

Sixth, the human science vision differs from the typical social science one because it asks itself to be useful. The goal of human science study is understanding that may be of earthly use to someone. In the social sciences that need not be the case. In current social science practice there continues to be a distinction between basic studies done without regard to their potential utility and applied studies that seek uses for results from basic research. In the past this cart-before-the-horse procedure has resulted in teaching machines, classroom behavior modification techniques, and similar irrelevancies.

The need for human science research in which practitioners become researchers is great, but practical obstacles to research by teachers is equally great. The principal one is lack of time. I marvel at the ability of conscientious high school composition teachers to survive the killing load of classes and papers in a normal school week. I am sure the task is not easier in other subjects. In the interest of our profession's need for important meaningful research, perhaps time can be found for teacher-oriented and teacher-directed research if the usual in-service programs with their complement of outside experts could be changed to programs for teacher self-service when colleagues could gather together as we did last spring in Ann Arbor to investigate problems of practice.

In fact, useful research need not take a great amount of time. During the last academic year, several members of the English Composition Board staff held bi-monthly hour-and-a-half meetings to study our reading and evaluation of student essays. Initially we intended to meet only once, but the dimensions of our interests soon convinced us that we should meet again and then again. In addition, and not at all irrelevantly, we found our work together interesting, stimulating, and fun.

The problem we studied was one which has been discussed continually since the beginning of the English Composition Board's program, one which has occupied our attention as we have assessed in excess of 20,000 entrance essays and countless student papers: what we do when we read student essays. We thought if we read together informally but independently—in contrast to the times when we must read and train together formally—and then examined from close at hand our judgments of each essay we might develop a better understanding of how our complex decisions are actually made.

Our procedures were simple. We all read the same essays chosen from among past essays written in response to the English Composition Board's entrance essay requirement. Separately, we evaluated the essays, giving them a score from "1"—exceptional, meaning exempt from introductory composition, to "4"—weak, meaning needs to take a special seven-week tutorial course in writing and then to repeat the exam. As each reader reported on his or her reasons for the score he or she gave a paper, the rest of us took note of the important statements characterizing the judgment.

After reading three or four essays, we recorded important recurring statements on the blackboard so we could consider them—what they had in common and how they differed. Initially, vocabulary posed interesting problems. As we discussed the essays, we discovered that several of us were using different terms for a single concept. Also, we found that on occasion we were using a single term for different concepts. Sorting out our terminology and agreeing on definitions for the words we used to describe aspects of the essays became an important part of our research. We had assumed that "flow" meant the same thing to everyone in the group. It was intriguing—and useful—to find that it did not.

By questioning, defining, and redefining recurring terms as we put them to use describing the essays we studied, we were able to bring our judgments of problematic essays into closer agreement than had been possible before.

Moreover, we recognized that there was more to our decisions than judging the essay at hand. We found that in our discussion of essays, we were often looking for the student writers behind the essays. While comments like, "I think this is a solid '2' essay" were frequent, comments like, "This student will do just fine in comp" were equally frequent or perhaps more frequent. We were not content to judge only the essay; we were trying to make decisions about the person who wrote it. Not only were we reflecting our commitment to place students in settings where they would receive appropriate instruction but we were also revealing something—and I'm not sure what to name it—at the center of the process of judging essays. We were reading, mindful that these essays were written in 50 minutes by entering students in a testing situation in response to a fixed topic and for a given audience: We were reading *contextually.* In so doing, we found that reading is always an interpretive process, an act of re-creation of the writer's circumstance by the reader. As we read, we asked ourselves, experienced teachers of composition, to consider how "forgiving" we ought to be and how to "forgive" accurately—yet consistently. We discussed the advice that social scientists offer us: Identify clear criteria and apply only those criteria during the evaluation process in order to attain higher reliability coefficients. We asked others—some beyond our campus—who are expert in judging essays to join us and share their thoughts about these matters with us. We evaluated holistic evaluation procedures themselves. We read. In the process—which is where one usually is in human science research—we decided once again there are no easy solutions. However, we had renewed our own interest in the hard, unresolved issues we face when we judge writing, issues which are not unique to our circumstance, issues which arise whenever interpretation of the meanings and intentions of others is called for, issues which differ in kind but not in principle from the interpretive acts of anthropologists and literary critics. By researching circumstances contextually we had come to see that context more comprehensively.

There's an irony here that should be noted. We were covering ground which others had talked about—some of them to us. But reading about or being told is always a little abstracted from the situation. Doing the analysis for oneself makes the writings of others relevant, clearer and more useful. To do research is to engage in dialogue with others who have considered similar problems. In the doing one becomes more aware both of the issues and of who one's colleagues are.

I don't think our experiences were at all unusual. The more we tried to understand, the more we learned about ourselves as readers, about the dimensions of the problem, and about what was still unclear. And these new questions led us to continue our meetings for an entire year—to continue to look from a new perspective at an issue which has always concerned teachers of writing—and to invite other experienced teachers of writing to read with us. As we proceeded we became much more certain both of the central criteria by which we judge essays and of the difficulty of specifying exactly how these criteria fit together in deciding about a particular essay. But the specific results of our research are not the subject of this paper. This is only an example to illustrate the power, the fascination and the intellectual interest which comes from a reflective turn of mind toward practice. What began for us as a commitment to one meeting became a year's work. But not really work; rather I would call it an opportunity, an opportunity to see that our practical problem was in fact an intellectually challenging puzzle of the first order that was able not only to engage us but had occupied others as well. An experience like ours could convince us teachers that our work is actually important.

It would take only the commitment of a small portion of time for a faculty group to become its own research group studying those aspects of practice which seem intractable. I doubt that difficult, longtime problems can be solved in the sense of finding *a* solution of which others can then be informed. The "solution" rather resides in the process of study itself which can invigorate, inform, and enliven practice. Our world as teachers is important. Our problems are of broad interest and significance. There is no better way to realize this than to take time to study them for ourselves.

10 A Comprehensive Literacy Program: The English Composition Board

Patricia L. Stock
English Composition Board, The University of Michigan

Readers of this book of essays, those of us charged with translating the abstract concept of literacy into specific programs and practices, will find no prescriptions for doing so here. One assumption that pervades all the essays in the collection is that there are no ready made programs or practices for teaching reading and writing—each one must be designed by those who teach for those who would learn particular subjects in a particular setting.

Does this assumption mean that educators who would develop programs and practices for teaching literacy cannot learn from one another? No, it does not. But it does mean that each institution within the larger social context described by Robinson earlier in this chapter must develop programs suitable to its own academic setting. As Bailey reports, even in Great Britain, where educational policy (such as that itemized in the *Bullock Report*) is shaped by centralized decision making and national examinations, educational programs are created by faculties of particular schools (such as the Abbey Wood School in London) who provide detailed guidelines for the implementation of policy. By extension, individual teachers must develop unique practices for teaching literacy, practices which address the needs of their students, the subjects they teach, and their purposes for teaching reading and writing. In their essays earlier in this chapter, Rueter and Dunn, Siegel, and White substantially illustrate this point.

Because I believe descriptions of our experiences as teachers contribute to our common sense and serve as metaphors—if not models—which may guide our practice, I offer the following description of the English Composition Board at The University of Michigan as an illustration of one faculty's effort to develop a comprehensive program for teaching literacy to all its students at all levels of instruction.

Michigan's comprehensive literacy program was developed in the College of Literature, Science, and the Arts in response to a specific need identified in testimony given in 1973 and 1974 at hearings of the Graduation Requirements Commission. During this internal review of the College's graduation requirements—the first such review since the 1940's—dissatisfaction was expressed by students and faculty alike with the quality of students' literacy both upon entering and leaving the College. The impact of the non-literate age that Robin Lakoff characterizes in her essay was making itself felt in institutions of higher learning. Faculty could no longer assign the quantity of reading material to students that it once did; students who had watched television an average of 6½ hours a day but were unpracticed in reading could not complete it. Faculty could no longer assign the themes and papers it once did; students who had learned to keep #2 pencils inside the lines and to reach out and touch distant grandparents by telephone were unpracticed in writing and could not compose complex, sustained discourse.

Responding to the observations and recommendations of the Graduation Requirements Commission, the Dean of the College, Billy Frye, consulted with Jay Robinson, Chairman of the Department of English, whose essay in this chapter bespeaks his interest in language and literacy. Robinson directed the Dean to Daniel Fader, architect of a program for teaching literacy which is widely used in schools throughout this country and in the United Kingdom (see Fader, *Hooked on Books*). The Dean asked Fader to serve as the chairman of the English Composition Board (ECB) and to develop a new writing requirement for the College. Fader and Robinson together were to spend the next two years soliciting the advice and enlisting the support of faculty throughout the College who were sympathetic to the theory of a comprehensive literacy program that fostered the systematic teaching of reading and writing in all disciplines. Among those colleagues was Thomas Dunn, Chairman of the Department of Chemistry, who writes persuasively about the importance of teaching writing in the sciences in the essay he co-authors with Rueter in this chapter. Dunn's conviction that the health and well-being of the sciences is dependent upon scientists' effective transmission of their ideas reflects the conviction of scholars at Michigan across the disciplines with whom Fader and Robinson conferred during 1976 and 1977.[1]

In March, 1977, confident that he had support from the majority of his colleagues in the College, Fader proposed an English Composition Board and a new graduation requirement in composition to the faculty. He proposed that students fulfill the requirement by completing:

> one course offered for credit in writing about any subject by any unit in the College, and identified by the instruction in writing that it offers, and two other courses offered for certification in writing by any unit in the College, and identified by the assistance in writing that they offer.

In all courses, frequent practice in writing was to be required and the ECB was to approve each as a course in writing.

In a vote of 59 (in favor)—62 (opposed), the proposal was defeated. Following the March 1977 defeat of what was a proposal for the teaching of writing by faculty in the context of their own subject area classes, Fader and Robinson resumed their meetings with faculty in all disciplines in the College as they turned their attention to four concerns and desires that their colleagues expressed about the new program:

1. That it should be based upon faculty assessment of all students' writing when they enter the College;

2. That it should require a composition course taught by the Department of English;

3. That the English Composition Board should reach out to the faculties of secondary schools and community colleges in the state for the purpose of improving pre-university instruction in writing;

4. That the Board should conduct or sponsor an extensive research effort to determine the success of all parts of its program.

In January 1978 a revised proposal calling for an even more comprehensive program than the March 1977 proposal was placed before the faculty. The following description of the proposal for the English Composition Board and its work testifies to the intention of its designers that the teaching of writing at Michigan be related to the teaching of reading in every unit in the College and that the administration of the program be thoroughly interdisciplinary:

The Board

The English Composition Board shall be composed of six faculty members, two from the Department of English and four from other departments or programs within the College. One member of the Board from the Department of English shall be the department chairman.

The Board shall be an agent of the College faculty, responsible to every unit in the College but the responsibility of none. Its budget shall be provided by the Dean and its chairman appointed by the Dean for a three-year term. The chairman's work for the ECB shall be considered half of his or her teaching responsibility.

The Board shall be responsible for offering immediate intensive instruction in English composition to all students who may present themselves or may be recommended by their instructors as needful of special help.

The Board's tutorial work shall be accomplished by both faculty members and graduate student teaching assistants (GSTA's) who have special interest and competence in teaching English composition. The ECB shall pay an appropriate portion of the salaries of both its faculty members and GSTA's; the Board shall supervise and train where necessary the GSTA's who teach for it.

The Board shall provide assistance and guidance in the transaction of teaching composition to faculty members or GSTA's who may request such help in planning or offering courses which carry with them potential credit or certification in English composition. The Board shall accept responsibility from the College Curriculum Committee for approving the writing component of such courses offered by any unit in the College.

The following description of the composition requirement to be administered by the Board testifies to the faculty's insistence that instruction in writing at the introductory level be the responsibility of trained composition teachers and that advanced instruction in writing be the responsibility of faculty in the disciplines:

The Requirement

All students entering the College for the first time must compose an essay before registering for their classes. According to competence demonstrated in this writing sample, students shall be placed in one of three categories:

1. *Tutorial:* A two-to-four credit tutorial, offered by the ECB, which must be taken in the first semester after matriculation; the tutorial course precedes the Introductory Composition course taught in the Department of English.

2. *Introductory Composition:* A four credit course, taught in the Department of English, which must be taken in one of the first two semesters after matriculation.

3. *Exempted:* No introductory composition requirement to fulfill before the upper-level writing course or program.

A writing course or program must be completed by all students, usually in their area of concentration, after their sophomore year.

As the English Composition Board began to implement the new writing requirement, it assumed responsibility for developing and administering two types of activities which were requested by the faculty but which were not part of the writing requirement: First, the Board incorporated into its program a Writing Workshop which had been initiated in the Department of English to provide the support of experienced composition teachers to all undergraduate students in the College at any stage of a writing task. Second, the Board prepared to offer in-service seminars and conferences on theory and practice in the teaching of writing to teachers of pre-university students who might enroll in The University of Michigan.

In effect the ECB took shape as a seven-part program, with six parts of the program within the College and one part beyond its confines. The six responsibilities within the College are the administration of an *entrance essay* required of all incoming undergraduates; *tutorial instruction* required of all students who demonstrate on the entrance essay that they need such assistance; *Introductory Composition* required of most students to make them more proficient writers; *writing workshop* support available to every student; *junior/senior writing courses* offered and required primarily in students' areas of concentration; and *research* into the effectiveness of all parts of the program.

The seventh part of the program includes five types of activities relating the teaching of writing in secondary schools and community colleges to the writing program at The University: *writing conferences,* intended primarily to inform pre-university teachers of the ECB's program of instruction and of its willingness to engage in outreach projects; *one-day and two-day seminars* conducted in secondary schools, community colleges, and universities throughout the state of Michigan and beyond, designed to familiarize faculties with the College's writing program and to discuss with teachers the current state of theory and practice in the art of teaching writing at all levels; *writing workshops,* held at The University of Michigan, designed to provide teachers with three days of intensive work in the teaching of writing; *extended curriculum and staff-development projects* undertaken as models with a few school districts which requested such service; and publication of *fforum,* the journal in which this group of essays was originally published, designed to provide teachers of writing a meeting place for mutual instruction and dialogue.

In June 1981, funded by a generous grant from the Andrew W. Mellon Foundation, the Board extended its outreach program by offering a three-day Conference on "Literacy in the 1980's." The Conference was preceded by one three-day workshop and followed by another. The first was for 175 teachers invited from sixteen states and the District of Columbia; the second, for 175 Michigan teachers who had attended either Writing Workshop '79 or '80 or one of the 215 ECB Seminars on the teaching of writing held in Michigan's schools from January 1979 through May 1981. The overlapping structure of this event—Workshop I→ Conference ← Workshop II—provided teachers of writing in Michigan and elsewhere with the opportunity to benefit from one another as well as from twenty representatives of the vocations, the professions, and education who delivered papers at "Literacy in the 1980's."[2]

Among the Conference speakers was William Coles who, earlier in this chapter, describes his conviction that only as students become alive to the power of language use will they have choices, will they be able to order their worlds and shape their experiences instead of being ordered or shaped by them. Other speakers at the Conference commented on other issues raised in this chapter: the impact of television and computerized print upon literacy; the dangers inherent in the proliferation of specialized languages such as those in science or government which exclude many from their messages; and the significant differences between spoken and written language and their effects upon inquiry and learning themselves.

Through conferences such as "Literacy in the 1980's" as well as workshops and seminars it has been able to conduct for teachers of writing, the English Composition Board has asked its colleagues in elementary schools, secondary schools, colleges, and universities to think about the teaching of literacy—as faculty at Michigan has—in terms of the issues addressed in this chapter. Members of the Board have also encouraged their colleagues to join them in the challenging enterprise of teaching literacy today.

Daniel Fader argues that complex as the teaching of literacy is in our age, it is within our reach and well worth our effort if we make a commitment to teaching it in every classroom at every level of instruction.

Just as periods of time for reading can be set aside daily in one class or throughout the school to provide models of adults and children reading in front of one another so can periods of activity in every subject be devoted regularly to the practice and discussion of writing. For the reluctant or inexperienced writer, the surrounding presence of the activity of writing in class after class is powerful persuasion to the act itself. To resist so much pressure so broadly applied is a heroic act of which few people are capable—especially young people, for whom peer pressure is least resistable of all. Furthermore, the use of writing in any curriculum as a means to the end of comprehending all subjects is persuasive of itself in the struggle to invest writing with the importance it possesses. . . . Finally, Writing Across the Curriculum offers a means for investing a young person's voice with an importance it may no longer possess in home or classroom. Homes with familial hours dominated by television and school with all hours afflicted by large classes are unkind environments for *nurturing the individual voice* (emphasis mine). The sense that one has something to say and someone to say it to, is a sense dulled by silence in the home and hordes in the classroom. That same sense, so basic to the belief that communication is worth the effort, is sharpened and expanded by the experience of writing at every opportunity. Inviting continuous, coherent participation in the process of communication . . . provides both student and process with an importance that nothing else in the curriculum can promise (*fforum*, Winter, 1981, pp. 54, 91).

Notes

[1] In the English Department, Professors Fader and Robinson consulted with colleagues who shared their interest in literacy and learning—Richard Bailey, later to design and direct research for the ECB; Michael Clark, later to direct the design of the ECB's assessment instrument; and Bernard Van't Hul, later to design and direct a new Introductory Composition program for the College. In other disciplines they consulted with the following faculty members who later joined them to become the first English Composition Board—Peter Clarke, Chairman, Department of Communications; Thomas Dunn, Chairman, Department of Chemistry; Harriet Mills, Professor of Far Eastern Language and Literature; and Wilbert McKeachie, Director of the Center for Research into Teaching and Learning and Professor of Psychology.

[2] The papers delivered at this Conference will appear in: Bailey, Richard W. and Robin Melanie Fosheim, Eds. *Literacy for Life: The Demand for Reading and Writing* (New York: The Modern Language Association of America, 1983).

2.

On Speaking and Writing

In this chapter a linguist and an educational administrator join teachers of English language and literature at every level of schooling to explore both the relationships that exist between speaking and writing and the specific implications of those relationships for the teaching of writing. The first three essayists explore the similarities and differences between speaking and writing: Chafe reports on the distinctions between speaking and writing which he and his colleagues at Berkeley have identified after examining an extensive collection of written and spoken data; Kroll identifies four principal relationships between spoken and written language each of which characterizes a phase during students' writing development; and Horner emphasizes that writers must provide their audience the contextual indicators that speakers and listeners always share.

A second group of essayists describes practices for teaching writing which are based upon students' talking with one another about their writing: Graves urges us to encourage even very young students to choose the topics of their writing and then to talk about their topics and their processes of composing stories with their teachers and with one another; Martin recommends that we provide students occasions for journal writing—for conversations in writing—which they may use as a language bridge between speech and writing; Macrorie argues that having writers face their readers not only makes the concept of audience concrete for them but also provides them with a mirror for their prose; Fader describes the voice to which he would direct each writer as she composes and defines this primary source of each individual's language for writing as her mediate voice-in-place between experience and expression; and Robinson recommends a pedagogy to teachers of basic writers that places heavy emphasis on revision and makes explicit the differences between speech norms and writing norms.

In their companion essays, Bailey reflects on the Ann Arbor Black English Case in which the central issue was the distinction between spoken and written English and in which he was a witness for the plaintiffs; and Hansen, Associate Superintendent of the Ann Arbor Public Schools, offers his retrospective views of both the case and the plans and activities which the school district developed in compliance with the verdict.

As she reflects upon all the essays in the chapter and contemporary research into the relationships between speech and writing, Couture urges us to look at what speakers and writers do that is similar rather than to narrow our focus to the distinctions between speaking and writing that have limited relevance for composition teachers.

11 Speakers and Writers Do Different Things

Wallace L. Chafe
Department of Linguistics, University of California, Berkeley

The activity of writing is fundamentally different from the activity of speaking. Among other things, people write much more slowly than they talk. And they have the chance to go back and change what they have written before anyone sees it, whereas speakers can't hide what they have said. Writers are isolated from their audiences; speakers are normally in face-to-face situations. Writers, furthermore, are likely to feel more accountable for what they say, since their product may stay around for a long time. It is interesting to consider how differences like these affect the nature of written language, as language. How do both the special nature of what people do when they write and the special circumstances in which they write lead to the special properties of written language?

Only recently have the unusual characteristics of the writing process received serious attention, and only recently have we begun to understand the distinctive kind of language which results from this process. Several of us at Berkeley have been looking at an extensive collection of written and spoken data, trying to learn more about what is involved in each of these distinctive uses of language.

Speaking, which people have been doing for a million years and which will probably always be the most common means of using language, is a fast-paced activity. We speak at an average of about three words a second, and we can't really slow things down very much without losing our listener's attention and our own train of thought. I suspect that this speaking rate in fact reflects the pace of natural thought processes (Chafe, "The Deployment"). Writing is nothing like this. We can write as slowly as we like, but we would have to be pretty fast at a typewriter to approach anywhere near the speed of normal speech. Writing is commonly a leisurely activity. Our thoughts, nevertheless, are likely to be jumping along at a much faster pace. Thus we have plenty of time to think about more carefully structuring the language itself as well as reviewing and revising it as we see fit. The result is a language which no longer consists of a sequence of brief spurts, as spoken language does:

> It's just a program of Victorian and Modern poetics.
> It's just a seminar. It's tangential to reality.

Instead it is a language which uses a variety of more complex syntactic devices—nominalizations, participles, complement clauses, attributive adjectives, and so on—to mold information into more elaborate, integrated products of deliberate creation:

Critics have used George Eliot's failure to accomplish her self-proclaimed goal of writing realistic novels as evidence of the impossibility of the realistic undertaking itself.

These two examples were produced by one and the same speaker/writer. They illustrate well how the integrated quality of written language, made possible by the slow, deliberate nature of its production, contrasts with the fragmentation of language which is spoken on the fly (Chafe, "Integration").

Walter Ong has pointed out the irony of the fact that a writer who may expect his product to be read by hundreds of thousands of people sets about his task by closeting himself with his typewriter. Isolated from his audience, a writer lacks the direct feedback and interaction enjoyed by a speaker; he also cannot share with his *reader* any of the immediate context and environment which he would have with his listener. Typical written language lacks the ego involvement, interaction, and liveliness of spoken language:

I'm feeling OK now (laugh), but uh I had last week I thought I was (laugh) dying. You heard that I fainted in the shower.

Evidence for the detachment of written language can be found, for example, in the impersonal references, use of passive verbs, and lack of reliance on shared context which characterizes written texts. Compare the following written example, produced by the same person, with the spoken example above:

Only by taping an event at which one is a natural participant is it possible to gather data which is not distorted by the presence of a non-participant analyst.

Written language, then, tends to be detached and distant where spoken language tends to be involved.

Finally, speakers seem willing to operate with a kind of hit-or-miss epistemology, not worrying so much about the ultimate truth of what they say, but trying on ideas for size. Spoken language is sprinkled with expressions that suggest the tentative origins and reliability of what is being said:

I think if I had gotten the police, I probably would have just gotten my things back.

Not only do writers have more time to ponder what they are saying, but they are likely to realize that their product will be read by a critical audience, that it may exist for a long time, and that it may be perused by many people. These factors impose a kind of accountability on a writer which does not normally constrain a speaker. The result is often that the writer assumes a more authoritative stance than the speaker, as evidenced by the words "specifically," "constantly," and "fact" in the following example of written language:

Since all puppet heads are specifically good or evil, the fact of struggle between the opposing forces is constantly clear, both verbally and visually.

The precise tone of much written language contrasts with the more hesitant tone which is typical of spoken language.

Qualities like *integration, detachment,* and *authority* are thus fostered by the process and circumstances of writing. They may appear in speaking too, of course, but in writing they are strikingly more prevalent. As we delve further into the speaking and writing processes and their products, we expect to be learning more about these differences. Both the teaching and the practice of writing should profit from a clearer knowledge of the ways in which writing is a very special use of language.

12 Speaking–Writing Relationships in the Growth of Writing Abilities

Barry M. Kroll
Department of English, Indiana University, Bloomington

It's not unusual to hear conflicting claims about the relationships between speaking and writing, as well as contradictory advice about the implications of these relationships for the teaching of writing. Some experts in the language arts stress the close connections between speaking and writing, believing that students should be encouraged to draw on the strengths of their oral language when they engage in written composition. Other experts stress the differences between speaking and writing; they observe that the demands of writing require new skills, and they believe that if students rely heavily on oral language skills and strategies, the quality of their written discourse will in fact suffer. Which of these expert claims are we to accept?

Paradoxically, each claim seems to be correct. One key to understanding this paradox is to recognize that the functional relationships between oral and written language change during the individual's development of writing skills. I want to suggest that there are, in fact, four principal relationships between oral and written language and that each of the four characterizes a phase during the student's development of the skills of writing. I call the four phases *preparation, consolidation, differentiation,* and *integration.* By attending to the ways in which the relationships between speaking and writing change for individuals during these phases, we are in a better position, I believe, to understand and promote students' growth in writing.

During the *preparation* phase, our primary pedagogical goal is to help each young child learn those skills which will enable him or her to engage in the first stages of independent writing. Obviously, a child must learn the "technical" skills of handwriting and spelling. But there is also a need for the child to develop the ability to "compose." Many language arts specialists agree that having a child dictate while the teacher writes out the child's sentences is an important aspect of *preparation* for writing, both because dictation provides practice in composing original texts and because dictation translates the connection between spoken and written language into concrete form.

Preparation leads into the next important phase in writing development, a period in which our goal as teachers is to strengthen written expression by drawing on the child's ability to talk well. This *consolidation* of a child's oral competence with his or her resources for writing is generally accomplished by the teacher's providing activities in which the forms and functions of writing are made similar to those of speaking. Many language arts specialists propose that children should engage in "personal writing" or exploration of the "senses" or "expressive writing"—writing which remains close to the child's experience, which addresses an intimate audience, and which provides a legitimate context for "talk written down." But *consolidation* can also involve such oral language activities as oral monologue, a form of speech which is like writing in that the communicator assumes full responsibility for sustaining the discourse.

Such *consolidation* of the child's oral and written resources may function to extend and strengthen the child's nascent writing abilities. However, since speaking and writing also differ in important ways, the child must ultimately master *differentiation* of the two modes. A child needs to learn that written texts— particularly texts with transactional functions—are often free from features which characterize the language of conversation and, furthermore, such texts are often particularly explicit in meaning. The compositions of inexperienced writers contain many stylistic features of oral language, such as the use of stock phrases or the use of "and" as an all-purpose joining device. Inexperienced writers often tend to write as though they were conversing with a reader who shares their context—as though writing were, like speaking, an interactive construction of meaning, rather than an autonomous production of text. This leads inexperienced writers to represent meaning in ways that are not sufficiently explicit— often these writers use ambiguous references, fail to define terms, omit transitional devices, and so on.

Thus, while we as teachers must encourage children to draw on their oral language resources during the early phases of their development as writers, we must actually curb their reliance on oral language during later phases of their growth as writers. Continued reliance on their oral competence might actually limit students' abilities to develop more specialized writing skills.

It seems important, therefore, that the focus in teaching shift from *consolidation* to *differentiation,* from writing assignments which allow students to draw heavily on spoken language to assignments which require students to use the increasingly explicit and autonomous discourse of literate texts. This shift in pedagogical emphasis from *consolidation* tasks to *differentiation* tasks does not mean that children must suddenly abandon their oral language resources, striving for an artificial, "bookish" style that is far removed from their experience and competence. During a period of transition children can continue to *consolidate* their oral and writing resources, even as they also begin to *differentiate* certain features of speaking and writing.

For mature writers the phases of *preparation, consolidation,* and *differentiation* come together in a systematic manner to produce *integration* of the complex relationships between speaking and writing. Mature writers both *consolidate* and *differentiate.* In fact, aspects of oral language continue to influence their writing: The expressive qualities most typical of speech ("voice," "tone," "expressiveness") distinguish the character of the texts of advanced writers.

In this essay, I have presented a model which suggests how teachers may use the relationships between children's oral and written language resources to foster children's growth as writers. Most models have limitations, of course. This model makes writing development appear more linear and uni-dimensional than it is. It also oversimplifies the difficulties that students can encounter in the transitions between phases, particularly in the important shift from *consoli-dation* to *differentiation*. Nevertheless, the model defines sequential relationships between speaking and writing which are pedagogically useful to those of us who teach writing.

13 Speech-act Theory and Writing

Winifred Bryan Horner
Department of English, University of Missouri

Speech-act theory is based on the premise that communication is a series of actions or interactions between a speaker (writer) and a hearer (reader). The theory contends that a speaker (writer) in performing the act of utterance (or writing) also performs a second act, the *illocutionary act,* in which he *intends* the utterance to do something. Thus, in making the assertion, "That dog is dangerous," a speaker may not only *intend* to inform his hearer but he may also *intend* to warn his hearer as well. Similarly, I may request you to turn up the thermostat by saying, "I am cold." In fact, all uses of language including much of our daily conversation is composed of such speech acts.

In making a request a speaker assumes that a hearer is both willing and able to perform the act, and the speaker may form a polite request by questioning the hearer's willingness or ability.

1. Would you mind closing the window.
2. Can you close the window.

It is important to note that these two utterances can be intended as true questions if the speaker feels that the hearer is either unwilling or unable to close the window: "Can you close the window" becomes a true question if the hearer has his arm in a cast.

As these examples suggest, meaning depends in part on the speaker's understanding of the feelings and desires of the hearer. When a wife requests that her husband wash the dishes by saying, *"Would you mind washing the dishes,"* he may respond by denying his willingness, "Yes, I mind—" while, at the same time, recognizing the intended request, "—but I will." In all our interactions with one another, we assume roles and attitudes for ourselves within certain contexts, and we presume roles and attitudes for others. And meaning is highly dependent on the relationship of speakers and hearers.

In non-fictive writing, the same rules apply, but authors and contexts must be reconstructed by the reader. A good writer will always assist his reader in making that reconstruction, because voices must be clear and contexts well established. In ordinary spoken conversation, speakers and hearers are physically attached to their texts; in written and recorded discourse, on the other hand, writers may be removed from their utterances by both time and distance. When I pick up a week-old Detroit newspaper, I am able to read it within the Detroit context of my experience and, furthermore, as a reader, I know that the news events being reported occurred a week ago rather than at the time of my reading. Hence I am able to reconstruct the context of place as Detroit and time as a week ago.

In written acts of communication, a writer must be especially aware of his readers; furthermore, he must make his readers aware of himself as writer. It is important that a reader know not only who the writer of a written text is, but also what the writer's purpose or intention is. According to the precepts of speech-act theory, in writing as well as in speaking, individuals are performing intentional acts. As a writer, one needs to recognize, to be constantly aware of his readers, and to establish his voice and purpose early in the discourse. In written discourse, since the author and the physical context are not present, it is especially important for the writer to establish the context, the purpose, and his identity as a writer as well as the identity of his readers. In the following opening paragraph from his well-known "Letter from Birmingham Jail," note how Martin Luther King, Jr. establishes his identity, his intention, the context, and his immediate readers.

> While confined here in the Birmingham City Jail, I came across your recent statement calling my present activities "unwise and untimely." Seldom do I pause to answer criticism of my work and ideas. If I sought to answer all the criticisms that cross my desk, my secretaries would have little time for anything other than such correspondence in the course of the day, and I would have no time for constructive work. But since I feel that you are men of genuine good will and that your criticisms are sincerely set forth, I want to try to answer your statement in what I hope will be patient and reasonable terms.

King imposes a role on his readers when he calls them "men of genuine good will" whose "criticisms are sincerely set forth." Although his immediate readers are his fellow clergymen, he is obviously writing for a larger audience. However, anyone who reads this essay must read it with the writer's conception of his readers in mind.

In the following opening paragraph from "What Life Means to Me," Jack London establishes his background in an equally forceful fashion.

> I was born in the working-class. Early I discovered enthusiasm, ambition, and ideals: and to satisfy these became the problem of my child-life. My environment was crude and rough and raw. I had no outlook, but an up-look rather. My place in society was at the bottom. Here life offered nothing but sordidness and wretchedness, both of the flesh and the spirit: for there flesh and spirit were alike starved and tormented.

Because contextual indicators are seldom physically present in written language, authors must make their intentions clear either directly or indirectly at the beginning of their essays. Sometimes writers declare their intentions directly in the opening paragraph, but sophisticated writers are often more subtle. Although written or recorded language can and usually does exist in time and place separated from its author and its original context, that fact does not mean that there is no context for their works. Readers will reconstruct contexts, complete with speakers, intended hearers, and purposes. Consequently, authors must make their voices and their purposes clear within their texts or they might be misunderstood. Every effective piece of writing must have what Wayne Booth calls a rhetorical stance.

> The common ingredient that I find in all of the writing I admire—excluding for now novels, plays, and poems—is something that I shall reluctantly call the rhetorical stance, a stance which depends on discovering and maintaining in any writing situation a proper balance among the three elements that are at work in any communicative effort: the available arguments about the subject itself, the interest and peculiarities of the audience, and the voice, the implied character, of the speaker (p. 141).

Speech-act theory recognizes that meaning in spoken discourse depends upon the interaction between the speaker and the hearer within a given context. So too, meaning in written discourse is equally dependent upon the interaction between writer and reader. Skillful writers establish the context, the purpose, and the relationship between themselves and their readers within their texts, so that meaning can survive long after the original writers, readers, and contexts cease to exist.

14 Break the Welfare Cycle: Let Writers Choose Their Topics

Donald H. Graves
Department of Education, University of New Hampshire

A seventh grade teacher left my writing workshop one Wednesday afternoon filled with renewed optimism only to return seven days later with that tarred and feathered look. She was a bit hostile to boot. "I told my class they could choose any subject they wished for their writing assignment this week. Well, you'd think I'd asked them to undress in public." Her glance at me said, "That was a pretty dumb suggestion . . . letting them choose their own topics.

"Some children asked for a list of good topics. Others asked outright, 'What topics do *you* (the teacher) like best?' More said, 'Our topics are dumb.' They pleaded, 'Give us the topics.'"

By the time most children reach seventh grade, they are unable to choose topics. This serious symptom is an indicator of many other problems in the life of the young writer. Children who can't choose topics see writing as an artificial act disconnected from their own lives. Writers need to know what they can command and defend, to put their voices on the line.

From the second grade on, we won't let them learn to choose topics. Instead, children go on writers' welfare, dependent on the teacher for everything, starting with the topic. Our reasoning seems to be: "Children are afraid to write; worse, they come to the page with nothing of significance to write about. We'll take care of both problems by giving them the topic."

The welfare trail begins. The child is fed a diet of snappy gimmicks: story starters, stimulating pictures, "dial-a-story" games, opening paragraphs, open-ended stories to complete, as well as teachers' favorite topics. It doesn't have to be this way. Children bring rich experiences and voices to the page.

Children show us much about topics and how we can better help them. Under a three-year grant from the National Institute of Education, Susan Sowers, Lucy Calkins and I have completed a study of the composing processes of young children from age six through ten. One small sector of data on topics is reported here to show the importance of topic choice as well as its implication for the teaching of writing.

Choice and Voice

Topics come easily to six-year-olds. They write about personal experiences, fantasies, and information books about prehistoric animals, weapons, weather, and animals. The sources seem unending. The children are confident; their voices boom through the print. For many these happy days don't last.

Developmental issues intrude. Somewhere between grades one and three the child becomes aware of the intrusion of audience. The audience includes the child himself. The child finds that other children as well as the teacher react differently to his writing. Until now the child supposed others had the same interpretation, registered the same feelings about his writing.

A sense of audience is intensified by the writer's growing ability as a reader. Good readers are overheard saying, "This is awful. I don't know what to say. What's a good subject to write about?" At this stage the child's critical skills outweigh his ability to produce a text satisfying to himself. The child looks for help. Instead of giving help, we induct the child into the welfare cycle. We ignore the resources the child already has to deal with—the problem of topic choice.

Help means leading writers back to their resources, their sense of territory, information, and voice. Help writers to speak about their topics. When teachers help writers to speak about their topics and how they compose them, children find renewal in the sound of their voices. They hear new information because teachers listen, reflect, and question writers in such a way that the writers teach the teachers about what they know. The children in our New Hampshire study were constantly speaking about their writing through formal and informal conferences. Note the voice, sense of process, and control of information by two nine-year-old children as they speak about their topics:

Andrea

I think I say "Little White Fish Jumped All Around Us" and I realized—How big are they? Why white? What did they look like? And I realized probably my whole story is like that—blah! Like I have, "I pressed my toes in hot sand." What was it like? How did it feel? So I'm going to do a whole new draft, rather than fix it up. I'll sort of follow along with the other draft, but in my own words.

Brian

When I wrote about the cat and the car running over it, it came to my mind. When we were riding down North Broadway and we saw a burning car . . . I could describe the car burning up—it was a Pontiac, burning in the night. Hey, a title! "Flames in the Night!"

Both children encounter problems but articulate a process to solve them. Andrea is highly critical of her piece about the fish but isn't discouraged. She'll do a new draft. Brian discovers a new topic and title in the midst of writing another. These children speak this way because their teachers have not only given them responsibility for their topics, but help to deal with issues in draft.

Topic Choice Helps the Writing

When writers know the choice is theirs and they write at least four times a week, they think about topics when they are not writing. When six-year-old John discovered a bat with his father on a Saturday, he rehearsed both topic and some of the text before he wrote about it on Monday morning. John knew he could rediscover what happened in the event through writing and that time would be provided for it when he got to class. Nine-year-old Amy is interested in foxes. She has chosen the topic. The night before she will write, Amy rehearses the lead to her fox piece. One of the significant findings in our study was the amount of "off-stage" thinking done by children who felt they controlled their topics.

Children who write regularly, yet have topic choice, are seldom without a topic. Their writing folders contain lists of "future" topics. These are topics they pick up from reading, other children, new experiences, or information they wish to know more about. Or, in the course of writing one topic, inevitably another more interesting one arises. It is saved for another day.

Teachers in the study placed great emphasis on the information behind the topic. The children were interviewed about the content in their topics; they were responsible for teaching the teachers about what they knew. This procedure appeared to result in two study findings as writers developed:

1. More problems of information handled in second or third draft were dealt with at the point of choosing the topic.
2. As children learned to choose and limit topics, the number of drafts diminished.

The Switch from Choice to Assignment

Writing is, after all, a tool for learning. It is meant to be used in mathematics, science, and social studies. It is *not* the exclusive property of personal narrative, fiction, or poetry. As part of any child's diet, writing needs to be used as a means of finding out, sometimes by assignment. Such writing can begin in the primary years. The central diet, however, still needs to be with the child's developing power in choosing the topic. The switch from drafts in personal narrative or personal topic choice can be made in a very short time frame.

By the second year of the study many of the eight-year-olds now turning nine had had considerable experience with topic choice and the use of successive drafts to clarify their subjects. In the second half of the fourth grade, the teacher moved the children into content writing. The switch from personal writing to writing in science and the social studies was barely perceptible. The children used more resources, interviews, had some work on note taking, but the actual composing in the new genre was hardly different from the personal writing. These children already knew what it meant to have supporting information, to organize toward meaning, to have more precise language to communicate their topic.

Choice and Responsibility

Children learn through the choices they make. Early on, first choices, even second and third ones are often poor. Fred wants to write about "space" but is swallowed up by the enormity of his choice. With help Fred may find he knows more about the space shuttle. He begins to learn the power of limitations, the meaning of choice.

Our data show children learn and benefit from choice. They think about writing when they are not writing. They learn the meaning of choice by thinking of information behind their topics. They find it easier to learn to revise in personally related themes because there is more depth to their understanding of the topic. Most of all, they learn the meaning of voice. They learn to put themselves into their pieces because they are able to defend the information in their topics.

We need to break the teaching cycle that places young people on writers' welfare. Children won't learn if we think for them. We want writers who will write and talk as if they knew their subject. Independence begins when writers choose their topics.

15 Contexts for Writing

Nancy Martin
Educational Consultant, London, England

I asked a six-year-old if he was a writer yet.

"Yes," he replied, "you just put down what's in your head."

True, but like all other activities, writing is sustained or constrained—by its context. It is illuminating to observe the different settings in which school writing is done, since these figure largely in students' expectations of themselves and of teachers. Most teachers set the topics, and most writing is graded: by producing the kind of writing their teachers seem to want, students hope to gain a good mark. Over the years they lose the six-year-old's sense of having things to say of their own. Meanwhile, teachers suppose that students cannot write without suggested topics and the incentive of marks—and indeed, for a time they cannot.

A College of Education student wrote:

> At secondary school it was always writing to please whichever teacher was
> teaching you. Essays all had to be very descriptive and interesting to the
> teacher we had, otherwise they were no good.

The circle of passivity is complete.

And then there are the constraints of time, occasion, and absence of audience
other than the teacher. However, the teacher who abandons the role of assessor,
to become an advisor, begins to change the picture. And the writing changes too;
it begins to take on the character of a conversation, one with reflections or
questions. That is to say, the writer's own intentions begin to operate, and the
teacher-audience is now seen as a real listener who may even be expected to
reply, in conversation or writing. Such are the expectations of the senior high
school boy who wrote this journal entry:

> I think I went fairly well (in a maths exam) after such a disastrous start, and
> this is probably because I enjoy maths so much this year. You would too if
> you had Captain Brown for a teacher. With a unique combination of nautical
> terminology and mathematical theory delivered at great volume through the
> smoke haze of the occasional Marlborough, one cannot help but pay attention.

What has happened here is the crucial change in the role of the teacher. By becoming a partner in—rather than a director of—the student's writing, he has
cleared the way for the student's own intentions. At first the student may not in
fact know his own intentions; but the way is now clear for the teacher to help
the student to discover them. Consider this log entry from a fifteen-year-old girl:

> Would you give me some English please. Would you give me an interesting
> book to read, for example a humorous one. I have finished all my Geography
> off. We have done a great amount of work in Geography since September.
> Can you also give me some work on my project because I am getting bored
> with just taking notes and putting my own views down on paper. I would like
> to do something different with this project. Today I started to answer those
> questions you set me on primitives but I am stuck so I will carry on with
> them on Monday with your help.

On the way to becoming an autonomous learner, this student has yet to find a
language, her own language; and she is on the edge of escape from the all-pervad-
ing school sense that you must use other people's language—the language you
may never manage. As a less fortunate study:

> I knew what he was on about, but I only knew what he was on about in my
> words. I didn't know his words. In my exams I had to change the way I
> learnt you know. In all my exercise books, I put it down the way I understood
> but I had to remember what I'd written there and then translate it into what I
> think they will understand, you know.

Written conversation would seem to be the language bridge; and the form of
writing nearest to speech is the journal. It has no set form and does not, therefore hold the anxieties for students that other forms of writing carry—no problems of topic sentences or beginnings and conclusions. In addition, a journal has

built-in rights and needs of reflection, comment, and questions. It can move from trivia to a student's deepest reflection and back; and it has the continuity which provides for sheer quantity, which is also an important element in writing progress. A seventeen-year-old student commented as follows on the effect of her journal writing:

> I found that with writing regularly, my ability to write improved enormously, not only in the quality of the result but in the ease of actually doing the writing . . . I often used my writing as a thought formulating process . . .

Given the writing that journals require and the confidence that they may foster, students will begin to move into other literary forms, whether in their journals or as additions to them. If it is made clear to them that all forms are welcome, some will write poems, or more formal descriptions of events, or narratives, or, by negotiation, essays which take up themes they have explored in their journals or their reading. They move into these transitions naturally if their teachers show them the possibilities. Of course the amount and quality from different students varies; but the students' access to autonomy in learning and to a language to match—that is the essential feature behind this kind of work. It turns upon a non-authoritarian relationship with their teachers. It is a matter of bringing personal involvement back into the education scene and thereby raising the level of achievement. To see journal writing and its attendant directions as just another kind of topic set by the teachers and marked in the usual way would be to mistake the situation totally. It is in effect a different curriculum which carries with it different forms of writing.

Of course, journals are not the only form of writing that students should do; nor is it invariably bad for teachers to set a topic for the whole class to do. But it is suggested that unassessed journals—written for the teacher and chiefly about the work in which the students are engaged—should form a major element in their writing. Where journals have been used in this way they have yielded rewards for students and teachers alike. The effect is to alter significantly the all-too-common authoritarian contexts for students' writing. Improved contexts—of reflection and conversation—significantly affect the students' freedom, as they learn on higher and higher levels, "to put down what's in their heads."

16 Language-using Animals

Ken Macrorie
Santa Fe, NM

At lunch today Joyce, my wife, told me she had read in *The New York Times* that, unlike most animals, the young of higher apes are able to identify themselves in a mirror and react, some going so far as to preen themselves before the glass. This afternoon I picked up a copy of *Unduressed,* a broadsheet of writing done by a student in a Winter 1978 class of mine. One story, by Lois, began this way:

When I was about two and a half, my parents, my brother, and I were watching TV. One of those terrible World War II movies came on where the Japanese pilots shoot at the Americans and scream jibberish to each other. I'm not sure whether it was just because the Japanese were so obviously the bad buys, but I suddenly realized that they looked *weird.*

Lois went on telling how she had called the Japanese "funnies," then looked over at her older brother and realized he resembled them. She began screaming in a sing-song voice, "Jimmy's a funny!" Eventually her father picked her up and placed her in front of a mirror which showed her she was a funny also. She became hysterical. The two Korean children had been adopted by an American family of German stock. "Since then," wrote Lois, "I've learned that people will accept me, Oriental or not, as long as I accept myself."

In the seminar where Lois's story was read aloud, the listener-readers were stunned. It was told simply and tersely with no embellishments, a Greek tragedy of recognition, touching fears of identity universal in all of us.

Six months later I was looking in a kind of mirror as I thought back over the experience of teaching 38 seminars in the last 14 years. The people ranged from 9- to 50-year-olds. As I stared at the glass of memory, I realized that I (and other teachers around the country who had directed similar seminars for a number of years) had before me a body of experience like that of an anthropologist who does field research. Week after week, month after month, year after year, we had observed groups of 10 to 30 people randomly chosen (within the selective processes of school enrollment) doing the same thing. They had attempted to tell of their experience truthfully, and were present to see the effect upon others who sat listening to the stories while holding a typed version of a narrative in hand.

At that moment I saw that some generalizing was justified. Writing is ordinarily read by an absent reader. That's its function—to provide communication between people who aren't in each other's presence. But in our seminars, the writers faced their readers, and perceived their body language, appreciative laughs, gasps of amazement at sensing common feelings, gulps, grunts, inarticulate "oh's," sharp intakes of breath, or glassy-eyed stares, all to be read as keenly as the listeners were reading the writing. I know about "creative writing" workshops, where for years writers have made up a critical audience for each other; but so often there they respond in what they consider "literary ways," careful to echo the teacher's pet critical attitudes or theories. Here, all responses were honored.

In the mirror I saw students who had begun the course writing freely, encouraged to concentrate on truthtelling and not worry about punctuation, spelling, or grammar, and then were further countenanced in the first three meetings by a prohibition set on responders against negative comments—"Positive remarks or nothing at all." Such a beginning encouraged that voice in their heads that speaks as most persons begin the strings of words that make up sentences and meaning on paper. Lois had written something shaking to us and to herself; the voice had supplied it in a flow.

Again and again in these seminars, writers use live metaphor, subtle alliteration, powerful parallel structure, significant rhythms, grabbing openings, and endings that let go. The situation frees them to be what they are—language-using animals. When the physical responses of the group are strongest, a paper that evokes them is often said by the writer to have "just written itself." Without realizing they are using a literary term, responders often say, "It all seemed to come from one *voice.*"

But when these same writers think they are being asked to write a "critical paper," they usually lose the flow of words in their heads and write Engfish, the labored, word-wasting, empty dialect of the schools. I'm beginning to understand why. Writing those papers, they revert to the common school experience—giving back the teacher's ideas—and the old feelings rise up in them, when they hadn't made themselves familiar with the actualities behind the ideas they were peddling. Unlike those few professional writers who write exposition powerfully, in most school writing students feel no ego satisfaction. Their work earns them no money. They won't lose their jobs if the writing is poor. If they're given a D or an F, they can always sign up for another section of the writing class. They know they're not writing for twenty other people, or hundreds or thousands, but for one—the teacher. It's wrong, this artificial, inhuman communication situation. It won't work. It never has worked. In the May, 1893, *Atlantic Monthly*, J. J. Greenough reflected upon "the great outcry . . . about the inability of the students admitted to Harvard College to write English clearly and correctly." He said the schools were requiring frequent written exercises that were corrected and commented on by the teacher, and asked, "With all this practice in writing, why do we not obtain better results?"

In the mirror I saw Lois's story about the "funnies" bringing about results in her peers. We have a way to go before the mirror shows powerful expository writing being read in writing classes. To bring that about we must put our students in situations where they feel a need to report, explain, or summarize.

Writing is an act that can be done well only through the initiative of the writer. It's like thinking, or breathing. No one expects us to learn to think by taking a class in which we fill out exercise books and are counted down for wrong thoughts. You may say, "That's exactly what we did in logic class," but remember, that logic class never made anyone logical.

In many places in the world these days people are beginning to understand the function of intention in writing. In his book *Personal Knowledge,* Michael Polanyi said that employing language is like employing a stick to reach a coin that has fallen under a table. We hold on to the near end but focus our attention on the far end. Our "focal awareness" is out there, and we have only a subsidiary awareness of the near end, which we are manipulating. And so, Polanyi says, we compose words, spoken or written. It is our intention that brings the words to us. Jimmy Britton and Nancy Martin, who helped found the London Association for the Teaching of English, have understood that truth for years and demonstrated it recently in the Program in Teaching Writing at the Bread Loaf School of English, Middlebury College, Vermont.

In the past, English teachers have ignored that truth. Traditionally we have set as our goal—as Roger Shuy of Georgetown University has pointed out—that students will master formal language from the outset, and not go through a natural sequence as they do in speaking, from babbling to casual to informal to consultative to formal language. Most people are seldom called upon to use formal language outside school, and yet in school students are seldom asked to employ any other. Asking them to write formally is—unbeknownst to most of us—asking them to have formal intentions. When they are puzzled or turned off by such a request—because they seldom have such intentions—we then devise an artificial situation for them, saying, "Imagine you're an editorial writer for a newspaper." A ridiculous request to children who have seldom read an editorial page, never written professionally, and are not experienced or knowledgeable in the kind of events newspaper editors usually write about. I'm not saying that children shouldn't be challenged to do something they haven't done before, but for such encounters they need the confidence that comes from having done well, and often, in other related tasks. School acts as if its job is to demoralize students by inappropriate challenges rather than to move them forward from success to success.

The perversity of such assignments as "Imagine you're an editorial writer for a newspaper" is laughable. We don't say to babies, "Imagine you're going to walk up that flight of stairs"—which would be a much more commonsensical command. Rather we put the baby down in front of the first step, in sight of something or someone the baby wants to get to above, and it begins to fall and crawl, slither and flop its way up, walking with arms and hands as much as feet. In less than a year that child walks upright with grace and confidence. The analogue is a child writing utterances in broken or fragmented American-English, moving through the stages of language from the most casual or informal to the most formal—as the occasion arises.

Recently on an educational television program I told of an elementary teacher who constantly encouraged her students to write for their own purposes. One day when a little girl complained that she had forgotten to bring her lunch to school, the teacher said, "Well, we can't stop our class work now for you, but why don't you write a note to the office secretary asking her to phone your mother, and I'll send it along with the attendance report." The girl did this and the lunch arrived at noon. She saw that writing works. When I finished telling the little story, the program host said, "Well, that's a whimsical example, but it makes a point." It was not at all a whimsical example. The writer of that note, who hadn't yet learned to spell conventionally with high consistency, at that moment began to write intentionally. In truth, in competence, in power, there is no other way to write. You can be sure that spelling, punctuation, and syntactic control will come to that girl much earlier than to children filling out exercise books to fulfill their teachers' intentions.

A movement emphasizing meaning before correctness in writing has begun. Teachers around the country are dropping the inane idea of creating imaginary audiences for student writers. In the *Foxfire* books, Eliot Wigginton long ago began publishing his students' investigations into the people and history of their region. Richard Lebovitz at Cape Hatteras School in Buxton, North Carolina, has been doing the same thing for several years.

The National Writing Project, based at the University of California in Berkeley, has recently published Anne Wotring's description of keeping a *Thinkbook,* in which she has recorded her struggles taking chemistry, a course that she had always been afraid of. She kept a log of everything that went through her mind as she took the course—a print of her thoughts that illuminates how we all think and write. It enabled her to master chemistry. The Center for Applied Linguistics in Washington, D.C., has published Jana Staton's description of the *Dialogue Journal* devised by a Los Angeles teacher who sets up an informal conversation between herself and students, most of whom are writing fascinating "complaints" about their lives in school.

Another simple way of allowing students to write out of their intentions is to ask them to report or comment on performances they have witnessed with critical awareness over the weekends—school plays, amateur or professional sports contests (in the flesh or on television)—whatever is apt to be covered by newspaper reporters or critics—and then to post both student and professional writings on bulletin boards in hallways for the whole school population to read. Students who speak with their peers outside school as expert critics should be encouraged to write as expert critics also, and to a real audience.

The possibilities for writing intentionally and usefully in school are innumerable, but our time-honored practice of making phony assignments blinds us to that fact. In my book *Searching Writing* (1980), I have presented the experience of dozens of high school and college teachers asking students to replace the conventional research or term paper with a story of their search for something that fulfills a genuine need in their lives. They talk to experts in the community before going to books in the library. Their report is a narrative of their wanderings, of their hits and misses. Its form helps them see how much an observer is always part of the observed. They meet authorities face-to-face, come to respect the work behind their assertions, and lose the urge to plagiarize. Their findings, and failures to find, pay off in their lives.

We need to make truthtelling and usefulness possible and probable in student writing. In the past we have supported writing in school newspapers, yearbooks, and other publications that is as specious and overblown as the worst writing done in government bureaucracies, business, industry, and the professions. We have unwittingly encouraged and nurtured Doublespeak. Let's forget that kind of writing and our part in it.

17 Narrowing the Space Between Writer and Text*

Daniel Fader
English Composition Board and the Department of English,
The University of Michigan

The three objects of the revising process provoke three kinds of activities that are separable rather than separate. Two of the three—text and audience—are conscious objects of attention for all experienced editors, whether revising themselves or another. The third, however, appears to be found only in the work of the few editors invariably regarded by their clients as effective and desirable colleagues in the remaking of a text. This third object of attention is the author him/herself.

Authors are as frequently forgotten by themselves in the revising process as they are by their external editors. When the editor who is not the author fails to read and retain the writer's stylistic signature, the product is likely to be a bastardized text unacknowledged by its author. When such mistreatment occurs, casualties are usually limited to the text and the relationship between editor and client; the author, unhappy, survives. This is not the case when author and editor are the same person.

The cruelest, most destructive editing I have seen in twenty-five years of curiously observing its practice is the editing inflicted upon self by clients, whether colleagues or students, in the process of creating what they identify as "drafts" of their material. Too often the drafts are hurricanes, violent blows that carry writers' language further and further from their possession with every new choice of word and every rearrangement of phrase and sentence. If at first their primary desire is not to obtain distance from their writing, then distance soon becomes the hallmark of their progress, their chief and sometimes their sole accomplishment.

How to account for the common phenomenon of devitalizing distance between writers and their texts? Two explanations recommend themselves—one because of its frequent occurrence in the testimony of writers who talk about the problem of distance in their own writing, and the other because of its utility in describing a densely inhabited but largely uncharted territory. Before offering and examining the explanations, let me cite examples of the affliction:

A. As both a woman who has been in the role of client and therapist, I strongly disagree.
B. The persistent economic woes that now plague the United States will not be vanquished, or even substantially curbed, until new currents of thought emerge within the federal government that will force it to commence with the difficult policies required to assuage our present problems.
C. I present this information to you in general exposition of the present efforts

being undertaken or projected in the area of basic English instruction (composition and language skills assistance/development) under the direction of or in association with this unit. I believe such information may be useful as a base for the determination of what further efforts and possible costs might be practicable in reference to basic English instruction efforts that could be relevant to the student focus of the new proposal.

Example A is taken from a letter to the *Ann Arbor News,* a daily newspaper publishing regularly if not memorably for 147 years; B is the first sentence of a paper written by a senior student for an Economics class at the University of Michigan, an institution where such opening sentences have been written regularly if not memorably for 162 years; and C is quoted from a document written by a university administrator for his administrative peers. The genesis of its form may date from creation of the first university administrator.

The woman writing to the *Ann Arbor News* is angry about a letter published a few days earlier in the same newspaper. The provoking letter was composed of equal parts of meanness and stupidity; having seen it, I watched with interest for its respondents, the best of whom wrote the sentence quoted here as Example A.

For the moment bypassing the question of the misplaced "both," I want first to ask her why she is "in the role of" client and therapist instead of simply being what she claims she has been—both a client and a therapist? She is angry, she is apt, and yet she invokes a metaphor of the stage to communicate her feelings. The actress who plays a role may be profoundly convincing in that role, but she is nevertheless not the thing itself. She is substitute and surrogate, a woman representing reality rather than being reality. In play or movie, such distance is acceptable because it is necessary; in writing, it is either nothing or less than nothing because it is neutral at best and diminishing at worst. Accepted by the reader, even accepted as convention, it always lessens the impact of the statement by not less than the difference between the personal and the conventional. Invoked by the writer, it resounds in the empty space between author and text.

The student writing to his Economics professor is provoked by financial chaos in the United States, by requirements of his course, and by demands of preparation for Law School (not necessarily in that order) to write this sentence which begins a lengthy paper. Although he is moved by all three of those provocations to the acts of conceiving and writing his paper, he is not enticed by any of them into a new (risk-taking) relationship to his subject.

Because I did not know the woman who had "been in the role of client and therapist," I could not ask her either why she had chosen that particular metaphor or if she understood its distancing effect. But I did know the senior student, who was also a member of my professional writing seminar at the same time that he was writing the paper for his Economics course, and I was able to ask him why he wrote what he did:

"Can you tell me what you meant by this first sentence?" I asked him. "Paraphrase it. Put it into other words." If I could only add a minute to my life for every time I've said that.

Having responded to other, similar requests from me, he handled this one easily. I wrote the words as he said them; the transcription omits all brief pauses and non-verbal sounds:

"Well ... yeah. ... America's worst economic problems won't be solved until the government ... until the government comes up with some tough new policies."

"Why didn't you write that?" I ask.

He doesn't take the question seriously, and he tells me why: What he had *said* to me might be all right for *saying* or even perhaps for writing in a *writing* class, but in an Economics class ... ? The words were too simple, too much like what you'd say rather than what you'd write.

"Why all this business of 'woes' and 'plague' and 'vanquished' and 'curbed' and 'currents' and 'emerge' and 'assuage'?" I ask.

"That's just the kind of stuff you use to write about Economics and ... and things like that," he replies. The lameness of it causes him to look away from me, and that part of our conversation comes to an end.

Both the woman who cast herself in the roles of client and therapist, and the young man who used the right kind of stuff to write about Economics and things like that—she by implication and he almost explicitly—are invoking the protection of distance to avoid the potential pain of unambiguous responsibility. In the case of the Economics student, the invocation is almost defensible (by him) because it is nearly conscious; but for the client and therapist, it is likely to be foolish in her own eyes were she to perceive the distance her metaphor achieves where she wants none at all.

The language of Examples A and B is practice and preparation for Example C. The brief and, at first, apparently direct statement of A is closely related in conception, if not in style, to the lengthy indirection of B. The most important difference between them is to be measured in degree rather than in kind. The distance inadvertently achieved by the writer of A with her single figure is more knowingly sought by the author of B in his metaphors of disease, battle, horsemanship, and hydrology, but only the species of the two texts is different. Both belong to the genus of writing significantly disabled by distance.

If A and B are of a kind, what then is C? Although its faults are as many as the grains of sand on the shores of the sea, and as nearly beyond human powers to enumerate, from one point of view it is describable as an extension of B—even as the same may be said of the relationship between B and A. The use of "I present" to open the initial sentence offers anything but the "I" of the personal statement, the "I" of "I think" that refers to the intellectual life of a real person. This "I" is of a piece with the "you," five words further into the sentence, that pretends to embody a real audience. Both are mechanical attempts to give human shape to language so dehumanized that the writer does not hear or see "pre/sent" as the second word and "pres/ent" as the tenth because no writer exists. No writer can be imputed to the text (in this, Example C is an extension of B) because no human agent can be perceived by the reader at the distance that the language creates. Where no responsible agent can be said to exist—the ultimate purpose of the prose that B is becoming and C has become—no individual responsibility can be assigned. If this is not an accomplished fact, it is at least the fervent hope and endeavor of such writers as the Economics student and the university administrator.

If the first and most frequent explanation of distance lies in the bad advice writers give themselves—abjure responsibility and thereby avoid pain—the second explanation lies in the bad advice that they are too often given by others, most notably linguists and teachers of writing. That advice is embedded in what seems to me to be the most serious common misunderstanding of the writing process:

The student who gave me the paper in Economics with the remarkable range of metaphor in the first sentence is now in my office to discuss his paper. After establishment of territoriality and order (he chooses to sit in the farther of two visitors' chairs but leans forward in a declaration of readiness; I stay behind my desk, lean back in my chair and try to appear more confident of helping him than I am), the following events take place.

I begin by asking him a question: "Do you think that you're familiar with the sound of your own voice?"

"Well, sure. I know what I sound like."

"And do you think that you know what I sound like? I mean, suppose somebody told you that I had said something and they had taken it down and this was it. Would you believe them?"

I show him two typewritten paragraphs from a piece of my own writing. He reads them slowly, a slightly puzzled frown narrowing his eyes. He looks up at me from beneath heavy eyebrows drawn together and makes a remarkable reply:

"Yes, and no. It sounds like you all right, but it's better than you talk. I mean, it's better than anybody talks, I think. What it really sounds like is you, the way you talk, but put through some kind of finishing machine so that all the pieces fit together better than when you said them."

Of course he is right with both answers. I know what most writers know about their own successful writing: that it is composed of their auditory vision of their available voice captured on the page, then revisited by their sense of their best voice contemplated in tranquility—a voice unhurried by immediacy and free of inadvertence. In that way I, as a writer, pass from captured vision to contemplative revision, from my voice in my ear to my voice on the page.

"Let me read the two paragraphs to you," I say to him, "and then tell me if you still think that they sound like me, only better." I speak the two paragraphs in a conversational voice, intending to enhance the illusion of conversation by scarcely glancing at the familiar words on the page. But now he does not look at me as I speak; instead, he looks at the rainwater flowing down the glass of my window. When I am finished, we sit briefly in silence.

"More yes," he says, still looking out the window, "but still some no. It's you all right, but it's not exactly you talking although it sounds more like you when you speak it. It's . . . it's just too good for talking."

Now we are ready, he and I, to go on to the more important part (for me) of our conversation. I remind him of where we began—with his claim that he knows what he sounds like—and of where we have come (to his assertion that my writing sounds like me speaking, only better); then I give him back only the first sentence from the paper he had given me two days earlier, and I ask him to read it aloud:

"The persistent economic woes that now plague the United States will not be vanquished, or even substantially curbed. . . . " he reads it first to himself. I can see the small movements of his lips as he practices his own words. He looks up at me, then launches himself into the sentence. The launching is not a success.

"Doesn't sound like me, does it?"

"Not much. Any ideas about why it doesn't?"

He has a few. We talk about the several voices he speaks with and the several other voices he writes with. He mentions the rare letter he writes, the somewhat rarer successful paper, and the differences between them. One big difference, he observes wryly, is that no one complains about his letters. But even he complains about his papers:

"It's like I was somebody else when I write a paper. Even when I'm pretty sure about what I want to say, most of the time I don't feel as though I've found the right words to say it with."

"Are you saying that you often feel as though you're writing with somebody else's words? That the ones you've found don't belong to you?"

"Well, maybe. Something like that, I guess. What I really feel, it's somebody else writing and *he's* writing somebody else's words."

As best I could, I recorded the foregoing conversation as it recurred in my memory in the minutes immediately following the actual exchange. The young man was taking a professional writing seminar with me because he was only too well aware of the chasm between his good training and better mind on the one side and his poor writing on the other. He had prevailed upon me for a place in the class—in spite of the fact that it was advertised as a seminar for competent writers who wanted to improve their writing, with admission by portfolio and interview—because he was so obviously quick-minded, serious, and distressed about the quality of his writing. As he had every right to be, for the sentence quoted from his paper was a fair example of his writing and he was committed to preparing for a career in legal scholarship.

At a late evening meeting in Santa Barbara, California, in 1967, Carl Rogers, psychologist and author, challenged a group of consultants to the U.S. Office of Education to explain to him why one of the persons among them, generally unknown to the rest who were generally well-known to each other, had seemed to guide and sometimes to dominate the day-long discussion of an exceptionally divisive question. He answered his own query by observing that the person was, for him at least, so apparently in visual command of his own voice that his words had an unusually close and illuminating connection to their meaning. It was, Rogers said, as though the person saw what he said before he said it, adjusted his words to the needs of meaning and audience, then released them only when he was satisfied with their condition. Had we noticed, he asked, that the person spoke in sentences?

These two events seem to me to be closely connected with each other although separated by almost fourteen years in time. Each illustrates a different aspect of the same problem, the single most significant problem of literacy in our time: Call it the unfamiliar personal voice; call it the blunted tool of written language; call it the decline of eloquence; call it the discomfort of students and teachers alike (not to mention virtually all other occasional writers who are neither students nor teachers) in anticipation of the act of writing and in contemplation of the language it produces.

By any name, it is as much the able student embarrassed by reading his own sentence aloud as it is the less able student embarrassed by his inability to write anything acceptable even to himself. By whatever name, it is a control of language so rare that a great psychologist should draw special attention to its presence. It is a control so rare that colleges and universities in North America are full of students who—in the very great majority—have no problems of interference from a dialect or another language, have been in school every year of their lives since they were five years old, and do not know that they possess a reliable means and measurement of effective expression. That instrument is the voice in which they *think* they speak, the voice they know as their own although it is a voice heard by no one but themselves.

I believe that each writer possesses *three* voices, the third being a metaphor for the mute eloquence of written language chosen and adjusted to reflect experience of words primarily seen but sometimes heard, then arranged according to the writer's selective rhetoric. This voice is the only one shaped by the requirements of permanence, for the other two are the voices of audible discourse and both are ephemeral although the second may be recreated at will.

The first voice is our instrument of speech—capable of enormous variety, subject to every influence of unpredictable demand. Left ephemeral, it is likely of success at all appropriate tasks; given the permanence of script, it suffers from inadvertence and indirection when not altered by translation.

If the first voice speaks for us, the second speaks to us: It is the bridge between language spoken and language written, the voice that *enables* the writer when the writer is experienced and comfortable enough to heed it. Unlike the first voice, it cannot be heard by anyone except the speaker, although it is no less real than the first voice which it both precedes and improves upon. This is the voice that speakers know as their own.

This is also the voice often unrecognized by those who emphasize the differences between spoken and written discourse—those differences being indisputably many and significant—when in fact the likeness is very great between the language we hear ourselves speaking (not the language we actually speak) and the language we write. This likeness, I believe, is the key to competent writing: The person familiar with the voice in her ear is the person prepared to take her own best counsel as writer.

I have said that this second voice both precedes and improves upon the voice used for speaking. The paradox is only apparent, for it is this voice-in-place (accumulated by practice, shaped by intention) that refuses admission to infelicity even as it reshapes the spoken voice for its owner's ear. It is to this voice-in-place and not to the spoken voice that the writer refers when he claims that what he has written "doesn't sound like me." It is to this voice-in-place that teachers of writing must send their students and editors refer their clients, including themselves, if students and clients alike are to possess a standard for competent writing more available and more reliable than the transitory judgments of others.

In long experience of teaching reading and writing by any name—whether seventh-grade English or graduate Shakespeare—I have never had a student who didn't recognize the discrepancy, where such a discrepancy existed, between the quality of her spoken and written voices. That my Economics student should have been acute enough to identify the difference between my spoken and written voices is testimony to the strength of his intellect; that he should have written the sentence he read aloud—he who by his own testimony was in school for his seventeenth consecutive year, spoke only standard-middleclass English, and had always been a good student—is testimony to the devastating effects of abusing the fact that we do not speak and write with the same voice.

In reference to the phenomenon of distance, common misunderstanding of the relationship between spoken and written voices—misunderstanding based upon failure to recognize the mediating role of the voice-in-place—has led writers to every authority but themselves. Since those authorities are always more distant than the writer from the writer's own accumulated and individual voice, writers obtain undesirable distance from their texts by just the quantity of language unreferred to the standard and judgment of their voice-in-place.

This is not in any way intended to diminish the important and unique work of the external editor—whether writing teacher, professional editor, or friend who is neither. Instead, recognition and use of the voice-in-place enhances that work because its invariable effect is to strengthen the sense of *personal* language that the writer relies upon to make appropriate linguistic and rhetorical choices. This is not the appropriateness of language to subject or audience, both of which are generally as accessible to external editors as they are to writers themselves; it is, rather, the fit of language to self that make impossible the disabling distance explicit in the vision of "somebody else writing [my papers] and *he's* writing somebody else's words."

No matter what the pathology of distance between author and text, the remedy is always the same and always efficient: Questioning of second and third semester freshmen at the University of Michigan who have had a one-semester Introductory Composition course leaves no doubt that those few students who *may* have thought, at the end of high school, that they wrote the language they spoke, have been powerfully re-educated. They have had a good course based on sound linguistic principles, and they know at least some of the very persuasive differences between colloquial and formal diction. Unfortunately, they have no idea that the voice they *think* they use for speaking is heard only by themselves and is not the voice by which they are known to their auditors.

Just as speakers afflicted with "ah" and "eh" and "you know" are not afflicted so much as afflicting, being themselves relatively free of pain because unable to hear themselves unless instructed in the hearing, so are all speakers retentive only of the intended shape and substance of their spoken words. Inadvertence, indirection, and non-verbal sound are filtered by the screen of purposive memory and disposed of as unfit for storage and recollection. Ask me not what I said, for I cannot tell you; ask me, instead, what I intended to say, and I will give you a privileged account of reality.

That remedy for distance which in my experience is always the same and always efficient, is to send clients to their voice-in-place as their primary source of language for writing. To direct writers to this source does not necessarily depend upon making the argument for the presence of a third voice mediate between the voices that are spoken and written. One is not dependent upon the other because the *argument,* as separate from the practice, is intended in part to free those of us who teach writing from thralldom to the linguistic truth of colloquial and formal differences. In the actual *practice* of writing, writers who turn first to themselves for judgment will always turn to their voice-in-place; their selective memory gives them no other choice.

And what then will happen to the conserving accuracy that is the most common rhetorical difference between spoken and written language? Will writing of the eighties become as surfeit with expansive and ephemeral personal voices as writing of the sixties was overwhelmed with confessional shouts and whispers? Will economy and constraint be the more difficult to obtain in proportion to the apparent freedom of self-reference? Not in my experience.

I believe that we have always referred our clients to their voice-in-place when we have asked them to "tell me what you meant to say; paraphrase it; put it into other words" and they have always responded from that mediate source. When my recalcitrant student was persuaded to make a new beginning by writing the words he had spoken—"until the government comes up with some tough new policies," we had no difficulty in agreeing that "comes up with" was more appropriate to speaking than to writing, and that "tough" wanted some thinking about. In his final version, he completed his sentence by advising the government to "develop(s) tough new policies based on economic facts rather than economic politics." With his own voice, processed through his own selective memory, he had built a bridge between experience and expression. We must, I believe, counsel all writers to do the same.

18 Basic Writing and Its Basis in Talk: The Influence of Speech on Writing

Jay L. Robinson
Department of English, The University of Michigan

Knowing how to use a language involves knowledge of many kinds, among them at least these three: knowledge of the meanings and functions of words and of word parts such as derivational and inflectional endings; knowledge of formal structures such as those for constructing words, phrases, and sentences and for connecting groups of sentences; and knowledge of strategies for using words and sentences to make language mean and to organize and communicate meaning in a way that is both purposive and effective. Let us call the first two kinds of knowledge *grammatical* knowledge, and the third kind, knowledge of *discourse*. Grammar is language in potential—a formal system that makes human interaction possible; Discourse is language in use—a product of human interaction.

A bald assertion: teachers of language use (following the lead of language scholars) have paid inordinate attention to grammar and have ignored discourse. A bold assertion: teachers of language use can improve instruction by focusing upon discourse—the strategies for making language mean and for making it communicate effectively.

Assuming that they are native speakers, students come to school with tacit knowledge of English grammar; and the older students are, the more likely they will be equipped with a comprehensive knowledge of that grammar. Even illiterates, if they know English, know the grammar of English save perhaps how to form learned plurals (*datum, data; phenomenon, phenomena*) or how to reach toward but not beyond the permitted range of syntactic options ("stealthily crept the intruder toward his sleeping victim, breathing hotly the while"). Such structures, of course, are learned from the pages of books, not from the lips of companions. Students also come to school with tacit knowledge of rules for English discourse: otherwise they could not talk meaningfully, purposively, and effectively, as of course they do. But the rules they are most likely to know are the rules for organizing and manipulating *talk,* not the rules for organizing and manipulating the written word. The younger the student, the more likely her reliance upon the rules for talking; the less exposure older students have had to reading and writing, the more likely their writing will be more like talk and less like writing.

In general, and putting aside for one moment the question of dialect difference, the same word- and sentence-level grammar underlies both spoken English and written English. Exceptions (like those suggested in the preceding paragraph) are those few forms that have existence primarily in print and those syntactic formations that are very bookish. The tacit grammatical knowledge students have

*Much of the material in this essay was worked out in collaboration with Bernard Van't Hul, who deserves jointly such credit as may accrue, but no blame. He and I developed these ideas with help from several groups of teachers, from high schools and colleges, in ECB workshops. The teachers who participated in those events will recognize Van't Hul's contributions as they will their own.

equips them as well to write as it does to talk, but in learning to write, students will have to learn *when* to use certain structures that they already know and how to edit sentences for compactness and grace. The *discourse* rules for talk and writing, however, differ significantly. In actual use, talk and writing do not resemble one another except in their basic grammar. The two modes are not organized in the same way, and what is meaningful and effective in talk is not necessarily so in writing.

For the inexperienced writer who is asked to produce a piece of written discourse, it is only natural to rely on the discourse rules he or she already knows. The result is likely to be something that resembles talk. Take this example, borrowed from Mina Shaughnessy's *Errors and Expectations* (pp. 19-20):

 1 First of all the system, don't really care about the students, schools are
 2 always overcrowded and the students get the, impression that really there
 3 are some teachers, just like students just to Be there, and the children
 4 performing below par is mainly the parents fault too, they really don't
 5 stress How important is, and that when they go to school they should try
 6 to do the Best they can instead they are encourage to learned Basketball,
 7 But in all the fault would lie on the state and government officials,
 8 Because really they don't care about children Education they're more con-
 9 cerned about what's your color or do your family have a good Income? and
10 really with all the pressure society put on the children they don't have
11 enough time to learned, But for the kids that are real Bright they can
12 make it through, But what about the kids that need a little extra Time so
13 with all this its too much, for them if a mother asked her child what did
14 you learned today, the average child would say nothing Because there is always
15 something going on Beside Educational, so when this kid is out of school he
16 or she has nothing, Because all those school years were just problems society
17 has push on the Kids, and when they hit the outside world they're not ready
18 not because they' are dumb, But society has effect them on the wrong side,
19 But who get the Blame? Always the children, if a kid could go to school and
20 learned, without meeting society, they would come out a Better product, and
21 could be ready to hit head on with society, over' all its all of our fault in
22 one way or another, but to put it plain society is more the blame, But then
23 again we the people make society up, but far as the children concerned not
24 that much, so I would suggest that society get on the good foot, because
25 whether they like or not we're the future

When read silently, as one would read any other student essay, this short theme is neither clear, coherent, nor effective. But when heard, from a reader who treats the theme as if it were a transcript of talk, the message makes sense, coheres, and conveys its point with force. Experiments with several groups of teachers who have listened to such readings have proved this to be true.*

*Van't Hul and I gave instructions like these: "Please listen as I read this English message. What I'll read was either spoken in the first place or written. Having listened to the reading, please guess which." We then followed the reading with questions about the effect of the message and the competence of the speaker/ writer. A majority of hearers always identifies the message as spoken.

A writing teacher's customary approach to such a theme is to treat it merely as a piece of writing and to evaluate it with expectations derived from reading written texts. Such a reading is likely to focus upon such faults as these: use of incomplete or ungrammatical sentences; failure to mark the boundaries of sentences with capitalization and punctuation; incorrect marking of such boundaries; "incorrect" verb forms; misuse of capitalization. The teacher who marks such faults is judging the theme against the grammatical and typographic norms of standardized written English. If she also judges the theme against discourse norms for "the standardized written English classroom essay," her paper-ending comments will likely include these: "The paper is badly organized"; "There are no paragraphs." In most cases, however, grammar and mechanics receive primary if not exclusive attention.

But suppose a teacher were to approach this theme not with expectations based on the norms of writing, but in the expectation that the theme reflects speech: that in writing it, this inexperienced writer has tried to make meaning using the grammar and discourse rules of his or her own talk. Directed by this latter expectation, a teacher's reading of the student's work will lead to strikingly different conclusions about the student's competence and needs. What follows is a step-by-step illustration of how a teacher might take such an approach:

Grammar: Sentences and Sentence Boundaries

Approach: (1) Ignore the punctuation provided in the original; (2) Read the theme aloud, trying to invest it with meaning; (3) Put a slash at the end of each sentence-like unit.; (4) Finally, read aloud each unit marked off by slashes.

When you are uncertain as to where a unit ends and another begins make a guess. (The slashes below are the author's guesses.)

```
 1   ¹ First of all the system, don't really care about the students,/² schools are
 2   always overcrowded and the students get the, impression that really there
 3   are some teachers, just like students just to Be there,/³ and the children
 4   performing below par is mainly the parents fault too,/⁴ they really don't
 5   stress How important is, and that when they go to school they should try
 6   to do the Best they can/⁵ instead they are encourage to learned Basketball,/
 7   ⁶ But in all the fault would lie on the state and government officials,
 8   Because really they don't care about children Education/⁷ they're more con-
 9   cerned about what's your color or do your family have a good Income?/⁸ and
10   really with all the pressure society put on the children they don't have
11   enough time to learned,/⁹ But for the kids that are real Bright they can
12   make it through,/¹⁰ But what about the kids that need a little extra Time so
13   with all this its too much,/¹¹ for them if a mother asked her child what did
14   you learned today, the average child would say nothing Because there is always
15   something going on Beside Educational,/¹² so when this kid is out of school he
16   or she has nothing, Because all those school years were just problems society
17   has push on the Kids,/¹³ and when they hit the outside world they're not ready
18   not because they' are dumb, But society has effect them on the wrong side,/
19   ¹⁴ But who get the Blame?/¹⁵ Always the children,/¹⁶ if a kid could go to school and
20   learned, without meeting society, they would come out a Better product, and
```

21 could be ready to hit head on with society,/[17] over' all its all of our fault in
22 one way or another, but to put it plain society is more the blame,/[18] But then
23 again we the people make society up, but far as the children concerned not
24 that much,/[19] so I would suggest that society get on the good foot, because
25 whether they like it or not we're the future/

Reading: When you read aloud each unit you have marked, you will find that
there *are* sentences in this theme. This is *not* the way the theme will read if you
pay attention only to the punctuation, if you read it expecting sentences to be
those units begun with a capital and ending with a period or some other terminal marker. Moreover, when you read aloud the sentences indicated by slashes,
you will find that most are complete and that most are grammatical, even though
many contain unexpected grammatical forms (*to learned,* for example, in Line
6). Sentences 2 and 4 omit words; sentence 12 can be read as a fragment and 15
is a fragment, though an effective one. But the remaining sentences have subjects,
predicates, and most other elements required by the rules of English grammar.

Judgment: This student knows how to *make* sentences, but not necessarily how
to recognize them once they are written down (in talk, sentences don't begin
with capital letters or end with periods). The student needs to learn how to
mark sentences with capitals and terminal punctuation, and (s)he needs to learn
the functional differences between commas and periods. But the student does
not need to learn how to make sentences; (s)he already knows how to do that.

Grammar: Verb Forms and Parts of Sentences

Approach: Underline all word forms and parts of sentences, phrases and clauses,
that seem ungrammatical. But jumping to no conclusions about these, ask yourself two questions: (1) Would these forms be normal in the speech of this student? (2) Are these forms the customary ones in nonstandard dialects of spoken
English? (To answer the second question, of course, you need to know something
about the grammars of the spoken dialects of English, as every writing teacher
should.)

1 [1] First of all the system, don't really care about the students,/[2] schools are
2 always overcrowded and the students get the, impression that really there
3 are some teachers, just like students just to Be there,/[3] and the children
4 performing below par is mainly the parents fault too,/[4] they really don't
5 stress How important is, and that when they go to school they should try
6 to do the Best they can/[5] instead they are encourage to learned Basketball,/
7 [6] But in all the fault would lie on the state and government officials,
8 Because really they don't care about children Education/[7] they're more con-
9 cerned about what's your color or do your family have a good Income?/[8] and
10 really with all the pressure society put on the children they don't have
11 enough time to learned,/[9] But for the kids that are real Bright they can
12 make it through,/[10] But what about the kids that need a little extra Time so
13 with all this its too much,/[11] for them if a mother asked her child what did
14 you learned today, the average child would say nothing Because there is always
15 something going on Beside Educational,/[12] so when this kid is out of school he

16 or she has nothing, Because all those school years were just problems society
17 has push on the Kids,/[13] and when they hit the outside world they're not ready
18 not because they' are dumb, But society has effect them on the wrong side,/
19 [14] But who get the Blame?/[15] Always the children,/[16] if a kid could go to school and
20 learned, without meeting society, they would come out a Better product, and
21 could be ready to hit head on with society,/[17] over' all its all of our fault in
22 one way or another, but to put it plain society is more the blame,/[18] But then
23 again we the people make society up, but far as the children concerned not
24 that much,/[19] so I would suggest that society get on the good foot, because
25 whether they like it or not we're the future/

Reading: Many of the forms in this theme do not conform to the usages of
standardized written English. Some are simply mistakes in *mechanics* that do not
reflect an influence from speech; others are *importations of colloquial forms,*
several of which reflect the fact that this particular writer speaks a dialect of
English that is non-standard. All inexperienced writers import colloquialisms
into their written texts; but most teachers, unfortunately, are far more impatient
with non-standard colloquialisms than with those found in dialects considered
standard. Yet both kinds of importation reflect the same process: An inexperienced writer is using the language (s)he knows best—the language of talk.

Mechanical mistakes

Line   4:   no apostrophe in *parents*
Line 13:
  and   no apostrophe in *its:* a common "spelling" mistake
Line 21:
Line 18:   use of apostrophe after *they* before full spelling *are.* (Apostrophes
          don't occur in speech.)

Colloquialisms

Line 11:   *real* as adverbial intensifier
          (Perhaps the alternation *child, children; kid, kids* throughout the
          essay; perhaps the phrase *get on the good foot* in Line 24, although
          semi-formal contemporary prose style is more accepting of such
          colloquialisms than at earlier times and in more formal contexts.)

Non-standard colloquialisms

Verb forms

1. No -*s* (-*es*) on the third person singular present tense of verbs. This reflects a
   feature of pronunciation in certain non-standard dialects.
       Line   1:   *don't* rather than *doesn't*
       Line 10:   *put* rather than *puts.*
       Line   9:   *do* rather than *does.*
       Line 19:   *get* rather than *gets.*

2. No -*d* (-*ed*) on certain past tense forms. This reflects a similar feature of
   pronunciation.

Line 6: *encourage* rather than *encouraged*
Line 17: *push* rather than *pushed.*
Line 18: *effect* rather than *effected* (or *affected,* if one wants to call this
also a failure to discriminate between two words pronounced
alike in most dialects).

3. The use of *-d* (*-ed*) where it does not belong. This is a feature of hypercorrection. Since the writer knows that *-ed* goes on some verbs and not others, and cannot trust his or her pronunciation as a guide, (s)he throws in a couple.

Line 6:
Line 11:
Line 14: } *learned* rather than *learn.*
Line 20:

4. Unmarked possessive. Also probably a feature of pronunciation rather than grammar, although the point is disputed.

Line 8: *children* for *children's*
Line 15: *beside* for *besides* is a related feature. (The *z* sound is not pronounced.)

5. Verb inversion in indirect questions: a syntactic feature of certain nonstandard dialects.

Line 9: *what's your color* rather than *what your color is.*
Line 9: *do your family have a good income* rather than *whether your family has a good income.*

Judgment: The writer is making errors, but the errors are not simple ones. Very few are random or careless errors (as is the missing *it* in Line 5, for example), and hence are not easily corrected simply by calling attention to them. Most errors show that the writer either does not know certain features of standardized written English, or else is so uncertain in her control of them as to revert to spoken alternatives; others are hypercorrections in which the writer aims at the correct written forms, but errs in doing so. The spelling *to learned* (Lines 6, 11, 14, 20) is a typical hypercorrection: the ending is added where it never occurs in standardized written English; the student knows that *-ed* is added to verbs, but puts it on the wrong verb form. To help a writer who makes mistakes like the ones in this theme, the teacher must first find causes for the errors that occur and only then try to help the student find appropriate remedies. Forms that are perfectly grammatical in nonstandard speech can be errors when used in writing; but the student is confused when a teacher merely calls all such forms grammatical errors without explaining that two grammatical systems are in conflict. To learn how to write, students need explanations that explain.

*   *   *

So far I have dealt only with the grammar and mechanics of the theme, not with discourse: What I have tried to suggest is that teachers will better understand the sentence- and word-level problems of inexperienced writers if they look for the origin of aberrant forms in the grammar of speech; and that once having found the origins of errors, teachers can more effectively correct them. This is an approach called "error analysis," and it has been the dominant approach in studies and textbooks that have dealt with dialect interference in writing. Error analysis is useful for teachers whose students are young or ill-prepared, and it is a clear advance over the traditional approach of "error marking," in which aberrant forms are merely circled and sometimes labelled, often inaccurately. But when restricted only to the domain of grammar, error analysis is a limited approach. Even if one were to correct every deviant grammatical and mechanical feature of the theme we have been analyzing, the result would still be more like speaking than like writing. Contrasts in *discourse* rules have to be noted if one is to perceive the crucial differences between talk and writing. Writers have to learn, and learn how to apply, the discourse rules of writing if they are to compose coherent and effective written texts.

Describing the rules of discourse is not easy. Discourse analysis is much less well developed than grammatical analysis as a sub-field in linguistics. And the variables one must deal with in trying to state discourse rules are both many and complex: Discourse is variable and highly sensitive to context—to persona, audience, topic, and genre. We know much less than we would like to know about talk and about writing. But we do know that talk, like writing, is highly organized, and that our students' own sense of the requirements of spoken discourse can enable them to intuit and then apply the rules of written discourse when encouraged to do so. Canny teachers can begin with talk and help students discover how it is shaped and organized; they can then move to writing and point out similarities and contrasts. We need not wait for a "Compendious Discourse Analysis of Written English," which will never be written anyway, and we can make effective use of such information as we have.

Consider the problems a talker must and does solve in order to make a meaningful contribution to an ongoing conversation. The talker must: (1) get the floor from those engaged in the conversation; (2) say something relevant to the topic under discussion (or else try to change the topic—always a hazardous ploy); (3) say something significant to the listeners (all talkers fear the "So what!" response); (4) hold the floor long enough to finish the message (conversation is competitive, and the task is not easy); (5) signal to the other participants that the message has come to an end. There are these other problems as well: Because conversation moves rapidly there is little or no time for planning how to organize the message that will be sent; because human memory is limited and talk transient (spoken words are gone even as they are heard) the information a talker sends must be immediately retrievable. A listener cannot flip back and scan earlier parts of a conversation. But in compensation for this last problem with talk, both listener and speaker are present and clarification can be requested and provided.

With these problems in mind, let's take another look at the theme.

Getting the Floor and Saying Something Relevant

A writer need not worry about getting the floor (though she has to worry about whether or not there will be readers); and because a writer sets her own topic (except in response to exam questions or writing assignments like them), saying something relevant is either not a problem or else is a problem of a different kind: For example, how to say something significant in a universe of discourse delimited by what has been written on that topic; or how to follow through a series of implications in a deductive sequence. Note how the theme begins:

1 First of all the system, don't really care about the students, schools are
2 always overcrowded and the students get the, impression that really there
3 are some teachers, just like students just to Be there, and the children
4 performing below par is mainly the parents fault too, they really don't
5 stress How important is, and that when they go to school they should try
6 to do the Best they can instead they are encourage to learned Basketball,

There is no general statement of topic, no thesis sentence. Instead, the theme begins in a way that appears responsive, perhaps to an assignment from the teacher: "Write an essay discussing why children don't do well in school." But in fact, the theme begins in much the same way a conversational response to a spoken question might:

Q: "Why don't students do well in school?"
A: "First of all the system don't really care about the students."

One expects an enumeration, and can imagine fingers thrust forward and bent down as the points are counted off. (A discerning teacher in one of our workshops, having guessed that the theme was a transcript of speech, said: "It sounds like something a person would stand up and say at a school-board meeting in response to an earlier speaker.")

Holding the Floor

Since conversation is competitive (everybody wants to talk), silence must be avoided by a talker who wishes to hold the floor. When a break in the flow of sound occurs, it is usually taken as a signal that the floor is open to another speaker. Talkers have many ways to keep sound flowing long enough to think up something else that is pertinent. One way is to use relatively meaningless phrases or words that serve only to keep the vocal cords vibrating, and another is to signal continuation by using conjunctions: Once an *and* or a *but* is spoken, a slight pause is possible because a speaker has signalled an intention to hold the floor. Consider the italicized sentence openers in the theme:

1 [1]*First of all* the system, don't really care about the students,/[2]schools are
2 always overcrowded and the students get the, impression that really there
3 are some teachers, just like students just to Be there,/[3]*and* the children
4 performing below par is mainly the parents fault too,/[4]they really don't

5 stress How important is, and that when they go to school they should try
6 to do the Best they can/[5] *instead* they are encourage to learned Basketball,/
7 [6] *But in all* the fault would lie on the state and government officials,
8 Because really they don't care about children Education/[7] they're more con-
9 cerned about what's your color or do your family have a good Income?/[8] *and*
10 *really* with all the pressure society put on the children they don't have
11 enough time to learned,/[9] *But* for the kids that are real Bright they can
12 make it through,/[10] *But* what about the kids that need a little extra Time so
13 with all this its too much,/[11] *for them* if a mother asked her child what did
14 you learned today, the average child would say nothing Because there is always
15 something going on Beside Educational,/[12] *so* when this kid is out of school he
16 or she has nothing, Because all those school years were just problems society
17 has push on the Kids,/[13] *and* when they hit the outside world they're not ready
18 not because they are dumb, But society has effect them on the wrong side,/
19 [14] *But* who get the Blame?/[15] Always the children,/[16] if a kid could go to school and
20 learned, without meeting society, they would come out a Better product, and
21 could be ready to hit head on with society,/[17] *over' all* its all of our fault in
22 one way or another, but to put it plain society is more the blame,/[18] *But then*
23 *again* we the people make society up, but far as the children concerned not
24 that much,/[19] *so* I would suggest that society get on the good foot, because
25 whether they like it or not we're the future/

Some of the connectives bear semantic or structural weight (*instead* in sentence 5, for example; *but* in sentence 10; *over' all* in sentence 17). Most, however, are importations from speech of those very necessary signals that say to other would-be-talkers, "You will wait, please, until I finish!"

Saying Something Significant, or How to Avoid "So What!"

The theme begins with topic focus upon an abstraction: *the system.* But focus quickly shifts to persons, as the following italicizings show (the italicizings are of sentence and clause subjects and of embedded subjects):

1 [1] First of all *the system,* don't really care about the students,/[2] *schools* are
2 always overcrowded and *the students* get the, impression that really there
3 are some *teachers,* just like *students* just to Be there,/[3] and *the children*
4 performing below par is mainly *the parents* fault too,/[4] *they* really don't
5 stress How important is, and that when *they* go to school *they* should try
6 to do the Best *they* can/[5] instead *they* are encourage to learned Basketball,/
7 [6] But in all *the fault* would lie on the state and government officials,
8 Because really *they* don't care about children Education/[7] *they're* more con-
9 cerned about what's *your color* or do *your family* have a good Income?/[8] and
10 really with all the pressure *society* put on the children *they* don't have
11 enough time to learned,/[9] But for *the kids* that are real Bright *they* can
12 make it through,/[10] But what about *the kids* that need a little extra Time so
13 with all this *its* too much,/[11] for them if a *mother* asked her child what did
14 *you* learned today, *the average child* would say nothing Because there is always
15 *something* going on Beside Educational,/[12] so when *this kid* is out of school *he*
16 *or she* has nothing, Because *all those school years* were just problems society

17 has push on the Kids,/[13] and when *they* hit the outside world *they*'re not ready
18 not because *they'* are dumb, But *society* has effect them on the wrong side,/
19 [14] But *who* get the Blame?/[15] Always *the children,*/[16] if *a kid* could go to school and
20 learned, without meeting society, *they* would come out a Better product, and
21 could be ready to hit head on with society,/[17] over' all *its* all of *our fault* in
22 one way or another, but to put it plain *society* is more the blame,/[18] But then
23 again *we the people* make society up, but far as *the children* concerned not
24 that much,/[19] so *I* would suggest *that society* get on the good foot, because
25 whether *they* like it or not *we're* the future/

The strongly personalized stance of the final sentence:

> So *I* would suggest that society get on the good foot, because whether *they* like
> it or not *we're* the future.

is thus anticipated in the focus upon persons in most of the preceding sentences.
Abstractions are okay in conversation, but only if their effects upon persons are
indicated, and especially upon persons like those who are talking together.
Otherwise, the conversation might well result in a "So what!"

Bringing the Message to an End

There are many ways to end a message in conversation (assuming that someone
else doesn't end it for you by interrupting). One is to generalize or sum up;
another is to bring reference back to present time (in narrative) or to the general
present. A useful device for bringing reference to general present in talk is use of
a proverb or aphorism. In this theme, there is a semi-conclusion in the form of a
summing up:

> *over'all* its *all of our fault* in one way or another

But that sentence evokes yet another comment:
> But then again we the people. . . .

So there is good use for an aphoristic statement:
> So I would suggest that society get on the good foot . . .

Organization

Writing can be planned: A writer has time for planning, and readers expect that
planning will be done. The customary expectation for the "standardized written
English schoolroom essay" is that it will be planned hierarchically, with alternating movements from the general to the specific and back again, in a scheme
something like this:

Generalization I
Specification I
Generalization A
Specification A
Generalization B
Specification B

Generalization C
Specification C
Regeneralization of I: A, B, C

Talking is rarely planned in advance, though a plan usually emerges as speakers cooperate in the task of making meaning. And talk is organized—as organized as writing is, though not in the same way.

The theme begins, as has been suggested, as a response—either to a real or to an imagined question:

Why don't children do well. . . .
First of all the system. . . .

And the pattern of implied question and response continues: sentence 6, for example, is a second response to the first implied question. And there are explicit rhetorical questions:

Sentence 10:   But what about the kids. . . .
Sentence 14:   But who get the blame?. . .

The use of the adversative *but* (sentences 6, 9, 10, 18) is further evidence of the dialectic structure of the theme. It is as if the writer imagines a conversing partner.

The theme is not planned as a series of movements from the general to the specific and back again. There is some analysis of generalizations for their component parts (for example, *"schools," "students," "teachers,"* comprise *"the system"*); but there is no consistent hierarchical arrangement. Rather, a topic is stated—usually as a response to an implied or rhetorically stated question—and thoughts about the topic are written down more or less as they come to mind: a pattern of message-making very familiar in talking, since the speaker must retrieve information instantaneously and has no time to order it in any other than a temporal sequence.

What finally holds the theme together—or at least can in an oral rendering—is the strongly projected stance of the author: the sense a hearer (or sympathetic reader) gets of a person worrying a question of personal concern and talking about it. The multitude of connectives that assert connection between ideas, even if they do not denote explicitly what the connections are, and the management of focus, even though the focus is subject to rapid shift, also contribute to overall coherence. These, too, are strategies, however, more customary and more effective in spoken discourse than in writing.

The theme is *not,* of course, a transcript of a monologue uttered in a conversational context. It was written down, and it is written text, and it consequently has features characteristic of writing as well as many characteristic of speech. Inexperienced writers produce what might be called transitional texts as they progressively learn the discourse and grammar rules of written English genres. By recognizing the oral features of texts, teachers can help smooth the transition.

*   *   *

In workshops with teachers concerned with the problems of basic writers, we at the English Composition Board have had an opportunity to analyze transitional texts like "First of all the system . . . " and to work toward two results: a list of the kinds of importation from speech one can find in texts produced by basic writers; and an outline of a pedagogy for dealing with the various kinds of importation. Here is a list developed by participants in our most recent workshop:

Influences from speech may be found in all of the following:

1. Strategies for finding and shaping meaning
    a. Predominance of dialectic organization:
    question and answer; assertion and counterassertion.
    b. Predominance of inductive movement: from example to generalization.
    c. Predominance of personal narrative; of narrative illustration used as evidence.

2. Rhetorical strategies (speaker-audience-topic relations):
    a. Predominance of highly personalized point of view.
    b. Tendency to rely on an extralinguistic context and to ignore the needs of an absent audience of readers:
    (1) Failure to contextualize the topic;
    (2) Failure to state crucial presuppositions;
    (3) Tendency to assume background knowledge necessary to meaning.

3. Organizational strategies
    a. Predominance of topic-comment arrangement.
    b. Predominance of linear sequencing, especially temporal sequencing.
    c. As a hypercorrection, mechanical imposition of an organizational pattern (Introduction: Three points: Conclusion) that does not fit the content or the needs of the audience.
    d. Heavy use of connectives, especially coordinating conjunctions.
    e. Non-denotative use of connectives (*so,* used merely as a connective with no resultive sense).

4. Manipulation of code (differences in medium):
    a. Loosely constructed sentences, with weakly denotative adverbial openings, and with relatively empty fillers.
    b. Use of colloquialisms and of non-standard colloquialisms; hypercorrection of forms.
    c. Overuse of slang or of colloquial jargon.
    d. Restricted range of word choice; repetition, use of clichés.

5. Management of the special conventions of writing (script or typographical features):
    a. Non-conventional or uncertain punctuation.
    b. Spellings based on pronunciation; hypercorrections showing uncertain knowledge.

A glance at the list will show the limits of error analysis when analysis is restricted to the domains of grammar and mechanics and does not extend to discourse features.

The pedagogy we have been developing places heavy emphasis on revision. Basic writers should be encouraged to create first drafts rapidly, worrying most about the problem of putting meaning into words and worrying little if at all about the demands of form. Once a text exists, it can be read and rewritten until it more closely resembles the norms of standardized written English of a particular genre. In a classroom discussion of examples, teachers can draw from students and then make explicit the crucial differences between speech norms and writing norms; and student writers can then revise their texts. The expectation is that student writers will internalize the appropriate norms and gradually modify their first drafts as well as later ones.

There are limits and dangers in this approach. We do not know much about the more important discourse rules of speech or of writing in their various genres: those that guide the translation of intention and conception into language. Knowing little, we may state rules narrowly and apply them over-rigorously, forgetting that both talk and writing in themselves are rich in diversity. Students must be engaged in trying to state the differences and thus be helping to formulate rules. If they are so engaged in a genuine act of discovery, we teachers acknowledge the vastness of our ignorance and thus avoid dogmatic prescription. In any work exploring differences between talk and writing, these must be the cardinal lessons: talk is every bit as good as writing; talk and writing differ only because they function differently in their human uses; sometimes writing that looks like talk is better than writing that looks too much like writing. It all depends, finally, on what a human being wants to do with her mouth or her pen.

These are the two more explicit messages this essay tries to convey: (1) Inexperienced writers, when asked to compose, use strategies and language forms that come readily to mind, especially when under pressure. The discourse strategies and linguistic forms used by inexperienced writers are likely to be those of speech. (2) A text does not exist until someone reads it. A reader creates a text on the foundation of certain preconceptions and expectations. Teachers should learn to expect in the writing of inexperienced writers strategies and forms derived from speech. In teaching writing, it all depends, finally, on what a teacher perceives in a student's work as a reflection of competence and need. There are talkers in all classrooms, and most of them can also learn how to write.

19   Litigation and Literacy: The Black English Case

Richard W. Bailey
Department of English, University of Michigan

Though it began with far different objectives, the litigation generally known as the "Black English" case ended in July 1979 with a decision that had as its central issue the distinction between spoken and written English. At first, the plaintiff children and their supporters wanted to draw attention to the disparity between school achievement and social class. As has long been recognized, children who are poor and black are less likely to do well in school than children who are not poor and not black. The "Black English" case began in 1977 with the plaintiffs' hope that the courts would address that issue.

Since it was opened in 1969, the Martin Luther King Junior Elementary School in Ann Arbor has been a model of what many parents and children hope their schools will be. Housed in a handsome, modern building in a suburban setting, the school is a racial mirror of the Ann Arbor community. In 1977, 13% of its 500 students were black, 7% Asian and Latino, and 80% white. Some children live in University of Michigan student housing, and many of them speak a language other than English at home. Children of students at the University of Michigan live in an environment where school and school values are highly prized: their parents have profited from education, whether in the United States or abroad, and most are working toward postgraduate degrees at the University. Children from the student housing area generally do well at King School and add interesting diversity to its population.

The majority of students at King come from affluent homes. Most of the housing in the immediate neighborhood of the school was constructed after 1970, when single-family houses began to be constructed on a lavish scale. One school administrator described his feelings during a visit to King School on a parents' night: the casual, after-work clothing of the parents, he said, was more elegant than his professional garb, and he liked to arrive early so he would not suffer the comparison between his well-used automobile and the "second cars" of the King parents. A central figure in the Black English case, this administrator had grown up in a large family in a poor urban neighborhood; but he did not recognize poverty because all his school friends came from similar circumstances. Even with a doctoral degree and a salary of $30,000, he felt acutely the difference between his income and that of most King parents.

As a consequence of affluence, many King School children have taken vacations throughout the United States and Europe. Their homes are well-supplied with books and magazines; most of them have visited museums, attended theatrical productions and athletic events; they feel at home throughout the Ann Arbor community; and are eager to learn in school, where they find parent volunteers to help them with extra tutoring, should they have difficulty, and a rich variety of extracurricular scouting and club activities.

One group of children is a dramatic exception to the general pattern of affluence among students of King school: children from the "scattered site" public housing development located within the King boundaries. All of the children from this project are black; most of them come from single-parent families; nearly none of them has had either "enriching" travel or the resources in the home that are routinely available to their schoolmates. Since the housing project is isolated from surrounding residential neighborhoods by a four-lane highway with no nearby traffic light, small children from the project are unlikely to have spent much time visiting and being visited by children they meet in school and are less likely to participate in scouts or clubs. They do play regularly, of course, with their neighbors in the project, those with whom they share common experiences and a common language, Black English.

Parents from the housing project have typically not completed secondary school, and at least some of them regard the schools with a mixture of fear and animosity. But a few of the parents place a very high value on education and see it as a means by which their children may escape from the cycle of poverty. Most of them, like the school administrator, are daunted by the affluence that prevails at parent-teacher meetings, and they are sometimes reluctant to press teachers for explanations of decisions made about their children's educational progress. Since designating children for special treatment opens opportunities and resources for extra help, the school moved to "label" many of the project children in the hope that extra assistance would improve their performance. Of the fifteen plaintiff children in 1977, three were categorized as "learning disabled" and two were identified as "emotionally impaired." Still others were being given speech therapy or experienced extra help from community volunteer tutors. Because their children were not doing well in school, despite the special attention given to them, four parents from the project accepted the help of the Student Advocacy Center and Michigan Legal Services Corporation in bringing the "Black English" suit in 1977. The schools, they felt, *could* help their children; the litigation would compel them to do so.

In 1978, after a series of legal maneuvers, the federal district court denied those arguments brought by the plaintiffs that would oblige the schools to eliminate "cultural and economic barriers." Nothing in the cited statutes, wrote Judge Charles W. Joiner, required schools to address the disparity between the affluent majority and the impoverished minority in the King School population. With that intermediate decision, the issue of "Black English" emerged as the principal issue to be litigated.

In 1972, as part of a series of amendments designed to eliminate busing for racial balance, President Nixon had sent to the Congress a series of prohibitions concerning the denial of equal education opportunity, among them "the failure by an educational agency to take appropriate action to overcome language barriers that impede equal participation by its students in its instructional programs." Eventually enacted into law in 1974, this provision was not immediately cited in suits brought on behalf of children whose "language barriers" impeded their educational progress. Most court decisions concerned with bicultural and bilingual education followed a different tradition, usually the "Lau Guidelines" that were issued by the federal government as a consequence of the Supreme Court's ruling that special help must be provided for children entering school with "no knowledge of English." The legislative history of the statute invoked in the Black English case did not specify precisely what "language barriers" were to be "overcome," and the Ann Arbor case was one of the first to provide a judicial interpretation of the language of that law.

In deciding in favor of the plaintiff children, Judge Joiner recognized that they suffered from the effects of "language barriers." As testimony by experts and the children themselves made clear, the children from the project used Black English in the home and in speaking to friends. It was the spoken language in which they were "most comfortable." In school, the children had variously mastered the skills of "code switching" that enabled them to speak in a more formal style of Black English generally intelligible to their teachers, a variety of English sharing some features with nonstandard varieties held in low esteem by most educators. While placement tests were not a major subject or argument in the case, specialists at King School had made use of tests that increased the likelihood that the children from the project would be given speech therapy or labeled "learning disabled" or one of the other categories that would lead to their being given "special treatment."

In working with small children, teachers are confronted by the differences between spoken and written English in a way that is different from the issues presented to teachers of older children and adults. When tested for reading readiness and "special needs," young children can be reached only through their ability to articulate in speech their responses to oral and visual stimuli. Teachers who are unfamiliar with Black English or other varieties of English that differ systematically from their own speech must be particularly sensitive to the difference between "errors" or "miscues" and the systematic features of language that differentiate dialects. This distinction is even more crucial for reading teachers who assist children in discovering the "alphabetic principle" of our written language. The "language barrier" identified in the Black English case consisted, then, of two parts: the use of Black English by the children and the uncertainty of teachers in interpreting the English they heard from these children in their classrooms. As Judge Joiner recognized, "the problem in this case revolves around the ability of the school system, King School in particular, to teach the reading of standard English to children who, it is alleged, speak 'Black English' as a matter of course at home and in their home community."

As Lee Hansen explains in the following essay, the remedy designed by the Ann Arbor schools in response to the Judge's opinion involved in-service training for teachers to make them aware of the feature of Black English and the interactional styles that promote good learning. As one of the children said in interviewing her younger brother, the issue ultimately resolves itself to the answers to these questions: "Do you be respectin' your teachers?" "Do your teachers be respectin' you?"

The main source of argument and ruling in the Black English trial involved the interpretation of the statutory phrase, "language barriers that impede education opportunity." Less noticed, however, is the fact that the defendants in the case were not school personnel but the Ann Arbor Board of Education. The decision rested on the Board's responsibility as an "educational agency" to provide teachers with current "knowledge" that bears on the ability of educators to open educational opportunities to all. As a precedent, the case has implications for Boards and administrators: they must make good faith efforts to keep teachers abreast of ideas and innovations that will make education more effective.

In his decision, Judge Joiner noted that the remedies to the problems raised in the case "involve pedagogical judgments that are for educators and not for the courts." Presumably, any reasonable course of action proposed by the Ann Arbor School Board in response to the decision would have been accepted by the court. A more recent case involving "language barriers"—*U.S.* v. *State of Texas* (506 F. Supp. 405 [1981])—mandates a more stringent standard: the "appropriate action" must be effective. As the court said in the case, "good intentions are not enough. The measure of a remedy is its effectiveness, not its purpose." The Black English case, then, is part of an emerging interpretation of a statute that will profoundly affect teacher training and in-service programs, our understanding of the nature of "language barriers," and the means by which we provide equal educational opportunity for all children.

As a district court decision, the *King* case has the effect of law only in the eastern judicial district of Michigan, and the Ann Arbor Board of Education satisfied Judge Joiner's required remedy by supplying teachers at King school with a year's program of intensive in-service workshops. For most of these teachers, the program was of considerable value, though, as Lee Hansen reports, "some were prevented from learning by their own linguistic and cultural attitudes."

In the wider sphere of litigation, the *King* case has been cited in a few related cases, but many schools have instituted or revived teacher training programs that deal with the cultural and linguistic differences that impinge on the teaching of reading and writing. In the Kalamazoo, Michigan, public schools—a district operating under a court-ordered desegregation plan—administrators voluntarily designed sessions to "sensitize" teachers to racial differences and their impact on scholastic achievement (see 640 F. 2d. 812 [1980]). Thus have enlightened school administrators responded to the *King* case through voluntary compliance.

Perhaps the most important consequence of the litigation that resulted in the Judge's decision has been the renewed attention paid to linguistic and cultural diversity and its importance for school programs. Every annual meeting of the National Council of Teachers of English since the decision has featured at least one session devoted to *King,* and professional groups of reading and composition teachers have explored the origins of the case and its implications for classroom practices. Renewed attention to the challenge of linguistic variety in American society through such meetings has thus been beneficial in raising the sometimes controversial issues litigated in *King* to a level of serious professional concern. (A substantial scholarly literature has also emerged; see the bibliography for citations of work by Labov, Sledd, Smitherman, Whiteman, and Zorn.)

20 The Black English Lawsuit in Retrospect: A Participant's Postscript

Lee H. Hansen
Ann Arbor Public Schools, Ann Arbor, Michigan

On July 12, 1979, after a long and often contentious litany of legal proceedings, Judge Charles Joiner ruled in the Federal District Court in Detroit on what was to become known as the "Ann Arbor Black English Case." The fact that all but one of the charges were dismissed was lost on most people. Instead, they turned their attention to the one indictment that Judge Joiner sustained: the charge of plaintiffs that the school system had permitted teachers to create a potential language barrier with plaintiff children, all of whom were black children of low income families from the Green Road Public Housing development and most of whom were purported to speak some variation of Black Vernacular English.

Since then, much has been written about the politics and legalities of the case. I do not propose to retrace that ground. Rather, I would like to share briefly what the Ann Arbor School System did to comply with the Judge's order, what has happened since, and what I have learned from the experience.

A Program of Compliance

As a result of that federal court order, the school district developed and implemented a program that had as its central focus the in-service education of the King Elementary School teachers. In his Memorandum Opinion and Order, Judge Joiner seemed to focus on two issues. First was the extent to which the King School teachers had knowledge and understanding of the linguistic and sociolinguistic features of the nonstandard English dialect Black Vernacular English (BVE). Extensive study of this dialect in the 1960s and early 1970s showed it to be a pervasive dialect among black people, but especially among urban lower socioeconomic black children, many of whom were labeled underachievers. Second, Judge Joiner pointed to the instructional barrier that could be created by classroom teachers who lacked an understanding and an appreciation of BVE. Consequently, the in-service program we developed and implemented sought to relate to both the linguistic and pedagogical issues raised by the court.

The in-service program itself took place during the 1979–80 school year and involved all classroom teachers, special teachers, and consultants who were assigned to King Elementary School. The first semester of that school year was devoted to 20 hours of workshop learning spread over five separate sessions. Instruction was provided by local school district staff in cooperation and consultation with Bill Hall and Roger Shuy, nationally recognized scholars in linguistics and dialectology. Upon completion of this formal workshop phase, it was the hope of the planning committee that in-service participants would:

1. be able to describe in general the concept of a dialect and dialect differences within the English language;
2. be sensitive to the value judgments about dialect differences which people often make and communicate to others;
3. be able to describe the basic linguistic features of Black Vernacular English as it contrasts with standard English;
4. have appreciation for the history and background of Black Vernacular English;
5. be able to identify without prompting the specific linguistic features by which they recognized a speaker of Black Vernacular English;
6. be able to discuss knowledgeably the important linguistic issues in code switching between Black Vernacular English and standard written English;
7. be able to identify possible instructional strategies that can be used to aid children in code switching between Black Vernacular English and standard English;
8. be able to distinguish between a dialect code switch and a decoding mistake when analyzing an oral reading sample;

Instructional activities were designed to help participants master each of the objectives above.

The focus of the second semester of 1979–80 was implementation of what had been presented during the first semester. With the help of a full-time language arts consultant, follow-up visits by Drs. Hall and Shuy, and the support of the building administrator and central administrative team, the teaching staff began to put into action what they had been taught during the first semester.

Again, it was the hope of the planning team that by the end of the second semester in-service participants would:

1. be able, using a variety of informal and formal techniques, to identify students in their class who speak Black Vernacular English;
2. be able to recognize specific code-switching problems encountered by individual Black Vernacular English speakers attempting to read standard English material;
3. be able, in the classroom setting, to distinguish between a dialect code switch and a decoding mistake as a student speaking Black Vernacular English is orally reading from standard English material;
4. use a variety of possible instructional strategies to help students speaking Black Vernacular English overcome code-switching barriers as they are learning to read standard English;

At the close of the school year a comprehensive evaluation was undertaken to assess the effectiveness of the program. That evaluation included an independent field assessment by Drs. Hall and Shuy, including classroom observations and 30-minute interviews with participating staff; an analysis of a questionnaire responded to by all King School staff; and case studies of the academic performance of each of the plaintiff children. As a result of this evaluation as well as our own "gut" feelings, many of us concluded that the in-service program had been quite useful in helping us to better understand and help the speaker of BVE who was an underachiever. We also concluded that the "court-ordered" attempts to assess student progress in light of the in-service program were premature and inconclusive. Finally, we confirmed what we had sensed all along: that, like any group of learners, there were individual differences among us participants with respect to the in-service program, its content, and its application. Some participants were already knowledgeable and enlightened. Others acknowledged a need to learn more. Some were prevented from learning by their own linguistic and cultural attitudes. Still others who had been stung deeply by the accusatory tone of the lawsuit and court trial viewed the whole in-service drama as punishment and were not equipped to learn effectively.

As a result of that evaluation, the central administrative team in the autumn of 1980 recommended that all professional staff, but especially those who teach the language arts, be encouraged to receive in-service training comparable to that received by the King School staff. To that end, the Director of Language Arts for the Ann Arbor Public Schools and his staff were directed to develop during the 1980–81 school year a set of instructional modules that can be used by each school to effectively study the issues and concepts raised in the King in-service program. Implementation will begin in October of 1981, as part of what we hope can be a larger in-service effort in our school district to improve educational opportunity and to implement the "effective school" research findings currently receiving national attention.

Some Reactions

The insights gleaned from the in-service program and, more generally, from the entire dramatic episode are many and diverse. However, among them are four observations that stand out in my mind from all the rest:

(1) In the final analysis there is no evidence that the agony of the under-achieving low-income black students is a univariate problem. The linguistic and sociolinguistic issues raised in the law suit can make an important contribution to our search for answers to the underachievement of students. However, they are not "lynch-pin" issues; attention to them alone will not suddenly dissolve the agony of black students' underachievement. Disproportionate attention to or commitment of resources to the issue of the language barrier to the exclusion of other equally important alterable variables would be tragic and undeserving of the public trust we all hold. We have a multi-variate problem for which we must seek multi-variate solutions; hunting for panaceas is no longer fashionable and never should have been. The rhetoric during and after the lawsuit has failed to recognize this critical reality.

(2) Contemporary scholarship suggests that the dominant issues surrounding school-based learning for a child who speaks BVE may be sociolinguistic rather than linguistic. There is little concrete evidence that anything inherent in the linguistic process of moving from BVE to standard English or back again is inhibiting to the process of learning to read. There is some evidence that unwitting but well-meaning educators, by their attitudes toward nonstandard language and by their ignorance of dialect variations such as BVE, may contribute to what is really a learning barrier, not a language barrier. If as teachers we unconsciously accept the prevailing societal view that nonstandard dialects are inferior and that they are symptomatic of other inferior features and characteristics in people, and, moreover, if we communicate that belief to our students who speak those dialects, then we may contribute to the underachievement of those students. If we associate Black Vernacular English with a reduced intellectual capacity, with laziness, with slowness, or with learning problems, and if we communicate those attitudes to black students in a variety of subtle ways. we have become part of the very problem we are conscientiously trying to resolve. All this is by way of suggesting that for *all* educators, a view of language and language development based on contemporary scholarship is important, even though it is not the only variable.

(3) Our in-service program set out to help all of us, teachers and administrators, examine and modify, as necessary, our attitudes toward language as a social phenomenon. In retrospect that was probably a mistake. Any kind of self-examination of attitudes and values is risky and threatening. To examine our attitudes toward language, and more particularly toward nonstandard dialects, under the accusatory pressures of a nationally highlighted lawsuit is totally unrealistic. Issues can be more profitably examined in the framework of teacher classroom behavior rather than attitude. If certain teacher classroom behaviors with respect to students' language patterns evoke certain responses from students that reduce learning, then we should spend our time apprising teachers of what those behaviors are and asking them to avoid those behaviors. We are not

asking teachers to change an attitude; we are asking them to examine and, if necessary, change a behavior. In a sense we are saying irrespective of what you believe about language and nonstandard dialect, it is in the best interest of *all* your students to avoid those teaching behaviors and foster these." We say that, knowing full well that as people modify their behavior, their attitudes cannot help but follow.

(4) Finally, as the controversies swirled around me, I could not help but be concerned by the prevailing attitudes toward language and dialect that emanated from the media, from other educators, and from the larger society. Some observers of the case to this day will insist that we were teaching teachers to speak BVE so that they could communicate better with BVE speakers and provide instruction in BVE. Even though we vehemently denied these assertions repeatedly, the misunderstanding persists. I was amazed to find some educated people who openly placed moral judgments and values on BVE as a dialect and others who openly felt that learning to communicate in standard English was not important. There were even a few from across the country who, in their written communications to us, strongly implied that anyone who "spoke that Black English" was inferior, ignorant, and illiterate. If these are widespread attitudes about language and its function in our society today (and I believe they are), then we who educate have failed our students and our society more generally. But where will the leadership to move our society toward an enlightened view of language and dialect come from if not from those of us who educate? Maybe we need a new beginning.

21 Speech and Writing Research in the Composition Class
Barbara Couture
Department of English, Wayne State University

Language is complex behavior. Equally complex must be the methods by which we research and teach that behavior. Certainly the previous essays in this chapter support this assertion. We teachers accept it without question, yet come Monday morning in the composition class, we systematically reduce our complex task to some prescription for language performance that can be taught within forty or fifty minutes. We send our students to an exercise in a sentence workbook ("Adding s and 's") or to a chapter in a composition text ("Structuring a Comparison"), and we make up packaged paper assignments ("Write about your first day at the university; include good and specific detail.") We want to adjust our teaching to acknowledge the multiple ways that language can work, yet we have too little time and too many students to teach. It is not surprising that when we apply research about language to the classroom, we often convert subtle conclusions drawn from linguistic observation to dogmatic maxims for language production— to something for students to do or not to do. This conversion process has been deceptively simple for teachers applying research on speech and writing to the composition class. And I fear many applications of this research have come to little good end.

Too frequently in my classroom observations of college composition teachers, I have heard things like this: "The problem with most of your writing is that you write like you speak. Because you don't read very much, you don't know how writing differs from speech." And in student-teacher conferences, I have heard things like this: "You know what your problem is? You don't say the 'ed' when you speak. That's why you never remember it when you write." Clearly, research on speaking and writing has finally touched the composition class, but not with invariably happy results.

Studies of differences in the form and function of speech and writing have been "raided" by eager teachers looking for ways to label error or to defend teaching methods. Many theoretical and empirical studies of the differences between speech and writing were not designed to explain how speech and writing are produced, how skills we employ naturally as speakers in different contexts translate to writing, or how language works as effective communication. Unlike the essays in this chapter, research on the differences between speech and writing does not explain how students can learn to express themselves in both modes more appropriately and effectively. Yet teachers adopt the conclusions of such research wholesale, making them "maxims" for the teaching of composition.

I find three "maxims" that have grown out of research on speech and writing to be potentially damaging when applied in the composition class. They are:

1. Speech and writing require different kinds of thinking;
2. Speech and writing are structured differently;
3. Speech and writing require access to different language codes.

I believe these research findings have limited relevance for the teaching of writing. They exaggerate distinctions that suggest the interference of speech in writing, and thus they ignore the very important ways in which our skills as speakers enhance our writing.

Maxim One: Speech and Writing Require Different Kinds of Thinking.

Maxim one is derived from three contrasting observations about how speech and writing record experience. These are: speech is concrete, while writing is abstract and general; speech is proverbial, reflecting "common sense," while writing is scientific, reflecting inductive logic; and finally, speech is fleeting and inconsequential, while writing is permanent and heuristic. Let's examine each of these claims as they distort relationships between thinking, speaking, and writing.

Because speech is concrete and writing is abstract, theorists tell us, thinking in writing is more difficult. Handling ideas in written language, Vygotsky claims, is complex not only because written language is often used to express relationships between abstract concepts, but also because written words themselves are more abstract than spoken words. Written language is one more step removed from the concepts it symbolizes because it lacks the "sensory aspect of speech" (1962, p. 98). Paralleling Vygotsky's claims, Foucault notes that Western writing systems involve an even greater degree of abstraction than Oriental writing systems because of the use of the alphabet to create words instead of ideograms:

> The ideogram . . . directly represents the signified, independently from a phonetic system which is another mode of representation. . . . Since writing refers not to a thing but to speech, a work of language only advances more deeply into the intangible density of the mirror, calls for the double of this already doubled writing . . . (p. 56).

Writing, these theorists tell us, is twice removed from experience, first removed from what it records and second from speech—the response closest to our physical selves.

This "foreign" quality of writing has been so successfully emphasized in composition classes that our students are convinced that writing has nothing to do with them. Our students need to know that writing is a mirror of speech, but more importantly they must understand that in that mirror is an image of themselves—"language-using animals" facing other selves, as Macrorie tells us earlier in this chapter. Our writing is not telling "the truth," it is rather "truth-telling," a personal, engaged record of our individual experiences. There can be very little that is abstract about that. Yet, empirical observation of writing in context shows that writing is in some ways more removed from experience than speech and, furthermore, that it is more logical in reporting experience than speech.

Olson's studies of the language of literate adults, preliterate adults (members of cultures that have never developed a written language), and children suggest several conclusions about differences in the logic of speech and writing. Speech, Olson found, is coded for action. Premises for argument in speech are "proverbs," that is, they are statements that reaffirm cultural assumptions for behavior, rather than draw conclusions based on inductive study. In speech, the values behind the words constitute their argument. The speaker who has the last word, whatever it may be, wins. In writing, Olson found, words are assessed logically— the winner of the argument is he who can draw the best conclusions from what was previously stated. Writing talks about the principle behind action—it generalizes particulars in such a way that true statements can follow from an inductive assessment of what is said (pp. 13–16).

This finding that writing is "logical" has suggested to some teachers that writing should lack rhetorical intensity. Opinion, attitude, personal conviction—these are functions reserved for speech. This view, of course, denies that the source of writing and speech is the same, a "truth-telling" author, communicating his or her truth, not "the truth."

A third observation of differences between speech and writing has led many theorists to remark that writing represents better "thinking" than speech. Writing is heuristic, or suited for directed, hierarchical thinking, because it is permanent. Speech is inconsequential, or useless as a building tool for complex ideas, because it is fleeting. Perhaps the most compelling arguments that writing directs thinking in a way speech cannot are those drawn from phenomenological observations of characteristics of the two modes. Barritt notes that the deliberateness of the communicative effort is reinforced in written communication by the existence of a tool (a pen or a typewriter), a place to write, a solitary context, a preestablished idea, an audience and communication purpose, and a permanent product. The possibility of reviewing the permanent record affords the communicator a "second chance" to develop the writing further and alter its affect (pp. 126-30).

The heuristic value of the review process for the writer perhaps has been most elegantly described by Emig in "Writing as a Mode of Learning." Here Emig suggests that reviewing what one writes helps the writer transform literal representations. When writers read the written record of their thinking, they experience a "revision" of what they thought they knew. Because speech is fleeting, here one moment and gone the next, it does not permit this opportunity for learning from thoughtful review of an artifact (p. 125).

None of the phenomenological differences observed between speech and writing "prove" that writing involves a different kind of thinking than speech. In fact, using this research to tell students that writing involves a different kind of thinking than speech can lead teachers to some awkward "moments of truth" in the composition classroom.

Can we, for instance, really help students by telling them that writing is "abstract," and if we do, will students believe that it must be profound, full of ideas and themes, never concerned with people and things—the everyday stuff of life we talk about to those we care about? Is it not the lack of the concrete, of the here-and-now, that makes some of our students' writing so terrible? Certainly some of our best literature, our most informative newscasts, our most handy reference works record everyday concrete things.

Can we say that writing is inductive rather than proverbial, analytic rather than supportive of cultural attitudes? This conclusion is proven false even when we examine scientific reporting. The development of argument in scientific discourse is often not inductive at all, but is made to look so through the use of "discourse performatives," language features which signal the development of factual argument, something we *should* believe (Gremmo, pp. 5, 27).

Furthermore, can we really say that writing is heuristic and that speech is not? After all, what is the process of revision that Emig described but an attempt to create a dialogue between self and paper, in the act of retrospectively structuring one's discourse to match what's in one's head, or a dialogue between self and a probable audience in the act of projecting an effective rhetorical structure? (Perl and Egendorf, pp. 125-26). What can encourage this kind of dialogue better than talk—talk in the classroom, talk about writing, about ideas, about talk itself?

Along with each claim that writing is more abstract, more logical, more thoughtful comes the underlying assertion that writing really is "better" than speech. And can we claim that? As Robin Lakoff points out earlier in this book, we really cannot: "Just as the human race has not been literate from its beginnings, neither has it been in agreement about the virtues of the written medium since the advent of literacy" (p. 12). In ancient Greece, the rise of literacy was viewed with suspicion. Plato called writing a poor substitute for good memory. In the twentieth century, Lakoff concludes, writing has taken a back seat to nonprint media; it is, in fact, an important skill, special to those who can use it, but hardly necessary for survival. We have little ground to stand upon if we persist in telling students that writing is more important or even as important as speech for our own survival or that of society.

Rather than persisting in comparing speech and writing as they support intellectual development, we should help students understand complementary relationships between the two modes that can help them as communicators throughout their lifetimes. We should tell students that our efforts to express both concrete and abstract ideas, analogic and analytic arguments, explicative and exploratory thinking can be realized in both speech and writing. Students who do not have experience communicating in writing do not need to be taught how to "think" differently, nor do they need to be taught new language functions. They do need, however, to know that some functions are "strikingly more prevalent" in writing than in speech, as Chafe tells us, making the use of writing special in some instances (p. 94). In examining the ways we do things differently when we speak and write, we stand a better chance of writing more effectively, not because we think writing is better or more important, but because we know that it is the mode best suited for special functions of language. More on this later.

Maxim Two: Oral Language and Written Language Are Structured Differently.

Some methods of teaching composition have been vindicated by research on speech and writing, primarily research which concludes that oral language is spontaneously developed, lacks embedding, and is dependent on context for coherence, while writing is planned, contains multiple embeddings, and is dependent on structural devices for coherence.

Sentence-combining practice, for instance, is justified by observations about typical grammatical differences in speech and writing. Speech, as Stalker notes, reflects the consistent use of "clausal rather than sentence syntax" and in speech "sentences that are completed are usually independent clauses (matrix sentences) with little or no subordination (embedding)" (pp. 276, 274). Mature writing, as Hunt has told us, includes more subordinated clauses and fewer independent clauses or clauses connected by coordinators (p. 307). Thus sentence-combining, which increases students' facility with subordinating structures (Mellon, pp. 51–52), can help them write "less oral" and "more mature" discourse.

The advice to "make more connections" or to "use more transitions," which teachers often write on student papers, is also supported by research on the structure of speech and writing. Speech, Crystal and Davy tell us, creates overt inter-sentence linkage through ellipsis, personal pronouns, articles, and determiners which cross-reference items previously stated (p. 112). Writing, however, involves more complex structuring, Emig tells us, establishing "systematic connections and relationships" through text features that signal the nature of "conceptual relationships" (p. 126).

We must remember, however, that most comparisons of the structure of speech and writing have examined spontaneous conversation and planned written composition. Gross differences are bound to be apparent. The function of spontaneous conversations is to explore, to find out what is going on, to explain what is happening moment to moment; its structure must be loose to allow for new possibilities. The function of written composition, on the other hand, is to communicate a planned message, to tell what one knows rather than to initiate dialogue. It is not surprising, thus, that linguists have found conversation to cover subject matter at random, to have no overall theme, to consist of utterances that are often incomplete and contradictory. It is also not surprising that linguists characterize writing as directed to one topic and composed of fluent and complete sentences (Crystal and Davy, pp. 95-121). Both teachers and students are aware that readers expect organization, standard English, and minimal error in written texts.

Planning composition instruction based on research that directly opposes typical structures in each mode really doesn't get us very far. For one thing, such instruction ignores the fact that we structure our language, both speech and writing, to respond to specific situations. Written expression will often closely approximate functions and structures "typical" of speech. When we ignore this, we overlook some very important kinds of writing. What's more, we imply that "typical" features are effective in every instance.

To insist, for example that speech is "random" while writing is "planned" is to discount the developmental kind of writing that Elbow, Macrorie, and others advocate. Many teachers underrate the importance of evolutionary writing as a step to finished composition when they ask to see only finished products instead of drafts. They often claim that, for many students, writing a single draft is an accomplishment; revising that draft is out of the question. These teachers have failed to teach students how to use writing as "planning." Graves has shown us that if we ask even the youngest writers to choose their own topics and to make those choices work through rewriting their drafts, they will write better prose. The stimulus to rewrite is the constant reactive input of both teachers and other students who read successive drafts. By breaking the "welfare" cycle, as he claims earlier in this chapter, by not giving students assignments which eliminate the "choice" to communicate effectively, we will help students *use* their writing to *develop* their writing. Teachers must begin to view the first draft as an opportunity for discussion that insures a more meaningful final product.

To assert that embedding and subordination are more desirable than coordination in writing is to ignore how language structure reflects purpose. Newspaper writing, some of our most readable prose, makes use of simple sentences connected by coordinators, rather than subordinators. This style, Crystal and Davy note, gives newspaper writing a sense of urgency and immediacy which maintains reader interest (pp. 184-85). The prose runs forward, rather than tracing backwards or spiraling inwards. Christensen claims that the most frequent sentence type in published prose of all kinds is not the complex sentence, but the cumulative sentence which presents an idea and then elaborates it with a series of free modifiers, explanations that are merely "added on" to the base loosely, as detail is added to a point in conversation (p. 156).

To urge students to "make more connections" is to urge them to use subordinators with abandon. Students following advice to make things connect may form prose habits that are hard to break. I found it very difficult, for instance, to convince a good freshman writer that the following paragraph contained dysfunctional connecting words:

To find the exact cause of rising costs is not quite clear; *however,* big city critics are putting the blame on stringent government aid and on insurance policies which finance expensive treatments and elaborate facilities with a blank check. This means that physicians will probably be reimbursed for just about any amount they charge. . . . *so, as you can see,* it is very difficult to beat a system which favors the physician. *Hence,* a stringent health insurance policy must be put into law in order to take this fee control from the doctor.

This student passage suffers from "connection" overload. It also reflects the writer's perception that subordinators and coordinators are things you insert between written sentences to *make* them connect.

An argument could be made that students misuse connectors, transitions, or structural markers in writing because speech requires no such features. Yet, features do exist in conversation which anticipate function. Paired sequences, for instance, can indicate intention to clarify, continue, or terminate discourse. Likewise, conventional strategies exist for introducing a topic so that it will be accepted by a listener or for suspending the "turn-taking" system so that one speaker may insert a story (Coulthard, pp. 69-92). As with any tool that has become so handy that we forget its importance to completing a task, the devices we use to structure conversation are so familiar, so directly functional, we do not easily recognize them without deliberate study.

Why, then, do comparable devices in writing, devices which direct the elocutionary force of discourse, pose such problems for our students? Could it be because most student writing is non-functional? In school, Britton tells us, students almost always write to teachers—an audience who will regard little they say as informative or engaging (pp. 63-64). It's perhaps not surprising that student writers fail to use features that clearly direct readers to functional intent. Or do students fail to signal functional intent in their writing simply because they haven't compared the different ways speech and writing both relate to external context? Teachers can help students discover how intent is communicated in both speech and writing through citing examples such as those Horner gives in "Speech Act Theory and Writing" in this chapter. By showing students how speakers and writers make language "do" something to listeners and readers, we can help students analyze their own prose as it clarifies purpose. But to do so we must accept the premise that meaning in written discourse depends upon "the interaction between writer and reader" as much as meaning in spoken discourse depends upon the interaction between speaker and hearer (p. 98).

Writers have to know which linguistic choices communicate which intent for which readers: They have to understand that discourse should be planned if the purpose is to inform rather than to explore; sentences should be short and coordinated if the purpose is to narrate with urgency; connecting devices should be used when they truly and correctly mark the intent of the statements which follow. As Robinson suggests in his essay earlier in this chapter, "Discourse is language in use" (p. 116), and teachers of language use can improve their instruction by focusing upon discourse, upon the strategies for making language mean and for making it communicate effectively. Writers who learn to avoid language that is structured like speech undoubtedly limit their potential to write effective prose.

Maxim Three: Speech and Writing Require Access to Different Language Codes.

Code, as defined by Gregory and Carroll, embodies the range of linguistic behavior to which an individual has access when communicating: "Code therefore determines which options will be selected as appropriate to a given situation" (p. 80). Codes that will dictate appropriate options in speech and writing are, of course, different. Yet there is great variety in the range of "correct" options in either speech or writing for a given situation, and options most typically chosen in speech may in some situations be most suitable for writing. As Kroll noted in an earlier essay, the skill to "differentiate" options that are more appropriate for one mode than the other is as important as the capacity to consolidate "oral and written language resources" and expand expressive possibilities (p. 95).

Composition pedagogy often assumes that the only "codes" students must control in writing are those which differentiate acceptable expression in both modes. Two codes most often referenced by writing teachers are "standard English" and the conventions of a loosely defined, authoritative yet personal style called the "writer's voice." In teaching standard English, teachers assume that they must fight the influence of local dialects, and in developing "voice" they must wage a war on clichés and aphorisms borrowed from speech.

I find it troublesome that some composition instructors feel that class time must be spent drilling students in standard English. Teaching standard English in the composition class emphasizes what students lack, the facility to switch from spoken to written dialects, rather than what most students have, a natural desire to communicate to others. Certainly, teachers cannot ignore individual differences in code facility, but neither can they afford to label differences "errors." Richard W. Bailey's and Lee H. Hansen's cogent summaries of the lessons learned in the Ann Arbor Black English case tell how the case brought national attention to what educators must know about speech dialects and language teaching. The Ann Arbor case informed teachers and the public about linguistic variation, Bailey notes, by showing why certain items in the speech of black children cannot be regarded as "errors," but rather as "systematic features of language that differentiate dialects" (p. 131). In the elementary grades, teachers must recognize how children learning to read will render written language into speech in ways that reflect their normal way of speaking. But in recognizing how Black English differs in specific and regular ways from standard English, they will teach best when they regard the language students use as a legitimate base for new learning, rather than as erroneous data. To Bailey's conclusions Hansen adds that teachers must also work to educate our society more generally about attitudes toward language variety. If teachers do not accept this responsibility, Hansen points out, "where will the leadership to move our society toward an enlightened view of language and dialect come from?" (p. 136).

I believe teachers can change attitudes toward language and improve writing instruction by taking the focus off dialectal differences in the composition classroom, by regarding dialectal differences as a potential for a range of individual expression, rather than as an obstacle to written communication. However, when teachers put mastery of standard English in perspective with the larger goal of encouraging individual expression in the composition class, they should not make "individual" expression a requirement for good prose. They should not urge each student writer, for instance, to develop a unique writing "voice." Asking students to write in their "voice," Schor notes, is to condemn them to failure:

> How many beginning writers have one "voice"? A nineteen-year-old who cannot decide on a major, who cannot see a job out there in his or her future, whose handwriting slants in a different direction in every paragraph, sometimes in every line? (p. 76).

When teachers tell students to write honestly, to find their own "voices," they ask students to do something that many of them are not mature enough to do. What's worse is that they ask students to do something most adults never do.

Adult speakers and writers change their language depending upon whom they're addressing, where, and when. The "codes" they bring to bear are those that work within the constraints of a particular situation. In many cases these codes are so definite that they constitute a "register" of language specific to a given context, such as the register of "CB radio talk" or "legal writing." Good writers must command many voices and make them their own. And this is, of course, what Fader tells us in his essay in this chapter. Writers make their texts their own by investing their selective rhetoric with a personal style. They meet the rhetorical demands of situation, neither by ignoring appropriate style in favor of personal expression nor by burying personality under the "register" the situation forces them to adopt. They control appropriate registers to make their texts communicate *both* their messages and themselves, authors with convictions, to others.

Teachers trying to get students to write with conviction would be more successful if they helped students discover the multiple "voices" they must employ when addressing different audiences for different purposes. How to inform students of the range of responses appropriate for a variety of specific contexts, however, is a big problem. Giving students a range of situations to address in writing won't insure that they make the best language choices for each situation.

We know that speakers depend to a large extent on feedback from immediate audiences to adjust their expression, and studies have suggested that good writers rely on an internal "monitor," checking their writing against rules and conventions for specific writing situations (Barbara Kroll, pp. 87–88). The job of teaching writing then boils down to "programming" students' writing "monitors" so that they can serve for all writing situations. What a hopeless task! We can't possibly teach what is appropriate for all situations. Fortunately for us, in real-life as opposed to classroom writing, few writers depend solely on their own judgments.

In business and industry, documents summarizing progress of a project, proposing a bid, or describing a procedure are often the work of a team of writers or are the end products of a series of rewrites that have passed from worker to co-worker to supervisor. In the real world, writers know when to adjust their writing to meet the needs of their audiences because their audiences are often right there telling them to do so.

I think teachers disregard the value of consultation in writing. Instead of showing students ways to gain expertise through talking with others, they burden them with the responsibility of being expert without any resources. Furthermore, by insisting that students work alone as writers, they encourage behavior that does not prepare them for writing tasks in corporate environments where team work and team writing may be essential. Teachers can better simulate the conditions for writing that are likely to be a part of our students' adult professional lives through applying the peer consultation techniques advocated by Macrorie, Fader, Martin, and Graves. Requiring students to write and critique in groups not only makes our teaching much easier and more effective, it also prepares students for writing in a context which integrates oral and written expression.

Teachers cannot continue to view speech simply as language conforming to codes which potentially interfere with good writing. If they do, they will miss the very significant fact that what we do as speakers to insure that our words affect others is very similar to what we must do as writers, that is, to keep talking—with other students, with instructors, with potential audiences—to get a feel for what they want to hear and read, and how they want to hear and read it.

We must be more open to ways to bridge that gap between speech and writing, to working with the two modes together so that students never forget that writing is not an academic exercise, but rather a special form of communication. We can encourage students to express themselves in writing almost as freely as they do in speech by not setting artificial limits upon what written language should be. I take heart in reading the writing of Nancy Martin's students which she included in her essay in this chapter. These students have found that, in their formal writing, they can better address their teacher as a real audience with a real interest in their prose if they regularly write to her in a journal. Teachers should view journals, outlines, first drafts, and notes of all kinds as a privileged kind of "talking to a reader" that is an essential part of the writing process. This talking insures the viability of the final product.

How, finally, should composition teachers regard the research that compares speech and writing? We need to think more carefully about how such research should influence teaching. It is important to know how writing differs from talk, but more important to know how writing works like talk. When we urge students to think inductively, to develop new syntactic patterns, to discover a personal style—in short, to make their writing different from their speech—we stigmatize facility in speech as a liability. We must look at research on speech and writing in hope of ascertaining what speakers do that is similar to what writers do. Writing instruction will then focus not on making student language "more literate" and "less oral," but on the mastery of operations that insure effective expression.

3.

On Reading and Writing

In this chapter, teachers of literacy and psychology explore the reciprocal relationship that exists between the processes of reading and writing. As they do so, these teachers remind us that reading is not a passive process, that readers invest texts with meaning as they read. In the first essay, Tierney reports on research which suggests that readers and writers negotiate the meaning of texts; and in the second essay, Bransford, Vye, and Adams remind us that writers implicitly expect readers to use past experience and prior knowledge to make meaning of texts.

In the next six essays, teachers at different levels of instruction describe practices they have developed to make the relationship between reading and writing explicit for their students. Hansen describes reading and writing instruction that teaches first grade students to assume responsibility for their own learning by focusing the students' attention upon what they do when they read and write. Torbe describes writing activities that not only provide secondary school students a variety of ways to respond to their reading but also reflect the mental activities in which they engage as they respond. Berthoff presents a theoretical framework for understanding the processes of interpretation and describes activities that require college students to reflect on their own processes of interpretation. Moffett urges teachers at all grade levels to encourage students to take responsibility for their writing by allowing them to write about readings they have selected themselves. D'Angelo asks students to analyze and imitate the writing styles of professional writers as one means of focusing their attention on the "literalness" of the writing activity. And Harkin describes a course she teaches to college students in which she asks them to articulate the processes by which they make required texts into readings that are meaningful to them.

In her essay Stotsky argues that teachers at all levels and in all courses should ask students to read texts that are increasingly rich and dense. And in our concluding essay, Wixson and I reflect on the other essays in this chapter as we urge our colleagues to teach reading and writing—together.

22 Writer–Reader Transactions: Defining the Dimensions of Negotiation

Robert J. Tierney
Center for the Study of Reading, University of Illinois

I believe that texts are written by writers who expect readers to make meaning, and they are read by readers who do the meaning making. I do not view writing as simply sharing information, nor do I view reading as a solitary activity in which the reader's responsibility is just to extract information more or less successfully. Writing and reading are multidimensional. They involve concurrently complex transactions between writers, writers as readers, readers, and readers as writers.

Writers as Readers

The suggestion that the writer is his or her own reader should not be considered novel. In conjunction with studying composing, revision and the difficulties writers encounter while composing, several researchers have begun to discuss the reading that occurs during writing (Atwell, 1980; Perl, 1979; Rose, 1980). Their research suggests that writers spend a great deal of time reading and rereading; that the reading which writers do serves different purposes (for example, distancing writers from their own work, problem-solving, discovering and monitoring the clarity of what has been written); and that the quality of these reading experiences seems closely tied to successful and less successful writing products. While these researchers have begun to define the nature of reading during writing in conjunction with the amount and nature of the text being read and written, less thoroughly investigated are questions of how, when, and why reading proceeds at different moments during a variety of composing experiences. Although we do not yet have complete answers to these questions, the notion of writers as readers suggests a view of reading-writing relationships which goes beyond a tendency to perceive reading and writing as separate activities whose influence upon each other occurs only at the level of overall reading and writing achievement.

Readers as Writers

To suggest that readers act as writers is less commonplace. But if one considers the processes involved in reading comprehension and written composition, the parallels between reading and writing are quite compelling. For example, consider the structure of the composing process as described by Flower and Hayes (1981) alongside a description of the reading process.

An examination of the two suggests that reading and writing hold many elements in common. The Flower and Hayes' model includes three major sets of elements: the task environment, long-term memory, and the processes of planning, translating, reviewing and monitoring. These same elements are integral to the reading process. A reader has a task environment, memory plays a key role, and reading proceeds by planning and by a type of translation and revision—all of which are monitored. Under planning, the activities in which readers and

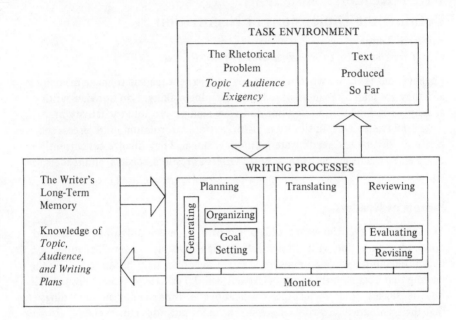

Flower & Hayes' Depiction of the Structure of the Writing Process

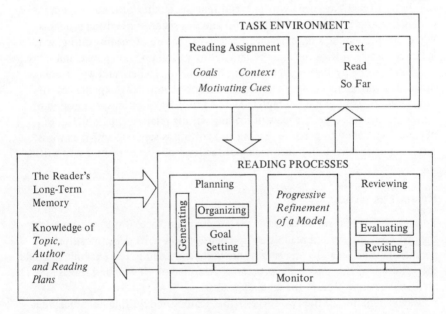

Parallel Depiction of the Structure of the Reading Process

Figure 1

writers engage are largely identical—namely, generating ideas, organizing, and goal-setting. Likewise, under translating, both readers and writers are faced with the same trade-offs over the number of ideas which can be held in short-term memory. And there is a sense in which readers, in their meaning making, do as writers do in terms of revision: editing and evaluating. Obviously, numerous other parallels can be drawn.

The recursive nature of composing is a property both reading and writing exhibit. Both are driven by a network of goals, some of which emerge during the formulation of ideas.

Reading and Writing As Multidimensional Transactions between Readers, Writers, Readers as Writers, and Writers as Readers

With a view toward defining some of the constraints operating upon writers and readers, I have been involved in a collaborative research project with P. Cohen in which we have tried to examine systematically the various facets of the writer-reader relationship by analyzing writing and reading as plan-based speech acts. Specifically, we have been trying to define how a contract to effect communication is achieved in light of constraints imposed by (1) the written mode, (2) writers' realizations of their intentions, and (3) readers' interpretations of those intentions. In so doing, we have found substantial support for the notion that readers act as writers, writers act as readers, and that readers interact with a projected writer, and writers interact with a projected reader.

During the course of this study, we recorded the interactions of pairs of adults—an expert and a novice—while one adult, the expert, provided instructions to the other adult, the novice, whose task was to assemble a model. The novice was unfamiliar with the model and the expert was thoroughly familiar with it and was responsible for providing all the necessary instructions for its operation to the novice. When the expert wrote to the novice, a think-aloud procedure provided us access to the intentions of both the participants engaged in the communicative situation. After a brief training period, writers were asked to think aloud about what they were trying to get readers to do; likewise, as readers read the text the writers produced, they were asked to think aloud about what they believed the author was trying to get them to think or do and to point at the parts of the model as they referred to them. We used split-screen video-tapes to merge transcripts of (1) the stated intentions of the writers, (2) the texts, and (3) the think-alouds of the readers.

As we examined the think-alouds of both writers and readers, we were particularly interested in the match and mismatch between them. At various points in the text the match between the writers' think-alouds and the readers' think-alouds was unusually close: If writers expressed concern for describing an object by a certain attribute (e.g., color), the readers would focus on the same attribute (e.g., color) during their think-alouds. This occurred regardless of the other attributes included in the text to describe this same object. Also, both writers and readers understood the function of certain descriptors without the writers' being explicit about their function: Frequently, writers described an object expecting—but not explicitly cuing—readers to identify, gather, and assemble the object; at other times, when writers identified an object which was not to be assembled, they cued their readers.

At points in the text, the mismatch between writers' and readers' think-alouds was apparent: Writers suggested concerns which readers did not focus upon, and readers expressed concerns which writers did not appear to consider. There was also a sense in which the writers' think-alouds suggested that at times writers assumed the role of readers. As writers thought aloud, generated text, and moved to the next set of sub-assembly directions, they would often comment about the writers' craft as readers might. There was also a sense in which writers marked their compositions with an "okay" as if the "okay" marked a movement from a turn as reader to a turn as writer. Analyses of the readers' think-alouds suggested that the readers often felt frustrated by the writers' failure to explain why they were doing what they were doing. Also the readers were often critical of the writers' craft, including writers' choice of words, clarity, and accuracy. There was a sense in which the readers' think-alouds assumed a reflexive character as if the readers were rewriting the texts. If one perceived the readers as craftspersons, unwilling to blame their tools for an ineffective product, then one might view the readers as unwilling to let the text provided stand in the way of their successful achievement of their goals or pursuit of understanding.

Taken together, these findings suggest that the processes of writing and reading involve shared plans. These plans are based upon the shared beliefs of participants (writers, writers as readers, readers, and readers as writers). Writers consider their readers as they compose text—they consider the transactions in which readers are likely to engage. At the same time, writers act as their own readers—they read and review what they have written as if they (the writers) assumed they were their own audience. Readers, as they comprehend text, respond reflexively and actively to what writers are trying to get them to think or do. These readers use knowledge of the world and the text cues to compose meaning: They recognize these cues to meaning making are provided by an author who is trying to get them to think or do something.

Another way to view the reading-writing relationship is as a variety of configurations which emerge from the following interfaces: a set of concerns (tacit or conscious) of writers for what and how the text might be negotiated by readers; a set of concerns of writers for what they as writers need to do (i.e., for purposes of accomplishing a task or communicating a message); a set of concerns (tacit or conscious) of readers for what writers are trying to do; and a set of concerns of readers for what they as readers need to do (i.e., for purposes of accomplishing a task or achieving an understanding).

Of relevance to language educators, this view of reading and writing provides a framework—albeit broad—for beginning to define how and why readers and writers make the decisions they do. In terms of how reading and writing are interrelated, it suggests the need to redefine the research and thinking regarding how reading and writing are interfaced. Rather than pursuing the global question as to how reading and writing influence each other in terms of achievement scores, the present view suggests coming to grips with how meaning making is constrained by and influences different types of reading and writing. This entails answers to questions such as the following:

How does the type of reading and writing that readers and writers do influence problem-solving (including discovering ideas, revision, etc.)?

How does the writing that readers do influence how readers perceive what they do as writers as well as what others do as writers?

How does the reading that writers do influence how writers perceive what they do as readers and what others do as readers?

Finally, from a practical perspective, if reading were viewed as composing and writing viewed as involving receptive as well as productive elements then some important and worthwhile implications for teaching emerge. The writing teacher might advise writers to assume alternative points of view of potential readers and to pursue different types of reading outcomes with their compositions in order to achieve a variety of distances from their work. If teachers help writers assess the comprehensibility, including the informativeness and sincerity, of their work, they might enable writers to acquire more sense of their power and role as authors engaged in a communicative exchange. Reading teachers might remind student readers that reading is akin to composing, might prompt a process rather than product orientation. They might emphasize efforts to help readers make meaning rather than outcomes and reading rates. For example, the role of reflecting, rethinking, and revising might be recognized and supported in reading as it is in writing lessons. Visualizing and networking of ideas might be viewed as integral to the early stages of reading as it is to the planning stages of writing. If teachers help readers juggle constraints and manage the information that they are seeking during reading, they might also enable readers to more thoughtfully control and assess coherent understandings. What we need are reading teachers who act as if their students were developing writers and writing teachers who act as if their students were readers.

23 Prerequisites for Comprehending Prose*

John D. Bransford, Nancy J. Vye and Lea T. Adams
Department of Psychology, Vanderbilt University

Dear Jill,

Remember Sally, the person I mentioned in my last letter? You'll never guess what she did this week. First, she let loose a team of gophers. The plan backfired when a dog chased them away. She then threw a party but the guests failed to bring their motorcycles. Furthermore, her stereo system was not loud enough. Sally spent the next day looking for a "Peeping Tom" but was unable to find one in the yellow pages. Obscene phone calls gave her some hope until the number was changed. It was the installation of blinking neon lights across the street that finally did the trick. Sally framed the ad

*Preparation of this paper was supported in part by Grant NIE-G-79-0117. The letter about Sally is adapted from a passage that was originally written by Nancy McCarrell.

from the classified section and now has it hanging on her wall.

Please write soon.

Love,

Bill

Most people have difficulty understanding the preceding letter about Sally. Their problem does not stem from a lack of familiarity with the words; the letter does not contain highly technical vocabulary. Each sentence in the letter also conforms to basic rules of English syntax, so syntactic abnormalities are not responsible for the fact that the letter is difficult to understand. Indeed, the hypothetical recipient of the letter, Jill, understands the message perfectly. Why is Jill able to understand while other English-speaking people are not?

The beginnings of an answer to this question were formulated several decades ago by the psychologist Karl Buhler, who argued that language comprehension depends on more than one's knowledge of a particular language. He emphasized that listeners and speakers (or writers and readers) must also share a common "semantic field":

> Given two speakers of the same language, no matter how well one of them structures a sentence, his utterance will fail if both parties do not share the same field to some degree. There are inner aspects of the field, such as an area of knowledge, or outer aspects, such as objects in the environment. . . . The structure of any particular language is largely field-independent, being determined by its own particular conventional rules, but the field determines how the rules are applied (cf. Blumenthal, 1970, p. 56).

Buhler would undoubtedly argue that Jill can understand the letter about Sally because Jill and the writer share a common "semantic field." In particular, Jill knows from previous letters that Sally has been attempting to do something: She has been trying to get her neighbor to move. Given this information, the letter makes much more sense. (Read it again.)

During the past ten years, psychologists have become increasingly sensitive to the fact that language comprehension involves much more than simply a "knowledge of one's language" (e.g., knowledge of vocabulary plus basic rules of syntax). People rely on their general background knowledge to fill in the gaps in messages; they actively contribute to the comprehension process by making assumptions and inferences. If you look again at the letter about Sally, for example, you will probably discover that you made a number of assumptions once you were informed of her goal. Thus, you probably assumed that the gophers were let out in the neighbor's yard, that the motorcycle and stereo noises were designed to bother the neighbor, that the Peeping Tom would have been hired to look in the neighbor's window, that the obscene phone calls were directed at the neighbor and that it was the latter's number that was changed, that the ad from the classified section said "House for Sale" and so forth. None of this information was supplied in the letter; it was supplied by you.

The letter about Sally is a "trick" passage; it was specially written to illustrate various facets of the comprehension process (for additional examples see Bransford, 1979; Bransford & Johnson, 1972; Bransford & McCarrell, 1974; Dooling

& Lachman, 1971). There is considerable evidence that the ability to understand any conversation or text requires the use of previously acquired knowledge to fill in the gaps in messages (e.g., see Anderson, 1977; Bower, Black & Turner, 1979; Bransford, 1979; Schank & Abelson, 1977). For example, consider the following story about the Ant and the Dove (cf. Mehan, 1977):

> A thirsty ant went to a river. He became carried away by the rush of the stream and was about to drown. A dove was sitting in a tree overhanging the water. The dove plucked a leaf and let it fall. The leaf fell into the stream close to the ant and the ant climbed onto it. The ant floated safely to the bank. Shortly afterwards, a birdcatcher came and laid a trap in the tree. The ant saw his plan and stung him on the foot. In pain the birdcatcher threw down his trap. The noise made the bird fly away.

Most adults understand the ant and dove story with no difficulty; they are often surprised when helped to notice the degree to which they spontaneously made inferences in order to comprehend it. For example, readers usually assume that the ant walked to the river and the dove flew to the tree, although this information was never explicitly presented. Similarly, readers realize that an ant might drown because it requires oxygen (it would be strange to worry about a fish drowning in a river), that the dove probably plucked the leaf with its beak and so forth. Basic information about doves and ants therefore plays an important role in guiding the inferences that readers make.

Additional sets of inferences must also be drawn in order to understand the ant and dove story. One important set of inferences involves assumptions about the characters' goals. For example, most people assume that the dove plucked the leaf in order to save the ant, that the birdcatcher's plan was to trap the dove and that the ant bit the birdcatcher in order to repay the dove for its previous favor. Note that none of this information is stated in the story; in each case it is generated by the reader. In fact, the passage never even mentions that the ant and the dove saw one another. The author of the passage didn't need to explicitly present this information because it was almost certain that readers would supply it. Indeed, communication would be extremely cumbersome if speakers and writers had to explicitly provide all the information necessary to comprehend.

Several investigators have asked whether people may sometimes think that they remember having heard or read information that, in actuality, was only inferred. After hearing the Ant and the Dove story, for example, listeners could be given a recognition test which included both actual statements from the passage plus information that was likely to have been inferred (e.g., "The dove wanted to save the ant"). Results from various laboratories show that listeners and readers falsely recognize information that never actually occurred in a story but that was likely to be assumed (e.g., see Bransford, Barclay and Franks, 1972; Johnson, Bransford, and Solomon, 1973; Bower et al., 1979; Graesser, Gordon, Sawyer, 1979).

Memory tests such as those just described can be used to assess the degree to which individuals spontaneously attempt to fill in the gaps in messages while comprehending. For example, one of the authors recently used this method to study the comprehension processes of three and four year olds. Children who participated in the study were first read several stories about situations that were familiar to them. One story was about Jack and his family going to a restaurant. It included information about sitting at a table, receiving a menu from the waitress, eating the food and so forth. After hearing the stories, children were presented with a set of test statements and asked to decide which ones were explicitly stated in the story and which were not.

The results indicated that children were highly likely to think that information which was typical of a situation (e.g., of a restaurant) had actually been stated in the story irrespective of whether it had or had not been stated. For example, the children were very likely to think they had heard "Jack's father paid for the food" even if this had not been mentioned in the story. On the other hand, the children were not likely to falsely recognize statements that were less typical but still could have occurred in the story (e.g., "Jack spilled his water in the restaurant"). This pattern of results shows that the children were not simply saying "yes" to each test item but were instead trying to decide whether they actually remembered the information. The fact that they falsely recognized typical information that was not actually presented suggests that even three year olds spontaneously activate organized bodies of knowledge (often called scripts or schema; e.g., see Schank & Abelson, 1977; Rumelhart & Ortony, 1977) in order to fill in the gaps in messages that they hear.

Note that the preceding study involved topics that were familiar to the children. In addition to the story about going to a restaurant, children who participated in the study heard stories about getting up in the morning and about going to a grocery store. Since even young children are familiar with situations such as these, they have developed knowledge structures or schemas that provide a basis for making inferences. However, there are undoubtedly many topics that are extremely difficult for children to understand because they lack the necessary schemas. For example, young children would probably be unable to understand the passage about Sally even when told of her goal because they lack information about neighborly relationships and about activities that cause irritation. Similarly, children would fail to understand that the ant and the dove were attempting to help one another if they lacked general ideas about cooperation.

One important educational implication of an emphasis on previously acquired knowledge or schemas is that educators need to be aware that students may fail to comprehend a story because they lack the knowledge presupposed by the writer. Students could know all the words in a text yet find it too difficult by virtue of their lack of familiarity with the overall text structure and goals (e.g., see Anderson, in press; Bruce, in press). Of course, a student's lack of familiarity is not the only cause of comprehension failure. Oftentimes, students have the requisite knowledge yet fail to use it. One reason for this failure may be the way in which the story is written. For example, many stories used to teach beginning reading are designed to be "simplified" for young readers. Unfortunately, many attempts to "simplify" stories result in cryptic texts that are extremely difficult to understand (e.g., see Beck, in press; Bransford, 1979). As an illustration, consider the following story from a beginning reader (cf. Beck, in press, p. 9):

I can run fast. I see a pond.
I must stop. I can't stop.
The pond is bad luck.

As was the case with the Sally "passage," the meaning of the story is unclear in spite of its familiar vocabulary and simple sentences. The intended message is that the person is running so fast that he or she is unable to stop in time to avoid falling into a pond. A large number of inferences are necessary in order to make this into a coherent message; young children may have difficulty doing so. They might therefore acquire the idea that reading is "word calling" and fail to develop an understanding of how to read a text for its meaning. A number of studies suggest that many students become efficient decoders yet poor comprehenders, and that they need to learn how to activate previously acquired knowledge in order to make information make sense (e.g., see Bransford, Stein, Shelton & Owings, 1981; Bransford, Stein & Vye, 1982).

In our work with poor comprehenders such as those noted above (see especially Bransford et al., 1982), we have found it useful to have them adopt the perspective of a writer who elaborates passages in order to make various inferences explicit. This helps the students become aware of the contributions they must make to the comprehension process and hence increases the number of inferences they make when they read. Ideally, experiences such as these should also provide important information about writing. Writers often think that their messages are "perfectly clear" because they are unaware that they spontaneously fill in the gaps in their own statements. They are often surprised when others cannot understand their products, or understand them in ways that are incongruent with their original intent. By helping students become more aware of the amount and kinds of inferences they generate in order to comprehend written material, teachers may also increase students' sensitivity to the types of information which must be incorporated into written material in order that it may be understood by readers.

24 First Grade Writers Who Pursue Reading

Jane Hansen
Department of Education, University of New Hampshire

Everyone knows writing is hard except children who are just beginning first grade. Twenty-three of them were asked, "Can you write?"

"Yes," answered every child.
"Can you read?"
Only two children said, "Yes."
Then the children were given journals and they wrote.
On September 17 Susan, who had said earlier she couldn't read, wrote:
MIMOMISHBE
BKIKRD

When she showed it to someone else she said, "I bet you can't read this, but I can. I wrote it. Want me to read it to you? 'My mom is happy because I can read.' "

Susan is part of a case-study research project on the relationship between reading and writing which three of us—Ellen Blackburn (the teacher), Don Graves (pp. 98-101), and I—began during the 1981-82 school year and will continue during the 1982-83 school year. In 1981-82, Don and I spent part of three days each week in Ellen's classroom in Great Falls School, located in a lower-middle class community in Somersworth, New Hampshire, an old New England mill town, studying three children who represented low, middle, and high achievement levels. We collected data about the reading and writing of these children on video and audio tapes, protocol forms, and in notes taken during frequent interactions and conferences with the children.

In order to make the relationship between reading and writing as obvious as possible to the children, we gave identical definitions to both reading and writing and created similar learning environments for their reading and writing periods in class: We defined both reading and writing as the process of composing a message; and during reading and writing periods in class, Ellen Blackburn expected the students to assume responsibility for their work. She taught them to make decisions, and as they gained knowledge about making decisions in writing and reading their sense of responsibility grew and they pursued messages. Their perseverance started with their writing. They wrote by learning about their writing process (Graves, 1982); they composed messages. The same applied to reading. During the reading period, they all had stories in front of them for the entire period.

In this class, students are provided frequent opportunities to read and write, and they interact with others as they read and write so they may gain feedback in order to improve. The classroom buzzes during reading sessions just as it does during writing sessions: Randy chooses to read with Carlos. Susan chooses to read with a group of friends. Marie curls up in a corner by herself. Ellen has a group with her, students of mixed reading levels who have chosen to read together. Interaction is important in this classroom because beginning readers need a lot of help; and they need to get much of that help from each other, because the teacher alone cannot answer all their questions.

During times when she meets with groups, Ellen teaches students to confer with each other the way she confers with them. She teaches them four types of interactions, or conferences, which I will describe separately although they do not occur discretely.

Initiating Conferences

An initiating conference occurs when children need to get started. They may need help in choosing topics for writing or selecting books to read. Each time they come to the writing table or each time the reading period begins, they decide whether to continue with texts they are currently working on or to choose new ones. For example, when children choose stories they may stay with them until the stories flow; or, if their choices are inappropriate, they may put the stories aside. This practice is posited upon the assumption that when children choose the topics of their writing or the stories they will read, they have an investment in the pieces: There is a message they want to create and they persist until they have done so.

One day Toby consulted George about his writing:

T: "Should I write about sledding or my new goldfish?"
G: "You have a new goldfish? Where did you get it?"
T: "My memere got it for me. You should see the aquarium it has. Maybe I'll write about that."
G: "Yeah, our whole class went sledding so everyone knows about that topic already."

Toby chose the topic of his writing—which could just as easily have been the topic of his reading—by consulting with a classmate. And the teacher honored the choice.

Comprehension Conferences

A comprehension conference helps children clarify messages. Such interactions begin when children read texts to others. The initial responses are focused on the content of the piece.

One day Carlos had just written this piece and read it to me:

As he touched another piece of paper he said, "I can't decide if I should add some more information to it."

Referring to his text, I asked why he had written he would never use the front brakes, and he explained that he might be thrown off if he did. I told him I didn't know that because I don't know much about dirt bikes and I wondered if it would be important information to add.

"I'm going to go talk to Jamie," he responded. "He has a dirt bike so he knows a lot about them." The responsibility for making the decision about what to do with his text rested with Carlos. He would seek advice, and he would decide.

The children in this class want their messages to be clear so they seek conferences until they are satisfied with their pieces. They approach their writing as something that can be revised as it emerges. They know their "drafts" improve their messages.

I happened to walk by Jon one day after he had written most of the text in Figure 2 about his grandma's knee operation.

I noticed he had cut his original story apart, pasted it on another sheet of paper, and had added new information in the middle as well as at the end. I asked Jon why he had cut apart his original story.

"Well, it didn't sound right."

"How did you know?"

"You see, when I read my first draft to Ms. Blackburn, then she read it back to me and it sounded funny."

"What sounded funny about it?"

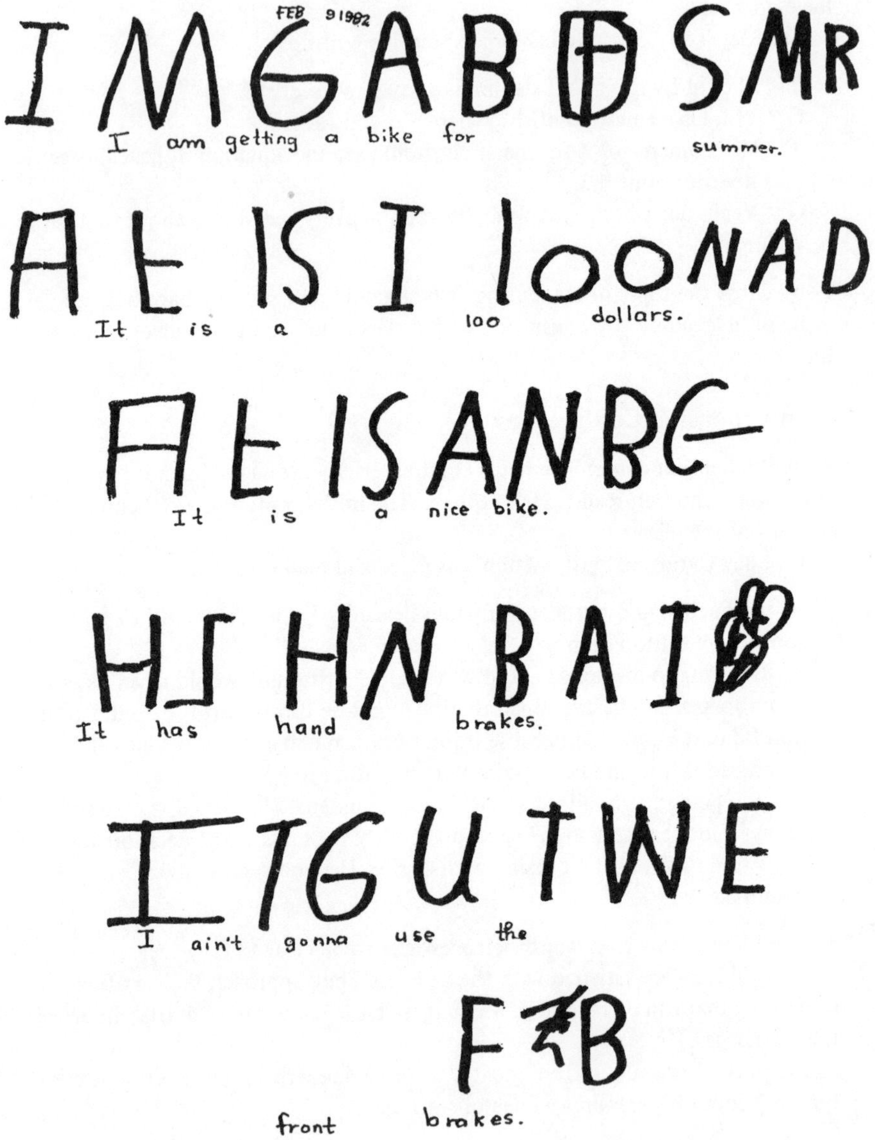

I MG A B D S MR

FEB 9 1982

I   am getting   a   bike   for   summer.

A E   IS I loo N A D

It   is   a   100   dollars.

A E IS A N B G

It   is   a nice bike.

H J H N B A I

It   has   hand   brakes.

I TG U T WE

I   ain't   gonna   use   the

F B

front   brakes.

Figure 1

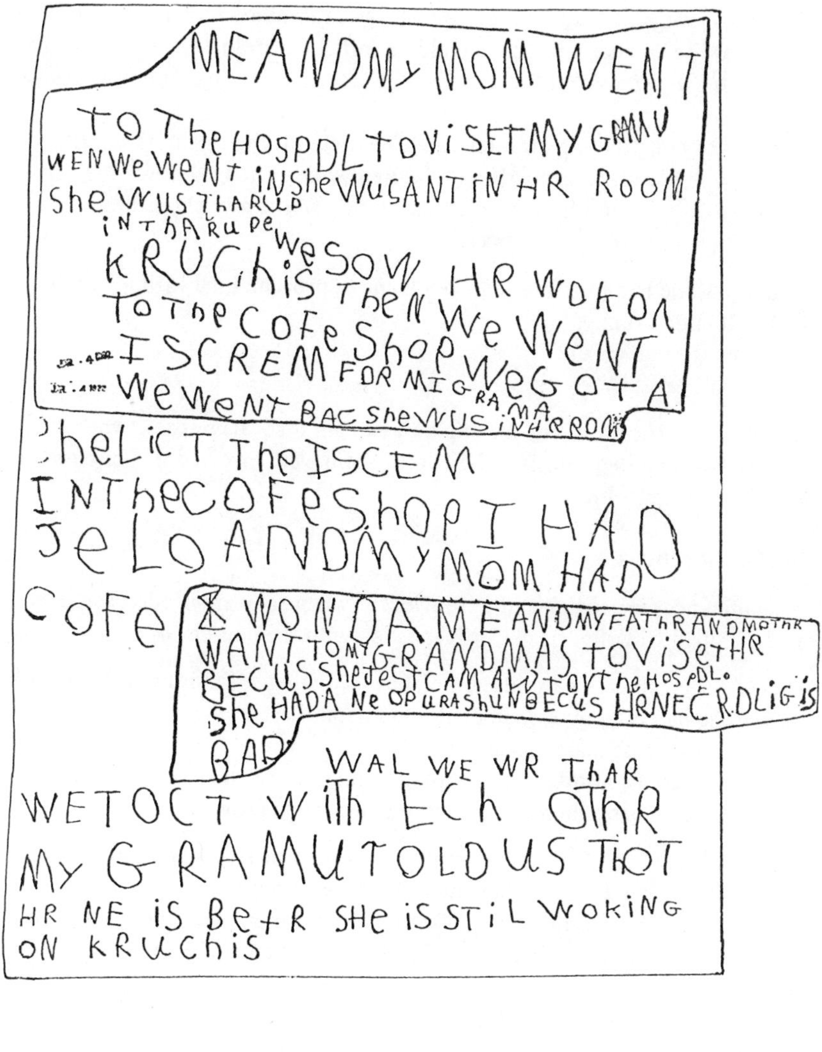

MEANDMY MOM WENT
TO THE HOSPDL TO ViSET MY GRMMU
WEN WE WENT iN She WUSANTIN HR ROOM
She WUS THARUB in She
iN THARUB De
KRUCIHiS WESOW HR WOKON
THEN WE WENT
TO THE COFE ShOP WE GOT A
I SCREM FOR MIGRAMA
WE WENT BAC SHEWUS iNHRROOM
:heLiCT THE ISCEM
IN THE COFE ShOP I HAD
JeLO AND MY MOM HAD
COFE X WON DA MEANDMY FATHRANDMOTHR
WANT TOMY GRANDMAS TOViSET HR
BECUS SheJeST CAM ALT TOYT THE HOSPDL.
She HADA NE OPURAShUN BECUS HRNECR DLiG iS
BAD
WAL WE WR THAR
WE TOCT WiTh ECh OThR
MY GRAMU TOLD US ThOT
HR NE iS BE+R SHE iS STiL WOKiNG
ON KRUChiS

Figure 2

"I had said we visited my grandma at her house and we visited her in the hospital, but we had visited her in the hospital FIRST, so I had to cut it apart and put that part first!"

No one told Jon to reorganize his piece. After all reorganization is a lot of work. Jon chose to reorganize himself because he was determined to make his message right. Just as the teacher gives these children initial control in the choice of their topics, she is careful not to take responsibility for an emerging text away from them.

The task of constructing meaning is not restricted to writing in this classroom. Rereading is as prevalent as rewriting. Children who get bogged down the first time through a story and find the message muddy frequently choose to reread; often they reread books many times.

One day Marie had just finished a book and approached me with a dejected look, "It ended funny."
"What do you mean?"
"I don't get it."

We talked about the book but she couldn't explain it so she reread it with a friend. By the time they finished the two of them were involved in a discussion about what it meant. I listened.

Skills Conferences

Skills conferences in reading and writing occur when they are needed and only after the individual writer or reader is satisfied with the content of a piece.

Don Graves conducted a skills conference in writing with Susan one day when he saw she had used quotation marks and parentheses.
"What do those marks mean, Susan?"
"Well, these (pointing to the quotation marks) are what you use when kids talk and these (parentheses) are what you use when grown-ups talk."

Because students write freely, concentrating on their messages and not worrying about spelling or parentheses, they are able to create texts.

The skills conferences in reading, like those in writing, place the skills in context. In a skills conference the teacher helps the children apply appropriate word attack skills to their texts. For example, the teacher may encourage a child who remembers seeing a word he cannot now identify to thumb back through the book to find it on a preceding page where he did read it. Sometimes children recognize a word as one they used in their writing but cannot identify it:

I was with Randy one day when he came across the word *what*. He couldn't identify it but said it was in one of his stories. He got his writing folder, found the appropriate story among four in the folder, found the right page, noted the word, and went back to his book. This took ten minutes, but he did not feel rushed. He wanted to figure the problem out for himself.
Like the other children in the class, he had confidence in his ability to learn how to read.

Process Conferences

The process conferences provide the thread that runs through all of the conferences. Although initiating, comprehension, skills, and process conferences may occur at different times, the teacher weaves process questions into all of them. The teacher does so to encourage children to talk about what they do. If children are to take the responsibility for their learning, they need to recognize why and how they make decisions about their learning activities, and the teacher's questioning them about the process in which they engage helps them to learn why and how they make decisions as well as why and how they might make better ones.

In writing conferences they talk about what makes a good topic or, in reading conferences, about what would be a good book to choose. They learn that writers write best when they write about something they know well. They know that writing begins with having something to write about; they think about writing on Saturdays when their family goes bottle digging. Some of the titles of their writing illustrate their topics: My Cold, Watching My Baby Sister Get Born, My Cousin Lisa, My Dad's Truck, My Broken Arm, and My Loose Tooth. When I asked one of the children what makes a good writer, the answer was, "Someone who does lots of things. I don't mean in school. We all do the same things in school. I mean on the weekends."

Similarly they choose their reading materials and reading method with an awareness of their needs. They select their reading materials—their own stories, the published stories of other children, basals, trade books, and books at the listening center—based upon their current interests. Often they choose to learn how to read stories they have heard before:

"Why did you pick 'Rabbit and Skunk' "?

"Because Amanda read it to me so I know the story. It helps to learn the words if you know the story."

As they evolve their own plans for their own reading programs, they plan with three books on their mind—one they can read well and enjoy reading over and over again; one they are working on; and one they intend to learn to read next. They know that in order to learn how to read they need to review, practice new stories, and try harder ones. And they decide when to read alone, when to read with a partner, and when to read in a group. If a child intends to learn how to read a new story and thinks it will be somewhat difficult, he often wisely chooses to read with a partner.

Children in this classroom talk about why different people understand things differently.

One day Randy explained how terrible the child in a story must have felt, "Well, I know of a time when I felt sad, and I REALLY felt sad."

"When was that?"

"When my dad moved out."

Another boy told a sad story about when his family used to live in Alaska. Then a third boy told about how he gets upset when his little sister messes up his things. Finally I asked Randy whether all children would be thinking about the same things when they read. Of course, he said they wouldn't; and of course, I asked why not.

"Because different things happen to all of us so the stories mean different things to all of us."

And within the skills conferences the children talk about how to use the skills. One day when Susan had chosen to read a published book of Reggie's, Ms. Blackburn asked her, "What will you do if you get stuck?"

"I'll sound it out."
"What will you do if you can't sound it out?"
"Ask Marie (the best reader among the girls)."
"Would you ask George?"
"Yep. He wrote it so he SHOULD know the words."

Because these children are in an environment where everyone talks, writes, and reads, they pursue composing with zest. It's the thing to do. They approach blank pieces of paper with ideas and they approach books with ideas. Print is accessible to them. They know where it comes from. The words on the pages of books are someone's story. That author has something to share. It is probably interesting and it would be fun to find out what it is.

One day Randy had read *The Three Little Pigs* to me from his basal. I asked him what he planned to learn how to read next.

"I don't know," he answered softly and wandered off across the room. Later, when I was leaving for the day, he cornered me, "I'm planning what I want to learn to read next. I'll have something to read to you next time you come."

The next time I arrived he greeted me, "Hey Mrs. Hansen, I have a book I'm learning how to read!"

When he finished *More Spaghetti, I say!* I asked, "Are you going to continue learning how to read this or are you going to go on to something else?"

"Oh, I'm going to finish learning how to read this. I don't know it too good yet. Then I'll learn how to read some others. You know Mrs. Hansen, there are only three months of school left!"

A few days later, Randy sought me out in the classroom, "I can read it excellent now. Wanna hear it?"

25 Writing About Reading

Mike Torbe
Local Education Authority, Coventry, England

There is reading; and there is writing. There is writing about reading, and whatever is written has been, and will be, read by someone, even if it is only the writer. The print in a book is the product of one person's imprinting blank paper with meanings that echo in a reader's mind in unpredictable ways; and one effect of that encounter between written word and mind may be that the reader wants to write something, too. Not always *write,* of course. Very often, *talk* is enough. Clayton, a 9 year-old-boy, is talking to his teachers:

> I'll always read story books. I'll never finish the story book, cos (sic) over the past 6 years I've read 700 books different, all different books, and about 300 all the same book over and over again. . . . I still read *Watership Down.* I read it last night. . . . At the beginning it seems ever so exciting, but when you get to the last page (of the first chapter) it seems all sad and horrible because of all the poison and all that. . . .

Clayton couldn't have written that. He had to talk it. When he was asked to write a book review, he could only write this:

> I have read *Watership Down.* It is a good book, it is exciting.

Because the form of the book review is one that no child would naturally choose, he cannot produce the easy flow of language so obvious in his talk. But writing about reading need not be like that. Clayton can write very differently when the form is one that allows him to say what he needs to. Puzzled by a key element in the book, he wrote to the author, Richard Adams.

> Dear Richard,
> I like your book Watership Down. Why do you call Hazel the Captain of all the rabbit who left the warren why don't you call Bigwig the captain.
> Yours sincerely,
> Clayton (8)

And when the cartoon film of *Watership Down* came to town, Clayton designed and made a poster advertising the film, to encourage all his school friends to share his enthusiasm. In these pieces of writing, he was able to express some of his feelings about what he had read.

The interaction between reading and writing is mysterious, but if we recognize what spontaneous language uses follow from our reading, then we can see what kinds of writing may enable readers to tap their responses to reading. I want to explore five types of inevitable processes of reading and understanding—*rehearsal, commentary, associative anecdotes, thinking aloud, enacting consciousness*—and to look at the writing that may go alongside them.

Leigh, a 13-year-old girl, shows us the most typical and familiar kind of writing about books, which is also representative of the most basic process—*rehearsal.* She does what we all do after an experience—she relives it by retelling it, partly for herself, enjoying the good bits. Her entry in her work diary for her teacher (and for herself) begins like this:

> I've recently read a book called *The Lotus Caves* by—I think his name was John Christopher. It's about two boys who live on the moon in a confined bubble and they decide to go and explore first base where the living quarters are, and they find a diary of a man who had disappeared. . . .

She continues by outlining the peak episodes of the story—rehearsing it and thus enjoying it again.

Paul, who is also 13, seems at first to be doing the same thing in his writing which is also a diary entry; but he is doing something more. He is offering a *commentary* on his reactions, capturing fleeting thoughts, and his language is, so to speak, transparent: One is conscious of what he is saying, not of how he is saying it.

> Today we finished *The Island of the Blue Dolphins,* and for me it was a relief that she had got off the island. I thought the book was over detailed. Every little movement Karana made was logged and spelled out. The book also lacked much action and I don't think I would have given it the Newberry Medal (Torbe, 1980).

Paul's diary entry seems recognizable to us as a child's writing, and we might assume it is a response and a kind of writing that we grow out of as we get older. But here is a mature, highly sophisticated university lecturer, musing on his own reading in precisely the same way, suggesting that the process of reflecting on response and trying to account for it is basic to all readers. He has read Rosemary Sutcliff's *Song for a Dark Queen.*

> Now this is frightening. The book won the Other Award. Why? Boudicca is a victim—raped, humiliated or insulted somehow by Romans who, being patriarchs, don't recognize her as Queen rather than widowed consort of Iceni—but her suffering makes her wicked . . . I saw it as frightening portent of British civil unrest. . . .

If we stay with another adult for a moment, we can see another characteristic response, in which what one reads subtly affects and controls what one writes, and *why* one might write. Kath is a mature student and has been reading Hemingway. Her log book has begun with general comments, but gathers intensity as the reading bites deep into her personal memories. Finally, she seems to forget the book, but in fact writes a cluster of *associative anecdotes* as a direct consequence of her reading, and as a way of testing the novel against her own life.

> I first read *The Sun Also Rises* when I was 17 (1949) and on the fringes of a similar group in Brighton, the most marked difference being their lack of money.
>   My involvement began quite simply by being picked up. A girl friend and I were waiting for our dates in the bar of the Pavilion Hotel one evening. . . .

These first kinds of writing—*rehearsal, commentary,* and *associative anecdote*— are all reflective. The writing serves to sort out thoughts, associations, and responses, and organize them for the reader. But there are other kinds of writing, much more enactive, writing which follows closely the contours of the mind, echoing the processes of understanding at the point of encounter with a text. An example is the *thinking aloud* that Meriel, who is 17, shows us here. She is faced with a Blake poem, *"The Garden of Love,"* which she has never seen before, invited to read it, and whenever she stopped or paused in her reading, to write down precisely what was in her mind at that moment. She numbers what she writes each time she stops. She wrote eight comments: I quote only the first five:

1. I find that I do not really understand the poem properly. If I read it again, it might help.
2. It's a very imaginative piece of writing. But I still cannot quite figure it out. My thoughts at the moment are all very confused.
3. This is the first time I have ever written my thoughts aloud quite like this.
4. I've been thinking what on earth I'm going to write about this poem.
5. I like the way it is written and the sort of words it uses. I find the whole poem a bit of a mystery and though I hate to say it a bit boring. That is probably because I can't tell what the author is trying to put over to me.

The writing is serving Meriel as a way in which she can learn about her response. The act of writing helps her to see what her response actually *is*. When she sees her own thoughts written down, she is so struck that she comments on that rather than on the poem. Writing like this, she is not only learning about the poem, and about her response to it, but is on the verge of discovering the power of writing as a process of learning, writing as a systematic way of inspecting your own thoughts.

This idea of interrupted reading, and of writing a commentary upon the process of reading and understanding, represents an important way of helping students to control their own reading and writing. A similar, but more refined, technique is shown in the next example, in which Cowper's poem *"The Poplar Field"* was presented to fourteen-year-old students piece by piece, first the opening two lines, then the whole of the first verse, the first two verses, and so on. The students were instructed: "Write down what you think that bit of the poem means, and anything the poem makes you think of. If you want to ask questions, write them down as well." Here is the opening verse.

> The poplars are fell'd: farewell to the shade,
> And the whispering sound of the cool colonnade!
> The winds play no longer and sing in the leaves,
> Nor Ouse on his bosom their image receives.

Here is what Stephanie wrote. Her writing gathers intensity as the meaning of the poem seeps in to her *consciousness:* she is not able fully to articulate that meaning, but she is *enacting* it in her own way. I cite her first two pages only, for brevity's sake. She is not too sure at first what a "poplar" is, and in fact when she worked it out (on her page 5) went back over what she had written. Her second thoughts are printed in bold-face.

1. What does poplar mean?
   The scenery is brightening up, the sun's coming out, and in the background the sound of the breeze. **Reminds me when a heavy shower has slowly withdrawn and the sun is starting to peer through shining on the ground, making shadows fall away.**
2. The air is silent, motionless, like a picture taken when everything is still. The river reflects the scenes of the trees, like a clear mirror. **But now the trees are felled there is no image reflecting in the river.**

The rhythms of her writing show her catching at the feelings at the heart of the poem. Though she is not yet able to express them as literary criticism, she is able to make her own writing re-enact those feelings. She transforms, for example, 'Nor Ouse on his bosom their image receives' into her own elegant version— 'like a clear mirror', and shows how a reader's response can pay homage to the power of the original by imitating its style or tone.

To conclude then. I am suggesting that these five processes are common, in some form or other, to most readers who want to respond in language to what they have read. Of course, not everyone does want to respond like that. Some readers always, and all readers sometimes, do not want to say or write anything about their current reading; but because these five processes, of rehearsal, commentary, anecdoting, thinking aloud, and enacting consciousness, seem to be natural kinds of response, they also represent natural ways for us to write about our responses when we want to, or have to.

They fall into groups, one of which I am defining as reflective, the other as enactive. They represent, I believe, mental activities which we engage in whenever we read either in talk or in that silent talk inside the head which is one kind of thought. Because they are so natural and perhaps inevitable, when we introduce our students to them, we can show that writing in certain ways can tap intellectual processes directly. Then the students discover not only that they are able to write in ways they did not know they were capable of, but also that the act of writing has an effect on their understanding of what they read. Writing about reading in these ways deepens and extends the students' response and understanding, and makes it possible for them to move on to the more public and formal modes of critical writing.

All these examples involve the reading of literature. Similar processes, and similar uses of writing can be applied to the reading of non-fiction. But that is perhaps another essay altogether.

26 How We Construe Is How We Construct*

Ann E. Berthoff
Department of English, University of Massachusetts, Boston

Literature has lately been exiled from many a composition classroom and for reasons which are all legitimate (in one way or another) and all pernicious. One doctrinaire contention is that the students' own writing should supplant literature because students can learn best how to write by learning to read what they and their classmates have written, treating their writing as they would printed texts. Some hold that there is simply not enough time to teach both reading and

*The philosophical argument for the claims made here about the centrality of interpretation is developed in *The Making of Meaning: Metaphors, Models, and Maxims for Writing Teachers* (Boynton/Cook, 1981). The "dialectical notebook" is described at length in *Forming/Thinking/Writing: The Composing Imagination* (Boynton/Cook, 1978).

writing. And there is a strong conviction among composition specialists that no writing teacher should be permitted to teach literature because all writing teachers, even those certified as composition specialists, are literature teachers in disguise; and, since their first loyalties are to the printed page, to poems and stories by authenticated writers, they will—given half a chance—desert the spurious for the real. The assumption seems to be that in teaching literature the teacher would be engaged in an enterprise which has nothing whatsoever to do with composition and, furthermore, that the only role literature could possibly play in the writing class is to provide prose models for imitation or to generate topics. It follows that if there is to be any reading in the composition classroom other than that of student texts, it should be of informational articles written in that "effective" prose proclaimed by rhetoricians as ideal, identifiable by its high readability rating and its decidedly unliterary character.

It is a delusion, however, to think that reading that kind of expository writing will necessarily teach those who read it how to write it. I like to remind my colleagues that when T. R. Henn, a Yeats scholar, was asked shortly after the Second World War to do something about the problems science undergraduates were having with their writing at Cambridge University, he chose to teach them to read tough poems.

The point is that critical reading can be a way of coming to know, of learning to learn and thus discovering some important things about writing, but *only* if it is taught as a means of making meaning. Arguably, that approach is most profitable when what is read is worth the trouble, when the text is literary. Even more crucial than the character of the text, though, is the *method* of teaching critical reading. Calling literature back from exile is fatuous if the reason is only that the "message" is more valuable than that of a *Reader's Digest* selection: The heuristic power of literature will not be released by asking "What is the author trying to say?" That non-question is generally matched by others: "What do you want to say?" "Who is your audience?" "Where is your thesis statement?" Literature taught as dressed-up message and writing taught as effective communication deserve one another.

Critical reading can replenish a student's repertory of syntactical structures and can create an interest in ways of deploying them; it can awaken the moribund auditory imagination, the chief cause of sentence errors. But the centrally important reasons for returning literature to the composition classroom is that it is a form of knowledge. The critical reading of literature can turn on the mind to it its own powers of making meaning; it is the best means we have of raising consciousness of the heuristic powers of language itself. If we can teach reading so that the mind is actively engaged in seeing "how words work" (I. A. Richards' definition of rhetoric), anything and everything that is learned in reading will be transferable to learning to write. The reason is that how we construe is how we construct.

Positivists enjoy derailing the argument I've been making by wearily noting that "literature" is hard to define; that some people might consider the instructions for cleaning a fish tank as beautifully textured as any poem; that students should not have to suffer the tyranny of their teachers' conceptions of just what is literature and what is not. The answer which must be vigorously returned to the weary positivists and others who see such skepticism as the true scientific spirit is that real scientists don't agree with them. As Robert Oppenheimer puts it, Einstein did not sit pondering the question "What is a clock?" Real scientists do not contemplate the meaning of such concepts as *Life* and *Time* and *Purpose;* they form hypotheses which they then test experimentally. I suggest that we follow the procedure set forth by C. S. Lewis in that excellent little book which all reading and writing teachers should read and re-read, *An Experiment in Criticism.* Lewis says that instead of declaring that we must read literature in a certain way, we should take as our premise that what we read in a certain way is literature. Put the fish tank instructions on the reading list if they can be read rigorously, energetically, thoughtfully, heuristically. Paulo Freire shows us how we can indeed convert anything to a genuine "text"—pictures, lists, aphorisms, slogans—by raising consciousness about the ways meaning is being made.

Constructing and construing: at the heart of both reading and writing is interpretation, which is a matter of seeing what goes with what, how this goes with that. Interpretation is a process analogous in many important respects to what we do when we make sense of the world. It has survival value: We and all our fellow creatures must interpret in order to stay alive. The difference between them and us is language: It is language that enables us to go beyond interpreting, to interpret our interpretations. This spiralling circularity empowers all the activities of mind involved in making meaning. We continually use meanings to find other meanings, use forms to find forms, use whatever intellectual activity in which we are engaged to find other intellectual activities. This is what I. A. Richards meant when he said that "all studies are language studies, concerned with the speculative instruments they employ." Our speculative instruments are the ideas we depend on in order to interpret our interpretations. They are our means of making meaning, in writing as in reading. Keeping reading and writing together will enable us to teach interpretation, to take as our point of departure what Vygotsky calls "the unit of meaning." That way, to strengthen one kind of meaning-making will be to strengthen the other.

I believe, with I. A. Richards, that what our students need most when they are studying English is "assisted invitations to find out what they are doing and thereby how to do it." What that means is that consciousness in reading and writing is not a debilitating self-consciousness but a method of thinking about thinking. Language is not just "verbal behavior" and it is not adequately modeled by motor skills. Language is our means of form-finding and form-creating, and it involves us in looking and looking again; in stating and re-stating; in trying out many how's to go with many what's. When we see forming as an activity of mind central to both reading and writing, we will have no difficulty finding ways to keep reading and writing together.

In this enterprise of teaching reading and writing as ways of making meaning, ways of interpreting our interpretations, the emphasis will have to be on process. That self-evident premise is not helping us as it should because we rarely develop pedagogies which are consonant with the kind of processes which reading and writing are. Reading cannot be represented by linear models derived from the way the computer processes "information" or the way we memorize nonsense syllables, any more than the composing process can be represented by such linear models as "Prewriting–Writing–Rewriting" or "Writer-based Prose–Reader-based Prose." We need ways of making the dialectical character of reading and writing apparent. We need models (and images) of the ways our expectations guide what we think we are reading, of the ways that "feedforward" (Richards) shapes the emergent meanings we are forming.

Let me suggest a way to get the dialectic going. I ask my students–all of them–freshmen, upperclass students, teachers in graduate seminars–to furnish themselves with a notebook, spiralbound at one side, small enough to be easily carried around but not so small that their writing is cramped. (School teachers who have tried this idea tell me, however, that their students insist on a note-book that will fit into the back pocket of their jeans.) What makes this note-book different from most, perhaps, is the notion of the double entry: On one side, reading notes, direct quotations, observational notes, fragments, images–verbal and visual–are recorded; on the facing side, notes about those notes, summaries, formulations, questions and queries and mumbles, editorial revisions, comments on comments are written. The double-entry format provides a way for the student to conduct that "continuing audit of meaning," which is Richards' name for the activity at the heart of learning to read and write critically. The facing pages are in dialogue with one another.

The dialectical notebook is for all kinds of writing, creative and critical; any assignment you can think up can be adapted so that it can teach dialectic. Suppose you want your students to read some nature poems. The writing assigned could be a record of ten minutes of observation and meditation carried out daily over a period of a week–descriptions and speculations in response to a seashell, a milkweed pod, a garlic bud, a chestnut bur, or any natural object (the odder the better) that can serve as a "text": Reading the Book of Nature is probably the oldest writing assignment in the world. Each day's writing should begin with re-reading the notes from the day before and writing a recapitulation of critical comment on the facing page. At the week's end, two paragraphs are assigned: (1) a description of the object, based on the right-hand entries; (2) a comment on the process of observing and interpreting, based on the left-hand side. Writers should be encouraged to move freely from one side to the other, from notes to recapitulations and back again, interpreting as they go.

Meanwhile, a poem could be assigned for study in another section of the double-entry journal, to be read and contemplated and responded to dialectally. On alternate days perhaps the pine cone or crab shell could be responded to dialectically. (The poem should not be about the object.) New poems might emerge and new ways of reading surely will. This kind of writing will encourage students to set aside the non-question "What is the author trying to say?" in favor of critical questions about what has been made. They can learn the art of interpretive paraphrase: "How does it change the meaning when I put it this way?" By teaching that how we construe is how we construct, the double-entry notebook assures that whatever is learned about reading is something learned about writing and that looking again will come to be seen as the way into interpretation.

In my opinion, the best texts for these purposes are those which demand that we read them as literature. To make this point, I juxtapose, for instance, Gerard

Manley Hopkins' "Inversnaid" with the Baedeker description of the same land-scape. After a couple of weeks with their dialectical notebooks, students feel a kinship with Hopkins because they have been discovering for themselves some-thing about the power of language—of words and images, metaphors and syn-tactical structures, of rhythm, rime, cadence, and so on. They come to see reading as a process of making meaning, discovering in their own parallel compos-ing how sources, constraints, emergent purposes work to find and create forms. These discoveries become their speculative instruments, fit for exploring the literary text which serves as the point of departure and promises safe return.

27 On Essaying

James Moffett
Consultant in Education, Mariposa, California

While doing summer institutes on writing I have frequently encountered teach-ers who will call every kind of writing that is not book-report, term-paper, essay-question stuff "personal" or "creative" writing (the two terms being interchangeable) and hence put it in a big bag that goes up on the shelf. Pri-ority goes of course to "exposition," which is equated with "essay," which is equated in turn with forced writing on given topics from books, lectures, or "current issues." In these institutes with teachers I break a class into trios in which members help each other, over several weeks, to develop subjects and techniques by hearing or reading partners' writing ideas at various stages of work-ing up the material. Some of this material is gleaned from memory, some is information obtained fresh by interviewing or observing, and some is feeling, thought, or imagination elicited suddenly by a stimulus such as a tune or other in-class presentation. The material may take the form of stories, dialogs, essays, or songs and poems. It soon becomes obvious that ideas stem from all kinds of material and take all kinds of forms and that the very limited sort of exposition used for testing enjoys no monopoly on intellectual activity; participants can see, often with astonishment, how loaded with ideas is this rich variety of writing they have produced.

When schools narrow the notion of essay to fit it to editing, they are violat-ing the whole tradition of the genre from its very inception to the present. College composition instructors and anthologists of essays have doted for years on George Orwell's "Shooting an Elephant," which they hold up to students as a model of essay or "expository writing." Please look closely at it even if you think you know it well; if a student wrote it, it would be called "personal writ-ing," that is, soft and non-intellectual. Orwell narrated in first person how as a British civil servant in Burma he was intimidated by villagers into shooting an elephant against his will. But so effectively does he say what happens by telling what happened that the force of his theme—the individual's moral choice whether or not to conform to the group—leaves us with the impression that the memoir is "expository,"—that is chiefly cast in the present tense of generalization and in third person. What we really want to help youngsters learn is how to express ideas of universal value in a personal voice. Fables, parables, poems and songs, fiction and memoir may convey ideas as well as or better than editorials and critiques. Orwell does indeed provide a fine model, but teachers should not let prejudice fool them into misunderstanding the actual kind of discourse in which he wrote "Shooting an Elephant" and other excellent essays, for this leads to a confusing double standard whereby we ask students to emulate a great writer but to do it in another form.

The Essay: An Attempt

Orwell wrote deep in a tradition of English letters, honoring the essay as a candid blend of personal and universal. It was resurrected if not invented during the Renaissance by Montaigne, who coined the term essai from essayer, to attempt. From his position of philosophical skepticism ("What do I know?") he saw his writing as personal attempts to discover truth, what he thought and what could be thought, in exactly the same sense that Donald Murray or Janet Emig or I myself might speak of writing as discovery. From Burton's *Anatomy of Melancholy* and Browne's *Urn Burial;* Addison's and Steele's *Spectator* articles; through the essays of Swift, Lamb, Hazlitt, and DeQuincey to those of Orwell, Virginia Woolf, Joan Didion, and Norman Mailer, English literature has maintained a marvelous tradition, fusing personal experience, private vision, and downright eccentricity, with intellectual vigor and verbal objectification. In color, depth, and stylistic originality it rivals some of our best poetry. Look back over Hazlitt's "The Fight" and compare it with Mailer's intellectual reportage of the Ali-Frazier fight in *King of the Hill* or "On the Feeling of Immortality in Youth" or "On Familiar Style"; DeQuincey's "Confessions of an Opium Eater" or "On the Knocking at the Gate in *Macbeth*," which begins: "From my boyish days I had always felt a great perplexity on one point in *Macbeth*"; or Lamb's "The Two Races of Men," "Poor Relations," or "On Sanity of True Genius." Consider too a book like Henry Adams's *Education of Henry Adams* for its simultaneous treatment of personal and national or historical.

Some essayists, like Montaigne and Emerson, tend toward generality, as reflected in titles like "Friendship" or "Self-Reliance," but tone and source are personal, and we cannot doubt the clear kinship between essays featuring memoir or eyewitness reportage and those of generality, for the same writers do both, sometimes in a single essay, sometimes in separate pieces; and Lamb and Thoreau stand in the same relation to Montaigne and Emerson as fable to moral or parable to proverb. The difference lies not in the fundamental approach, which is in any case personal, but in the degree of explicitness of the theme. "I bear within me the exemplar of the human condition," said Montaigne. Descending deep enough within, the essayist links up personal with universal, self with self.

Writing and Reading

These essayists frequently write about their reading, and they love reading. They set, in fact, a model for writing about reading that is very different from writing-as-testing, because they have selected what to read according to their own ongoing pursuits, and, because they cite ideas and instances from books in mixture with ideas and instances drawn from everyday experience, thus fusing life with literature. Many openly framed assignments that I have long advocated will elicit from students exactly the kinds of essays that constitute our fine heritage in this flexible form. They call for the writer to crystallize memories, capture places, "write a narrative of any sort that makes a general point applying beyond the particular material," "put together three or four incidents drawn from life or reading that all seem to show the same thing, that are connected in your mind by some idea," or "make a general statement about something you have observed to be true, illustrating that truth by referring to events and situations you know or have read of." The point is to leave subject matter to the writer, including reading selections. Any student who has done such assignments will be better able, strictly as a bonus, to cough up some prose to show he has done his homework than if he has been especially trained to write about reading.

Transpersonal, Not Impersonal

Schools mistreat writing because the society suffers at the moment from drastic misunderstandings about the nature of knowledge. Applying "scientific" criteria that would be unacceptable to most real scientists making the breakthroughs out there on the frontier, many people have come to think that subtracting the self makes for objectivity and validity. But depersonalization is not impartiality. It is, quite literally, madness. Einstein said, "The observer is the essence of the situation." It is not by abandoning the self but by developing it that we achieve impartiality and validity. The deeper we go consciously into ourselves, the better chance we have of reaching universality, as Montaigne knew so well. Transpersonal, not impersonal. It is an undeterred faith in this that makes a great writer cultivate his individuality until others feel he speaks for them better than they do themselves. Teachers should be the first to understand this misunderstanding and to start undoing it, so that schooling in general and writing in particular can offset rather than reinforce the problem.

Here are two examples of what we're up against—one from a famous current encyclopedia and one from a leading publisher, typical and telling symptoms. Most English majors probably sampled or at least heard of Sir Thomas Browne, a very individualistic seventeenth-century master of an original prose style, a writer's writer much admired by successors. Of his *Pseudodoxia Epidemica* Funk and Wagnalls *Standard Reference Encyclopedia* says, "Its unscientific approach and odd assemblage of obscure facts typify his haphazard erudition," and then concludes the entry: "Despite Browne's deficiencies as a thinker his style entitles him to high rank among the masters of English prose." What this verdict tells me is that the writer of that entry felt overwhelmed by all the books Browne had read that he had not and that he knew far less than he should have known about the enormously important and complex networks of thought and knowledge, called esoteric, that after several millenia of evolution still had great influence on Newton, Bacon, and Descartes (who displayed at times equally "irrational" intellectual behavior). The encyclopediast's judgment on such a writer as Browne is nothing but smart-ass chauvinism: permitted to poison basic information sources, it makes "science" as deadly a censor as ever the Church was during its Inquisition.

We can avoid producing Brownes in our school system by having all youngsters read and write the same things—a goal we have closely approximated—and then their approach will not be unscientific, their assemblage odd, their facts obscure, nor their erudition haphazard. And we will have ensured that no one will be able to emulate the great essayists we hold up as models (or even read them with any comprehension). Real essaying cannot thrive without cultivation of the individual. Who would have any reason to read anyone else? (And I want to know how Browne's style could be worth so much if he were merely raving.)

The second example is personal. When I received the edited manuscript of the original edition of *Student-Centered Language Arts and Reading, K-13* back from the publisher, I was aghast. "My" editor had rewritten sentences throughout the whole book to eliminate first-person references and other elements of the author's presence and voice. This included altering diction and sentence structure at times to get a more anonymous or distanced effect. Faced with the appalling labor of restoring all those sentences, I called the editor, furious. She said righteously, "But we always do that—it's policy." It never occurred to her to exempt, or even to warn, an author who wouldn't be publishing the book in the first place if he weren't regarded as some kind of expert in writing.

Remove the Double Standard

You can't trust your encyclopedia, your publisher, your school administration. And you can't trust yourself until you learn to spot how you too may be spreading the plague, as Camus calls it. The double standard in "Look at the greats, but don't do what they did" naturally goes along with our era of Scientific Inquisition, which is really technocratic plague. Teachers stand in a fine position to spread infection. If you let yourself be convinced that "personal" or "creative" writing is merely narcissistic, self-indulgent, and weak-minded, then you have just removed your own first person.

28 Imitation and the Teaching of Style

Frank J. D'Angelo
Department of English, Arizona State University

It may seem incongruous for someone who has written a text entitled *Process and Thought in Composition* to advocate an approach to writing that stresses the imitation of models. The imitation of models suggests a product approach to the teaching of writing, whereas a heuristic approach puts the emphasis on the process. This seeming dichotomy is not a real one, however, for the imitation of models mediates between process and product.

What is imitated is not merely the form or structure of the original model, but more importantly the grammatical and rhetorical principles that underlie the structure of the model. These principles are the elements that model the writer's cognitive processes. They are analogs of the composing process.

Imitation is a process that focuses the writer's attention on the "literalness" of the writing activity. This literalness is one of the meanings we give to literacy. But it is also a process that enables a writer to go beyond the letter, so that the principles a student learns in imitating models can be applied to other kinds of writing tasks. To teach students to imitate, then, is to teach them to make full use of literacy, that is, to participate fully in the processes of reading and writing.

In this paper, I would like to discuss some strategies that teachers might use to teach imitation in the classroom and that students might find useful to develop their skills in reading and writing. These strategies consist of a close reading of the model, followed by an intensive study of the features of the text, and two kinds of writing assignments—stylistic analyses and imitation exercises.

Close Reading

I ask students to read the model carefully before coming to class, making annotations on their copies of the model. In class, we reread the selection. Then, I proceed inductively, asking questions about the context, the dominant tone, point of view, arrangement, sentence structure, diction, and so forth. I encourage students to relate the various features of style to the writer's intention. I also guide students into a discussion of the effect that a stylistic feature has upon meaning, tone, or dominant impression.

We use short selections from literary works, such as the opening paragraph of Harper Lee's novel *To Kill a Mockingbird* or the opening paragraph of Stephen Crane's "The Open Boat," but from time to time I will introduce non-fiction models such as "The Emerald Tree Boa" from *Snakes of the World,* "The Crumbs of One Man's Years" from Dylan Thomas's *Quite Early One Morning,* or "The Scoliae" from J. Henri Fabre's *More Hunting Wasps,* especially models that may be similar in form, but different in rhetorical purpose. For example, I may pair a non-fiction narrative, such as W. H. Hudson's account of his encounter with a snake when he was a young boy, in *Far Away and Long Ago,* with a fictional narrative, such as the passage in Marjorie Kinnan Rawlings's novel *The Yearling* where Jody encounters two bears. In both of these narratives, the writer focuses first on the action, then on the observer's reactions to the action. This kind of pairing raises interesting questions about genre, technique, and intention.

Each model is selected because it has certain characteristics of arrangement or style that might reward our study. For example, I use the following selection from Ray Bradbury's "A Sound of Thunder" which emphasizes the cumulative sentence, concrete and specific diction, and the extensive use of figurative language. The passage is organized skillfully in space and in time. In this passage, a dinosaur (Tyrannosaurus Rex) is seen by a group of hunters from a distance where it looms above the trees. When it moves in close, Bradbury describes it in great detail, moving from the legs, to the thighs, to the cage of the upper body, to the head itself, and then within the head, the mouth, the teeth, and the eyes. The beast then moves off "into a sunlit arena . . . with a gliding ballet step."

It came on great oiled, resilient, striding legs. It towered thirty feet over half of the trees, a great evil god, folding its delicate watchmaker's claws close to its oily reptilian chest. Each lower leg was a piston, a thousand pounds of white bone, sunk in thick ropes of muscle, sheathed over in a gleam of pebbled skin like the mail of a terrible warrior. Each thigh was a ton of meat, ivory, and steel mesh. And from the great breathing cage of the upper body those two delicate arms dangled out front, arms with hands which might pick up and examine men like toys, while the snake neck coiled. And the head itself, a ton of sculptured stone, lifted easily upon the sky. Its mouth gaped, exposing a fence of teeth like daggers. Its eyes rolled, ostrich eggs, empty of all expression save hunger. It closed its mouth in a death grin. It ran, its pelvic bones crushing aside trees and bushes, its taloned feet clawing damp earth, leaving prints six inches deep wherever it settled its weight. It ran with a gliding ballet step, far too poised and balanced for its ten tons. It moved into a sunlit arena warily, its beautifully reptile hands feeling the air.

From *A Sound of Thunder* by Ray Bradbury

This is a masterful description by Ray Bradbury, one that will repay a detailed analysis with your students.

To illustrate the balanced sentence, I use the opening paragraph of Harper Lee's *To Kill a Mockingbird.* To illustrate abstract and impressionistic diction, Latinate words, and archaic words, almost anything by Edgar Allan Poe will do. I have used passages from "The Fall of the House of Usher" and "The Island of the Fay" with great success. I have also used passages from Joseph Conrad's "The Lagoon" to illustrate impressionistic diction, sentence rhythm, and sound devices. I use certain passages from Virginia Woolf's *The Waves* in which there is a "riot" of metaphor. In brief, I try to lead students through an intensive analysis of style to get them to realize that the same principles of style *can be found in any kind of discourse.* Their use and their effect, of course, will vary as their context and the writer's intention varies.

This kind of close reading and analysis provides *material* for the stylistic analysis papers that they will subsequently do. It also provides the rhetorical *means* for a second kind of writing, the imitation of models. In this kind of class, teachers and students use a *subject-specific heuristic* rather than a more general heuristic such as the tagmemic heuristic. The heuristics implicit in our teaching are not always clear to our students, so this is one way of our being explicit about what we do. Both kinds of heuristics are important, but in imitation exercises, we aim at something more specific and limited.

Stylistic Analysis

After a class period or two, I give the first kind of writing assignment, a stylistic analysis of the features of the model. The purpose of this assignment is to insure that students *understand* the rhetorical and grammatical principles that they will subsequently *use* in their imitations. Another purpose is to reinforce their reading skills, since they must necessarily read the model carefully in order to write about it. To help them write this paper, I suggest strategies they might use for dealing with the context, the tone, the stylistic features, etc. In brief, I introduce them to the conventions of doing this kind of writing.

Guidelines for Writing a Stylistic Analysis

1. Provide a *context* for the discussion of style:
   a. Mention the author's name, title of selection, etc.
   b. Give any other background information that may be needed.
2. Make a *general introductory statement* about the overall effectiveness, or lack of effectiveness, of the style.
3. Make *other general statements* as needed.
4. Discuss the *dominant impression* of the passage as a whole, its *structure,* and *meaning.*
5. Take up one *feature* of style at a time:
   a. Use a single paragraph for each feature.
   b. Or combine several related features in a single paragraph.
6. Give *examples* of these features by quoting from the text or by paraphrasing.
   a. Incorporate examples into your own text.
   b. Offset the examples.
7. Discuss the *effect* of the stylistic features on meaning, tone, rhythm, etc.
8. Conclude with some general remarks about the effectiveness of the style, summarize, etc.

To illustrate how students carry out the assignment, I am reproducing a passage from Poe's "The Fall of the House of Usher," followed by a stylistic analysis of the passage by one of my students:

During the whole of a dull, dark, and soundless day in the autumn of the year, when the clouds hung oppressively low in the heavens, I had been passing alone, on horseback, through a singularly dreary tract of country; and at length found myself, as the shades of the evening drew on, within view of the melancholy House of Usher. I know not how it was—but, with the first glimpse of the building, a sense of insufferable gloom pervaded my spirit. I say insufferable; for the feeling was unrelieved by any of that half-pleasurable, because poetic, sentiment, with which the mind usually receives even the sternest natural images of the desolate or terrible. I looked upon the scene before me—upon the mere house, and the simple landscape features of the domain, upon the bleak walls, upon the vacant eyelike windows, upon a few rank sedges, and upon a few white trunks of decayed trees—with an utter depression of soul which I can compare to no earthly sensation more properly than to the after-dream of the reveller upon opium: the bitter lapse into everyday life, the hideous dropping off of the veil. There was an iciness, a sinking, a sickening of the heart, an unredeemed dreariness of thought which no goading of the imagination could torture into aught of the sublime. What was it—I paused to think—what was it that so unnerved me in the contemplation of the House of Usher?

Stylistic Analysis of Poe's "The Fall of the House of Usher"

Susan Horn

The opening passage of "The Fall of the House of Usher," a horrifying tale by Edgar Allan Poe, establishes the undeniable sense of gloom and depression which permeates the entire story. The story begins with a single horse and rider approaching the House of Usher, the home of Roderick Usher and his sister, and the setting for Poe's tale of terror and insanity.

Poe sets the tone for the passage through a variety of devices, one being the sentence structure. He uses extremely long sentences to create a feeling of endlessness and rambling. Although the average length is 40.8 words, each sentence is unique. There is no dominant sentence type. Instead, a wide assortment is used:

Sentence 1 . . . . . . periodic
        2 . . . . . . periodic
        3 . . . . . . loose
        4 . . . . . . balanced
        5 . . . . . . balanced
        6 . . . . . . rhetorical question

This irregularity establishes a sense of uneasiness and distress, the same feeling that the narrator experiences.

Diction is another method that Poe uses to express emotion. Details such as "the clouds hung oppressively low," "a singularly dreary tract of country," and "the melancholy House of Usher" are abstract and impressionistic. They don't describe the environment; rather, they characterize the feelings of the narrator. Poe projects the narrator's sentiments onto inanimate objects such as the clouds, the countryside, and the house, thus creating the identical sensations in the reader. He also describes the surroundings with words that are uncommon and even archaic. "Domain," "reveller," and "aught" build an impression of antiquity in the reader's mind. An eerie sense of gloom accompanies these terms that are reminiscent of the Gothic, further developing an atmosphere of dreariness and uneasiness. This atmosphere is compounded by the abundance of negative and depressing details. For example, phrases such as

a *dull, dark,* and *soundless* day,
bleak walls, *vacant* eyelike windows, *rank* sedges
the *bitter* lapse into everyday life
no *goading* of the imagination could *torture*

all paint a dreary, dismal portrait. The use of negatives in various forms further illustrates this point. Words such as "*in*sufferable, *un*relieved, *un*redeemed," and "*un*nerved," add to the negative, decaying feeling. They symbolize the absence of growth, the deadening of life and perhaps more significantly, the deadening of the narrator's spirit. Each of these aspects of Poe's diction contributes to the powerful sense of gloom and despair that pervades the story.

Another device that adds to this sense of depression is sound effects. Alliteration is used several times to achieve different results. The repetition of "d" sounds in the first sentence, "*D*uring the whole of a *d*ull, *d*ark, an*d* soundless day in the autumn of the year," initiates the dreary mood of the passage, while in the sentence, "There was an iciness, a sinking, a sickening of the heart," a sinking feeling is produced by the repetition of "s" sounds. The "o" and "au" sound in words like "whole," "autumn," "soul," "thought," "goading," and "paused," sounds like moaning, as if someone were in extreme pain. Poe also repeats certain words, but for a slightly different purpose. Instead of creating a sense of gloom, he establishes a rhythmic pattern. In the fourth sentence he repeats the words "upon" and "the," and in the fifth, "an" and "a."

> I looked *upon* the scene before me—*upon* the mere house, and the simple landscape features of the domain, *upon* the bleak walls, *upon* the vacant eye-like windows, *upon* a few rank sedges, and *upon* a few white trunks of decayed trees—with an utter depression of soul which I can compare to no earthly sensation more properly than to *the* after-dream of the reveller upon opium: *the* bitter lapse into everyday life, *the* hideous dropping off of the veil. There was *an* iciness, *a* sinking, *a* sickening of the heart, *an* unredeemed dreariness of thought. . . . "

The effect on the reader is that of fear and horror. Poe achieves a feeling of motion by a building up of details; the reader is caught up in a mounting display of frightening, distressing details. This repetition of sounds and words further contributes to the depressing, horrifying tone of the passage.

In this passage from "The Fall of the House of Usher," Poe combines sentence structure, diction, and sound effects to project a feeling of depression and impending gloom to the reader as well as onto the environment. By creating a sense of dreariness and uneasiness, he almost warns the reader of the terror to come later in his story. Poe is able to transfer the reader from an objective observer to one who is personally involved in the tale.

The following student stylistic analysis is a bit longer and more detailed. It is based on the opening paragraph of Harper Lee's *To Kill a Mockingbird*. I am including both the model and the analysis so that you can judge how successful the student was in carrying out the assignment:

> Maycomb was an old town, but it was a tired old town when I first knew it. In rainy weather the streets turned to red slop; grass grew on the sidewalks, the courthouse sagged in the square. Somehow, it was hotter then: a black dog suffered on a summer's day; bony mules hitched to Hoover carts flicked flies in the sweltering shade of the live oaks on the square. Men's stiff collars wilted by nine in the morning. Ladies bathed before noon, after their three-o'clock naps, and by nightfall were like soft teacakes with frostings of sweat and sweet talcum.
>
> People moved slowly then. They ambled across the square, shuffled in and out of the stores around it, took their time about everything. A day was twenty-four hours long but seemed longer.

A Stylistic Analysis of the Opening Paragraph of Harper Lee's *To Kill a Mockingbird*

Rachel Mason

This passage from Harper Lee's *To Kill a Mockingbird* is an excellent description of Maycomb, the small Southern town where the narrator spent her childhood. In the story, most of Maycomb's citizens are prejudicial and resistant to change, and the young narrator becomes confused and bewildered by their cruel treatment of a Negro being tried for rape. The description of the town is very important, because by knowing the characters' environment, the reader can often better understand their actions. Also, by realizing the townspeople's unprogressive lifestyle, the reader has further insight into the story and perhaps will feel more involved. In the paragraph, the author illustrates the stagnant, aimless mood of the town through her imaginative story-telling and style of writing.

The overall structure of the paragraph is narrative, with some expository details. Lee first describes a group of inanimate objects (streets, grass, courthouse), then animals (dog, mules), and finally humans (men, ladies). The reader pictures the people last, and by then already has a clear impression of a tired town from the preceding descriptions. Perhaps this organization was meant to stress that the whole town seems tired and worn out, not just the citizens. The actual features Lee describes in each category are chosen randomly, and this contributes to the lazy feeling of aimlessness. In giving her portrayal, the author makes general statements and follows them with examples that support the statements:

GENERAL: Somehow, it was hotter then:
SUPPORT: a black dog suffered on a summer's day;
SUPPORT: bony mules hitched to Hoover carts flicked flies in the sweltering shade of live oaks on the square.

GENERAL: People moved slowly then.
SUPPORT: They ambled across the square,
SUPPORT: shuffled in and out of the stores around it,
SUPPORT: took their time about everything.

The supporting clauses are very specific and therefore help to clarify the general statements for the reader. To say that "people moved slowly" gives the reader a vague image, but saying that they "ambled" or "shuffled" enables the reader to picture their actual movements. The examples in the clauses are descriptions of common everyday things which many people are familiar with (dogs, mules, trees), and thus it is easier for them to imagine Maycomb and feel involved in the story. Also, many of the examples are old-fashioned (bony mules hitched to Hoover carts, streets turned to red slop) and thus help to set the time period of the story. Lee's observations and comments are stated simply and are similar to those a child might make. This style reflects the plainness of life in Maycomb and also emphasizes that the story is being remembered through the impressions of a child.

The point of view in the passage is first person, singular and the use of the word "I" implies a personal involvement in the story, but the relatively objective nature of the narrator's statements make her seem detached. She makes very matter-of-fact observations:

a. Men's stiff collars wilted by nine in the morning.
b. . . . grass grew on the sidewalks . . .
c. People moved slowly then.

When she states that "*People* moved slowly then" instead of "*we* moved slowly then," it seems as though she is setting herself apart from the citizens of the town, and when she says " . . . it was a tired old town when I first *knew* it," instead of "when I first *lived there*," she seems to be disassociating herself from Maycomb. Some of her phrases suggest negative impressions (tired old town, streets turned to red slop, courthouse sagged, bony mules), but she makes no attempt to emphasize the town's positive aspects. Also, she says that "a day was twenty-four hours long but seemed longer," as if to imply that she was bored living there. The one impressionistic word (tired) and the single figure of speech (Ladies . . . by nightfall were like soft teacakes with frostings of sweat and sweet talcum) may be Lee's attempt to show that, although the town is tired and uninteresting, the narrator has imagination. This adds contrast to the story, and makes it much more interesting. The narrator's use of past tense (Maycomb *was* an old town . . .) suggests that she has since moved away; perhaps she was dissatisfied with the lifestyle or disillusioned by events during her childhood.

Instead of using subjective, impressionistic diction to emphasize the first person point of view, Lee chooses concrete, specific words that work together to provide distinct images:

1. Men's stiff collars wilted . . .
2. . . . streets turned to red slop . . .
3. They ambled across the square . . .
4. . . . sweltering shade of the live oaks . . .

These images are easily understood, and so the narrator's impressions are effectively conveyed and help the reader to feel well acquainted with Maycomb. The diction is very appropriate; words such as "tired," "ambled," "shuffled," and "sagged" have specific connotations which add to the impression of an old, slow-moving town, and words such as "suffered," "sweltering," and "wilted" help the reader to feel the heat of a steaming summer day. Most of the words are Anglo-Saxon and quite simple, symbolizing the uncomplicated, routine actions of the people. Even the one impressionistic word (tired), and the only figure of speech in the passage (Ladies . . . were like soft teacakes with frostings of sweat and sweet talcum.), are plain and simplified. As stated before, this may emphasize the ordinary lives of the people, or it may be a reminder that the narrator is remembering the impressions of a little girl, as a child would be unlikely to use complex, impressionistic words and phrases.

Lee's simple style is also evident in the sentence structures she uses. Her long compound sentences have the effect of many short sentences because they are broken by punctuation and because the conjunctions are omitted. This results in slowing down the movement of the passage by making the reader pause after every few words, and thus contributes to the static quality of the passage:

Ex. A (1)   In rainy weather the streets turned to red slop;
       (2)   grass grew on the sidewalks,
       (3)   the courthouse sagged in the square.

Ex. B (1)   They ambled across the square,
       (2)   shuffled in and out of the stores around it,
       (3)   took their time about everything.

Although each example is one long sentence, each seems more like three short ones. This effect can be illustrated more clearly by rewriting Example B:

> Some ambled across the square, *while others* shuffled in and out of the stores around it, *taking* their time about everything.

Though the meaning of the new sentence is essentially the same, it flows more smoothly than the original, giving a stronger impression of unity, action, and even progression, which Harper Lee tries to avoid.

The dominant sentence structure in the passage is that of balance and parallelism. The shape of these sentences impedes the action, because each sentence falls back on itself, repeating a similar structure over and over. This helps to convey a sense of deterioration, and reinforces the image of a declining town:

> In rainy weather
> the streets turned to red slop;
> grass grew on the sidewalks,
> the courthouse sagged in the square.

Each of the three clauses has a subject, a verb, and a three word prepositional phrase. Each clause in the sequence has the same structure, and they form a parallelism. Short simple sentences which imitate the structure of their surrounding clauses are also used, illustrating the same idea of parallelism:

> Somehow it was hotter then:
> a black dog suffered on a summer's day;
> bony mules hitched to Hoover carts flicked flies in the sweltering shade of
>   live oaks on the square.
> Men's stiff collars wilted by nine in the morning.

The ideas in the clauses of each sentence are related, and the arrangements of each are similar: an adjective, subject, verb, and prepositional phrases. This parallelism is used constantly throughout the passage and creates a continuous repetition of ideas and structures, impressing upon the reader the monotony of life in Maycomb. It also reflects the narrator's implied feeling of boredom with the town.

In many of the sentences, the clauses seem interchangeable because they present such similar ideas, and this open-endedness contributes to an aimless feeling of repetition. The clauses can be rearranged without drastically affecting the meaning of the sentence:

ORIGINAL: a. They ambled across the square,
                    b. shuffled in and out of the stores around it,
                    c. took their time about everything.

REARRANGED: c. They took their time about everything,
                    a. ambled across the square,
                    b. shuffled in and out of the stores around it.

REARRANGED: b. They shuffled in and out of the stores,
                    c. took their time about everything,
                    a. ambled across the square.

Thus, the repetition of ideas and structures strongly reflects the stagnant, listless mood of Maycomb.

Lee also uses sound parallelism, through alliteration and assonance. The rhyming words seem to come in pairs, with only a few exceptions. Some examples of alliteration are *f*licked/*f*lies, *s*weat/*s*weet, *g*rass/*g*rew, and *s*uffered/*s*ummer's. Examples of assonance include s*u*ffered/s*u*mmer's, h*i*tched/fl*i*cked/st*i*ff, and d*ay*/sh*a*de. The sound repetition adds to the feeling of boredom and monotony. When Lee says that the ladies were like "*soft* teacakes with frostings of *s*weat and *s*weet talcum," the softness of the "sw" sounds illustrates her idea. The other soft "s" and "f" sounds throughout the passage help emphasize a feeling of listlessness.

Through her description of Maycomb, Harper Lee effectively conveys the narrator's image of an old, unprogressive town. Her writing is clear and uncluttered and her ideas are easy to understand. Also, the reading is made enjoyable by her clever, imaginative descriptions. Altogether, Lee's style holds a simple charm that makes her work appealing to readers of all ages.

Imitation Exercises

The next assignment is one in which students must imitate as closely as possible the structural and stylistic features of the original. I suggest certain subjects that they might want to consider in doing this assignment, but more often than not I encourage students to provide their own subject matter, based on their own knowledge and experience. Not only do students learn that certain kinds of stylistic features will not be appropriate to all subjects, but they also learn how important it is to be able to choose the proper set of features that will communicate their intended meaning. This calls for more than slavish imitation. It calls for a thorough understanding of stylistic alternatives.

The following student imitations exemplify how two of my students carried out this assignment. The first example is a student imitation of Harper Lee's *To Kill a Mockingbird*. The second is a student imitation based on Poe's "The Fall of the House of Usher." You might wish to compare these imitations with the original passages previously cited.

Broadmor School

Susan Horn

Broadmor was an old school, but it was a tired old school when last I saw it. In rainy weather water dripped through the warped ceiling; paint peeled off the walls, the litter collected in the hallways. The playground seemed desolate then: the wind blew empty tetherball chains against their poles; the broken merry-go-round gingerly rested its tired carrousel against the decaying ash trees of the lot. The teeter-totter lay there motionless. Rotting swings hung silently, stirred abruptly in the breeze, then gradually ceased their movement like a rocking cradle left unattended.

People moved slowly then. Teachers dawdled in the break room, chatted before and after each class, barely made it through the day. The workload was tolerable but seemed overwhelming.

The Town of Quartzwell

Tom Howell

Throughout the morning of a dusty, dry, and silent day in the summer of the year, when the sun beat down unmercifully on the flat, arid land, I had been passing alone, on horseback, through a lonely tract of desert; and at length found myself, as the sun climbed ever higher overhead, within view of the abandoned town of Quartzwell. I know not how it was—but with the first glimpse of the ghost town, a feeling of unbearable uneasiness overtook my person. I say unbearable, for the feeling was unrelieved by the knowledge that this was just an ordinary, abandoned town, and the same scene could be seen throughout Death Valley. I looked upon the scene before me—upon the old, decrepit buildings, and the simple wooden boardwalks of the town, upon the hard-packed dust road in the town's center, upon a few motionless, brown tumbleweeds—with an utter depression which I can compare to no feeling better than that of the rider when he comes upon the newly decayed remains of an animal, white and dried by the desert sun, the feeling of bitter emptiness when encountering death. There was an emptiness, a bareness of the heart, an unredeemed blankness of thought which no use of reason and logic could bring me out of and back into the reality of the present. What was it—I pondered—what was it that so unnerved me in the contemplation of the long abandoned town of Quartzwell?

Follow-up

After each kind of writing assignment, I bring my students' papers to class, read them aloud, comment on the relative strengths and weaknesses of each, and make suggestions for improvement. I reinforce this procedure by writing marginal and summary comments on their papers and by student conferences. As often as I can, I discuss the possible applications of what they are learning in my class to other classes. My hope is that the principles of writing they learn in doing these exercises can be applied to other kinds of writing situations.

To illustrate the kinds of problems I try to anticipate in my students' writing and to exemplify the kind of advice I give them to help them improve their papers, I am reproducing below two kinds of student papers, a stylistic analysis and an imitation, with marginal and summary comments:

A Stylistic Analysis of "A Sound of Thunder"

Too vague and general

A clear, distinct example of style can be found in the excerpt from "A Sound of Thunder" by Ray Bradbury. The story concerns a (pssage) back *Proofread more carefully* through time to the prehistoric era in order to

by a group of hunters hunt one of the most awesome beasts that ever existed--the noble Tyrannosaurus rex. While the hunters watch, transfixed, as the huge dinosaur emerges from the forest and moves into a nearby clearing, Bradbury takes the opportunity to conjure *This is a more meaningful statement* up an image of the beast so rich in detail and

I'm not sure I understand this. The passage is imaginatively written, but in what way is imagination an "element" of style? movement that it almost breathes. Although the writer's imagination is obviously the most important element of the composition, many other ingredients of style are still essential to the passage's effectiveness.

The overall movement of the paragraph is narrative; that is, it gives a sequential account of the dinosaur's movement out of the wooded area, toward the group of hunters, and then into a clearing. Thus, Bradbury makes the description an integral part of the plot and keeps the story flowing, rather than stopping the story momentarily *good* and thereby risking the possibility of losing the reader's attention. This technique works especially well in an adventure story such as "A Sound of Thunder" because as the plot builds, the reader becomes more involved and is anxious to know what will happen next.

The actual description of the dinosaur is spatial, and so creates another sense of movement, narrowing this time from a spanning overall glance to an upward inspection of the beast's legs, thighs, body, arms, neck, head, and finally, the mouth, teeth, and eyes. When the beast begins to move, these neatly arranged descriptions blend

together easily, creating a sharp image in the
reader's mind.

Keep ideas parallel Although the average sentence length is
relatively short when compared to other modern *2. that of*
writers, each word has been carefully chosen to
contribute to the expository, detailed nature of
the selection. The diction is mainly concrete,
specific, and metaphorical, with Bradbury making
extensive use of figurative language and both
what do you mean by sound imagery? visual and sound imagery. The body of the dinosaur
is described as a "great breathing cage." The
head, "a ton of sculptured stone," is supported by *The wording is confusing.*
a "snake neck," while "each lower leg was a piston,"
and the "pebbled skin" is likened to the "mail of
a terrible warrior." The images seem to cluster *Give examples of these image clusters.*
into patterns, giving impressions of balance, size,
and power. Also, present, active participials
This sentence ought to go with your discussion of parallel structure and word and phrase repetition. such as "gliding" and "exposing" depict action
vividly and work to enhance the rhythm.

The relatively short sentence length helps to
create excitement by enabling the story to move
quickly. Bradbury uses mainly two kinds of
sentences throughout the passage: *the* series and *the*
cumulative. The series moves in order from *sentence*
general words to more specific choices, as in the
following:

> "Each thigh was a ton of meat, ivory,
> and steel mesh."

What? The concrete, specific word choice? Not so! It's the "placement" of the words in a series that creates the parallelism. The words are balanced between concrete, general
choices such as "thigh" and "meat," and concrete,
specific choices such as "ton," "ivory," and "steel
mesh." This creates a grammatical parallelism in
the sentences, and Bradbury carries this parallelism
beyond the sentences to the whole paragraph through
the use of a coordinated arrangement of phrases and
clauses. However, the cumulative sentences
dominate the paragraph, and their rhythm tends to
give a sense of movement of the beast, as in this
vivid example:

> "It ran, its pelvic bones crushing aside
> trees and bushes, its taloned feet claw-
> ing damp earth, leaving prints six inches
> deep wherever it settled its weight."

The free modifiers, built carefully upon the base, result in a rhythm which may even be termed poetic.

The overall tone of the paragraph gives the reader the impression that the dinosaur is a mechanical, evil creature, controlled not by thought, but by cold instinct. This "machine" image is carried (subtley) through the passage in *sp.* words and phrases such as "oiled," "watchmaker's claws," and "piston," and is also implied by the spatial description, which details each part separately and then describes the parts working together as a whole. The sheer massiveness of the animal also contributes to the mechanical image, because most creations today which are that huge have been designed by man. The impression of evil stems from the use of words such as "great evil god," "gleam," "teeth like daggers," and "death grin." The dinosaur's eyes, "empty of all expression save hunger," suggest that the beast is not accustomed to thinking rationally.

good point

a nice observation

Yet, underlying these impressions, there is a clear sense of respect for the huge creature, a kind of reverence for nature, made evident by Bradbury in phrases such as "sculptured stone," "delicate arms," and "a gliding ballet step, far too poised and balanced for its ten tons." As well as helping the reader to picture the dinosaur more clearly, the various moods of the passage enable *the reader* to imagine that she, herself, is a character in the story, watching with the same awe as the hunters on the bridge.

Respect? or is it "awe"?

I wouldn't go this far.

he or she

Bradbury's ability to capture and hold attention, mainly through creative diction, makes reading "A Sound of Thunder" quite enjoyable. The reader's imagination is gently guided and never strained, and the short sentences rarely grow tiring. The plot unfolds neatly, with no unnecessary wandering, and builds just slowly enough to create excitement. For a first taste of Bradbury's work, the selection was not only palatable, but quite savory.

This is a good first paper, one of the best I've received. You do a fine job of discussing the narrative movement and the spatial description. Your discussion of the imagery is fairly good. There are times, however, when your statements are too vague (what do you mean by "a clear, distinct example of style"? Besides, this can be said of any writers work.) and general; occasionally inaccurate ("a kind of reverence for nature"); or imprecise (Bradbury uses "sound imagery"). All in all, your writing is clear, interesting, and to the point.

The Runner

Brenda "striding" suggests one kind of motion, "gliding" another.

The runner came on light, rhythmic, stream-
lined, striding legs. He glided thirty yards
ahead of half of his opponents, a graceful
athletic god, swinging his curved pendulum arms
close to his glistening wet chest. Each lower leg
was an extension, a limb of solid muscle, working *an extension of what?*
in unison with the other, flying weightlessly over
the track like the wings of Mercury's feet. Each *What is being compared? The legs? The flying? Weightlessness?*
stride was identical, effortless, and elastic.
And from the perfect chest cage of the upper body,
those ~~his~~ two solid arms pumped consistently at his side, *Are a conductors arms at his sides?*
arms which controlled and directed the pace like a
conductor, while his legs obeyed its orders. And
the ~~his~~ head itself, a floating buoy, supported his
fleeting form. His cheeks billowed, inhaling and *This is a good image.*
exhaling the air in shallow breaths like a
trumpeter. His eyes were frozen on the finish, ice
Eyes "frozen" fine. — But why like "ice particles"? particles, empty of all desire save victory. He
entered the final stretch in a faint knowing grin. *?*
He sprinted, his (cadent) strides brushing the *Some nice descriptive details* *too formal*
cinder and lime, his spiked feet flying across the
hot track, leaving prints barely visible wherever
he planted his stride. He sprinted with a gliding *These details are contradictory*
gazelle gait, far too graceful and lithe for his
excruciating pace. He flew over the finish line
eagerly, his exhausted arms stretched to the sky
in victory.

Brenda, I like your choice of subjects. You've captured the sentence rhythms of Bradbury's style nicely, and some of your descriptive details are effective. You do a good job with literal descriptive details ("his spiked feet flying across the hot track"), but you've got to be more careful and precise in your use of figurative language ("he sprinted with a gliding gazelle gait"). Occasionally, your figures do not fit the action or the content, or you'll use words to describe the action that are at odds with one another.

The imitation of models is not a mere slavish copying of a model, but an emulation of the best features of a writer's style. It mirrors the writer's cognitive processes, leading the student writer to a discovery of new effects.

29 Theory and the Individual English Teacher

Patricia Harkin
Department of English, Denison University

The recent burgeoning interest in reading theory has encouraged many members of our profession to change the way they teach introductory literature courses to make them reflect what we now know—empirically and theoretically—about what happens when human beings read literary works. Such change is healthy, but it is not without practical problems. Chief among them is the fact that the literature curricula of universities and high schools are organized, not around the teaching of reading, but around literary history and genre theory. Moreover, these curricula tend to assume the determinate meaning of texts: Instructors teach students the meaning of literary texts that authors intended. As a consequence, a teacher who offers a thorough-going "reader-response" course in introductory literature/composition in an English department which offers only traditional upper division courses in historical periods or literary genres may be said to do herself and her students a conceptual and political disservice.

Imagine, for example, a student who hears in a Freshman English course that reading is a radically private activity wherein readers make meaning, and then moves to a sophomore survey where it is announced that the meaning of *Paradise Lost* was intended by John Milton (who didn't like surprises) and that we can best find that meaning by clearing our minds of preconceptions and letting the poem come to us. My hunch is that the student is less likely to be enchanted by the theoretical diversity of the Humanities than to decide that the English Department has a coherence problem. The teacher of the introductory service course experiences this problem as a set of conflicting inclinations—to formulate a teaching procedure which responsibly grounds itself in the firm and cogent data of recent reading theory but at the same time to preserve and advance those methods of literary analysis which we used to call "training," and that still remain (in the language of legislators and administrators and parents) "basic."

One solution is to offer students a poetics of reading—a carefully developed system of language which describes, not a poem, but the process of reading it. In this essay I shall propose a course design which modifies Wolfgang Iser's *The Act of Reading* (1978) to produce a plan which asks freshmen first to raise their process of reading to consciousness and then to begin to articulate that process and finally to describe their own reading acts clearly and coherently enough so that others can understand them. My claim is that Iser's *Act of Reading* is a valuable conceptual ground for the introductory English course because its informed and far-reaching use of gestalt theory, speech act theory, semiotics, and phenomenology is responsive to the state of our knowledge of the process of reading and because it is amenable to description in terms that we associate with the methods of traditional literary analysis.

Iser's success at bridging this conceptual gap is most clearly demonstrated in his conception of the "implied reader," the key term in his theory. For Iser, the "concept of the implied reader designates a network of response—inviting structures, which impel the (actual) reader to grasp the text" (p. 34). The concept of implied reader does not posit a biographical or historical person, or group of persons, or even set of attitudes; rather the concept is a phenomenological construction which includes "the reader's role as a textual structure, and the reader's role as a structured act" (p. 35). The concept of the implied reader is a set of capabilities, or possibilities—imaginary functions to be performed by actual persons as they follow the text's instructions for the production of the signified, for the making of the aesthetic object. Every text contains such instructions. They were put there by the author (consciously or not) because a literary work is, after all, a communication. But not every reader is identically capable of following these instructions, or willing to follow them. Thus it is that individual readings differ, even though the process of reading can be described in terms which remain the same within Iser's system. Basic to the theory is the assumption that the reader behaves as if he or she is to be communicated with. Therefore it follows that, whatever the state of their preparation for literary study, individual readers are potentially willing to perform the structured act of reading—willing to follow the instructions to be found in the world for making its meaning. When readers follow instructions they are following *textual structures;* these textual structures evoke *structured acts.* In practice structured acts are inseparable from their performance, for textual structures exist only as they are perceived. My point is a simple one: When we concentrate on the process by which a reader performs the structured act of reading, we are responding to the data that contemporary reading theory has generated; when we examine the textual structures that evoke these acts, we are in touch with traditional methods of literary analysis.

One significant structural act is *consistency building,* the process by which readers form gestalts by linking together disparate segments of a literary work in order to form a whole that is, for a given reader, at a given moment, consistent. Consistency building operates both on the level of the text's referentiality and on the level of formal unity. Consistency exists between the tenor and vehicle of a given metaphor and among the several image patterns of a given text. A reader of Wordsworth's "I Wandered Lonely as a Cloud," for example, will find consistency between daffodils and people in communities as well as among the speaker's various and changing references to daffodils within the form.

Iser gives the name *wandering viewpoint* to the structured act which enables readers to grasp the literary work by allowing themselves to be caught up in and transcended by it. For example, readers of *Tom Jones* would experience the wandering viewpoint as a series of subtle shifts whereby they sometimes adopt the narrative perspective of Tom, sometimes of the other characters, sometimes of the narrator, and sometimes of the role marked out by Fielding for the reader. This flexible conception of wandering viewpoint is not to be confused with the traditional notion of point of view. The difference is easily seen in a story like Joyce's "Clay," where the point of view is third person omniscient but the reader's wandering viewpoint continually shifts from the perspective of Marie to that of the characters who pity and scorn her.

The structure of *theme* and *horizon* is that by which the reader is understood to concentrate on, or hold in consciousness, one set of textual data at a time. A theme, then, is whatever is present to the reader's consciousness at a given reading moment. We might make the perspective of Marie, or Allworthy into theme in *Tom Jones*; or we might connect textual segments to make community into theme in "I Wandered Lonely as a Cloud." Horizon is the background of remembered textual segments against which a given structure is made into a theme.

It is important to remember that the "product" of these "processes"—a reading—is not necessarily a record of the author's intention, although it is a meaning. A reader makes meaning by filling in *gaps* between given elements (words) of a text. Gaps, for Iser, are places where information is not given. Joyce, for example, *gives* certain information: Dante tells Stephen Daedalus that the eagles will pluck out his eyes if he does not apologize; Stephen is punished for being without his glasses; Stephen has a conversation with the Prefect in which it is asserted that beauty is that which is pleasing to the senses. If a reader chooses to establish a connection among these textual segments and to make a theme of Stephen's way of seeing, then that reader has perceived and filled gaps among those givens. Gaps in a literary text are themselves indeterminate—they may or may not be perceived by a reader; different readers perceive different gaps; different readers fill the same gaps in different ways. Nevertheless, the meaning produced by each individual reader is, for that reader, for that moment at least, determinate. A rereading can, and usually does, produce a new meaning.

In order to fill gaps, readers need to be aware of a text's *repertoire,* all the extra-textual reality to which it refers. Repertoire includes the social, political, and literary norms and commonplaces that were in place at the time of the text's production. It is, therefore, a much broader notion than the traditional one of setting. A story like Philip Roth's "Defender of the Faith" is set in Camp Crowder, Missouri, in the last year of World War II. Its repertoire includes a system of values having to do with Judaism, racial and religious prejudice, and patriotism. Iser believes that valuable works of literature distinguish themselves by requiring their readers to call into question the thought systems that they invoke or represent.

With this brief introduction to Iser's frameworks, it is possible to describe the introductory composition and literature course I teach in which I use a traditional anthology, require such traditional kinds of writing as a library paper and interpretive essays on fiction, poetry, and drama, and employ traditional language for literary analysis. My course is unlike traditional ones, however, in that it abandons the notion that the text is an object with determinate meaning. Course discussion and writing assignments are designed to evoke the reading skills I believe significant and to encourage students to employ them.

The terms or concepts in Iser's system are easy enough to explain to first-year students, and they produce immediate and perceptible results in students' discussions. To illustrate repertoire, I begin the course by assigning a short story from the department's anthology—one that explicitly and evocatively grounds itself in an ethnic experience—the experience of being a Jew or a Black or a Southerner. The key is to find a story with whose repertoire some students will and others will not be familiar. Roth's "Defender of the Faith," already mentioned, is an excellent example, Frank O'Connor's "First Confession" another. Students quickly see that unless they understand dietary laws or the necessary conditions for receiving the sacrament of penance, their response to character is not so rich as the response of some of their peers. They see too that those peers respond more fully, not because they are "better in English," but because they are Jews or Catholics or whatever.

In designing writing assignments at this early stage, I begin by focusing narrowly, asking students to close one gap. For example, I ask students to distinguish the perspectives of the narrator and the grandfather in "Battle Royal," and then, with reference to one or two incidents in the excerpt from Ralph Ellison's *Invisible Man,* stipulate the clues that suggest to them that one or the other is to be preferred. Later, I move to studies of more complicated questions of narration. When students can stipulate the moments in "Clay" or "Araby" when their viewpoints wander from one narrative perspective to another, they are ready to discuss irony with conceptual cogency.

An assignment on repertoire provides an excellent correlate with library research—especially these days when students have read so little—because it allows me to assign a text, like Joyce's *Portrait,* one that ordinarily would be dismissed as too difficult. The assignment asks the student to experience the difference between repertoire and the formalist notion of setting, and to test Iser's assertion that the text does not merely refer to its repertoire, but rather forces the reader to call into question the social, cultural, and literary norms that were in place at the time the text was written. Obviously, freshmen readers need to determine what these norms were before they can perceive them as being broken. A typical social norm, for example, would have to do with notions of Jesuit education and its techniques and its values at the time Joyce was writing *Portrait.* In order to prevent the reduction of repertoire to setting, it is helpful to ask students to list as many as possible of the clues in the text that point to its repertoire. In the *Portrait* example, such a list might include the elder Daedalus' naive belief that a Jesuit education will help Stephen get a good job, the conversations between Stephen and the rector about vocations as well as the conversations between Stephen and the Prefect of Studies about aesthetics. Considerable class time must be devoted to discussing the commonplaces that implicitly ground the beliefs expressed by the characters. Here, research is crucial. Students find contemporary accounts of Jesuit education, or investigate the Society's own accounts of the importance of logic, etc. Thus informed, class discussion might produce the following generalization:

> Many Irish Catholics at the turn of the century believed that Jesuit education was prestigious because Jesuits were highly intelligent men who were trained specifically to be teachers. Such education was an important force for training young people to behave morally and to become economically successful.

Class discussion can turn on the question of how the text makes that commonplace seem invalid. Here, students' responses are likely to be quite specific and personal. One might notice that Father Dolan punishes Stephen unjustly, and that the Rector's handling of Stephen's complaint evades the issue of justice. Another might point to the fact that the Prefect of Studies lacks a rudimentary understanding of Stephen's aesthetic, etc. The class as a whole will see the repertoire of a complicated text being called into question, while individual members of the class prepare personal articulations of the judgments they have been led to make by this kind of questioning. My favorite response in one class discussion of this text came from a young woman who actually researched the *Ratio Studorium* and discovered that, when Father Dolan punishes Stephen in Book One, he violates no fewer than three rules for the conduct of discipline established by the order. This information allowed her to perceive several other instances of hypocrisy within the Society of Jesus and to produce a thoughtful essay on that aspect of Stephen's motivation for leaving the church.

What I like best about this assignment is that students' research has information as its object rather than professional interpretations of the text, interpretations whose assumptions they neither recognize nor understand. The writings students produce for this assignment lack the eclectic hodgepodge of half-understood conclusions because the assignment demands a genuine encounter with the text.

Consistency building, the next important element of Iser's system, lends coherence to discussions of poetry. Class discussions of Roethke's "I Knew a Woman," for example, usually evoke "consistencies" involving grass and hay imagery, or motion-stasis, or death-life oppositions. These discussions lead to the question of how the patterns discussed are themselves consistent with the relationship that the poem describes.

In the consistency building/poetry sections of the course, I shift the writing emphasis to revision and to argument. In an in-class writing assignment on Roethke's "I Knew a Woman," I ask students to characterize the speaker, his beloved, and the nature of their relationship, on the basis of one or more consistencies they have found in the text. Then I ask them to analyze three short professional readings of the poem. What occurs, of course, is that the students encounter in these professional essays other readings of the poem which are mutually exclusive and which call their own into question. Usually the discussions revolve around some issue on which the students want to achieve closure. Is she dead or did she leave him for another guy? I know of no better way than this to teach indeterminacy because students have a stake in the argument. Having already written about it, they usually evince some interest in refuting the professional readings, or at least in looking carefully at the evidence adduced, and deciding on its relevance. Techniques of argument become important to them because they realize that both claims and grounds in these arguments are functions of the reader's hypothesis, the reader's reading. Students have to see that the closure for which they so strongly argue is of their own making. Finally I ask students to revise their essays. I encourage them to come up with a thesis about the indeterminacy of the text itself and their response to it. This revision, then, is not just a matter of fixing comma splices and dangling modifiers but precisely a re-vision, a re-thinking in another conceptual context.

Iser's description of the shifting structure of theme and horizon makes a useful overview for the work students and I have been doing. It allows students to respond to texts at a higher level of generality than questions about individual strategies in individual works allow them. I prefer to work with theme and horizon in the context of a relatively accessible play, like *Death of a Salesman*, so that students can perceive that a given theme is perceptible to them at a given reading moment only against the horizon of other perspective segments.

Finally, the last writing assignment I give on drama calls for a full-scale reading of a relatively uncomplicated text. Students are expected to produce a valid argument in a paper using all of the critical and analytical vocabulary they have met during the course appropriately and consistently. By stipulating the specific element of the reading process which warrants their readings, students might, for example, respond to Charley's assertion at the end of *Death of a Salesman* that "Nobody dast blame" Willy Loman. In preparation for composing these papers I ask students to work in groups which focus on one element of reading. One group might attend to "the American Dream" as repertoire for *Death of a Salesman* and as a rationale for finding Willy neither wholly blameless or blameworthy; another group might work with "success" or with "being well-liked" in the context of theme and horizon; another might probe consistent patterns of language about dreams or sports or apartment houses; still another might look at how the reader's wandering viewpoint prevents determinate sympathy for any one character.

What distinguishes these writing assignments from traditional ones is the requirement that students stipulate and describe the reading process. Such requirements go far toward countering vagueness: A writer who *must* point to the moments when his or her sympathy shifts from Willy to Biff and back again cannot depend on *Masterplots*. By asking students to form a coherent account of what happens when they read, moreover, these assignments enable students to read texts which have not been "taught" critically.

The course I have just described offers instruction in a very basic skill, critical reading; it offers a way of getting Joyce and his ilk back into the classroom, from which they have lately been displaced in an effort to get students in; it offers a conceptual coherence not available in traditional belles lettres; and it offers an opportunity to discover why human beings need fictions. In many ways it is a beginning—an introduction to literature which provides instruction in literary analysis and, through repertoire, a very sophisticated technique for doing literary history. As such, it is coherent with traditional and nontraditional upperdivision literature courses. It is an introduction to composition and to argument; as such it is coherent with advanced writing courses. It is an introduction to reading theory; as such it allows students to begin to perceive the theoretical reading spectrum from Hirsch to Bleich. It is also, I like to think, a preliminary skirmish in the conceptual revolution that must occur in Humanities departments if they are to survive the current crisis.

30 A Meaningful Model of Written Language Development for Teachers

Sandra Stotsky
Writing Consultant, Brookline, Massachusetts

For decades, many linguists have stressed the primacy of oral language and seem to have viewed writing as simply the transcription of speech. For example, Greenberg writes in *Psycholinguistics:* "The linguist views writing . . . as a derivative system whose symbols stand for units of the spoken language" (Osgood & Sebeok, p. 9). This assumption has led some educators to believe that writing is little more than "speech written down."

On the other hand, composition teachers, especially at higher levels of education (e.g., Shaughnessy, 1977), have frequently observed that poor writing is often considered poor precisely because it seems to reflect the patterns, structures, and lexicon of the spoken language. Moreover, scholarship in still another academic discipline suggests that academic writing, at least, cannot be regarded merely as an alternate form of the spoken language. Snell, a professor of the classics, points out that philosophical and scientific discourse was deliberately created by the ancient Greeks to develop knowledge because the structures and lexicon of natural language were not suitable for that purpose. He states that academic discourse lives today in other languages "by virtue of taking over, translating and elaborating upon the original Greek" (Snell, p. 50).

The claim that academic language is unlike natural language suggests that it cannot be acquired, spontaneously and effortlessly, in a natural language environment, but, instead, must be learned through deliberate exposure to it and by formal instruction in it. Indeed, the practices of most teachers of academic writing would appear to support these views. Unfortunately, what these teachers lack is a theoretical framework that supports their practices. What seems to be needed is a model of written language development that not only acknowledges the differences between the language of formal schooling and the language of daily life but also suggests how developing writers acquire their competence with this special language. The purpose of this essay is to provide such a theoretical framework.

The model I am presenting in this essay is a synthesis of ideas that can be found in the writing of many different psychologists; however, its broad outlines have been suggested explicitly in the work of Vygotsky and Luria particularly. We might perhaps call this model an epistemological model of written language development because it seeks to explain how we come to know—and, hence, be able to use—the language of formal schooling. According to this model, writing, although initially dependent upon spoken language while students learn to decode and encode written language, becomes increasingly independent of spoken language and more influenced by written language itself. Although the language the developing writer reads is usually far richer and more complex than the language he can write, the model suggests that students' writing may gradually become like the language they read with continuous experience and instruction in reading and writing this language.

The basic assumption of the model is that oral and written language differ both in their origins and in their purposes and, accordingly, are qualitatively different in nature. Vygotsky (1978) writes: "writing . . . is a new and complex form of speech" (p. 118). Luria writes: "written speech (differs) from oral speech in its origins and in its structural and functional features" (p. 141).[1] Simon writes that written language does not arise as a "twin" to spoken language; it may share some common elements but requires other resources for its full development, using different means to achieve different goals (p. 323).[2] Bruner *et al.* suggest the following differences between written and oral language:

> All the semantic and syntactic features that have been discussed in relation to concept formation—a rich and hierarchically organized vocabulary, as well as the syntactic embedding of labels—become necessary when one must communicate out of the context of immediate reference. It is precisely in this respect that written language differs from the spoken (p. 310).

In order to explain how the language of beginning writing can be transformed into the language of mature writing, the model must address two critical issues: (1) how the reader derives meaning from written texts; and (2) where the writer derives meaning from in order to produce written texts. Figure 1 presents a preliminary version of the model in order to show what happens in beginning reading and writing. In this figure, and in the next one as well, the circles represent the four language processes of listening, speaking, reading, and writing. The direction of the arrows indicates whether the process may contribute to the development of meaning and thought or to an expression of meaning and thought—or to *both*. As Figure 1 indicates, the language learner first derives meaning from the spoken language of others; moreover, his own speech may also contribute to the development of meaning and thought. The language learner learns to read primarily by decoding and fusing written symbols into sounds that have meanings he recognizes from his experience listening to the speech of others (Luria, pp. 411–413). Thus, as a beginning reader, he derives meaning from written texts on the basis of meaning gained from experience with spoken language. The written texts he reads with understanding may be less rich and complex than, or as rich and complex as, what he can understand aurally, but they cannot be richer and more complex than what he can understand aurally. What he understands aurally sets a ceiling on, or gates, what he can understand in written texts.

During this period, as Figure 1 also indicates, inner listening continues to develop. Inner listening refers to our ability to "hear" inner speech and would seem to be presupposed by the existence of inner speech (see Sokolov, p. 568).

Sources of Influence on the Development of
Meaning and Thought at the Onset
of Literacy Training

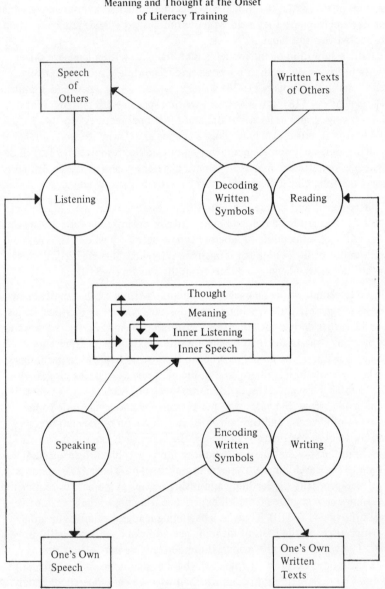

Figure 1

In the pre-school years, inner listening may simply be the internalization of external listening.

Eventually, with enough reading experience, the beginning reader no longer has to translate written symbols into sounds in order to understand the meaning they signify but can understand the meaning they signify directly. The reader now goes directly from print to meaning. Vygotsky (1978) writes:

> As second-order symbols, written symbols function as designations for verbal ones. Understanding of written language is first effected through spoken language, but gradually this path is curtailed and spoken language disappears as the intermediate link. To judge from all the available evidence, written language becomes direct symbolism that is perceived in the same way as spoken language (p. 116).

The direct influence of reading upon meaning—and thought, too—is shown in Figure 2, a more fully developed model. It is possible that the development of inner listening facilitates the understanding of written language as "direct symbolism."

At the point when written language can be understood as direct symbolism, something very significant can occur in the reading process. Up to this point, the reader has understood written language on the basis of his understanding of spoken language. Now, however, the reader can go beyond the limits of his spoken language experiences. His level of listening comprehension no longer sets limits on his level of reading comprehension. The reader now can learn to read written language that is richer and more complex than his spoken language.

How can the developing reader come to understand written forms and patterns of language that differ from those he has heard? In general, in almost exactly the same way he has learned to understand greater complexity in oral language—through continuous exposure. Just as the language learner learns to understand greater complexity in oral language through frequent exposure to more complex oral language, so, too, does he learn to understand more complex written language through continuous exposure to more complex written language. New meanings are gradually incorporated through frequent experiences reading them; in other words, the beginning reader uses the same processes for absorbing the lexical richness and density of written language that he uses for absorbing or internalizing more complex oral language.

How more precisely does the developing reader go beyond the limits of the level of his comprehension of spoken language? This is not spelled out by Vygotsky or Luria. One may hypothesize that the development of the reader's ability to understand as "direct symbolism" written forms of language that are familiar to him may gradually enable him to understand as direct symbolism some written forms of language that are unfamiliar to him. These newly acquired semantic/syntactic forms and structures then provide the context for the developing reader to understand other written forms of language that are also unfamiliar to him. In this way, written forms of language that differ from forms in the reader's spoken language system function as new resources that serve to accelerate growth in understanding written language beyond the level of listening comprehension. It is in this way that literacy nourishes itself. Eventually,

Sources of Influence on the Development of
Meaning and Thought at Higher Levels
of Literacy Training

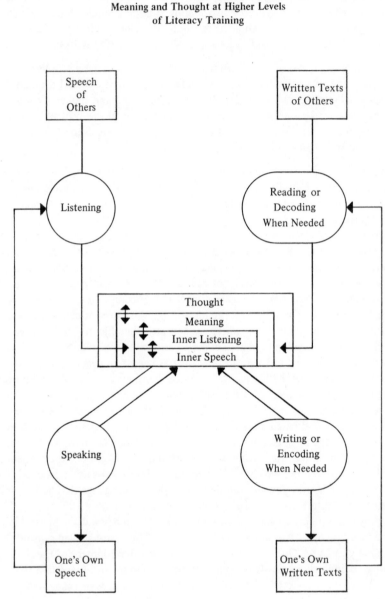

Figure 2

mature readers can absorb language visually that is far richer and denser than spoken language. (Indeed, it is difficult to listen to language that is as dense and as rich as the mature language we can read.)

Now let us turn to the development of writing. As Figure 1 indicates, the beginning writer may encode spoken language directly or he may encode from inner speech, which in the pre-school years is the internalization of external speech. In either case, the only independent source from which the beginning writer derives meaning is the spoken language. Written language that is of greater richness and complexity than the oral language he can comprehend cannot influence his writing because his experience with spoken language determines what he can understand, and hence, absorb from written texts. So long as what the beginning writer reads must be translated into meaningful sounds for comprehension to occur, his writing cannot be richer or more complex than the language he has heard. The language of beginning writing will therefore be very much like speech written down.

How is the language of the beginning writer transformed into the language of more mature writing? Here one may hypothesize that the development of the ability to understand written language directly, together with frequent reading experiences at progressively more difficult levels, enables the developing writer to internalize written forms of language that differ in quality and density from the language he experiences aurally and, eventually, to use or reproduce them in his writing. With sufficient experience and instruction in reading and writing, the mature writer can produce language that is far richer than the language he speaks. (Indeed, we cannot easily produce language orally that is as dense and as rich as the language we can write.) Note that by positing a source of influence on meaning that is not gated by the writer's level of listening comprehension, the model in Figure 2 accounts for the writer's ability to use or produce language that is richer and denser than his spoken language.

As suggested by Luria, inner speech develops even more after the onset of literacy training. Thus, Figure 2 also shows the direct influence of writing upon inner speech. Luria writes:

> Because it delays the direct appearance of speech connections, inhibits them, and increases requirements for the preliminary, internal preparation for the speech act, written speech produces a rich development of inner speech which could not take place in the earliest phases of development (p. 143).

Because meaning and thought are related but not identical in this model (see Sokolov; Bruner *et al.*, pp. 43–44), the direct influence of writing upon inner speech and inner listening means that meaning and thought are also enhanced by writing.

Finally, Figure 2 shows that what one has written becomes in its own right a text to be read and "listened to" directly. Critical reading of one's own text during the revising process may become at least as great a stimulus for mental activity and intellectual development as the reading of others' texts. Ong asserts that written words make possible "psychological operations so complex as to defy total description" ("Beyond," p. 8).

It is important to note that in this model, speech itself is affected by written language development. However, it is possible that the longer established habits of speech, the speed with which it must be produced, and its lack of permanence probably keep speech less complex than writing at all levels of development. The relative slowness of writing and the objectified nature of written language enable the writer to produce or work out forms of written language that the nature of spoken language precludes.

What are the pedagogical implications of this model? If the significant characteristics of mature written language are not present in spoken language and are therefore not a part of the language learner's natural language environment, then the density and richness of mature written language cannot be absorbed through oral language experience and practice. Teachers will need to provide students with regular exposure to increasing levels of textual density to help them absorb the lexical richness and density of written language (see Stotsky, forthcoming, for a discussion of this issue). They will also have to provide them with regular practice in writing about their own ideas and what they are learning about the world around them to help them use this language and develop mastery of its resources. Note that this model does not suggest that students should not engage in oral language activities; such activities are valuable for their own sake. What the model does imply is that oral language experiences are not a substitute for reading and writing experiences.

The model of written language development that I offer here accounts for the knowledge the mature reader/writer has of the language he understands and uses. The model is based on the assumption that the structure and substance of written language is qualitatively different in nature from the structure and substance of spoken language. Although experience with spoken language determines meaning in beginning reading and writing, the model indicates that the relationship may be very different at higher levels of literacy development; not only may reading and writing influence each other, but they may also influence meaning in oral language as well. In effect, the model postulates a reciprocal relationship, even a multidirectional one, among the four language processes: oral language may influence written language, written language may influence oral language, and reading and writing may each enhance the other directly in different but equally profound ways. Because the model not only supports the goals and activities of teachers of academic writing but is itself supported by empirical evidence (e.g., see the review of the literature by Stotsky, 1982), it may be useful as a theoretical framework for both pedagogy and research. Moreover, because this model suggests how literacy at its higher levels provides readers and writers with a wealth of resources to think with as well as about, it can help us to explore how the mind develops new meanings and creates ideas that previously did not exist.

Notes

[1] Although the word *speech* is used in the English translations of Vygotsky's and Luria's statements, it seems to make better sense to understand the word as *language,* since neither Vygotsky nor Luria considers writing as "speech written down."

²The original passage is as follows: "La langue écrite naît chez l'enfant; parturition douloureuse. Et elle ne naît pas soeur jumelle de la langue parlée, mais nouvelle Eve, elle lui emprunte ses éléments et non pas ses aliments car elle se nourrit à d'autres sources, ne vise pas les mêmes buts et dispose d'autres moyens techniques."

31 Reading and Writing—Together

Patricia L. Stock and Karen K. Wixson

English Composition Board and School of Education, The University of Michigan

Reading and writing teachers most certainly are aware that an intimate relationship exists between reading and writing. Yet, we rarely acknowledge this relationship in our instruction, preferring to keep reading and writing separate "subjects." This is due, at least in part, to the models for the development of language skills which have traditionally served as the basis for instructional practice. These models typically present the acquisition of reading and writing skills as part of a developmental hierarchy which proceeds from listening, to speaking, to reading, and finally, to writing (see Figure 1). Furthermore, models of this type assume that "a firm foundation is required at each level before the next skill level can be effectively added or integrated" (Lerner, p. 254). With such a model as the basis for instructional practice, it is not difficult to understand why there has been so little integration of reading and writing instruction.

However, activity in the fields of psychology and linguistics during the past 50 years has resulted in a new approach to studying language activities—psycholinguistics—and to newly conceived models of language learning and use that place listening, speaking, reading, and writing within a cognitive-linguistic framework. The essence of this view is that language is a medium of communication which is grounded in thinking. Proponents of the view—psychologists, linguists, and sociologists as well as theorists and teachers of reading and writing—have elected to describe their insights in terms of a superstructure of language use which is formed by the set of relations among sender, receiver, and message, and the set of reciprocal relationships which exist between listening and speaking, reading and writing (see Figure 2).

Within this framework for thinking about how the processes of language are interrelated and especially about the interrelationships between reading and writing, lies an approach for teaching literacy. Indeed, it is precisely this framework and this approach toward which theorists are leading reading and writing educators today. Some of their ideas appear to be particularly salient for our purposes.

First, a cognitive-linguistic view of reading and writing which emphasizes the relationships inherent in language use focuses our attention on the *process* of communicating through written language, not the *products* of this process.

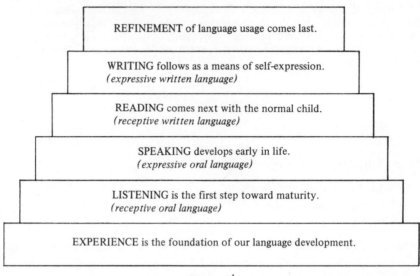

Figure 1[1]

Development of the relationship of the elements of the language arts

Traditionally, our instructional efforts have been directed at the products which result from either reading or writing—on written texts themselves and on accurate reading and writing of them—rather than the processes which enable readers/writers to become effective meaning makers. In the name of teaching students to read, we have focused our instruction primarily on training behaviors such as expressive, errorless oral reading and accurate question-answering. Similarly, in the name of teaching writing, our instruction typically has focused on training students in good penmanship, spelling, grammar, and punctuation. When the emphasis is placed on products, there is no apparent relationship between instruction in reading and writing; therefore, it is logical to treat them as separate subjects for instructional purposes. However, when the emphasis is placed on process, the interrelationship between reading and writing can be seen clearly and, therefore, it is obvious that the two should be integrated in instruction. It follows that models which focus our attention on the processes involved in the

	ENCODING *DECODING*	
VERBAL-IZATION (basic)	speaking———listening	ORAL
LITERACY (derived)	writing———reading	WRITTEN

Figure 2[2]

The two levels of verbal coding

effective use of written language bring us one step closer to instruction which focuses on the reciprocal relationship between reading and writing.

Second, when emphasis is placed on the process of communicating through written language, it is clear that the language user (i.e., reader/writer) is at the heart of the process. Whether reading or writing, the function of the language user is the same—to make meaning. When viewed in this context, it is obvious that we cannot separate reading from writing any more than we can separate the reader from the writer; and that instructional efforts should be directed at the language user rather than the material to be read or to be written because it is only in the language user's processing of text that meaning is made. When the instructional emphasis is placed on language users, we can see that procedures which are directed at improving their skills in one area are likely to influence their skill in the other area. As Berthoff remarks, the way "to strengthen one kind of meaning-making will be to strengthen the other" (p. 168).

Third, when emphasis is placed on each language user's processing of text as the source of meaning in reading and writing, then it is obvious that meaning can vary and that we must be concerned with the factors that influence meaning making. Meaning making is dependent on the interrelationship between factors which are both internal and external to the language user. Language users' knowledge and experience, their perceptions of text and the nature of various communicative events are all sources of variation in the process of meaning making. Similarly, meaning making is influenced by the functional properties of the communicative event itself. It is the interrelationship between the factors associated with the language user and the function of the communicative event which defines the dimensions of instruction in reading and writing.

Function is a concept that is not easily defined. However, for instructional purposes it can be characterized as a combination of the following contextual variables: 1) the *purpose,* or communicative intent, of the written language event; 2) the *setting* in which it occurs; and 3) the *mode,* or genre, in which the language is written.[3] In writing instruction the writing itself is the task, whereas in reading instruction it is necessary to create a task which will make the meaning resulting from comprehension visible. In practice, task requirements in both reading and writing instruction frequently play a major role in determining the nature of the meaning making process which occurs. However, it is our belief that function should serve to define the task, rather than the reverse. Therefore, we conceive task as implied by the functional variables of purpose, setting and mode. In sum, our instructional task is to teach language users effective methods for making meaning within the context of a particular written language event— in so doing, we, too, make meaning.

What we have described here is a theory of the relationship between reading and writing which can serve as a basis for instructional planning. The focus of the theory is the language user (reader/writer) as meaning maker. The two types of written language events in which language users may participate are reading and writing. Within each type of written language event, the function of the event, as defined by purpose, setting, and mode determines the nature of the meaning individual language users will make as they comprehend or compose. The interrelationship between reading and writing exerts its influence on the meaning-making process in the form of either the author (i.e., the reader's perception of the function of the writing event which produced the text) or the audience (i.e., the writer's perception of the function of the predicted reading event.) The meaning making which occurs within the context of specific written language events is ultimately referred to as either comprehending or composing.

This theory presents reading and writing as a communication system in which the reader/writer functions as a meaning maker. In other words, reading and writing are viewed as part of the same process—communication—and readers and writers are viewed as partners in that process.

What are the pedagogical implications of this view of reading and writing? First, and perhaps most important, this model implies that the goal of both reading and writing instruction is the same—to teach effective communication through written language. This suggests that the best way to accomplish this goal is to *teach reading and writing together.*

The theory also suggests that the focus of *reading and writing instruction should be reading and writing activities.* James Moffett and Betty Jane Wagner (1976) point out that traditional composition instruction is not writing. Rather, it is a body of prescriptions and proscriptions *about* writing. This is also true for reading instruction. Moffett and Wagner conclude that learning generalizations about language will not improve either writing or reading. Stephen Judy states the case emphatically, "Literacy programs should be based on reading and writing experiences, not principally on the study of literacy-related skills" (Judy, *The ABC's* p. 82).

The theory we present further implies that *the basis of instruction should be the communicative function of the reading and/or writing event for the language user.* Too often, students are asked to engage in reading and writing activities which have no meaning for them. As a child told one of us recently when asked why she read in her reading book: "Well, it gives me something to do!" It is questionable if reading for the purpose of learning to read or writing for the purpose of learning to write is sufficient to produce in our students the type of internalized knowledge of those activities which we are seeking. Using *function* as the basis for instructional activities has several other advantages as well. First, it permits us to introduce our students to a variety of forms of written language and their uses. Traditional instruction in reading and writing focuses primarily on the small subset of written forms which are most common to academic settings. Many students leave our classrooms ill prepared for the variety of reading and writing tasks which confront them outside an academic setting. However, when function is the starting point for instruction, there is no limit to the variety of written forms that can be studied or the skills for reading and writing which can be taught.

To illustrate the functional approach to the teaching of reading and writing which we propose here, we shall describe a series of activities we have developed to teach reading and writing together. It is important for us to state what may appear to be obvious because what is obvious is at the heart of our approach: The activities we describe here—like all meaningful learning activities—were created with a specific class and a specific setting in mind, a secondary school English class about to study John Hersey's novel *Hiroshima.* Although the class and the subject guided our choice of materials and the activities we constructed, we believe that language/learning events such as the ones we illustrate here are as appropriate for teaching elementary school children and adults in professional schools as they are for secondary school students.

The goals for the materials and activities we have developed are as diverse and complex as our students, ourselves, and the environment in which we all inter-act. Through them, we want our students to participate in language experiences that will not only prepare them to read Hersey's work of literature but will also immerse them in the study of a subject which is new to them. We want them to discover that studying a new subject can be a frustrating experience, initially; that the frustrations they may experience when first reading and writing about a topic are often the result of their unfamiliarity with the topic and the texts rather than of their inabilities or shortcomings as readers/writers; and that these frustrations abate and fade as learners talk and listen, write and read their way to understanding. In summary, we want students to experience the power of language as a heuristic for learning even as they learn to read and write more effectively.

Within this broad framework, five specific goals guided us as we developed the activities: (1) to provide students with occasions to learn to read and write effectively for a variety of purposes and settings, and in a variety of modes; (2) to have them make explicit for themselves a number of their implicit linguistic and/or cultural intuitions about reading and writing and written texts; (3) to introduce them to how different human interests and activities shape the discourse of literate texts; (4) to provide them instruction in techniques for reading and skills for writing; and (5) to have students begin and complete a project which requires them to select a topic for study and to read and write extensively on that topic in preparation for communicating their understanding to others.

Once in the classroom, we initiate this study by asking students to do 15-20 minutes of freewriting about Hiroshima in their journals: We suggest that students write what they know about the city of Hiroshima, or what they have heard about it, or whatever questions they may have about it. When students finish writing, we discuss Hiroshima, beginning with what they have written. Our students, born a quarter of a century after WW II, have as many questions about Hiroshima and the atomic bombing of that city as they have facts or opinions about it. Class discussions begin with students' offering tentative opinions, uncertain facts, and proceeding to pose questions about the city and the events which made it famous. Their discussions lead them back to opinions and on to more questions about the atomic bombing of the city. Some students line up on the issue of whether the city should have been bombed, insisting on the necessity for the bombing or condemning its immorality; others watch from the sidelines and listen; still others share personal anecdotes:

S1:   My uncle was on the USS *Missouri*; he saw the Japanese emperor sign the surrender through his binoculars.

S2:   No.

S1:   Yes.

Talk is encouraged, for the more information, the more questions, the more opinions, and the more personal history our students invest in the subject, the more intellectual curiosity they will bring to the reading and writing we ask of them. Some of them will begin to read and write for particular purposes of their own making; others will depend upon our guidance.

We provide that guidance after this first session of writing and talking about Hiroshima, when we ask students to free write again. This time we ask them to focus their attention upon a controversial issue implicit in the topic:

Do you think the U.S. should have dropped an atomic bomb on the city of Hiroshima? Explain the reasons why you think as you do. If you do not have an opinion on this topic at the moment, explain why you are unable to form an opinion. What facts or issues make the problem too complex for you to make a decision about it?

Before they write, we explain that we will be reading and writing together about Hiroshima and its bombing for several weeks and that as part of our study we would like them periodically to write about the bombing and their opinions about it and to reread their previous writings so that they may reflect upon their opinions about the topic over time to see if reading, writing, listening, and talking about it change their opinions and/or their reasons for holding their opinions. After these writing and discussion activities have helped students to identify issues and questions which interest them in the subject matter to be studied, we begin our study of the processes of reading by having students divided into small groups to read together six passages from longer texts written about Hiroshima.

Because we want students to learn that effective readers and writers read and write differently for different purposes, we supply students a purpose for their reading, knowing full well that many students are already reading to satisfy their curiosity about the topic we have introduced or a specific aspect of it. Before we guide students' reading with our purpose, we assure them that we know that readers often have more than one purpose for reading and that they will read for our purpose most effectively, if it becomes one of their own.

These are the directions we give them:

Among the six passages you have in your hand are a speech, a poem, a scientific report, an encyclopedia article, a true-experience account, and a social science essay. As you read these passages together, talk about them and decide which is which. Be prepared to explain to the class all the reasons you can find for identifying each passage as you do.

In fact, students have almost no difficulty identifying each text accurately; furthermore, their explanations for why they are able to identify the modes or genres of the texts serve both to demonstrate to them how sophisticated their linguistic/cultural intuitions are and to give them confidence as readers and writers.

For example when they identify the encyclopedia article (Excerpt A), they cite as their evidence the conventional physical features of the passage such as the bold-faced heading of the piece, the initialed signature to the article, the size of the print, the minimal paragraphing, and so on. They also note other conventions: The first sentence is a fragment which functions like an equation, Hiroshima=; the passage is laden with information; new facts are presented in each sentence; there are no sentences that function exclusively to connect or to relate one sentence to another; no words are wasted, and so on.

* * *

Excerpt A[4]

HIROSHIMA, a seaport, capital of Hiroshima prefecture, in southwestern Japan. Population (1960) 431,336. The town of Hiroshima grew up on the delta of the Ota river, where the Mori clan built a castle in 1591 which survived until 1945. From the Meiji era (1868-1912) to World War II, the city was a military centre. On Aug. 6, 1945, Hiroshima was the first city to be struck by an atomic bomb— dropped by the United States air force. The greater part of the city was destroyed, and about 75,000 people were killed or died later as a result of the bombing. Reconstruction was commenced immediately after the end of the war. New permanent buildings were begun about 1950 under a city-planning scheme. Bridges are important as the city is split into six islets by the river delta, and recovery began with the rebuilding of the Inaribashi bridge. Being the largest city in the Chūgoku and Shikoku districts, Hiroshima has many administrative offices and public-utility centres. The chief modern industries include the Matsuda truck factory, the Mitsubishi shipbuilding and machinery factories and the Kirin brewery. The city produces 80% of the needles used in Japan.

* * *   (R.B.H.)

When students comment upon the content and form of the sentences, we as teachers can take advantage of the occasion we have created to ask students why the sentences are structured as they are. Students can begin to direct their attention to the communicative function encyclopedia articles serve—how readers' and writers' purposes intersect to produce meaning in this particular setting. Discussions about the function of the discourse which is found in an encyclopedia article can provide teachers occasions for demonstrating how human interests and activities of people shape texts.

> T: Why are the facts of this experience recorded for others to read?
> S1: So that we can learn from the past.
> T: How much can we learn about the past from this piece?
> S1: Well, the facts.
> T: What facts?
> S1: Where the city is. What happened. That kind of general thing.
> S2: It's only meant to give you an overview. You're supposed to go to other books, longer books for other facts, for more details.
> S3: Or to a novel, like the one we're going to read.
> T: What facts do you get in a novel?
> S4: You don't get facts in a novel. Novels are fiction.
> S3: You get facts, facts about what it's like to live through it. What it's like to get bombed. People who write novels are interested in feelings and problems and those kinds of things.

Discussions like these help students to identify the functions of different forms of discourse and to recognize why the meaning readers make differs with the form in which writers shape their messages and why writers choose to compose in different genres. The discussions can make clear that different people have different interests, occupy their time differently, look at the world with different expectations, and therefore find different things in it. The nature of uniquely human ideas shapes not only human activities in the world but also what human beings make of those activities in written texts.

The same observations students make about the structure and content of the sentences in the encyclopedia article can lead to meaningful instruction in and skills for reading and writing—meaningful because the instruction can be related to the functions of the text. Teachers can introduce these strategies and skills to their student readers/writers as potential—even necessary—aids to the activity of meaning making. For example, meaningful lessons in topics which teachers often find difficult, and sometimes less than interesting, to teach—topics such as mechanics (punctuation)—can grow out of the careful reading of this encyclopedia article. One such lesson dealing with the use of the comma might develop in this fashion.

The teacher might ask students: What is the *subject* of this article? No doubt they will reply: Hiroshima. She can then ask what are some of the *predications* about Hiroshima in the article. Students may answer: *Hiroshima is* a seaport capital; *it grew up* on a delta; *it was* a military center; *it was* the first city struck by an atomic bomb; and so on.

At that point, the teacher might note that students are drawing their information from one sentence after another. She might indicate that after the introductory sentence fragment in the text, there are ten complete sentences, seven of which begin with the *subject* of the sentence immediately followed by what is *predicated* about that subject. She can ask students to identify those seven sentences by telling her the *subjects* and *predicates* of them so she may write them on the chalkboard.

After the subjects and predicates of the seven sentences have served to identify them, the teacher can ask what the subjects and predicates of the three remaining sentences are. Then he can ask what mark of punctuation precedes the subject in these three sentences and then ask students to speculate on why the comma is used in that place consistently.

Activities such as this one lead students to form hypotheses about mechanical and linguistic conventions from a functional perspective. They suggest that writers place commas before the subjects and predicates of sentences when the subjects and predicates do not open those sentences because this mark aids readers who are trying to determine the writers intended meaning for the sentence. They suggest that the mark of punctuation in part helps the reader's eye to learn from the writer's pen, what a listener's ear might learn from a speaker's voice. They begin to talk about marks of punctuation as mutually recognized conventions available to readers and writers as they are about the business of making meaning together.

Discussions like this can lead teachers and students as far into theoretical and/ or practical language study as their imaginations and information will take them. For example, during such a discussion, one of us once recognized a student who commented on the spelling of *centre* (1. 6). Students at first delighted in finding an error in an encyclopedia, but they soon began to explore other explanations for the spelling:

S1: I've seen it like that.
S2: Yeah, well somebody spelled it wrong.
S3: Oh, no, sometimes *theatre*'s like that too.
S3: I know, I know it's English, you know, not American–English.
S2: Oh, yeah, that's right.
S3: Where is this from–this article.
S1: Some English encyclopedia, I bet.
S3: It is?

Each of the other five passages we ask our reading/writing students to identify– like the encyclopedia article–provides occasions for them to probe a different mode or genre of text and to rehearse both its conventional characteristics and the human interest and activities that shape it. The texts also provide students occasions for instruction in skills of reading and writing.

Excerpt B provokes questions about the communicative function of scientific discourse–even as it provides occasions for demonstrating how the vocabulary and syntax of technical language, cohesion in texts, the use of graphic aids, and so on, influence the meaning making process. Reports such as Excerpt B also raise theoretical questions on the nature of scientific argument: Is the purpose of scientific argument to gain consensus among scientists? To persuade others of the correctness of one scientist's methods? or findings? or theories? Excerpt B can also lead to analyses of the powers and constraints of ordinary language, technical languages, even symbolic languages, and of how the visible discourse itself in scientific texts facilitates the meaning making process.

Excerpt B[5]

In another report, shown in Table II, the incidence of salivary gland tumors per 10^c persons per year in Hiroshima City in 1953–71 was 1.8 in exposed (36 cases) and 0.7 in unexposed, that is, 2.7 higher among exposed; the rate of malignant tumors in exposed was 10 times higher than in unexposed. Two peaks of salivary gland tumor were found, in 1960–63, and in 1967–70. Furthermore, there was a tendency for the incidence to be higher, as the exposure distance is shorter.

Stomach cancer is the most common malignant tumor among the Japanese, and the mucosa of the gastrointestinal tract is said to be sensitive to radiation. In 326 autopsy cases of stomach cancer in Hiroshima and Nagasaki in 1961–68, no dose-effect relation could be established. However, in a survey of death certificates and autopsy cases in 1961–74, a higher prevalence rate was observed in those exposed to a dose of more than 200 rads.

The occurrence of malignant tumors with different localizations without statistical incidence to exposed dose was described in other papers. Studies on individual malignant tumors need to be continued.

Table II. Rate of Incidence of Tumors of Salivary Gland Divided by Sort of Exposure in Hiroshima City (1953-1971)

	Total Ex-posed	Directly Ex-posed	Early Enterer in City	Non-exposed
Total tumors				
Observed cases	36	31	5	30
Rate of incidence*	1.8	1.9	1.4	0.7
Malignant tumors				
Observed cases	19	17	2	5
Rate of incidence*	1.0	1.0	0.6	0.1
Benign tumors				
Observed cases	17	14	3	25
Rate of incidence*	0.9	0.9	0.8	0.5

*Rate of incidence per year per 100,000 persons. Standardized in five years of age classes according to census 1960.

* * *

Excerpt C from the speech delivered by Harry Truman leads to discussion of discourse in which persuasion not consensus is the author's intention for his audience. It also stimulates discussions about the difference between talking and writing, listening and reading as well as lessons on denotations and connotations of words, on how the vocabulary and syntax speakers/writers choose as they construct meaning facilitate reconstruction of meaning by listeners/readers.

* * *

Excerpt C[6]

SIXTEEN HOURS AGO an American airplane dropped one bomb on Hiroshima, an important Japanese Army base. That bomb had more power than 20,000 tons of T.N.T. It had more than two thousand times the blast power of the British "Grand Slam" which is the largest bomb ever yet used in the history of warfare.

The Japanese began the war from the air at Pearl Harbor. They have been repaid many fold. And the end is not yet. With this bomb we have now added a new and revolutionary increase in destruction to supplement the growing power of our armed forces. In their present form these bombs are now in production and even more powerful forms are in development.

It is an atomic bomb. It is a harnessing of the basic power of the universe. The force from which the sun draws its power has been loosed against those who brought war to the Far East.

Before 1939, it was the accepted belief of scientists that it was theoretically possible to release atomic energy. But no one knew any practical method of doing it. By 1942, however, we knew that the Germans were working feverishly to find a way to add atomic energy to the other engines of war with which they hoped to enslave the world. But they failed. We may be grateful to Providence that the Germans got the V-1's and V-2's late and in limited quantities and even more grateful that they did not get the atomic bomb at all.

The battle of the laboratories held fateful risks for us as well as the battles of the air, land and sea, and we have now won the battle of the laboratories as we have won the other battles.

Beginning in 1940, before Pearl Harbor, scientific knowledge useful in war was pooled between the United States and Great Britain, and many priceless helps to our victories have come from that arrangement. Under that general policy the research on the atomic bomb was begun. With American and British scientists working together we entered the race of discovery against the Germans.

* * *

In contrast to the form and language of the speech—shaped as they are by the speech's function—the poem, Excerpt D represents the shaping of language for artistic purposes—to capture the multiple motivations that make up specific human drama. The poet's uses of the cadence of oral language and the graphics of written language become sources of discussions about the function of written discourse in the arts and the humanities as it may be contrasted to the function of written discourse in government and science and to the visual nature of written discourse. This excerpt also provides the occasion for skills' lessons on concrete and abstract uses of language.

* * *

Excerpt D[7]

In a Surrealist Year

In a surrealist year

of sandwichmen and sunbathers
dead sunflowers and live telephones

house-broken politicos with party whips
performed as usual
in the rings of their sawdust circuses
where tumblers and human cannonballs
                filled the air like cries
   when some cool clown
           pressed an inedible mushroom button
and an inaudible Sunday bomb
      fell down
catching the president at his prayers
              on the 19th green
   O it was a spring
           of fur leaves and cobalt flowers
when cadillacs fell through the trees like rain
     drowning the meadows with madness
while out of every imitation cloud
          dropped myriad wingless crowds
            of nutless nagasaki survivors
   And lost teacups
   full of our ashes
   floated by

             *   *   *

The true experience account of the bombing—Excerpt E—can lead to discussion of the power of expressive writing, for the writer-as-reader as well as for others who might also become readers of the text. The richly figurative language in the text informs students that informal speech and writing is often as poetic as the language in Excerpt D.

             *   *   *

Excerpt E[8]

Ah, that instant! I felt as though I had been struck on the back with something like a big hammer, and thrown into boiling oil. When I abruptly came to again, everything around me was smothered in black smoke: it was all like a dream or something that didn't make sense. My chest hurt. I could barely breathe, and I thought. 'This is the end.' I pressed my chest tightly and lay face down on the ground, and ever so many times I called for help. . . .

Through a darkness like the bottom of Hell I could hear the voices of the other students calling for their mothers.

At the base of the bridge, inside a big cistern that had been dug out there, was a mother weeping and holding above her head a naked baby that was burned bright red all over its body, and another mother was crying and sobbing as she gave her burned breast to her baby. In the cistern the students stood with only their heads above the water and their two hands, which they clasped as they imploringly cried and screamed, calling their parents. But every single person who passed was wounded, all of them, and there was no one to turn to for help. . . .

             *   *   *

The excerpt from the social science essay (Excerpt F) is included to provoke discussions about how the form of discourse mediates the communication process between writers and readers. Students can tackle ethical—even moral—questions about forms of discourse when they address issues such as: What meaning is to be construed by readers, is intended by the writer from the form of this discourse?

*   *   *

Excerpt F[9]

Before describing postwar problems, let us consider what we mean by an acceptable level of risk. We could start by asking, "How much tragedy can we live with and still not have 'the survivors envy the dead'?", but we will start with a more moderate question: "How dangerous or hostile a world would we be willing to live in and still call it a reasonable facsimile of a Russian or American standard of living?"

Nobody in either country would worry about a situation in which one thousand workers were engaged in some hazardous occupation which inflicted on each worker one chance in a hundred thousand per year of a fatal accident. Over a full year there would be approximately 99 chances in 100 that none of the workers would be hurt (see Table 5). Over a fifty-year period there would be better than an even chance that no worker would have been hurt. However, this attitude may change if the entire world population is subjected, as a result of some governmental action, to the same level of risk.

Table 5   Acceptability of Risks

Peace

$$1 \text{ thousand workers} \quad \times \quad \frac{1}{100,000} \quad = \quad 0.01/\text{year}$$

$$0.01 \quad \times \quad 50 \text{ years} \quad = \quad 0.5 \text{ workers}$$

$$3 \text{ billion people} \quad \times \quad \frac{1}{100,000} \quad = \quad 30,000/\text{year}$$

$$30,000 \quad \times \quad 50 \text{ years} \quad = \quad 1,500,000 \text{ people}$$

Postwar

$$180 \text{ million Americans} \quad \times \quad \frac{1}{100,000} \quad = \quad 1,800/\text{year}$$

$$1,800 \quad \times \quad 50 \text{ years} \quad = \quad 90,000 \text{ Americans}$$

Because the world's population is so large (about three billion), one chance in a hundred thousand of a fatal accident per year means that on the average 30,000 extra people per year would be killed. Over fifty years, 1,500,000 would die prematurely. While these are large numbers, something like this might result if many governments engaged in vigorous programs of weapons testing. Many people feel that any peacetime government action that could result in such a large number of casualties is intolerable.

We are concerned here, however, with the consequences of a war. One might well ask, "If a few bombs in the distant Pacific or Soviet Arctic will cause so much damage, would not a lot of bombs close-in be totally catastrophic?" The answer depends on how one defines "totally catastrophic"; a catastrophe can be pretty catastrophic without being total. Unfortunately, in order to make some necessary distinctions I will now have to treat some aspects of human tragedy in an objective and quantitative fashion even though some readers will find such treatment objectionable. I will tend to ignore, or at least underemphasize, what many people might consider the most important result of a war—the over-all suffering induced by 10,000 years of postwar environment. Instead, let us ask two questions: Can society *bear* the economic burdens caused by the increased sickness, malformations, and deaths? What view should a reasonable (non-hyprochondriac) individual hold toward his own future?

The reader can easily see that from the viewpoint of these two questions, decision makers might define a postwar world as "tolerable" if death rates increased by about one per cent for tens of thousands of years, even though this might mean that at long length the war would cause the premature death of more people than are now alive. ...

*   *   *

In all of the activities suggested above and the myriad others implicit in the material, communicative language events become the class's medium for studying the uses of written language. As we ask students to listen and talk, read and write their way to better understanding of written language use in class, we also ask them to read and write alone outside class. For example, one of the tasks we assign them is to read and write about an article from the October 1978 issue of *The Progressive* magazine. Specifically, we ask them to read the article with pens in hand, recording in their journals what they have to know in order to comprehend the article. Our purpose is to have them use writing as a means of making their processes of reading explicit for themselves.

The following brief excerpt from the article illustrates the challenge it presents to readers.

*   *   *

The Day the Bomb Went Off
*Erwin Knoll and Theodore A. Postol**

It was a sunny summer morning in the Chicago Loop. The usual bumper-to-bumper jam of cars and trucks. On the sidewalks, the usual crowd of shoppers, tourists, messengers, office workers heading out to an early lunch. It was Friday.

At 11:27, a twenty-megaton nuclear bomb exploded a few feet above street level at the corner of LaSalle and Adams. First the incredible flash of light and

*Erwin Knoll is the editor of *The Progressive*. Theodore A. Postol is a physicist and nuclear engineer on the staff of the Argonne National Laboratory. He is a member of the Chicago Committee for a Nuclear Overkill Moratorium (NOMOR).

heat: In less than one-millionth of a second, the temperature rose to 150 million degrees Fahrenheit—more than four times the temperature at the center of the sun.

The roar followed immediately but there, in the center of the city and for miles around, no one was left to hear it. There was only the heat. And the dust.

Imagine that it happened. We will not speculate here on why it happened—on whose fault it was, on the series of diplomatic bluffs and blunders and miscalculations here and there that made it happen. It happened.

Even in the macro-magnitudes of nuclear weaponry, a twenty-megaton bomb is large—the equivalent of twenty million tons of TNT, though such comparisons have little meaning. The yield of a twenty-megaton bomb is some 1,500 times greater than the yield of the bomb that was dropped on Hiroshima thirty-three years ago.

The United States does not admit to deploying any twenty-megaton bombs in its nuclear arsenal. With its superiority in missile numbers and missile accuracy, the United States prefers weapons of lower yield. But the Soviet Union's 200 SS-9 intercontinental ballistic missiles are believed to carry warheads in the twenty-megaton range, and they—along with lesser bombs—are presumably targeted on the fifty largest cities in the United States.

In the event of a nuclear war, a total of some 100 to 200 megatons would be directed at a metropolitan area like Chicago's.

The bomb that exploded in the Loop left a crater 600 feet deep and nearly a mile and a half in diameter. The crater's lip, extending almost to the shore of Lake Michigan on the east, was 200 feet high and would be, after the cloud of radioactive debris and dust had settled or dissipated, the tallest "object" visible in the area of the blast.

For the moment, though, there was just the incandescent fireball, rising and expanding outward at enormous speed, reaching a height and breadth of three or four miles, illuminating the sky, so that 100 miles away, over Milwaukee, the flash blinded the crew of a Chicago-bound airliner.

Around Ground Zero, everything—steel and concrete skyscrapers, roads and bridges, thousands of tons of earth, hundreds of thousands of people—was instantly evaporated.

At the edge of the fireball, a thin shell of super-heated, super-compressed gas acquired a momentum of its own and was propelled outward as a blast of immense extent and power, picking up objects from disintegrating buildings, snatching huge boulders and reducing them to vapor that would solidify, eventually, into radioactive dust.

Three seconds had elapsed since the bomb went off.

A high-altitude blast at one to three miles above ground level would have inflicted considerably greater blast damage, but the surface blast has its own "advantage": By maximizing the amount of debris sucked up in the nuclear explosion, it multiplies the long-range radiological effects, threatening the survival of living things hundreds of miles from the target area. And even the blast radius of a surface detonation is powerful enough to ignite fires more than twenty miles from Ground Zero—more than thirty miles if clouds help to reflect the flash.

Within a minute, the familiar shape of the mushroom cloud began to form over Chicago, symmetrical and strikingly beautiful in various shades of red and reddish brown. The color was provided by some eighty tons of nitric and nitrous oxides synthesized in the high temperatures and nuclear radiations. In time, these compounds would be borne aloft to reduce the ozone in the upper atmosphere.

The mushroom cloud expanded for ten or fifteen minutes, reaching a mature height of twenty to twenty-five miles and extending seventy to eighty miles across the sky.

*   *   *

The tone of the essay, the point-of-view from which it is written, the genre in which it is written, even the typeface in which it was printed shift back and forth between the real and the imaginary, the authoritative and the fanciful. Our students record their initial disorientation and eventual satisfaction as readers of the essay, readers who are striving to negotiate meaning with the authors. This exercise provides occasions in class for students to read excerpts from their journal records of their reading processes. These sessions demonstrate to students that we read in as many styles as we write and, furthermore, that most of us make similar meanings of texts. We explore why this is so: How much of the meaning we make of texts is a function of the way they are written and printed? Of the culture and conventions we share with each other and with authors? Of rules of discourse that we know intuitively? Of our individual perceptions? As readers gain a sense of their active role in the reading process, they learn that they are crucial participants in the meaning making process.

This activity is a natural bridge to discussions of the composition of *The Progressive* article and the processes by which writers construct their meaning. Discussion shifts from the audience of our student readers to the authors of the essay—Knoll and Postol—their training, talents, interests, and the text they wrote. Students understand that *The Progressive* essay is powerful and effective not only because the authors are apparently committed to communicating about a topic which concerns them but also because they have researched the topic. They have done their homework, and, therefore, they have something significant to write about. Something others are interested in reading about.

After students have read and written about Knoll and Postol's "The Day the Bomb Went Off," we distribute copies of a collection of essays about nuclear warfare which appeared with the Knoll and Postol essay in the October 1978 *Progressive.* These essays provide us another bridge. We ask students to read these essays in preparation for the project in which they will first read and write extensively on a topic of their choosing and then share their understanding of the topic with us. Our practice is to ask several students to read each essay in *The Progressive* in preparation for a class discussion that begins with the articles written about nuclear warfare by different authors and goes on to deal with the interpretation of the essays by the individual student readers who make meaning of them. Discussions move back and forth between the topics of the composition and comprehension of the essays. Such discussion leads students both to realize that the essays in *The Progressive* were published together because they bespeak a particular point-of-view about the subject— a point-of-view either palatable or distasteful to students depending on their particular point-of-view toward the subject—and to speculate upon why the editor of the magazine, who presumably published essays compatible with his point-of-view, chose to co-author an essay in the magazine himself. Among other speculations students offer are this one: None of the other essays cover an aspect of the subject he wished to cover in his collection.

When students identify that individuals sometimes write because they know something or hold a point-of-view which they have not read elsewhere, we remind them that such writings are often important contributions to knowledge, and we invite them to contribute to one another's knowledge and ours by first reading widely to inform themselves about a subject of interest to them and then by writing with authority about the subject. We ask students to choose the topics of their intensive reading and writing because we want them to recognize how reading and writing can function as means of learning what they want or need to know as well as what we want them to know.

As they study to fulfill the assignment, students work in groups of three or four so that they may both benefit from one another's perspectives and counsel and so that they may enjoy the social benefits of collaboration. We divide the assignment into sequenced stages and give at least three class hours a week over to workshop sessions on the project for two reasons: to demonstrate that comprehending and composing take time and to enable us and the students to model reading and writing behaviors for one another over the five-six weeks it takes to complete this project. During the first two-three weeks we ask them to:

1. Read as many texts as time permits dealing with the topic you wish to study.
2. Comment in drafty journal-writes upon both the content and shape of the texts you are reading. As you do so: Identify the mode or genre of each text, the audience and purpose for which you think it was written, and the situation or setting in which it was produced or published; and comment upon the ease or difficulty you had reading each of the texts.
3. Share the texts you find most interesting/informative/useful with your group members. Discuss them together.
4. As a group, select a series of eight-ten of the most effective essay length texts from among your reading which argue for a perspective toward your subject which has emerged during your group discussions.

After they have read widely and selected readings they could recommend to others, we ask them to spend three-four weeks fulfilling the following activities:

1. Organize the collection of essays you have selected in an anthology for the audience of our class and for two purposes: (1) to inform us about the topic which interests you and (2) to persuade us to assume your perspective toward that topic.

2. Identify aspects of the topic or issue which are not adequately covered in the material you have collected.

3. Plan, compose, and polish one piece of writing each, to be included in your group's collection. The piece may be an essay, short story, several short poems or one long poem, a report of original research, and so on. Your original work is to cover aspects of your topic or approaches to it which you believe have not been covered in the eight-ten texts written by others which you have collected.

4. Make a Table of Contents of your selections in the order in which you would like us to read them. Write a Preface to your collection collaboratively. Your Preface should describe your texts, your purpose and the rationale for your arrangement of them.

5. Title and bind your anthology and add it to our classroom lending library.

The anthologies that eventually line a shelf in our classroom represent hundreds of hours of communicative language events distilled into texts—texts collected and composed by the language users in our classroom—texts focusing upon topics which reader/writers selected to study themselves. In fact, the texts which inspired the activities and excerpts on Hiroshima in this essay were developed as the result of one student's work to fulfill this project.[10]

We have found that when we have students select materials and topics for their own reading and writing, the texts they collect for us as well as those they write for us are as interesting to us as they are to our students. We have also found that as students read and write texts, mindful of the functions those texts are to serve, they become increasingly effective at both comprehending discourse written by different authors and for different audiences, purposes, and occasions and composing discourse for different audiences, purposes, and occasions. They come to understand that discourse is shaped by and for language users whose task it is to make meaning.

Notes

[1] From Ralph E. Kellogg. "Listening," in Pose Lamb (ed.) *Guiding Children's Learning*. (Dubuque, Iowa: William C. Brown, 1971) p. 118.

[2] From Moffett, James and Betty J. Wagner. *Student-Centered Language Arts and Reading K-13*. 2nd Ed. (Boston: Houghton Mifflin, 1976) p. 11.

[3] For the conception of function which we present here, we are indebted to the theory of language use developed by Bernard Van't Hul, Professor of English Language and Literature at the University of Michigan. In his heuristic acronym MAPS, Van't Hul reminds us that effective language use meets the demands peculiar to the *M*edium or *M*ode in which it is delivered (for example in speech or writing; in a friendly letter or medical report, and so on) and is suited to the speaker's or writer's *A*udience, *P*urpose, and *S*ituation. Van't Hul calls his acronym "warmed over Aristotle"—warmed over with insights gleaned from contemporary scholarship in language and linguistics.

[4] "Hiroshima," *The Encyclopaedia Britannica* (1972) p. 522.

[5] *A Call from Hibakusha of Hiroshima and Nagasaki:* Proceedings, International Symposium on the Damage and After-effects of the Atomic Bombing of

Hiroshima and Nagasaki, (July 21–August 9, 1977), Tokyo, Hiroshima, and Nagasaki.

[6] *Public Papers of the Presidents of the United States: Harry S. Truman: 1945* (Washington, D.C.: U.S. Government Printing Office, 1961) pp. 197–200.

[7] Lawrence Ferlinghetti, "In a Surrealist Year."

[8] From Sen. John Culver, "Unthinking the Unthinkable," *The Nation* (Jan.6–13, 1979).

[9] Kahn, Herman, *On Thermonuclear War* (Princeton: Princeton University Press, 1961), p. 3.

[10] We are thankful to Mary Haller, one of Stock's students, who collected texts about Hiroshima and to Miriam Pemberton, Assistant Director of Introductory Composition at the University of Michigan from 1981–82, who collected a broad range of discourse on the topic of Hiroshima with us.

4.

On Writing as a
Way of Learning

In this chapter, theorists and teachers describe the power of writing as a means of learning. Britton, whose work has broadly influenced the movement to insure that writing is required across the curriculum, begins by reminding us that our concern for our students' use of written language in all subjects is a concern for the quality of their learning. Baker supports Britton's thesis as he argues that writing is "our supreme means of understanding, of discovering our thoughts, of learning, of grasping things in the mind, of intellectual maturity" (p. 224).

In the next seven essays, teachers describe practices and courses they have developed to enable students both to learn to write and to write to learn. Murray describes seven elements that characterize an environment in which students can become authors—authorities. Elbow offers eleven ways to ask students to write by focusing their attention on the uses of writing instead of upon the writing itself. Young provides analyses of four pieces of student writing to illustrate the benefits of composing for different functions. Next, Reiff and Middleton and then Odell demonstrate how teachers can create and structure assignments to provide students with opportunities for significant learning. And last, both Isaacson and Meiland describe courses they teach in which writing serves as the primary means of instruction.

In the final essay, Fulwiler reflects upon the other writings in the chapter as he argues that teaching writing and reasoning is, in fact, teaching the basic skills that make "systematic articulate thought possible."

32 Language and Learning Across the Curriculum

James Britton
Professor Emeritus, University of London

I think we need to be clear at the outset that a concern for Language Across the Curriculum is not, in the final analysis, a concern for language—for the oracy and literacy of the students we teach—but a concern for the quality of learning in all subjects. This is politic—for how could teachers of the other subjects be persuaded that what the English teacher is paid to do must be shared around amongst all members of staff? But it is far more than politic: It is no less than a challenge to all teachers to consider the processes of learning, both in their own subjects and in the whole curriculum. It is a challenge to them to make a much needed, little heeded distinction between rote learning and genuine learning—little heeded because our policies for school organization and pupil evaluation tend to blur that distinction. What has to be realized is that learning is not a uni-directional process (what the teacher "gives off," the pupil absorbs) but an interactional one, essentially social in nature—teachers and students learning with each other and from each other. Only in this way can what is learnt in school subjects effectively become a part of an individual's total learning pattern, his world-knowledge and his self-knowledge—in practical terms, his "know-how" in the here and now, and in terms of a wider understanding his "theory of the world in the head," as Frank Smith has called it (1971, p. 11).

The view I am taking—that knowledge is a process of knowing rather than a storehouse of the known—is easily ridiculed. A story went the rounds some years ago of an inspector who asked a pupil, "Where is Newcastle?" and the pupil replied, "I don't know where Newcastle is, but if you'll tell me where it is, I'll tell you why it's there." A more recent story—and I know this one is true—will serve to turn the tables: a geography teacher in an Australian school was being rated by an angry parent. "My son isn't learning anything in your lessons. He doesn't even know the names of the principal ports of Australia." The teacher (sticking his neck out): "Well, Madam, do you?" Her reply: "Of course I don't, but I learnt them when I was at school!"

To Michael Polanyi, scientist and philosopher,

"Knowledge is an activity which would be better described as a process of knowing. Indeed, as the scientist goes on enquiring into yet uncomprehended experiences, so do those who accept his discoveries as established knowledge keep applying this to ever changing situations, developing it each time a step further. Research is an intensely dynamic enquiring, while knowledge is a more quiet research. Both are for ever on the move, according to similar principles, towards a deeper understanding of what is already known" (1969, p. 132).

---

*It may be useful to readers to recall the distinctions Britton makes between transactional language—"language to get things done"; expressive language—language "that might be called 'thinking aloud' "; and poetic language—"language as an art medium" (Britton *et al.,* pp. 88–90).

To view knowledge as a "quiet form of research" constitutes, as I have suggested, a challenge to our conception of the learning process. A science teacher at a London conference on Language Across the Curriculum made his response to the challenge in these words:

> "There seem to be two different and conflicting goals in science education: one is to teach a body of accepted knowledge, the other is to teach the process by which that knowledge has been acquired. One of these goals—the former—continues to be dominant in science teaching today, but I believe the latter goal—the process of science—is by far the most important. The way we work is bound up with the way we use language, and a change in emphasis from science as knowledge to science as process would require, amongst other things, a change in the way we use language" (Martin, *et al.,* 1976, p. 165).

Many teachers in science as well as the humanities are shifting the focus of their pedagogy from product (knowledge) to process because they are coming to new understandings of the relationship between language and learning. Those of us who are interested in this relationship have learnt a great deal from Vygotsky, the Russian psychologist, about the way talking and writing function as means of learning (the way infant speech, for example, lays the foundations for adult thinking). Recently, thanks to the labors of four American editors, we have a posthumous work by Vygotsky which gives his views about writing in greater detail (Vygotsky, 1978, Chpt. 8). He claims here that mastery of writing comes from using it to satisfy some need or fulfill some intention—something out and beyond the act of writing itself—just as speech is acquired in infancy for the purpose of understanding and controlling the environment. It is difficult at first to see how utterly opposed this is to the traditional view in schools that writing is learned by practicing it under the guidance of an expert who will tell you how well or how poorly you have performed.

Looking at the curriculum as a whole, then, I want briefly to suggest three purposes that writing might achieve for children in school.

First, there is that of establishing and maintaining a satisfying personal relationship with the teacher. If we take an interactional view of learning, it follows that we cannot effectively teach strangers: development of a personal relationship is essential. Journal writing—a written dialogue between pupil and teacher—is one very useful way of doing this. Take for example these extracts from the journal of a nine-year-old girl in a Toronto school (with her teacher's responses):

Jan. 20th, 1978. After my rough copy of my project I am going to rerange my project around. I am going to put growing up first page. What monkeys do to eat in second page. Why do monkeys make faces page three.

(Sounds interesting!)

Jan. 25. It was interesting. Did you think it was very interesting or interesting or just a little interesting? . . .

Feb. 20. When you were away the class had other teachers. The first teacher's name was Mrs. G. and the second teacher's name was Mr. M. They were both nice teachers. You know sometimes I wish you were my mother.

(Lots of the time I wish I had a little girl like you!)

Feb. 21. It's too bad I'm Chinese because if I was English you could adopt me.

The second purpose appropriate to writing in school is *learning* in the widely accepted sense of that word: organizing our knowledge of the world and extending it in an organized way so that it remains coherent, unified, reliable: building into our knowledge-from-experience the knowledge we take on trust from other people's experiences. I have before me a splendid example, a seventy-page book on marine animals produced by fourth- and fifth-grade children in a California school. Chapter One begins: "The sea is a radiant water galaxy. It's a world of its own in a special way. Under its foam crested surface, there exists a universe of plant and animal life. With the tiniest microscopic beings to the most humungus creature that ever lived, the sea is alive!" (*Our Friends in the Waters,* a Book on Marine Mammals Written by the Kids in Room 14, Old Mill School, Mill Valley, California, 1979).

I shall call this kind of learning Learning I in order to distinguish it from my third category of purpose, Learning II. In Learning I, we are in fact organizing the objective aspects of our experience; in Learning II we are organizing the subjective aspects of our experience, and though it is a familiar enough process, we do not usually recognize it as learning. The principle of organization of Learning I is, in essence, *logical*: that of Learning II is *artistic*. In the terms devised by the London Writing Research Project, Learning I employs language in the role of participant—a spectrum from Expressive to Transactional; that of Learning II is language in the role of spectator—a spectrum from Expressive to Poetic (Britton *et al.,* Chpt. 15). As the stories children write (whether autobiographical or fictional) become "shaped stories," more art-like, they move from the Expressive towards the Poetic. The more "shaped" they become, the more effectively they enable writers to explore and express their *values,* those ways of feeling and believing about the world that make us the sorts of people we are. I think you will sense this happening in the little story written by a six-and-a-half-year-old English girl:

There was a child of a witch who was ugly. He had pointed ears thin legs and was born in a cave. He flew in the air holding on nothing just playing games.

When he saw ordinary girls and boys he hit them with his broomstick. A cat came along. he arched his back at the girls and boys and made them run away. When they had gone far away the cat meeowed softly at the witch child. the cat loved the child. the child loved the cat the cat was the onlee thing the child loved in the world.

In a subject-based curriculum (as far as *using* language is concerned), Learning I will be the principal focus for lessons in science, history, geography, social studies, while Learning II will be the principal focus in English lessons.

Whether the topic be marine animals or ugly witches, what teachers and students say and write makes learning manifest. Thus there is in every classroom evidence of one kind of learning or another—neither of which a teacher can afford to ignore. Further, it is my experience that when teachers of different disciplines study such evidence jointly, important pedagogical and curricular issues come up for discussion.

33 Writing as Learning

Sheridan Baker
Department of English, The University of Michigan

The Practical Stylist arose directly from an article I wrote, as a young Instructor of English, against the new "Communication Skills," touted to replace old-hat freshman composition. Communication Skills was to include Speaking, Listening, and Reading, along with writing, not very strongly capitalized. It included a lot of listening to speech in hallways and playgrounds, pasting up bits from newspapers, magazines, and advertisements, watching people communicating through gestures and postures, and responding to movies and each other in darkened theaters. This new playschool almost crowded writing out completely, at best demoting it a clear seventy-five percent, and ignoring it as one of our most essential and powerful means of learning.

The new course took its cue from the new linguistics, whose slogan was "The spoken language is the language." Writing, newly described as a pale and imperfect imitation of speech, moved to the edges of education, and almost completely out the doors. The man whose article I answered in my first step toward *The Practical Stylist* was Ken Macrorie, then of the English department at Western Michigan University. He too eventually wrote a couple of textbooks, still representing his early stand against the square ideas of traditional composition, providing a kind of south pole to my north. A few years ago, and twenty-five years after our initial confrontation in the pages of an academic journal, Ken Macrorie and I finally met, for the first time, on a panel at a conference on composition where we aired our opposite views.

Macrorie believes that composition should be purely autobiographical. Students write best about what they know, he says, and they know themselves best. His students write first-person confessionals and complaints, sounding off as they produce an admirable number of pages—fluent, emotive, and, of course, interesting, like all human turmoil. The agonized "I" dominates throughout: "I . . . I . . . I . . . ," like the kindergartener's "show and tell" promoted to paper. Lively, yes—but oblivious to the greatest advantage composition has for a student.

Composition is a way of learning. It teaches us how to move from the circumscribed self-center of childhood and adolescence into mature thinking, how to generalize from our attitudes, emotions, hunches, and private ideas into mature and valid thought. It moves us from self to object, from emotional expression to rational thinking. The emotive and expressive is always with us. What an education should develop constantly is our rational and intellectual powers, not so readily operative as to need no encouragement. And composition, reasoning through language, does this better than anything else.

In *The Practical Stylist,* I urge two points: (1) writing leads to maturity, in the only places we mature significantly, in our attitudes, in our minds; (2) writing discovers our thoughts for us, as we try to produce them, clarify them, grasp them, and state them, on paper.

My point about maturity is this. If you say "I liked that film," you state a personal and historical fact, of no more consequence than "She went over to the neighbors'." If you say, "This film is good," you transform the personal report into an evaluation, an intellectual proposition to be illustrated as valid before the whole universe. This is growing up, this shift from believing that ideas are good because *you* hold them to realizing that they are good because they are good, and can be so demonstrated. Writing confirms this realization as you persuade others that what you believe true is indeed true. Writing reveals that you can trust what you think, not because it is *yours*—that kindergartener's "I"—but because it has demonstrable validity. So writing is one of our essential means of realizing our maturity. Writing teaches us that our ideas are valid, not merely personal and adolescent whimsies, and it teaches us to think as we attempt to prove those ideas so.

Writing is realizing. By writing we make our intangible floating notions into something as near to a solid reality as thoughts can come, objectifying them, and seeing them, *realizing* them, for the first time. W. H. Auden once summed up the process succinctly: "How can I know what I think till I see what I say?" He is explaining how writing poetry is a "game of knowledge, a bringing to consciousness, by naming them, of emotions and their hidden relationships" (Arnheim, pp. 173–174). But what he says applies to all writing, and not merely to emotions but to all we know, feel, sense, or vaguely intuit. Auden's sentence contains the anatomy of language as cognition, and recognition: *know, think, see, say*. The *saying* on paper puts our unformed thoughts before our eyes so that we *see* what we have been *thinking* and turns it into *knowledge*. Again, we *realize* our thoughts. Certainly, our common metaphor for understanding—"Oh, I *see*"—pays tribute to this power of writing. Speech alone does not serve so well. It vanishes with our breath, as it follows the circlings and repetitions of extemporaneous thought. We can think straight only on paper. And the process leaves our thoughts clearer and our speech straighter and more fluent too.

The process of writing, in fact, expands our capacity to think as nothing else can.[1] Aside from trying to solve mathematical problems and puzzles and playing tough intellectual games like chess, our intellectual beings—our physical brains, in fact—are never so intensely engaged as in the process of writing an essay. Writing is hard, and we shy away from it precisely because it demands such intense engagement. It is solving continuous sets of complex problems, finding the idea, from among myriad choices, by fitting the word to it. Writing is so highly valuable because it exercises our highest capacity so fully. And it increases that capacity. The old-fashioned notion that thinking makes our brains grow seems indeed to be true. Professor Mark Rosenzweig and his associates at the University of California have for some time been demonstrating by scalpel, calipers, and scales that the brains of thinking rats grow as compared to those of rats who don't have to think to eat. The problem-solvers develop bumps on their cerebral cortexes, enlarging that cortex far beyond those of the nonthinkers, to whom everything is given but the necessity to think. The brain is muscular after all. Problems develop its brawny powers. And writing is a kind of moment-by-moment problem-solving that exercises us along the very frontiers of thought itself, developing our most valuable capacities.

Thus writing does physically develop our ability to think, as it also helps us in each instance to discover and clarify our thoughts. I suppose we all know this from our own experience of writing and rewriting. But somehow we have failed to use this, our most efficient means of learning, in all our classrooms, whatever the subject. Mina Shaughnessy, in her excellent *Errors and Expectations* (1977), notes that in the British equivalent of our high school, students write about 1000 words a week in all their classes as against 350 in the good American high school and zero-zero-zero in a very great many. In all fields, writing does teach us. Like many others, Charles Darwin discovered this obvious but neglected truth:

> I have as much difficulty as ever in expressing myself clearly and concisely;
> . . . but it has had the compensating advantage of forcing me to think long
> and intently about every sentence, and thus I have been led to see errors in
> reasoning and in my own observations or those of others.[2]

We need to convince ourselves, all over again, of what Darwin discovered: Writing can bring one to think rationally, to uncover errors not only in reasoning but in what seems to be factual, empirical observation, until the struggle with thought and words reveals those observations to have been misinterpretations of what we thought we saw.

Writing gives us ourselves engaged with knowledge. The view that freshman composition is a dull exercise in platitudes, excluding the self, overlooks that necessary engagement. If it is dull, the self is not engaged. But we do not need the egocentric "I," the personal confession, to stir that engagement. Any subject of personal interest will bring self and subject together in language alive with personality and objectified for public inspection—and a sense of personal achievement. Language, and particularly as realized through writing, is rational thought, or rationalized thought (to borrow a seminal concept from James Harvey Robinson's book of some years ago, *The Mind in the Making*). We need words to get hold of, to grasp, in a rational, conceptual way, ideas provided by our minds below the level of language. Language comes from the left lobe of the brain that controls our right thinking, from the hemisphere able to achieve analytic thought, but it also comprehends, as best it can, the tumbling mists of thought and intuition in the darks of the right lobe containing our holistic and non-verbal beings, our inner selves. Language and writing thus get things together—reason and instinct, left and right. Writing our language out is like spinning a straight thread from the woolly heaps of whatever we have in our minds.

Ideas and language are not identical, as any effort to express our ideas in writing soon illustrates. As the transformational grammarians have reminded us, we can express the same idea in a number of different ways. We have something to say, even though we don't quite know what it is or how to say it. But we must say it in the only words we have, those supplied us from infancy by the public community we share. As James Moffett recently observed, our subjectivity is not so private as we usually think, since the inner speech from which we elaborate and edit all our utterances is acquired from our public culture (Moffett, "Writing, Inner Speech, and Meditation," 1981). We simply compose from the subjective fragmentary chaos a realized objective cosmos, from disorder to order, from hunches to sentences. We find the words that lift the thought up into the light, that fit it, like the shell of a snail, embodying it, giving it form and being. Again, only on paper, by writing and rewriting, can we get the fit, make the thought visible, bring it into some kind of nonsubjective being where it will bear inspection both from ourselves and others. In short, we discover it fully for the first time.

Writing formulates our thoughts. It is our supreme teacher. All of us know that having to write about something is our most effective means of learning about it, grasping it for ourselves as we try to explain it to others. We should use this elemental means of learning in every classroom. Do you want to understand how an internal combustion engine works? Get the basics in mind, and then write out your understanding for someone else, adding details and connections you hadn't even thought were there. You will understand it as never before. Writing is our supreme means of understanding, of discovering our thoughts, of learning, of grasping things in the mind, of intellectual maturity. Reading a book is following a stream of understanding. Writing one is a whole Mississippi. The simplest page of freshman writing demonstrates this process. Writing is discovery of thought. Writing is learning. Writing is maturity. We should use it in all our classrooms for all it is worth.

Notes

[1] From here on, I borrow from my "Writing as Discovery," *ADE Bulletin*, 43 (1974), 34–37.

[2] Darwin, Charles. *The Autobiography of Charles Darwin and Selected Letters.* Ed. Francis Darwin (NY: D. Appleton, 1892; repr. NY: Dover, 1958), p. 65.

34 First Silence, Then Paper

Donald M. Murray
Department of English, University of New Hampshire

I came to teach at the Wyoming Writing Project in Gillette, and John Warnock told me to shut up, sit down, and write.

I was in the right place. Writing begins when teachers give their students silence and paper—then sit down to write themselves.

That isn't all there is to teaching writing, a demanding craft that is backwards to most traditional teaching. We have to create an environment in which our students can become authors—authorities—on a subject by writing about it. Then they may learn to write by teaching us their subject, listening to our reaction to it, and revising their text until we are taught.

It isn't easy for me to be a student to my students' writing. I want to be the authority, to initiate learning, to do something—anything—first, to be a good old American take-charge guy. I keep having to reeducate myself to get out of the way, be patient, wait, listen, behave as I was commanded to behave in Wyoming.

This attitude, of course, is what I have to reteach myself day after day, year after year as a writer: to create quiet, to listen, to be ready if the writing comes. I am a writer and a teacher, and those of us who are, each day, both teacher and learner have to teach ourselves what we teach our students. We experience the difficulty of learning at the writing desk what so glibly can be said behind the teacher's desk—"be specific," "show, don't tell," "give examples," "make it flow."

It is our job as writers to create a context in which we can write, and it is our job as teachers of writing to create a context that is as appropriate for writing as the gym is for basketball. To do that I think we must consider seven elements.

Silence

Emptiness. Writing begins when I feel the familiar but always terrifying "I have nothing to say." There is no subject, no form, no language. Sometimes as I come to the writing desk I feel trapped in an arctic landscape without landmarks, an aluminum sky with no East or West, South or North. More often I feel the emptiness as a black pit without a bottom and with no light above. No down, no up. Soft furry walls with no handholds. Despair.

That's the starting point for good writing, an emptying out of all we have said and read, thought, seen, felt. The best writing is not a parroting of what others have said—or what we have said—before. It is an exploration of a problem we have not solved with language before. I have circled this question the editor of *fforum* placed before me, "What are the contexts in which effective writing can take place?" I write this text to solve that problem, first of all, for myself. I wonder if I have anything to say; I fear I do not, but I start making notes. I do not look so much at what others—and I—have said before, but what I find being said on my own page. The emptiness began to disappear when John Warnock gave me the gift of silence. I sat. I waited. The well began to fill.

We must begin our personal curriculum and our classroom curriculum with John Warnock's gift of silence. How rare it is that we encourage—even allow—our students freedom from busyness, moments of stillness, relief from the teacher's voice—quackity, quackity, quackity.

How rare it is we allow ourselves stillness. I try to start each day with fifteen minutes in which I just stare vacantly out of the window into myself, notebook open, pen uncapped. My vacant staring must be as disturbing to others as a class of students looking out of the window into themselves is to some administrators. It must seem a sign of mental illness, evidence of an acute cranial vacuum, proof you have left the company of those around you and become, in fact, a space shot. When my mother-in-law lived with me she took such staring as a social signal that conversation was needed. When I visit in other homes, or people visit mine, my early morning vacuity (indication to me that I am having my most productive moments of the day) causes them to leap into social action—quackity, quackity, quackity.

We must begin our writing curriculum with quiet, an unexpected and terrifying but productive, essential nothingness.

Territory

Emptiness cannot be maintained. The silence will fill and, if we filter out what is trivial, what we have succeeded at before, what we know, we will see and hear what surprises us. In the writing course the student is surprised at what he or she is in the process of knowing.

Again we have to turn our curriculum away from what is traditional and even may be appropriate in other subjects but is not appropriate for the learning of writing. In most courses our students come to us knowing they are ignorant of the subject matter, and we work hard to convince them of that ignorance. In the writing course our students come to us thinking they have nothing to say, and it is our responsibility to help them discover that they have plenty to say that is worth saying.

The beginning point is, again, a kind of nothingness, a responsible irresponsibility on the part of the teacher. No talk before writing, no assignments, no story-starters, no models, no list of possible topics—nothing that reveals you think the student has nothing worth saying and makes the student dependent on you for subject matter. Students will, of course, plead for a life preserver—a topic, any topic, even what I did on my summer vacation—but if you toss it to them they will not learn how to find and develop their own subjects, the basis of the writing process.

Instead of assignments—our assignments—the student is challenged to find his or her own assignments. We may have to help by drawing out of our students, in class and in conference, what they know. We may have to have our students interview each other, and then tell the class about the subjects on which the person interviewed is an authority. We may have to have our students list the subjects on which they are authorities, including jobs and out-of-class activities. But those are all crutches we use when we cannot stand the silence. It is far more responsible if we have the courage to wait.

Time

Waiting means time, time for staring out of windows, time for thinking, time for dreaming, time for doodling, time for rehearsing, planning, drafting, restarting, revising, editing.

I seem, to some of my colleagues, prolific, yet most of my writing evolved over years. Some of the things I am writing this year have written roots in my files that go back for ten or twenty years. The psychic roots go deeper. We cannot give our students years within an academic unit that is measured in 4 to 14 weeks, but we must find ways to give them as much time as possible. This means fewer assignments, in most courses, with frequent checkpoints along the way to make sure that time is being used.

Students need, as writers need, discipline applied to their time. There should be a firm deadline for the final copy—announced in advance—and then deadlines along the way, perhaps for proposals, research reports, titles, leads, ends, outlines, first, second, third or even fourth drafts. There may be a quantity demand: a page a day, or five pages a week, but pages that may be notes, outlines, drafts, false starts, edits, revisions, as well as final copy.

Time for writing must be fenced off from all other parts of the curriculum. This is not easy, because we have so many pressures on us, and we try to double or triple up. Many teachers are still trying to assign a paper on a reading, correct the first draft for grammar, and say they are teaching literature, writing, and language. Writing should, of course, be used to test our students' knowledge of literature, but that is only one form and a limited, schoolbound form of writing.

We must encourage writing that isn't bound by the limits of someone else's text and isn't restricted to a single form. Students must find their way to a subject worth exploring, and find their way to use language to explore it. Dr. Carol Berkenkotter of Michigan Technological University used me as a laboratory rat in a 2½-month naturalistic protocol. She discovered that more than 60% of my time—sometimes much more—was used for planning. We must give our students a chance to sniff around a potential subject, reminding ourselves of what Denise Levertov said, "You can smell the poem before you see it." We need time for this essential circling, moving closer, backing off, coming at it from a different angle, circling again, trying a new approach.

This circling means that the writing curriculum is failure-centered. If failure is not encouraged we will only have meaningless little essays plopped out like fast-food patties to our explicit measure.

Good writing is an experiment in meaning that works. The experiment that works is the product of many experiments that fail. The failure is essential, because through trying, failing, trying, failing, we discover what we have to say.

Need

Out of time and territory need will arise. Too often, as writing teachers, we use words such as "intention" or "purpose" too early with our students, as if such matters could, all of the time, be clarified early on with a formal strategy and specific tactics established before we know what we want to say and to whom we want to say it. The need to write on a subject at the beginning is much less than obvious purpose. It is an itch, a need to wonder about, to consider and reconsider, to mull over, to speculate.

As we give ourselves space and time we find we experience what can only be described as a sort-of-a-sensation, or a pre-sensation similar to the aura that precedes the migraine.

My mind fills by coming back to clustering specifics. Everything I read, see, overhear begins to relate itself to a particular concern. This concern is certainly not yet a thesis statement or a solution or an answer. It isn't even a hypothesis, a problem or a question. But as I give it words in my head and on my notebook page it begins to become a vision. I see a shadowy outline of a mountain range I may choose to map. I begin to have questions, I begin to define problems that may be fun to try to solve.

I have begun to be my own audience. I write to read what I have written not so much to find out what I already know, but to find out what I am knowing through writing. It is an active process. Dynamic. Kinetic. Exciting. This is what motivates the writer and the writing student: the excitement of learning and that peculiarly wonderful, significant, egocentric experience of hearing the voice you did not know you had.

Writing also satisfies the need to make. Years ago I wrote a story on General Foods and discovered they had created mixes that were too simple and foolproof. They had to back up and, as one executive said, "allow the housewife to put herself into the mix." A strange image, and perhaps a sexist one, but their marketing research revealed the need of making. Writing is a particularly satisfying kind of making, because we can make order out of disorder, meaning out of chaos; we can make something solid out of such powerful and amorphous materials as fear, love, hate, joy, envy, terror.

This brings us to another fundamental need, one we all, as teachers of writing, normally avoid. Beside my own typewriter is a quotation from Graham Greene: "Writing is a form of therapy; sometimes I wonder how all those who do not write, compose or paint can manage to escape the madness, the melancholia, the panic fear which is inherent in the human situation." The need to write above all else comes from the need to reveal, name, describe, order, and attempt to understand what is deepest and darkest in the human experience.

Process

The need demands process. There has to be a way to deal with the volume of information and language that crowds the writer's head and the writer's page. Quantity itself is both a problem and an opportunity—an abundance of information allows us to select and order meaning.

Too often students are forced to write without information or with just a few stray fragments of information they attempt to string together with a weak glue of stereotypes and clichés. It isn't easy to write without information. When students collect an abundance of information, however, they need to make distinctions between pieces of information—to decide what is significant and what is not—and then to follow the flow of the important information towards meaning.

It is of little value to teach skills and techniques, the processes of others, to students who do not put them into use in significant ways. Students who need techniques will develop them, and will start to share their tricks of the trade with other students who need them. Then the waiting composition teacher can pounce.

The teacher sees one student making a significant word choice, and the instructor broadcasts that to the class during the time for a class meeting when the day's writing is done. The instructor sets up pairs and small groups of students, inviting them to share their solutions and their problems. The instructor posts or publishes evolving drafts and outlines and notes to show how members of that particular class are making writing work. The teacher writes in public, on the blackboard, or with an overhead projector, revealing the teacher's own struggle to use language to achieve meaning, and inviting help from the class along the way. The instructor, in conference and in class meeting, shares accounts, techniques, and other tricks of the trade from professional writers at the moment the student defines a problem and seeks solutions. The teacher doesn't correct or suggest one solution, but gives the student alternatives so the student will decide which way to turn.

Most important, however, is the testimony from student writers who are writing well. The instructor calls attention to those pieces of writing that are working, and invites the student to tell the instructor, and the class, the process that produced the effective writing.

The case histories, first of all, instruct the writer. Usually the student has written by instinct, but when the student is asked to tell what he or she did, the student discovers that the writing was a rational process. It can be described and shared. And, of course, as the student describes the process that produced effective writing to others, the student reinforces that process.

Now students begin to work in a context of shared success. Those who write well are teaching themselves, each other, and the teacher how writing is made effective. They practice different styles of thinking and of working. They write in diverse voices and discover alternative solutions to the same writing problem. They find there is not one way to make writing work but many.

These solutions and skills flow into a coherent process. There are some things that are especially helpful when planning a text, others to help produce a text, still others to make the text clear. These techniques overlap and interact, because writing is a complex intellectual act, but the class discovers that underneath the contradictions there is a rational reason for most writing acts—don't be too critical in the beginning or you won't discover what you have to say, don't be too sloppy at the end or the reader won't be able to figure out what you've said.

It is vital that the process is drawn out of the class experience so the class learns together that each writer is capable of identifying and solving writing problems. Learning will not stop with this class. This class will not be dependent on this teacher; this class will graduate individuals who know, through their own experience, that they can respond, rationally and skillfully, to the demands of the writing tasks they will face in the years ahead.

Text

The principal text—and this from the author of writing texts—of the writing course should be the student's own evolving writing.

We have the responsibility to free our students from the tyranny of the printed page. They have been taught there is a right text, and it is printed in a book. They have been taught that the teacher has the code that will reveal the meaning of that text.

Writing is not like that. There is no text; there is a blank page, and then, with luck and work, a messy page. Language is trying to discover its meaning. The writer writes not knowing at first what the writer's own text is meaning, and then has to perceive the potential meaning in the confusion of syntax, misspelling, poor penmanship, and disorganized, searching thought.

Decoding a messy, evolving student text is a frightening challenge for most teachers, because they are untrained for this task. But writing teachers and their students have to learn to read unfinished writing. The use of finished models by far more talented writers is of little help unless the students see their early drafts, their clumsy and awkward sentences, their false sense, their early drafts that document how badly they had to write to write well.

Students publish their drafts in small group and whole class workshops where the writer is asked, "How can we help you?" I prefer to publish only the best drafts from the class to show good writing being made better. The text in the writing course is not what was once written, but what is being written.

Response

The writer needs response when it can do some good, when the writing can be changed, but in school we too often respond only when the writing is finished, when it's too late.

Professionals seek out writers who can help them when it counts. I call Don Graves, Chip Scanlan, or others, for I am blessed with many good writing colleagues—or they call me. We read a paragraph or two over the phone that needs a test reader right now. Not for criticism, not even for confirmation, but mostly for sharing.

Experienced writers need test audiences early on, and it is the challenge of the writing teacher to become the person with whom the student wants to share work that is still searching for meaning. It is also the responsibility of the writing teacher to create a community within the class that makes such sharing contagious. And as the drafts move toward a completed meaning the writer needs test readers who can become more critical and still supportive.

Writers need colleagues who share the same struggle to make meaning with words. As we write—student and professional—we practice a lonely craft, and we need writer friends who can reassure us, remind us of past successes, suggest possible alternatives, give us a human response to a changing text. Sometimes the writer's needs are specific—Will this lead make you read on? Do you understand my definition of photosynthesis? Have I gone off track on page 4?—but most of the time the writer simply needs to hear, by talking at someone else, what the writer, himself or herself, has to say about the text. The writer, after all, every writer, is continually teaching himself or herself to write.

Teachers should not withhold information that will help the student solve a writing problem. The most effective teacher, however, will try by questioning to get the student to solve the problem alone. If that fails, the teacher may offer three or more alternative solutions, and remind the student to ignore any of them if a solution of the writer's own comes to mind.

Central to the whole business of response is faith and trust. The teacher must have faith that the student can be the student's own most effective teacher, and must trust that student will find a way through the lonely journey that leads to effective writing. The student will feel that faith and trust. It will goad, support, challenge, comfort the student. And faith and trust given may be returned, especially to teachers who reveal their own lonely journeys as they use language to discover meaning.

These standards are high. The teacher believes you can write far better than you ever believed you could write. There is pressure on the student, and there are standards. At the end of the unit there is a delayed but meaningful evaluation. Students are graded on their final work of their own choice. The grades are based on accomplishment. The students have worked within contexts that allowed them to work well. Now their work is ready for measure. The private act of writing—born of silence—goes public.

35 Teaching Writing by Not Paying Attention to Writing

Peter Elbow
Department of English, SUNY, Stony Brook

"Pay more attention to your writing!" we say to students when they write badly. "Pay more attention to writing!" we say to teachers in all disciplines as we try to encourage writing across the curriculum. Good advice, but it's just as important to spend some time writing without paying attention to it. It's important in writing courses, where excessive self-consciousness can knot writing up or make it coy. It is also important in subject matter courses since writing-without-paying-attention-to-it is a way to work on writing without taking any time away from, say, biology or economics or modern drama.

In this short essay I avoid the hard advice I offer elsewhere about how to pay more and better attention to writing. (See *Writing with Power,* New York, Oxford University Press, 1981.) Here, I limit myself to what is easy: eleven ways to write without paying attention to it.

When we pay attention to our writing, it is as though we are looking out the window but focusing our gaze on the pane of glass. Imagine the relief that comes from letting our focus pass *through* the pane to the green scene outside—the relief that comes from doing lots of writing in a course but not thinking about it as writing. This is not so much teaching writing as *using* writing, but the benefits of using writing are sometimes superior to the benefits of teaching it. Besides, using writing takes much less teacher time than teaching it and doesn't require teachers to be experts in writing. To accomplish this shift in focus, we must use writing as input and use writing as a way to get other jobs done.

Writing as Input

Think of the famous recipe for cooking grandfather sturgeon: nail it to a cedar plank, roast it for fourteen hours, throw away the fish, eat the plank. We think of writing as output—as a movement of information from the writer to the world. The mental event disappears but the writing remains for others to read. But it helps also to think of writing as input or as a movement of information from the world to the writer. You can throw away the writing and keep the mental event. The writing isn't the point, the point is to produce a change inside the writer's head: to help her understand or remember something better or to see something from a different point of view. When you care more about the mental event than the writing, the writing suddenly gets much easier. Here are four ways to use writing as pure input.

(1) Students will get much more out of any lecture if it's shortened by ten minutes and that time is given to freewriting. They will get much more out of reading if they freewrite at the end of each section or chapter. Freewrite after a

film. Taking notes won't be so important because students will *remember* ideas and conclusions and reflections they have worked out for themselves.

Freewriting is writing without stopping, writing whatever comes, writing no matter what—even if it means writing "my mind is blank, what is there to say" over and over. This process is not usually feasible or humane to require of students unless you do it too and make it clear in advance that you will never require students to show what they have written to you or to anyone else. Some students may want to share parts or all of what they have written, which can be lovely, but it's important not to put pressure on others to do likewise. Perhaps I should call these uses "focused freewriting" since they involve writing *about* the lecture, reading, or film. But the principle still works: "Write without stopping. Sacrifice to the goal of not stopping every other consideration: making sense, the needs of audience, thoughtfulness, correctness." When people are unfamiliar with freewriting the process momentarily heightens their self-consciousness in writing, but it quickly leads to that odd-but-soon-natural condition of writing without thinking about writing. In extremely self-conscious people, that initial self-consciousness can persist through two or three freewritings.

(2) I like to start discussions with ten minutes of freewriting. One reason so many discussions are tiresome or useless is that students haven't yet chewed over the reading or lecture or some previous experience enough to have something thoughtful to say. Or they haven't yet changed gears from their previous class or activity. A freewriting at the start can help them assimilate the material and reach some exploratory conclusions they are interested in sharing.

The freewriting helps by getting people warmed up and getting their minds turning over. There is something oddly infectious, too, about sitting and writing in the same room with others, even though no one is communicating with anyone else. The shared activity and safety often help people have more to say. (Students often tell me they get more ideas in this setting than when they freewrite at home. Something about community.) Finally, freewriting helps separate two very different activities needed for a good discussion: figuring out what you think and saying what you think. Many students who don't contribute to discussions and seem shy really just need more privacy to figure out what they think.

(3) I sometimes like to pause for five or ten minutes of freewriting after a hard question arises in a discussion—before anyone responds. The writing gives students a chance to jot things down, collect their thoughts, get to a safer position for responding without fear of saying something silly. Everyone interacts with the question and therefore almost everyone carries something away—not just the person who talks. This activity is particularly useful when the question is hard personally rather than just conceptually, for example, "Can anyone think of an example from her own life of this phenomenon we are discussing?" After playing with memories on paper, students can see them in perspective, can be less threatened, and can more easily decide what to edit out. The student ends up with more control and is thus more likely to be willing to share an answer.

(4) I like to use freewriting at the end of the seminar or class period. The

object here is for people to reach some closure, some conclusion, so that they actually *carry away* with them some of the benefit of the discussion. Students benefit more from their individually worked out inferences than the nice ones we work out for them. Something pleases me, in addition, about the symbolism of ending on a note of privacy and separation, each person drawing her own conclusions and then going home.

Remember, however, that this must be freewriting. It musn't be judged, evaluated, handed in, or even shared (unless a student chooses to read some of what he wrote as part of an ensuing discussion). Emphasize that students should *not* try to produce a good or sharable product but rather use the writing process to explore their own thoughts and perceptions. But do press them to keep their pencils moving even if it means writing "stuck, stuck, stuck." The benefits of the process are lost if the student sits there chewing the pencil or staring off into space. Encourage them to write down the thought and feeling of stuckness—to *write out* the perplexity, not carefully but just as a record of what happens when stuck. This usually leads to a surprising path out of the perplexity and provides a model for writing out one's meta-thoughts when having difficulties in more serious pieces.

Notice that these activities all involve writing but they do not feel like "working on writing"—rather working on biology, economics, or modern drama. And though these tasks are all easy and painless, we must be willing as teachers to exercise unambivalent authority to make them happen because students at first will have trouble with writing that does not hurt and does not count.

Writing as a Way to Get Another Job Done

There are lots of jobs we can do better with writing than with talking or discussion—and here too we get students to put their attention on the job rather than on the writing. In the following seven activities we do not immediately throw the writing away, indeed it is output *for* an audience, *for* communication. But we do not care about the writing, we do not try to make it good, we do not ask readers to evaluate it or even pay attention to it as writing, and it's probably thrown away after it's read.

(5) At the beginning of a course it's helpful for the teacher and students all to write rough, informal pieces telling what they want from the course, what their positive and negative expectations are, what it will take to maintain their commitment and investment, what they need from the teacher and from each other, and what special strengths they can offer. If the teacher reads all these rough pieces, she can estimate how much conflict or disappointed expectation there is likely to be, and she can think about what adjustments—if any—she might want to make in how she will teach the course. It's even better—for people's writing and for the class—if everyone reads all the pieces.

(6) I find it helpful periodically to end a class with a freewriting as follows: "Please write for ten minutes about what's been going on for you this class period. The process of reflecting will help you, but it will also help me in my teaching if you're willing to hand it in. I want to know what's happening with you. But you don't have to hand it in or sign it. I won't grade or evaluate it. It will help me to know if you're frustrated." These pieces of writing are quick

and often interesting to read, they help my teaching, save on office hours, and give me early warning of potential disasters.

(7) If your course requires an interview for entrance or if a student wants to drop it or switch sections or make some change, it's helpful to preface the conversation by asking the student to sit down for ten minutes and write out her reasons informally—as though in a casual letter to a friend. This helps students find *more* reasons, yet it shortens most interviews. Some students are bothered at first because they feel at a disadvantage writing about their ideas as compared to talking about them, but I can usually convince them that I'm not asking them to create a document that will be the basis of judgment but rather just to write down things that I can read as a springboard for our talking.

(8) Most teachers are familiar with the usefulness of requiring students to keep a journal of thoughts and reactions to reading, classes, and other course activities, but for those who are not, I wish to recommend it. Traditionally teachers collect these journals a couple of times a semester and read around in them to make sure students are keeping them and to get a sense of what's going on with students.

(9) In a subject matter course I like to ask students to write a *think-piece* each week. A think-piece is not a paper, but it isn't freewriting either. I ask for two or three pages that explore an issue or start to develop a train of thought about the week's reading. This isn't freewriting because I ask students to throw away weak and irrelevant passages and to make the writing genuinely clear and coherent at the level of the sentence and paragraph. It's not a paper either because it need not be clear or unified or well argued as a total train of thought. It need not necessarily draw a final conclusion—though I encourage students to be braver or more outrageous about drawing conclusions because these pieces are ungraded trial runs. I tell them it's fine for a think-piece to record an unsuccessful struggle with a perplexity or perhaps even to offer three unrelated insights. I do not ask that they be typed, merely written so I can read them easily. I tell them that the easiest way to produce a think-piece is to do three to five pages of freewriting and then save the best parts, arrange them, and clean up the language. (See "Cut and Paste Revising and the Collage," Chapter 14, in *Writing with Power.*)

The test of a think-piece is whether it reads comfortably, coherently, and interestingly out loud. I urge them to write to the other students more than to me. I make sure that on the day think-pieces are due I use the first ten or fifteen minutes for students to read their pieces in small groups. No feedback, but perhaps some discussion after all are read. I collect them and read them, but the only feedback I give is to draw straight lines in the margin next to parts I find interesting, useful, or well done. I don't grade them, simply insist that they be done.

(10) Self evaluation. At the end of a course, I like to ask students to write a self-evaluation of their own performance: to write informally about what they are proud of and not satisfied with, and what they could do differently next time to make the experience more fruitful. If I think students will not be frank in these pieces because of fear of influencing me in my grading, I ask them to hand them to, say, the department secretary or some third party who will not show them to me until after I have submitted my grades. Indeed it isn't neces-

sary that I see them at all; but they do help me in thinking about my teaching, and if I think I might have to write a letter of recommendation for these students, I try to save a copy.

(11) Teacher evaluation. Frank evaluations of me are helpful to my teaching. They make a good writing task. They are usually more frank if students know I will not read them until after I have submitted my grades. I like to find playful and metaphorical ways to prompt this writing. (For example, "Write a letter that starts, Dear Peter Elbow, There is something I have been meaning to tell you." "What movie actor will play me when they make the film?" "What directions should be given to this actor for playing me?" "What sides of you does my teaching bring out and what sides does it leave unused or hidden?") And then on to more direct questions. (See Chapter 9 of *Writing with Power* for more questions for self-evaluations and teacher evaluations.)

I assume that in addition to these nongraded writing tasks most teachers will assign a certain number of regular papers that will be commented on and graded as writing. But it's my contention that if a mathematics faculty member assigns no papers at all—or if an economics teacher is naughty enough to assign no papers at all—she will nevertheless give considerable help to her students in their writing by assigning nongraded writing activities such as those I describe here.

"Nongraded." Of course I cannot pretend that these eleven writing activities will have no effect at all upon a student's grade. They permit me to know the student better. But I do not evaluate them at all as writing or even as thinking performances. That is, I do not hold it against a student if what she writes is wrongheaded, dumb, silly, or incomprehensible—as long as it represents some investment or risk. I try to encourage students to view these writings as adventures and I find what looks like deplorable writing in this kind of task often correlates with better writing after reflection and revision. I can't resist being prejudiced against someone who does not try at all in these pieces, does not take any risks. And I suppose that's all right: If I let "good class participation" help the grade just a bit, it's not too inconsistent if I count "good participation" in these nongraded writings. But I am currently experimenting with trying to make them genuinely risk-free. In any event, I find most students do use the opportunity to explore and risk: They are relieved at the chance for nongraded writing that nevertheless goes to an audience.

And I reiterate: These are all ways of *using* writing, not teaching it; they take no time away from the subject matter; and they require no knowledge or confidence in writing on the part of the teacher.

Graded Writing

In closing, I would like to make four suggestions about graded writing—writing to which teacher and student *do* pay attention.

(1) Two or three short papers produce more learning and improvement than one long one—even if the total time spent is the same. There's a limit to how much any single paper can be improved, no matter how hard one works on it or how many drafts one puts it through. The student learns more if she gets reinforcement for the strengths of the paper, gets feedback on *no more than two*

important recurrent problems, and then is invited to call it a day on that paper and write a different one.

(2) It is possible to get most students to take writing through stages—to get them not just to revise but actually to rethink. I like to require that they hand in a careful draft well before a final draft is due. A careful draft is one step farther along than a think-piece because it tries for unity, organization, and genuine conclusions. But still it's a draft, there's room for the student to change her mind, and she's not punished for weaknesses that are overcome in the final version. I insist that the student get some feedback from peers and if possible from me. Indeed, I prefer to put more of my reading-and-commenting energy into the draft than into the final version. This gets me out of the typically counterproductive situation where much of my commentary on papers and exams is really justification for the grade—or is seen that way. Students often experience my commentary on the final version—even if I am trying to help them—as a slap on the wrist by an adversary for what they have done wrong. No wonder students so often fail to heed or learn from our commentary. But when I comment on revisable papers or practice tests I'm not saying, "Here is why you got this grade," I am saying, "Here is how you can get a better grade." Furthermore, when I read final versions as evaluator I can read faster and not bother with much commentary.[1]

(3) Learning is minimized when there is only a term paper due at the end. This means feedback is treated only as evaluation and is wasted as feedback on future writing. If it really does make sense to have a term paper due at the end, I try to make sure that the student has already received feedback on an earlier draft—from me and from other students—so that what comes in at the end represents learning and improvement. On the final draft, I give the student credit for improvement.

(4) It does not follow necessarily that if you require an important piece of writing you have to read it. You can require students to turn out a short paper every other week, require that one or more other students give feedback to each paper, and frankly admit that you will collect the stack of them once or twice a semester and read only half of each student's writing, although you will look through it all to be sure it was done and that feedback was seriously given. Students need help in learning to treat writing as a transaction between peers and colleagues instead of only treating it as something given to teachers. Student writing suffers from the fact that its only audience is teachers with whom students have such convoluted authority relationships. (See Chapter 20 of *Writing with Power*, "Writing for Teachers.")

Notes

[1] Obviously it takes more time for us to read working drafts and final drafts too, no matter how quickly we read final drafts. So I think it's reasonable to save time in two ways: (1) Do not require students to revise every draft. This permits you to grade students on their best work or what they have learned, not on how poorly they may start out. In addition it is easier for students to invest themselves in revising if it's on a piece they care about. (2) In giving feedback on drafts, wait until you have drafts of two papers from a student in hand before

you give feedback. When I have only one paper in hand I often feel, "Oh, dear, everything is weak here; nothing works right; where can I start?" When I have two drafts in hand, I can always say, "This one is better or potentially better for the following reasons. It's the one I would choose to revise." And with two drafts there's a much better chance of finding genuine strengths. By emphasizing these strengths, I can increase the chances of the student's consolidating and gaining control over what was perhaps only a shaky or even accidental achievement. I can make a positive exercise out of talking about what *did not* work and how to fix it.

36 Value and Purpose in Writing

Art Young
Department of Humanities, Michigan Technological University

If students are to become proficient writers and active learners, they can and should use writing for a variety of purposes in classes across the curriculum. In my own classes in literature and philosophy, I assign writing tasks that require students to use writing in the following ways: 1) *to communicate* information to a particular audience, 2) *to learn* about certain subjects, 3) *to express* themselves and order their experience, and 4) *to assess values* in relation to material they are studying. While these four functions of written language are neither mutually exclusive nor exhaustive, I have found it useful to segregate them so that the unique value of each can be studied and practiced and so that I can offer the different and distinct response to each discrete piece of writing that its purpose dictates.

I have been designing assignments and responding to student writing based on these four functions of written language for several years. In order to encourage students to become confident, fluid, and effective writers, I assign them a variety of writing tasks that range from research papers, interpretative essays, journal entries, speculative pieces, poems, stories, and graffiti to reflections in writing on the experience of doing a particular writing assignment.

Let me share with you a suggestive student response to each of the four writing functions I have defined as a means of demonstrating *the value of writing to the writer.*

Writing to Communicate

When the primary function of writing is to communicate, then the writer has the dual obligation of arriving at a coherent understanding of the material and of presenting it in an attractive, efficient way. This dual obligation of writing is familiar to us all, and we spend a great deal of our professional lives assisting students to become proficient in it. After completing an analytic paper for a course, one student wrote about the obligation of a writer this way:

> By writing a formal paper, you want to get an idea across clearly, neatly, and concisely. You want your reader to be able to go through it and understand immediately what you are saying without having them stop and ask questions—about your purpose or grammar and spelling mistakes. You write a

formal paper to make sure you don't make mistakes, to make sure you're organized, and to make sure you don't leave anything out, but by using an outline, a rough draft and proofreading.

(John)

John clearly understands one of the major purposes of the formal paper—to present the paper as neatly, concisely, and correctly as possible in order to assist and engage a demanding reader. On the other hand, what John does not give us in this brief writing is any sense of the discovery or the commitment of the writer to the topic. John's statement is not atypical, and it apparently comes from years of instruction in only this one function of writing. It is the result of frequent teacher response which centers on a list of "do's" and "don'ts," and a practice in which the utilization of an outline and the frequency of spelling errors provide the main substance of teacher evaluation, at least as remembered by John. One irony, of course, is that John wrote this informal piece of prose for a teacher, and his main purpose was to please the teacher with his understanding of what the teacher undoubtedly wanted to read.

In spite of the fact that responding to students' formal writings which are offered up for evaluation remains one of the most difficult things teachers do, they must do more than just respond to the form of students' texts. It is important that instructors respond to content as well, suggesting what might be, even as they criticize what is. Beyond this common-sense advice is some practical advice. Teachers who provide instruction in the writing of formal papers—papers which are designed primarily to communicate information to readers—must attempt to engage students in the entire process of writing, from prewriting to proofreading, from identifying a perspective toward a topic to composing that perspective. John, for example, needs to understand that his relationship to his topic will have an inevitable effect on the quality of his paper, both as he and his readers perceive it. His teacher's responses to his papers can and must teach him the importance of his presence in his texts.

Teachers can also respond to students' informal writings such as the one John wrote. The purpose of such responses should not be critical or evaluative, but rather exploratory and communicative in order to open up a student-teacher dialogue concerning familiar perceptions regarding writing and the writing process. By having students share their informal writings with each other a teacher can broaden the dialogue into a conversation involving the whole classroom community. In such conversations each individual can evaluate his or her own written statement and perceptions in light of those of the group. Asking students to react to the writing of a formal paper, then to share their reactions with one another, promotes discussions not only of the value of the formal paper as a means of communicating knowledge, but also of the value of the informal written statement as a means of discovering knowledge both for the individual and for the class.

Writing to Learn

When the primary function of writing is to learn—to reach a secure understanding of new information, either for no immediate pragmatic end or as a step to mastering information in preparation for a formal paper or a test—then the writer is free to discover ideas and to play with language without the constraint of pleasing a demanding reader. Here is an example of a student writing his way toward an understanding of Emily Dickinson's poem "I started early, took my dog—":

> This particular poem is very perplexing. Even after quite some time of study I don't understand the meaning. I've even had problems with the overt meaning of the words.
>
> The poem seems to be about the sea—about how she (Emily) stands in a wave and then runs from it—back to dry land. But what do the dog, mermaids, frigate, mouse, and the town represent—why are they added? The dog and the mouse especially don't seem to have any meaning to the poem if it is just about the sea. Therefore the sea must be a metaphor or something.
>
> The mermaids in the basement speak of mermaids from the depths as the frigate in the upper floor speaks of a ship on the sea. When the ship extends its hempen hands, it seems to be beckoning to her to come out there—But she just seems to stand there until the waves wash on her and try to pull her in. Then she realizes that she can't be a part of the sea so she moves toward the land with the water close behind. As she gets closer, the sea "realizes" it can't go with her so it retreats.
>
> Overall the poem speaks of two worlds, both different and distinct from the other. E. D. is part of one and observes the other. This could be the recurring theme that nature is separate from humanity.
>
> (Ralph)

Ralph has written a piece of prose which begins by documenting his confusion about the meaning of the poem and concludes by stating his newly discovered understanding of the poem albeit a tentative understanding as the "could be" of the last sentence implies. In between the first paragraph and the final sentence Ralph has used written language as a tool for learning about literature, as a tool for discovering what he "knows" about this unfamiliar and strange poem. Ralph's piece of writing exhibits many of the characteristics we associate with writing-to-learn as distinct from writing-to-communicate: an admission of ignorance and the desire to learn, a self-questioning which is not rhetorical (*why are the mermaids added*?), a dialogue with the self (*if this be true, therefore the sea must . . .*), a rehearsing of what is known in order to find patterns and make sense, and finally, a conclusion which ends where most formal papers usually begin—with a statement of thesis to be developed and supported in the body of the text. The purpose of this writing task for Ralph was not to communicate understanding to others, but rather to learn about the poem for himself and for whatever contribution he might make to the class' understanding of the poem during class discussion of it. This kind of writing has little value to the scholar doing research on Emily Dickinson, but it has immense value to Ralph as a student of literature.

All students' written attempts at discovery will not necessarily be as successful as Ralph's. Teachers must be positive and supportive in response to students' writings for this purpose. At times teachers' responses to such writing may encourage students to pursue other directions for speculation and writing. In cases where students seem to have achieved an understanding of a significant topic in the course (when they have discovered a valid interpretation of a poem), they can be encouraged to develop that understanding into a formal paper, to communicate their knowledge in a way that will make it useful to others. However, tasks that ask students to write in order to learn need not always lead to writing for communication. Writing to learn is valuable in and for itself. Furthermore, because tasks which ask students to write in order to learn are brief and do not make the conventional demand that they be composed for readability, they can be assigned frequently as a tool for learning in all disciplines.

Writing for Self-Expression

When the primary function of writing is to express the self's perception of reality and to order experience, then the primary goal of the writer is to personalize knowledge—that is, to make it his or her own. One way individuals do this is by making new information fit their perception of reality. All of us need to symbolize knowledge in order to handle it, and written language can be a valuable tool in this process. Here is a student reflecting on the experience of reading Emily Dickinson's letters:

> They had a moral code. Now I understand, mind you, that some people rebelled against it, but at least there was something to rebel against. They knew where they were, and so the courageous ones could strike out on their own, from someplace to someplace. They had a culture. We either don't have one or have one too embarrassing to admit to. I can never decide which, I think maybe I'm just writing this on a bad day, because even though I'm no Puritan, I think I would rather be there than here. The only thing this has to do with Emily D. is that I started feeling this way reading her letters.
>
> (Joyce)

This piece of writing by Joyce serves a different purpose than the one by Ralph which we examined previously. Joyce is not attempting to interpret Dickinson's letters; rather she is attempting to relate the experience of reading the letters to her own life. She is providing a personal context for reading the letters through an expression of her feelings and thoughts on the subject. Notice how Joyce's statement exhibits many of the characteristics associated with the self-expressive function of language: the use of "I" to personalize and order experience, reflections on her own value system, the primacy of feelings (even though she— like many student writers—does not trust that her feelings will produce meaningful information), the use of unsupported generalities for speculation, and the evaluation of the experience of the reading rather than the meaning of the reading. In this brief writing Joyce has provided her own motivation for reading Emily Dickinson's letters. She has also produced a statement which she can refer to as she reads further in the letters, to see in what ways her experience of reading them changes with her *good* or *bad* days, and whether her desire to "be there [rather] than here" remains constant.

Teachers' responses to this kind of writing cannot be critical because the purpose of the task is to be expressive and reflective, not analytical and communicative. However, teachers can respond to such writings in ways designed to encourage the self-expressive enterprise and to create a more meaningful context for studying Emily Dickinson. For example, a teacher could respond to Joyce's writing by asking her to make a list of "embarrassing" characteristics in contemporary culture and a parallel list of admirable characteristics in Dickinson's. Another brief writing task the teacher might ask of Joyce is to reflect on what her lists mean in terms of her personal value system. By assigning self-expressive writing tasks and then responding encouragingly, teachers can assist individual students in establishing personal contexts for studying the subject at hand.

Writing to Assess Values

When the primary purpose of writing is to assess values, writers engage in discovering what they believe about a particular experience or piece of information. Although such engagement can be encouraged in many ways, I find creative writing assignments related to understanding the subject matter of the class to be a particularly effective way of shaping and sharing values. Here's the response of a student who has just completed an assignment to write another final chapter to Kurt Vonnegut, Jr.'s novel *Player Piano:*

> I think that I actually do enjoy creative writing and just the opportunity to be able to have anything you want happen to the characters. It is true that I usually tend to depict them pretty much as before but I still get the chance to see what it is like to be an author. That provides me with more motivation to do the other assignments. Looking back just now, I realize that when I have some character do something it is mostly likely to be in the manner in which I see that group in which the person can be classified. That is, I have women doing what I see as the role of women. Doctors doing what I see as the role of doctors, etc. I suppose that that is, actually, an indication as to what I am like, believe and see is important.
>
> (Steve)

After Steve had written a three-page chapter in the style and spirit of Vonnegut's *Player Piano,* he wrote the reflection of his work printed here. This piece of writing demonstrates many characteristics that students share when they write about their creative writing tasks: a sense of enjoyment and freedom and power, a better understanding of reading fiction because they have tried writing it, a better understanding of the particular novel being studied, and a personal assessment of their reading and writing experiences.

If we examine Steve's brief writing closely, we notice the first three sentences appear to rehearse statements which may be considered predictable responses to a teacher's assignment requesting a brief evaluation of a creative writing experience. But in the sentence beginning "Looking back just now . . . " the tone appears to change to one that recounts a genuine discovery, what for Steve was a fresh insight called forth by his own creative writing, his own reflection, and the opportunity his brief and informal writing provided him for discovery. In other words, this reflective writing task not only afforded Steve the opportunity to evaluate his prior experience, it also provided him the opportunity for new discovery about the nature of literature and about himself as a student of literature.

There appears to be something both personally liberating and personally inviting in writing in fictive, poetic, and dramatic forms that allows and encourages individuals to involve their own value systems in their compositions. Thus creative writing can play an integral part in liberal arts courses whose goals include self-knowledge and assessment of values in relation to material being studied.

Teachers should respond to creative writing assignments in ways that encourage students to probe and clarify value-related issues. For example, a teacher might ask Steve to do still another informal writing assignment growing out of his creative writing in which he articulates more specifically how he sees women and their roles, doctors and their roles, and whether he considers his vision on these matters to be similar to Vonnegut's as portrayed in *Player Piano.*

All students will not make a discovery as dramatic as Steve's; however, by having the class share their perceptions with one another, a teacher may assist Steve's classmates in making similar discoveries about how their writing reflects their values. Teachers' responses that encourage such dialogue demonstrate to students the value of their own writing as individual records of each person's journey into learning, values assessment, and communication. They demonstrate by practice the purpose and the process by which we make knowledge right with the self and experience meaningful. Such a purpose is one of the ideal goals of many liberal arts classes in literature, philosophy, history, and other disciplines; it is a purpose which can be more fully realized by using writing to serve different functions in the learning process.

The teaching of writing and the teaching of liberal arts are alike as humanistic callings. While we are proud to teach the survival skills of writing, reading, interpretation, and critical thinking, we are also privileged to teach whole persons— persons with thoughts, feelings, and beliefs. These persons should be engaged in the quest for self-knowledge even as they seek mastery over the academic subjects we teach. Indeed, both quests must become one if new information and technical competence are to be meaningful to the individual. As the cry of "back to the basics" lingers with us, we would do well to remind ourselves of this point. I believe that by systematically allowing writing to serve various functions, teachers encourage students to grow as their talents and competencies do.

37 Folklore of/and the Research Paper

Helen Isaacson
English Composition Board, The University of Michigan

When I first began to teach folklore, I had already been teaching writing for a long time. I had become aware that there had taken shape in the composition classroom what folklorists call a monster legend. A group of stories, rumors, and beliefs had developed and clustered around that piece of writing usually assigned by composition teachers as the final project of the semester: the research paper.

Students envisioned this final effort as monstrously large: four or five times the size of an ordinary paper; as terrifying: it could determine the final grade; as supernatural: humans had better learn the proper magical formulas—"Single-space within the footnote, double-space between the notes"—if they wished to survive. Above all, it was mysterious: What was the meaning, the purpose, the very nature of the Thing called Research?

Research becomes less fantastical if we examine how researchers in a particular discipline work. I ask the members of my folklore class not only to read what folklorists do, but also to become folklorists, to conduct original research in the field.

My students collect items of folklore from "informants" or "tradition bearers"—friends, family members, colleagues, or strangers who have some lore to pass on. The lore can be stories, songs, jokes, riddles, beliefs, customs, or any of the long list of items that interest folklorists. As collectors, students use a variety of techniques and sources to learn as much as possible about the function and context of the lore. They have collected such wide-ranging materials as: "Haunted House Tales," "Pregnancy Lore," "College Pranks," "Theater Folklore," "Traditional German Recipes Spanning Four Generations," "Cures for the Common Cold," "Superstitions of Athletes," and "Place Legends of Ann Arbor's Arboretum." This collection project enables students to learn about research as they engage in the complex of thinking/inventing/investigating/writing activities that comprise the research process.

Students begin the process by choosing a topic, which I ask them to discuss with me to ensure that the project has a reasonable scope and a clear purpose. Often a student has a personal reason for selecting a subject: "I want to learn how and why the religious beliefs of my family have changed over four generations," or, "I want to understand a very strange series of occurrences that made certain members of my family conclude we might be living in a haunted house." From his or her statement of purpose, the student researcher develops a series of questions and one or more hypotheses. These questions and suppositions determine the particular research to be done. For example, the student who wished to understand her family's religious views decided to interview family members about how they celebrated or remembered how they used to celebrate the religious holiday of Passover. As the research progresses, students' questions or hypotheses may change, be added to or discarded. The student whose house was the scene of extraordinary events speculated at one point that her home might have been disrupted by a poltergeist.

At any stage in their investigations students may discover they need information from secondary sources. I suggest that before beginning their fieldwork they read background material on their subject in order to feel more confident and be more competent to do their observing and interviewing; check a fieldwork handbook[1] to help them develop a set of questions and a plan for getting the most useful material from informants; and read selections from an archive I maintain of student collection reports. The archive not only offers ideas and models to students beginning their research but also assures them of a potential audience of future researchers.

The assignment sheet[2] I give students offers a model for the written research report, but students may adapt the model to suit their own needs. Indeed, the form of the research paper both shapes and is shaped by the complex of activities that comprises the individual research process.

The Assignment Sheet
for the
Folklore Collection Project

Areas of Folklore Studies:

   I. Traditional Verbal and Performed Art
       A. Prose Narratives
          folktales, legends, memorates, myths, jokes, anecdotes
       B. Folk Poetry
          rhymes, toasts, etc.
       C. Folk Songs
       D. Proverbs
       E. Riddles
       F. Folk Speech
          proverbial similes and metaphors, curses, the dozens, etc.
       G. Music and Dance

  II. Traditional Products and Processes: Arts, Crafts, Architecture
       A. Visual Arts
          such as Pennsylvania Dutch decor and designs
       B. Crafts
          quilts, toys, furniture, etc.
       C. Architecture
          barns, weathervanes, fenceposts, etc.
       D. Foods
       E. Occupational Techniques
          farming, fishing, hunting
       F. Instruments
          fiddles, dulcimers, special tunings, picking styles

 III. Traditional Attitudes: Beliefs and Associated Custom and Ritual
       A. Folk Medicine
       B. Stereotypes
       C. Taboos
       D. Magic
       E. Festivals
          (and the costumes, food, dances, narratives, etc. associated with
          them)

Please Note:
The above list is, of course, incomplete.

Some Titles of Projects in the Archives:

Folklore of Magoffin County, KY.; Haunted House
Tales of Adolescents: What Happens on Hell Night;

How They Scare the Pledges; Theater Folklore;
College Pranks; Ethnic Jokes; A Stereotype:
Cruelty of Catholic Nuns in Parochial Schools;
Folklore of Beauty Aids; How to Cure a Cold.

Suggested Steps to Follow in Doing Your Paper

1. Choose a topic carefully. Choose one that you think will be fun or (preferably *and*) useful. Consult with me and hand in a written Project Proposal. Be prepared to change to another topic if the first one doesn't work out.
2. Look at a book or article on your subject. You will feel more confident and be more competent when you do your field work if you have some background on your topic. Look at some of the papers in the archives in my office to see what others have done before you. You may want to use some of the materials you read in making your analysis of the data.
3. Consult a book on field work and write up a plan of how you intend to proceed. Make sure you have a good set of questions to ask your informants.
4. Think about yourself in relation to the project. Try out some of the questions on yourself, on your friends. Do your first interview with the informant you know best and feel most comfortable with.
5. Write up the project (see model below). As you write, you may find you need to do additional field or library research.

Some Things to Remember When Doing Field Work:

Try to find out where, when, and from whom the informant learned the custom, tale, belief, etc. You might want to ask:

What is the use (function, value, meaning) of this to you?
Can you describe the situation in which you tell (sing, perform) this item?

The Collection Project Should Consist of:

1. Title page. Please hand in two copies of this page. I will return one with comments and grade. Keep a copy of your paper. Unless you specify otherwise, the paper you hand in will become a part of the Archives.
2. Table of Contents.
3. Introduction. Explain what you have tried to do, describe the group you are studying, give local history. See Introduction to *South from Hell-fer-Sartin* for a model introduction to a collection of lore.
4. Description of Field Methodology, brief narrative of general collecting experiences, problems, etc.
5. Proper Documentation of Informants. (See informant sheet.)
6. Data on Collector. (See collector sheet.)
7. Transcription of representative samples of the lore you have collected together with any tapes, photographs, charts, etc.
8. Analysis of Traditions Collected. Although you may refer to secondary sources in your analysis, remember that your main job is to write about the raw data you have collected. You should sort or categorize your material in some meaningful way and discuss the function of the material. Why do the informants do this, believe this, remember this? How does this fit into their lives? Why does this kind of lore continue to exist? Look for a pattern.

9. Bibliography of library and archives materials consulted.

Please Note:
We can discuss in conference
variations of the above suitable to your project.

When term after term I found the research reports submitted by my folklore students so much more enthusiastically and competently written than the research papers of my composition students, I decided to bring folklore into my composition course.[3] I hoped that by assigning my composition students some modified version of the collection project, that nonetheless leads them through a step-by-step process of inquiry, I could make the Monster Research less mysterious.

I begin by conducting a workshop on collecting techniques, and then students practice interviewing each other before going out to collect information from friends, roommates, fellow workers, and others. I use data collected from the class to teach such skills as classification-division and basic elements of analysis. For my composition students I limit the choice of lore they study to superstitions and folk remedies, since these items are among the easiest to collect. One of my students collected theater superstitions from members of her drama class; a hockey player collected superstitions about winning and losing from his teammates; several students collected cures for colds, or hangovers. These students became actively engaged in their research; this is too often not the case when students do only library research for a traditional term paper assignment. The following is a composite sequence of several exercises and assignments for using folklore to teach research and various writing skills as well.

Folklore in the Composition Class

An Assignment/Exercise Sequence
(meant to be shortened or otherwise modified to meet individual needs and tastes)

On Collecting Folklore
(a subject about which teachers and students learn they already know a great deal)

1. Collecting Demonstration. Instructor acts as Collector or Field Worker; students are Informants or Tradition Bearers. Superstitions and folk remedies are easy to collect in the classroom. During the course of the demonstration, students learn that they already know something about the subject. They do use home remedies (one teaspoon of sugar in a glass of water cures the hiccups), they do write with a "lucky" pen when they take exams (or know someone who does).
2. Interviewing/Collecting Workshop. Students in groups practice on each other before going out into the field.
3. Library Research. Folklorists, of course, usually do considerable research before going into the field. Some library research may be assigned in addition to field work, or the instructor may wish to bring to class something like the following from *The Ann Arbor News*. Articles on certain kinds of lore appear

regularly in newspapers and popular magazines and confirm for students that folklore is available all around them.

> ### Sure-fire hiccups cures
> #### By Joe Graedon
>
> Q—At a dinner party the other night I got an embarrassing case of hiccups, and I went through a real torture treatment. Everybody and their uncle had a different cure:
>
> One person had me glugging water until I spilled it, another one almost suffocated me making me breathe out of a paper bag, and one man gave me a bear hug guaranteed to cure my hiccups—or break my ribs. Nothing worked, so as a last resort they all outdid themselves trying to scare the hiccups out of me.
>
> Please tell me, is there a sure-fire simple cure for the hiccups?
>
> A—You came to the right place with this question. I've got three dandy hiccup cures so if one fails you can always fall back on another and they're a lot less traumatic than the misery your friends put you through.
>
> My favorite and most successful remedy is the spoonful of sugar trick. Swallow a teaspoonful of dry, white granulated sugar. Researchers theorize that the sugar granules stimulate the phrenic nerve in the neck and interrupt the hiccup reflex.
>
> If that "sure-fire" treatment fails twice, you could try the vinegar cure. A jigger of vinegar down the hatch should do the job. But if that, too, falls short, the latest remedy I've discovered requires a lemon wedge well soaked with Angostura bitters. Gobble it down quickly (without the rind) and watch those hiccups disappear.
>
> Lest you think these treatments are a little weird or no better than your friends' attempts, we assure you they all come from the prestigious pages of the New England Journal of Medicine.

4. Field Work. Students go outside the classroom to do field work (they sometimes like to work in pairs). Informants can be friends, family, members of their theater, athletic, or social groups.
5. Classifying the Materials. The data collected by the class serves as material for a class session on classification-division.
6. The Collecting Experience. Class session on narrative writing. Assignment: Write a short narrative of your collecting experience that would make a suitable introduction to your collection of lore.
7. The Informants. Assignment: Write a descriptive sketch of one of your informants that emphasizes those details that would help a reader better understand the lore you collected.
8. Point of View. Assignment: Write on the relation of Collector to Collection. Reflect on how your own anti-superstition bias or your own hypochondria affects your view of the superstitions or folk remedies you collected.
9. Analysis of the Collection. Students' raw data is used for class session on analysis. Assignment: Write an analysis of your own data.

The relative success of folklore collection assignments is due surely to a number of reasons including the charm of the subject and the step-by-step approach. But it is due mainly, I believe, to the nature of original field research. Such research gives the investigator—professional or student—the awesome responsibility of collaborating in the creation of the primary source materials; the quantity, the scope, and the quality of the data depend upon how compatible a working relationship exists between interviewer and informant. Such research gives investigators control over the source materials; when they evaluate and analyze their data, they work as "experts" with interviews they have conducted and materials they have collected. Indeed this sense of control and authority may be the key element in providing students with a successful learning experience.

Notes

[1] Suggested reading for doing folklore field work: Kenneth S. Goldstein's *A Guide for Field Workers in Folklore* (Hatboro, Pa.: Folklore Associates, Inc., 1964) remains the classic in the field. Includes important chapters on Problem Statement and Analysis, Pre-Field Preparation, and Rapport Establishment and Maintenance. Richard M. Dorson's *Folklife* (University of Chicago Press, 1972) is an excellent collection of essays and includes advice on Collecting Oral Literature, Recording Material Culture, and Recording Traditional Music. Barre Toelken's *The Dynamics of Folklore* (Boston: Houghton Mifflin Co., 1979), includes sections on Being a Folklorist and on Folklore Research, plus a very useful, nearly-verbatim Fieldwork Transcript.

[2] Atelia Clarkson, a former member of the English faculty at Eastern Michigan University, generously shared with me her ideas and materials for a collection project when I began to teach folklore. Teachers interested in using folktales in their classes should consult the anthology she edited with Gilbert B. Cross, *World Folktales: A Scribner Resource Collection,* which contains appendixes on "Folktales in the Elementary Classroom" and "Folktales in the College Classroom."

[3] I was encouraged to give a folklore assignment in a course in English composition by the enormously successful results that followed Eliot Wigginton's decision to send his high school English class out to find and record traditional materials in the area of Rabun Gap, Georgia. The magazine of the articles the students write and edit, *Foxfire,* continues to flourish, and anthologies of selections from the magazines continue to find a mass audience.

38 Methods of Thinking and College Education

Jack Meiland
Department of Philosophy, The University of Michigan

Six years ago, I was offered the opportunity to teach a freshman seminar called "Introduction to the University." I accepted the offer on the condition that I could change the focus of the course. It seemed (and still seems) to me that students are plunged into college work without its aims and methods being explained to them. They are in the same position as a person who is asked to play a game of chess without being told the rules of the game or what counts as winning. So I created a course in which the focus was on intellectual methods in the various

252 fforum: Essays on Theory and Practice in the Teaching of Writing

disciplines and on questions of aims and methods which cut across the disciplines. I taught this material for two years. During the third time around, I became extremely dissatisfied with the papers that the students were writing. These were analytical and critical evaluations of arguments and essays.

I suddenly realized that I was giving assignments and writing critical comments on students' papers without explaining to them what I wanted. I was telling them what not to do without telling them what to do. So one day I walked into class and said, "You don't know at all what to do with these assignments; this must stop"—with which sentiments the students totally agreed. During that session and the following several weeks, I went step-by-step through the process of argumentation and of constructing an argumentative paper. I described the steps but especially emphasized the reasons why each step should be included—for example, *why* a good piece of argumentation raises objections to arguments previously given. The students participated enthusiastically, primarily by asking questions about the role and purpose of each step as we went along.

Their questions showed me that they did not understand the first thing about intellectual method. They did not understand what an argument is or why arguments are given. They even had difficulty in distinguishing among intellectual questions, positions taken in response to those questions, and arguments given for those positions. It was not their fault; instead, it was the fault of their teachers. No one had ever told them these things. No one had ever tried to teach them basic intellectual skills, and yet those same teachers expected them—required them—to do intellectual work. These class sessions were some of the most intense sessions I have ever taught. The attention of every student in the class was absolutely riveted on what we were doing. Students said repeatedly that this was the sort of thing they had come to college to learn; they had been disappointed when they did not find it in their other courses. They felt that at last the sacred mysteries of academia were being revealed to them. And that is indeed one of the aims of my course: the demystification of college work and of the academic world generally.

Because my colleagues were criticizing student writing at the same time that I was discussing the purpose of the argumentative paper with my students, I asked some faculty what they felt to be the great defects of student papers. The most serious faculty complaints were not, by and large, about grammar or about writing style. Instead, the most frequent complaints were that students did not know how to develop and organize their ideas. They did not know how to formulate their ideas clearly, argue for their ideas, develop replies to possible objections, uncover hidden assumptions, discover the implications and consequences of a position, and so on. The students' problem, that is, was not a problem in writing in a narrow sense of that expression; instead, it was a problem in thinking. Students' responses to my description of argumentation and faculty complaints about student writing reinforced me in my decision to teach basic skills of thinking in my course.

My assessment that college students do not know how to think and are not taught how to do so by current practices in higher education is reinforced by a report which appeared in the December 9, 1981 issue of *The Chronicle of Higher Education*. It is a report of a study of the writing of law students at the University of Texas Law School:

The widespread complaint that many lawyers are poor writers was described at a legal-education conference here (New York) as somewhat off the mark.

Law students do not have much trouble with formal grammar or with recognizing errors in other people's writing, said Dean John F. Sutton, Jr., of the University of Texas School of Law. The main problem, he said, pointing to research findings at his institution, is that students don't know how to organize their thoughts.

"Most law students do not have a writing problem," agreed James M. Douglas, Dean of the School of Law at Texas Southern University." "They have a thinking problem."

The striking implication of this report is this. All law students are already college *graduates*. If they have a "thinking problem," then it seems clear that colleges are failing in the teaching of thinking even though the teaching of thinking is one of the chief officially-declared purposes of most colleges.

I repeat that this is not the students' failure. It is the failure of college faculties. Apparently college teachers think that students learn basic techniques of thinking in their courses. But their own complaints about student writing, let alone studies like the one just quoted, show that they are not teaching these techniques—or at least not teaching them effectively so that the students actually learn them. Colleges are simply not providing students what they need.

Students sense this. Often they will take a course in logic in order to learn to think. But courses in logic usually do not fill this need either. All too often, an introductory course in logic will concentrate on the following: giving a logical analysis of arguments in ordinary language, detecting formal and informal fallacies, setting up symbolic systems, and deducing theorems of logic. The last of these is obviously of interest only to those interested in the properties of deductive systems; it is of no help in learning to argue and to theorize. The logical analysis of everyday arguments is useful, but it does not go nearly far enough. Neither it nor the detection of fallacies in already-constructed arguments helps the student to learn to *construct* arguments. Nor do most textbooks on English composition take up the slack. In many cases their chapters on writing the argumentative paper consist solely of lists and descriptions of informal fallacies taken from logic texts. Is it any wonder that students in my course say "This is the first time anyone has told me what to do rather than what not to do." One cannot teach students to think and to argue merely by telling them what mistakes of reasoning to avoid. This is like trying to teach someone to play chess by teaching him the traps and strategic situations to avoid. To teach effectively, we must tell students what to do.

Students need to be taught intellectual skills directly and explicitly. There are many intellectual skills necessary for effective thinking. I have already mentioned a few of these: identification of issues or problems; specification of what is problematic about an issue—why it needs to be discussed; why it is important; why obvious or easy solutions won't work (thus bringing out the full and essential nature of the problem); description of various alternative positions or theories; eliciting of hidden assumptions, and so on. These and many other skills must be taught to students as early as possible in students' college careers so that they may use the rest of their college work as conscious and deliberate practice of those skills. This is what much college work is supposed to be, anyway. When we assign a term paper to students, we do not expect the students' papers to be a contribution to human knowledge. Term papers are exercises intended to improve the students' skills and their understanding of the material. These exercises would be much more effective if the students understood which skills the assignment was an opportunity to practice and if the student had been told how to do the work required. A good piano or violin teacher does not simply tell the students to do this or that exercise. Instead, the teacher carefully explains exactly how to do the exercise and exactly what the exercise is intended to achieve.

I teach various skills of thinking by teaching the associated forms of writing. For example, I teach the skills of argumentation by teaching students to write argumentative papers. This makes the teaching of these rather abstract skills much more concrete and meaningful for students. It also enables students to measure their progress: If their papers get progressively better, they know that their thinking is getting progressively better.

A course which teaches skills of thinking must have some particular content in order that students may think about particular issues and topics. I choose topics of various types for discussion. Among them are these: creationism and evolution, technology and society, freedom and morality in scientific research. The creationism-evolution topic is perfect for my purposes. It surfaces periodically in the media, and this assures students that these techniques of thinking have practical application to issues of real concern in our lives. Moreover, this topic has at least four different aspects: educational policy and decisions about what to teach; the nature of scientific theories; political, social, and legal issues connected with separation of church and state; and liberal toleration of opposing views. Such topics illustrate the value of carefully identifying and distinguishing different issues and of carefully determining the relevance of various positions and arguments to each issue. I use materials of all kinds, ranging from letters to the editor and newspaper articles to scholarly articles and books to materials I compose myself. The following reading selection and related activities illustrate how I provoke students to identify and distinguish issues about a topic in preparation for discussing the topic in class, for preparing an inquiry paper about the topic, and for critiquing each other's writing about the topic.

University Course 101, Section 1

Paper Assignment: Analysis, Interpretation, and Argumentation

December ??, 1981: Mr. Washington George, Director of Americans for Moral Purity, an organization with headquarters in Rockrib, Massachusetts, held a press conference yesterday at which he spoke out against "moral laxity" in the United States.

"Some of our citizens," declared Mr. George, "tell us that we have no right to enforce our views on the American people. They tell us that even though they themselves believe that abortion is wrong, they favor freedom of choice by each individual. This is a nonsensical position. If they believe that abortion is morally wrong, then they have a moral duty to take action against abortion. What else can it mean to have moral beliefs?

They may reply that what it means is that they themselves would not have abortions, that abortion is wrong for them. But if abortion is wrong for one person, it is wrong for everyone. That is what it means for a type of action to be wrong."

1. What is the issue, problem, or question being discussed here? (There may be more than one, but present what you take to be the *main* question.) Explain and support your answer by showing how the various statements made by Mr. George are related to this main issue.
2. If there are any arguments in the above passage, state them clearly and fully, explaining how each argument (if there is more than one) is different from each other argument.
3. Does Mr. George make any hidden assumptions (that is, assumptions which he does not state explicitly)? If so, state these assumptions clearly and support your answer by referring to specific statements by Mr. George, showing how the statements you cite are related to these assumptions.
4. What might be some of the consequences, acceptable or unacceptable, of adopting Mr. George's view? Present some argumentation to show that these are indeed consequences, again referring to specific statements in the news conference.
5. Can any objections be raised to Mr. George's view? Explain.
6. Can any arguments be given for the position that Mr. George opposes? Explain by giving such arguments or by showing why such arguments cannot be given.
7. Which of these two views, Mr. George's or the view which he opposes, do you favor? Explain why by arguing for your answer. If you accept neither, explain why, again arguing for your answer.

To illustrate how students respond in writing to these topical assignments and how they receive constructive written criticism to their writing, I offer the following examples. The first is the inquiry paper one student, Bill, wrote in response to the question of whether universities should accept donations regardless of how donors have acquired their money. The second is the critique another student, Caroline, offered Bill after reading his paper. The third is the comment I wrote to Bill after reading his paper and Caroline's critique.

Bill's Paper

¶1.   Universities and Accepting Donations

Should a university accept donations regardless of how the donor acquired the money? This is a question facing many colleges in America today. Colleges get their support from many different sources. For example, colleges receive money from such sources as the federal and state government, corporations, private citizens, and anonymous donors to name just a few. With all the different sources, one wonders how this money was acquired. Should the university accept donations from reputable sources which list exactly where they received their legally earned money as well as donations in which the money comes from anonymous or questionable sources which acquire it through uncertain means.

¶2.

I feel that a university should not accept money regardless of how the donor acquired the money. How the donor acquired the money is very important. Many universities overlook where donors acquired the money for their donations because they need the money. I disagree with this procedure because the money may have been illegally obtained, maybe even from the university itself.

¶3.

I feel that universities should not accept these donations because the money often comes from sources who acquire the money illegally. It has been estimated that 15% of all the anonymous donors of money get the money through criminal means. Many universities do not check out how the money is acquired and therefore they take all donations whether they are acquired legally or illegally. Many times the criminals who are donating their illegally acquired money are trying to attain respectability in their community. When they gain this respectability, they use it as a front to gain respectability in their community. Once they have gained this respectability, they use it as a front to continue their illegal activities. Because of the hugh amouts of money that they acquire, even a large donation by our standards would not harm them financially in return for the respect and public image that they gain. Oftentimes the money that they acquire is taken from innocent innocent citizens, wo, because of their financial lose, may not be able to contribute money to the university. It is reported that 40% of the American public supports universities in one way or another while crimes against the innocent citizen increase 5% per year.

¶4.

An objection that can be raised to the foregoing argument is that universities desparately need money and if the donations go for a good cause, it does't matter whether the money was acquired legally or illegally. Also many times the criminals that donate money to gain respectability want a new chance at life. They want to start over and get a good legal job. their first step in the right path is to donate money to a very needy cause, the universities. Universities are failing financially and need money desparately. Last year, tuitions for all univesities natonwide increased 8%. The federal government, the largest contributer to universities, announced that they were voting on whether to limit their aid to colleges so that they could build up the defense budget. This situations comes at a time when college deficits are at an all-time high. Universities should take all donations, even illegal ones, to educate the young who, when they are older, may donate their own money. Therefore, the university is in a way paying for itself. The donations from all sources, legal and illegal, are a means to an ends of the colleges' self-sufficiency. There is proof in the fact that over 63% of college graduates contribute donations that add up to 15% of the total cost of running the college.

¶5.

A reply to this objection is that athough universities need money, much of the money that they need is wasted on red tape and beurocratic mismanagement. Therefore, the money which is gotten from illegal sources is not really needed at all and should be discontinued. In a study of university spending, it was discovered that through some economic cost-cutting, university budgets could be cut by 13%. This more than accounts for the illegally acquired donations from anonymous donors. thus, the illegal donations could be eliminated without increasing the university deficit.

¶6.

In conclusion, my arguments has not been refuted sufficiently enough to change my position that universities should accept donations regardless of how the donor acquired the money. I believe that universities should make a through check to see how or where the donor acquired the money. Finally, I believe that if the donor acquired the money through socially accepted means, than the donation can and should be used to help out a needy university.

Caroline's Critique

Critique of "Universities and Accepting Donations"

Clarity through Argumentation:

para. 2, *sentence 3*–when you make an assumption like this, you should have some authority or study to back it up, and you should include this in your paper

para. 3 almost this entire para. is asserted as fact. Don't write your own hypothetical situations as if they actually exist; if they are true, tell me how you found out about it

para. 3 this argument seems ludicrous; I don't see how you can correlate the two statistics in the last sentence

paras.3, 4, 5 you don't tell me *why* "questionable" money should not be accepted

para. 5 what should universities do with "questionable" money from known sources? How much is donated by anonymous donors?

Clarity through Organization:

Argumentative form is used very well in your paper. I see clearly an intro., (with question), position, argument, objection, reply, concl.

para. 4 put why the university needs money and should accept any they can get in the beginning of this para., then make a separate para. for each objection

My Comment

I agree with Caroline in a general way. You're getting the idea about organization. You do understand what arguments, objections, and replies are and roughly how they are related to each other. That's good. But I also agree with her that the actual argumentation in the paper is somewhat loose and needs to be tightened up.

I will mention only one or two points here. In paragraph 3, you give a certain argument down to line 14. At line 14, it seems to me that you start in on a new argument. I grant that it's an argument which perhaps supports the same conclusion. But it does seem to be a different argument, and the trouble is that you spring it on the reader with no warning or explanation of what it is. In fact, I'm not even sure that it is a new argument. I'm only sure that there seems to be a change at line 14, and it leaves me puzzled as to what is going on.

I want you to think more about the relations between objections and arguments. Is the objection in paragraph 4, lines 5-9 an objection to the argument (or arguments) which you give in paragraph 3? If so, just exactly how is it an objection? What exact point in the argument does it object to? You should tell the reader so that the reader will be convinced that it's an objection to the argument rather than, for example, an objection to the position. You *say* that it's an objection to the argument, but just saying so doesn't make it one.

At the beginning of paragraph 3, you talk about anonymous donors. Then you give the argument that donors often give money to gain respectability. But it's difficult to see how an *anonymous* donor can gain respectability in this way—after all, he can't gain respectability if no one knows who he is (since he's anonymous)!

You've got to proofread your papers before turning them in. Typos mar the paper. Get in the habit of turning in work without typos now, and this will pay off in your later job or profession. If this were a job application, you would not get the job because the typos show that you are not sufficiently careful and painstaking.

Jack

In teaching inquiry and argumentation, I deal with particular topics, particular readings, and particular theories. My principal aim in discussing this material with students is not to decide which theory is better than other theories, but instead to explain the intellectual motivation behind each move made by the theorists. Why does the theorist feel the need to say this at this point in the inquiry? In this way, I hope to give students a sense of the structure of inquiry. Theorists make the moves that they make at this or that point not from whim but instead because of objective intellectual imperatives. The very nature of inquiry forces a theorist to make this or that move. But one is forced to make a given move only if one has a particular end in view. For example, a very popular intellectual goal is explanation. The natural sciences are often said to aim at explanations of natural phenomena. Explanation is not the only goal that one could have. One could aim instead at categorization or at appreciation. And even if one chooses to aim at explanation, different sorts of things may be regarded as explanations by different inquirers. An explanation of a tribal ritual couched entirely in materialistic terms may satisfy some anthropologists and completely fail to satisfy others.

In conveying the structure of inquiry to students, I constantly strive to exhibit alternatives, both in methodology and in goals. I try to set each piece of inquiry in a context created by eliciting the fundamental (and often hidden) presuppositions of that inquiry. In this way, methods and goals—and hence results—which at first seemed inevitable and absolutely valid to students are seen to be dependent on human choices. Knowledge is seen to be a human construction responding to particular human needs and purposes. We need to combat the view which Lewis Thomas describes so well in talking about the teaching of science:

> But science, it appears, is an altogether different kind of learning: an unambiguous, unalterable and endlessly useful display of data that only needs to be packaged and installed somewhere in one's temporal lobe in order to achieve a full understanding of the world ("The Art of Teaching Science," *The New York Times Magazine,* March 14, 1982.)

Tom McMillen, a Rhodes Scholar, now a professional basketball player and aspirant to political office, describes his education in this way:

> In high school and at Maryland I was, more or less, a grind. . . . I had a retentive memory and I took in whatever information was given. Then I regurgitated it when I was asked. At Oxford, they not only expected me to take in information but also to speculate about it, analyze it, and create something from it. I was in a daze for a few months, but it was one of the most important experiences of my life. I learned how to think and to enjoy it (*Sports Illustrated,* April 5, 1982, p. 49).

To make what I am saying more concrete, I want to recount briefly two experiences recently reported by students because I think that they are paradigmatic of the kinds of experiences that we ought to be producing for our students. The first experience is that of a young woman, a sophomore, who was taking two psychology courses simultaneously. These two courses covered the same topics and content, but they were at different levels of sophistication; one was intended for freshmen and sophomores and the other for seniors. The woman found that everything that she was being taught as fact in the lower-level course was being questioned and sometimes rejected in the upper-level course. This coerced her to meditate on the aims of the sciences and on the nature of knowledge in a way which advanced her education rapidly and led her to a much more sophisticated grasp of intellectual method. She came to a more skeptical attitude and a critical awareness in dealing with intellectual matters. The second student had a course from a history professor who emphasized conflicting interpretations of various historical events. The student would read one historian and become completely convinced by that historian's account. Then he would read another historian on the same topic and be completely convinced by that historian's very different account. This proved to be an extremely illuminating experience for the young man, producing some of the same effects in him as the two psychology courses produced in the young woman.

All of this is old-hat to teachers. Teachers' reactions to what I have just said are likely to be: "Of course, there are different interpretations of a given historical event. Of course, knowledge in psychology is hypothetical and subject to revision. We know all that already. There is no revelation for us in what you are saying." My reply is this: Of course, there is no revelation *for teachers* in this. That is because teachers are professionals and have had the experiences which lead to these attitudes. But we must remember that we are teaching students. Our courses are mainly for the benefit of students. And consequently we must pay close attention to the situations of students—to their states of mind, their attitudes, and to what they need. We must remember that students come to us from high school where critical thinking is not necessarily encouraged, where they are asked to do "research" reports which consist mainly of recording materials from various references, where pieces of knowledge are often presented to them as incontrovertible facts to be memorized. College is, or anyway should be, different from high school. And it should be different not just in presenting students with more difficult knowledge. It should be different in that it raises students to a more sophisticated intellectual level by giving them valuable perspectives on intellectual activity.

Those of us who are college educators must ask ourselves several basic questions which we cannot repeat too often. What we do is take students in their late teens and have them spend four years in a college. The questions are these: On what grounds do we have students spend four years in college? What do we hope to achieve by doing this? In particular, if we do not regard most of our students as pre-professionals in one or another field of inquiry—that is, as probable graduate students—then why do we attempt to fill them with knowledge? The usual answer is that there are certain things that one must know in order to get along well in the world. But is this so? Are there some specific pieces of knowledge of which this is true? Most colleges implicitly answer "no" to this question, since they allow students to gain degrees by taking widely varying programs of courses, with the result that there is no group of pieces of knowledge deemed essential for everyone to know in order to get along well in the world. By what right, then, do we encourage young people to spend four years with us when they could be doing other productive things with their time? The answer I have been suggesting is that we prepare them for the rest of their lives by helping them to develop certain attitudes toward knowledge and certain skills which increase their intellectual independence and which help them become the kind of individuals they already want to be.

Unfortunately, most instructors rarely say anything explicit about intellectual skills and ways of thinking. Instead, they may feel that students can and should absorb ways of thinking by osmosis. Some instructors have told me that even if they wished to talk with students about analytic approaches or methods of thought, they would not know what to say. Others profess lack of interest in intellectual method, preferring to practice it rather than talk about it. Yet one would think that if the purpose of college work were to impart "helpful approaches" and "valuable methods of analysis," as Derek Bok, the president of

Harvard puts it, college instructors would attempt to give direct instruction in these topics or at least regularly make remarks about them in teaching the material of the course. They generally do very little of this. If the ultimate purpose of college education is the imparting of ways of thinking, it would seem appropriate to attempt to give direct instruction in ways of thinking rather than leave it to chance and osmosis.

We can approach this same matter in a slightly different way by asking this question: If we, as a faculty, are involved in liberal education, what is it that we intend to liberate the students from? Those educational theorists who emphasize the transmission of knowledge would answer this by saying that students are to be liberated from the darkness of ignorance and falsehood by teaching them the truth about history, society, the individual, and nature. These theorists would continue by saying that one major purpose of teaching students the truth about these matters is to allow them to formulate beliefs and make decisions on the basis of knowledge on the grounds that beliefs and decisions based on knowledge are better than those based on ignorance and falsehood. My own answer to this question is that we should aim to liberate students from domination by dogmatism and by experts. This includes liberating students from dependence on teachers too. We should want to put students in a position to make up their own minds. Happily, this coincides with what students want, too. They want to learn to be independent individuals, people who can weigh evidence and claims for themselves and form independent opinions rather than be blown back and forth by every intellectual, cultural, and political fad or impressive expert who comes along.

If this is our aim, or one of our aims, in education, then the study of methodology and an examination of the goals and limits of the major fields of inquiry are not subjects appropriate only for graduate students or professional students. They are essential for undergraduates too, in order that students may orient themselves in a sea of conflicting claims and exploding knowledge and make intelligent judgments and choices.

Intellectual methodology includes both such specific skills as analysis and argumentation on the one hand and "the rules of the game" (the moves and purposes of inquiry) on the other hand. Teaching intellectual methodology to undergraduates not only leads them to think critically and independently, but it also helps students to integrate their studies. As Professor Jonathan Z. Smith, Dean of the College of the University of Chicago has put it, "To dump on students the task of finding coherence in their education is indefensible. Colleges shouldn't be allowed to collect tuition on that basis." (*Time Magazine,* April 20, 1981, p. 50.) By showing students that some basic intellectual principles and intellectual techniques and skills apply to all fields of inquiry, we give them a sense of common purpose and of the unity of knowledge. By talking about cognitive frameworks and about world views, we show them how seemingly disparate data and theories can be integrated into an intellectual whole.

At the present moment, there is a great unease in the academic world over the effects of financial retrenchment. But there are signs of even greater and more important unease over the type of education that colleges now provide. A friend at the State University of New York at Buffalo writes, "I find it puzzling that U.S. colleges give the strong appearance of trying to get students to think for themselves, and yet in any area that I have had to judge students the result seems to be the opposite (viz., indoctrination in vague and shallow views, alienation, authority-worship, an almost studied inability to agonize over a problem)." Professor Bernice Braid of Long Island University tells of a recruiter for IBM who complained that IBM "finds itself hiring well-educated, or at least well-certified, personnel at relatively high salaries, only to have to invest a year or more in training them to think." At the same time, she finds a dangerous decline in morale and confusion about purpose among college teachers:

> We, as a group of teachers, seem less sure that spending time in the classroom produces anything. . . . This is merely another way of observing, then, that the professor of 1960 was both likely to be interested in his own field and certain that the pursuit of knowledge in some larger context was useful and/or significant. The professor of 1980, on the other hand, having lost faith in the enterprise of teaching itself, and perhaps having drifted, however imperceptibly, away from the values implicit in scholarly pursuit, finds it difficult to generate prophetic fervor, or just plain energetic curiosity. (*Forum for Honors*, XII:3, Spring 1982, p. 6)

I believe that these two phenomena, failure of colleges to do their job properly and decline in faculty morale, are related to one another. Colleges advertise that they produce critical and independent thinkers. But the way in which colleges proceed on a daily basis—namely each professor teaching the specific content of his or her narrow specialty—has, in my opinion, clearly failed to achieve this goal. No wonder, then, that college faculties are confused and demoralized about teaching. This basic problem may now be hidden by the financial crisis which education faces, but it will remain and be even more serious long after we have coped with the financial crisis. It is even possible that if colleges did their job better, a grateful public and a grateful business community would provide colleges with sufficient funds.

We need to teach students to think critically and independently. We need to provide them, not with more knowledge, but instead with greater understanding—understanding of the nature and limits of inquiry and of the knowledge which inquiry produces, and understanding of the fundamental features of the modern mind (such as those listed by William Daniels: positivism, reductionism, relativism, and determinism). This is our aim in University Course 101.

But college education should go even beyond this. One of the topics about which we can and should think critically is the way we live. Socrates is generally acknowledged to be the greatest teacher in Western civilization. Socrates inquired, but he did not inquire after knowledge for its own sake. His purpose was to find out how a human being ought to live and, secondarily, how society should be arranged so as to make the best life possible. He inquired into the patterns and principles of Athenian behavior so searchingly, and he suggested alternative ways of living that were so at odds with Athenian habits, that the Athenian citizens felt challenged by him in the most fundamental way. This was Socrates' purpose as an educator. Today we live in a certain way. For example, many of us are extreme individualists, with the result that we have a fragmented society peopled by social atoms. Many of us evaluate everything in terms of our own self-interest, our own desires. Strikingly, this is particularly evident in today's colleges where students evaluate everything by asking the question "What will it do for me?" (Usually they wonder whether this or that will help them get a job or into medical school or law school.)

One important point to be made about critical thinking is that it can easily be justified to students by precisely their own evaluative standards. We can show them exactly what the ability to think, read, and write will do for them. We can show them in concrete detail how this ability can help them get jobs and do well in those jobs or in professional schools. (Remember Prof. Braid's IBM recruiter.) This is yet another reason why college education should emphasize intellectual skills and methodology—it is easy to motivate students to learn these things. Learning these things makes excellent sense to them.

But once they learn these skills, colleges should encourage students to use those same skills to examine their own values and those of society, just as Socrates did with the youths of Athens. It is by no means clear that self-interest should be a person's only, or highest, value. It is by no means clear that our society should be as atomistic as it now is. Perhaps the teaching of critical thinking and a critical examination of world views and values would lead to an increase in the number of college graduates who are able to create meaningful and significant lives for themselves.

39 A Model for Designing and Revising Assignments

John D. Reiff
English Composition Board, The University of Michigan

James E. Middleton
Division of Communications, Humanities, and Social Sciences,
Williamsport Area Community College

In one of the English Composition Board's first seminars on the teaching of writing, a faculty member explained with frustration, "I've been giving this assignment for five years, and my students still haven't gotten it right!"

Why did class after class—student after student—keep getting the assignment wrong? When we, the faculty member's colleagues, looked at this assignment, we realized we wouldn't have known how to "get it right" either. While he was clear in his own mind about what he wanted, our colleague's written assignment failed to convey those expectations to his students or us: Unintentionally, he'd been getting what he asked for. His experience caused us to re-examine our own assignments which had failed to elicit writings we expected from our students.

In order to understand the assignment-making process better, we began to think about assignments as acts of communication between teacher and student. Our thinking led us to ask ourselves important questions: To what extent do students fail at writing assignments because we, their instructors, fail to communicate our expectations to them effectively? Are there criteria we can use both to evaluate our assignments and to revise them for greater effectiveness?

As we began to examine the assignment-making process with faculty and teaching assistants in writing courses across the curriculum, we saw that every assignment presents students not only with a complex set of demands but also with a series of opportunities to which they may respond—with explicit decisions or, as often happens, with unexamined assumptions. In order to make the assignment-making process a more explicit activity for us and for our students, we developed a systematic description of the elements of writing assignments as a basis (1) for revising our current assignments and (2) for designing new ones. We believe that as instructors make their expectations clearer to students, students' chances to succeed at assignments are increased significantly.

Goals for Writing Tasks

We see three conceivable goals, singly or in combination, for any writing assignment. One goal is discovery: Students are asked to write in order to clarify their ideas or feelings, uncover new information, integrate new material, understand a process or relationship, or in some other way generate new learning. Journals and other ungraded work commonly occasion this sort of writing-to-learn, but this goal may also be primary in more formal assignments.

A second goal is communication: The task for students here is to organize and present their ideas or feelings appropriately and effectively for specific readers, either real or hypothetical. With this goal in mind, the instructor will specify elements of the students' rhetorical stance—perhaps creating for them a hypothetical persona, situation and purpose, perhaps aiming drafts of their writing at the real audience of their peers. The case study, which analyzes a situation and recommends a course of action to a real or hypothetical audience, is an excellent example of the assignment focusing the student on the act of communication.

The third goal—and the one students are most apt to assume unless there is explicit discussion between instructor and student to counteract that assumption—is performance. Students are keenly aware of this "hoop-jumping" aspect of assignments, and their anxiety about performance may block both discovery and communication. They may define performance in superficial ways—attempting simply to show that they did the readings, or to show control over surface errors while producing a shallow empty text—or anxiety about performance may also reach to the core of the writing task. Students trying wholeheartedly to engage their material may feel blocked by awareness that their writing will be judged by readers more expert than they. Writing to what James Britton calls the "teacher-as-examiner" is a task unlike any found in the world outside of school: Students are expected to write as if they were experts writing to peers, while in fact they are novices trying to impress experts. Convinced of the implausibility of discovering and communicating ideas new to an expert reader, the student most often hopes to merely impress the expert instructor by avoiding error.

Instructors may alleviate these problems in at least four ways:

1. by defining some writing tasks as private writing, outside the range of evaluation,
2. by setting up writing tasks which allow students to generate information that is in fact new to the instructors,
3. by directing students writing to an either real or realistic audience other than the teacher, and
4. by evaluating students' success explicitly in terms of their discovery or communication.

Even as instructors alleviate students' problems by carefully defining the purposes of assignments, they must vary the criteria with which they evaluate those assignments; for example, if an assignment generates a series of leading questions about relevant topics, or if it conveys a particular view of the course material, to an appropriate audience, the student writer can be said to have performed well on the assignment.

Product

While instructors often remain silent about their goals in a given assignment and about the rhetorical stance those goals may entail, they almost always specify some of the features they want in a final product: "Compare and contrast X and Y in 3-5 pages," "Examine the causes of A," or "Discuss the use of P and Q in the work of Z." And so on. Like a contractor's specifications for a bridge or highway, these specifications tell student writers what the finished product must contain or must be able to do. "Compare and contrast X and Y" directs decisions about subject (which must be comparison/contrast). In addition, this example gives minimum and maximum lengths for the product (3-5 pages). Such an assignment expresses the instructor's desire for the students to master a particular method of organization or body of material, and it also enables the instructors, in evaluating performance, to measure a given paper against an ideal three-to-five-page comparison and contrast of X and Y.

Process

Such an assignment does not tell students how to develop that written product. The benefits of a carefully crafted assignment may be lost by students who dash off their papers late in the night before they are due, making only a few typographical changes in the first draft. Help in development may come through the processes the assignment specifies—the activities the students must complete as they work on their papers. Specified processes might include pre-draft conferences, outlines, preliminary thesis statements, group discussions, or required revisions. If students are required to submit a first draft, either to instructors or to peer readers, and then to make substantial revisions of those drafts, they must reflect upon their ideas as well as the form they have given those ideas. Specifying processes such as these in an assignment requires that students abandon the quickly-written "first-draft paper" in favor of the more carefully developed one.

Revising and Designing Assignments

Whether or not instructors speak to each of these elements of an assignment, students must make decisions or act on assumptions about them all. They must envision a goal or purpose for writing (often performance) and a rhetorical situation (often that of novice trying to impress expert reader—a difficult situation in which to perform); they must decide on subject and structure (often these elements are determined by the teacher, at least in broad terms); and they must use some process to create the paper (too often combining the techniques of avoidance, of staring blankly at an empty page, and of filling up the blank page with last-minute desperation). Considering the decisions students must make, the instructor may want to revise assignments to guide those decisions more carefully—not necessarily by specifying every element, but so as to make clear which aspects of this complex interchange are fixed by the instructor and which are left open for students to decide. A graphic representation of these elements and their relationships to one another is presented in Figure 1 (p. 268).

The instructor may choose to design a sequence of assignments which, throughout the term, systematically vary the elements about which students must decide. One such sequence might move from teacher control to student control. Initial assignments might be tightly structured by the teacher, with purpose and rhetorical situation specified, subject and structure defined, and checkpoints built into the pre-writing, drafting, and revision of a paper. Such assignments would make students aware of the elements with which they must deal and would demonstrate both the freedom and the constraints implicit in those elements. Later assignments might progressively turn over to students more and more decisions about a writing task. The final assignment in the sequence might require students to devise a rhetorical situation and purpose: to specify a subject and a process of composing, and then to meet the requirements that those specifications demand of them.

Alternate sequences of assignments might be designed around other models of development. Richard Larson suggested at CCCC, in March 1981, that an assignment sequence should move students from the private and concrete to the public and abstract. The journal assignment below, taken from the writing course that one of us teaches on the Vietnam War, represents private and personal concrete writing that would be most appropriate at the beginning of such a sequence:

> Divide your journal into three sections, the first of which is your reading log. Draw a line down the middle of each page of the reading log; label the left column "Passage" and the right column "Response." As you read the assigned readings, use the left column to describe any passages which puzzle you, intrigue you, anger you, or elicit some other response from you. Use the right column to set that response down.
>
> The second section is your writer's sketchbook. Use it for any informal writing you do in class, and for times outside of class when you want to reflect on the discussions or readings and their connections to your experience. Ideas you set down in your sketchbook may be beginning points for more formal writing you do in the course. I will read material from this section only if you ask me to do so.

The third section is for letters. Each week I expect you to write me a letter at least a page long about your involvement in the course; each week I will write a letter in response to yours. You can use your weekly letter to discuss the issues of the course, to discuss problems in a paper you're working on, to suggest changes in the class, and of course to respond to issues I raise in my letters to you. This letter exchange is one way for us to extend discussion between us beyond what our time in class allows.

The final assignment in this course on the Vietnam War is a research paper—developed through draft and revision—whose real audience is both other students in the course and students who will take the course the following year. Whereas the journal writing is personal and concrete, the research paper is aimed at a public not fully known to the student writers, and it demands that they answer a research question by constructing an argument—by supporting generalizations with concrete evidence. Specified processes vary as students move through the assignments in this sequence.

It is of course essential that each instructor evaluate student work in accordance with what assignments require. In those areas where assignments are most specific, instructors should indeed ascertain students' ability to meet expectations. But instructors must also recognize that areas left open for students' decisions may pose more complex problems and may lead to unanticipated choices. The entire interchange—from the instructor's first speaking or writing the assignment to the students' finally submitting the finished product—is a process wherein teachers and students together can negotiate the assignment's meaning. The more clarity that instructors can bring to this process of negotiation, the more able students will be to form a personally meaningful conception of the assignment and its potential.

THE WRITING ASSIGNMENT AS A COMMUNICATION EXCHANGE

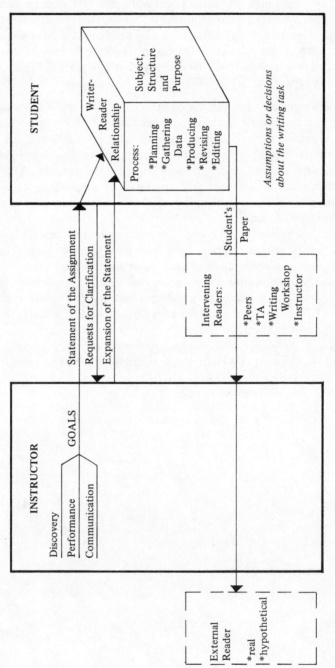

Figure 1

40 How English Teachers Can Help Their Colleagues Teach Writing

Lee Odell

Department of English, Rensselaer Polytechnic Institute

Increasingly, colleagues in other disciplines are recognizing the importance of writing and are looking to us English teachers for help as they try to improve the writing of students in, say, history or biology. Frequently, our colleagues' notion of help is expressed this way: "I know. We could collaborate. I'll read students' papers for content and you read them for grammar and style."

When we decline this invitation—as I think we must—we invite a series of questions: "Well, what can you (or will you) do? What do you English teachers know that will help me with my students? More important, how can we teachers of history (or science or . . .) help students with their writing without losing sight of our subject matter?" From my experience in working with colleagues in schools and colleges, here are several suggestions as to how we might respond to these questions.

We Need to Address Colleagues' Concern about What They Call "Grammar."

As we and our colleagues go over selected student papers, we can show them how to categorize errors. We can help them answer such questions as these: Which errors appear to be the result of careless proofreading and which seem to reflect a basic misunderstanding of, for example, the basic structure of a sentence? Which types of errors appear in the work of more than one student? Which types of errors could be eliminated by a brief explanation and which require the attention of a skilled tutor in a writing workshop?

Answers to such questions will enable our colleagues to focus their efforts and set realistic goals for students. Once these goals are set, of course, there are no magic solutions to the problem of improving punctuation, spelling, and usage. What's needed is a certain amount of hard work guided by these principles: Students must know what the teacher will and will not accept; they must have a reasonable amount of explanation as to what certain errors are and how they can be corrected; colleagues in other disciplines must take responsibility for seeing that students have edited their papers. This last point is particularly important in light of an experience one high school English teacher reported to me. Most of this teacher's students used complete sentences in their essays, yet their social studies teacher complained that these same students turned in papers filled with sentence fragments. When the English teacher asked students about this, several of them shared one student's feeling: "Oh, well, that's social studies, not English. He [the social studies teacher] doesn't really care about that stuff."

We Must Expand Our Colleagues' Notions of What "Writing" Is and of What Kinds of Assignments Are Possible.

For many of our colleagues, writing is a synonym for expository essay or term paper. Of course we want to help colleagues with these two types of writing. But we should point out that writing can take various forms, many of which need not be graded, or even read, by the instructor. Toby Fulwiler has done a very thorough job of explaining how short, in-class writing tasks can help students synthesize material that is being presented or can enable students and teachers to identify students' misunderstandings of a given topic (Fulwiler, 15-22).

In addition to showing colleagues how to use frequent, in-class writing assignments, we need to identify colleagues in other disciplines who give well-focused, stimulating writing assignments. We may find fewer of those colleagues than we would wish, for many people simply assign a report or term paper and turn students loose in the library. At best, this sort of assignment may require students to do some useful synthesis. But at worst, this type of assignment tends to become little more than a cut-and-paste job based on secondary sources and distinguished by a lack of independent thought on the part of the student. Fortunately, there are colleagues in other disciplines who give quite different assignments. Consider these examples for which I am indebted to Susan Burke (eighth-grade teacher), Doris Quick (high-school teacher), and Gary Goseen (university professor).

From a Middle School Social Studies Class:

On the basis of class discussion of consumer rights and young people's important role as consumers, identify a specific consumer complaint you have, and write a letter to the organization against which you have a complaint. Your letter must explain the complaint clearly and reasonably and describe a course of action that would solve the problem you are complaining about.

Read the attached excerpts from a diary in which a soldier in the American Revolution describes the hardships of life in the Continental Army. Using his diaries as evidence, write a letter in which you persuade the Continental Congress to provide benefits to veterans after the war with England is won.

From a High School Chemistry Class:

Assume you have removed the following pieces of chemistry equipment from your lab table. [The list included 20 diverse items such as Bunsen burner, asbestos gauze, evaporating dish.] You have three drawers in your lab table and each piece of equipment must be logically placed in one of the three drawers. Label the drawers and write a one page paper in which you describe your system for storing the equipment, and persuade your classmates that your system is efficient and logical.

Explain by means of analogy or model system any topic in chemistry we have discussed this year. Your audience will be students who are taking the course next year and who are having trouble understanding the topic you are explaining. Your paper (if good) will be retained in the teacher's file and used as supplementary material for those students who are confused about a given concept.

From a University Anthropology Class:

On the basis of our discussions and readings about communication among non-human primates, explain your answer to this question: Could Washoe [a chimpanzee who had learned some elements of human language] "think" a poem?

Attend a religious ritual and analyze it (following procedures discussed in class) as a symbolic statement of essential characteristics of the social groups involved.

The Age of Innocence and *Tom Sawyer* deal at great length with the theme of socialization in American life of the nineteenth century. Using an analytic approach demonstrated in class, analyze a character of your choice from each novel as he or she reaches a "compromise" with society.

As we identify people who make assignments such as these, we will expand our own notion of what is possible in writing about, say, anthropology. We will also improve our credibility with our colleagues, since our suggestions can be based on the actual practice of colleagues and are not simply the product of an English teacher's fevered imagination.

We Must Help Colleagues Be More Sensitive to Audience.

We should encourage colleagues to think about such questions as these: What are the characteristics of the audience(s) for whom their students will write? For a given assignment, what may students assume about their audience's knowledge, biases, expectations? What constraints must students accept when they write for a particular audience? One response to these questions is to claim that students are writing academic discourse for an academic audience. This, of course, is true. But we must not over-simplify our conception of an "academic audience." Its characteristics and expectations may be more diverse than one might think. One way to test this speculation is to remember the last time we attended a common paper-grading session, one at which—with no prior training or discussion of criteria—we and our colleagues read and graded a set of essays. In my own experience, comments made at those sessions indicate that people are using different sets of criteria and are attending to different aspects of the writing, some responding to diction and syntax, some to organization, some to what Paul Diederich refers to as "quality of ideas." Thanks to recent work by Sarah Freedman, we have reason to think that for some readers "quality of ideas" weighs most heavily in the evaluation of a piece of writing (Freedman, 161-64). But even here it is possible for academic audiences to vary quite widely.

To illustrate this last point: As part of my work in *Writing Across the Curriculum* I have had occasion to read a number of student papers (complete with instructors' grades and comments) from a number of disciplines. Teachers of business courses frequently give students a set of facts about a company and ask students to recommend policies that the company should adopt. In evaluating students' papers, these instructors seem concerned with matters of practicality: Have students identified one or more specific courses of action for the company to follow? Given the information at hand, does it seem likely that the company in question could and would follow the writer's recommendations? In economics courses, instructors seem most concerned with how accurately students apply economic theory to new sets of data. In at least one political science course, the instructor places great emphasis on the imaginativeness of students' synthesis of materials studied.

Practicality, accuracy, imaginativeness: these are not the only criteria by which instructors judge the "quality of ideas" in students' writing. But these criteria do suggest the different values held by audiences for which students will be expected to write. If we can help colleagues give students a clear idea of the audience for whom they are writing, we will probably do a favor for our colleagues as well as for their students.

We Need to Help Colleagues Recognize the Intellectual Demands of Specific Assignments.

And we need to help devise ways to show students how to meet those demands. Consider the following history assignment, which asks students to write about a nineteenth-century novel in which the narrator purports to be describing life in Boston in the year 2000.

> Suppose that you had never heard of Edward Bellamy's novel *Looking Backward.* One day while killing time in the College Library, you came across a dusty, mutilated copy of the book. As you began to read *Looking Backward,* it seemed reasonable for you to guess, although you could find no date of publication, that the book had to be written after a certain date and probably before another date.
>
> What is the narrowest time frame you would choose? Write an essay in which you defend your choice with specific references to customs, institutions, inventions, or anything else the narrator mentions.

In order to determine when the book was originally published (and thereby formulate one's thesis) one might:

—focus on inventions and customs mentioned in the book;
—identify inventions and customs not mentioned in the book but known to us today;
—determine dates (e.g., the date at which a particular invention was made) for things that are mentioned and for things that are not mentioned in the book;
—consider alternate conclusions about the publication date of the book and explain how those conclusions are less plausible than one's own.

Without presuming that this brief list identifies all the intellectual work a writer might engage in, I want to use this list to make two points. The first is that the intellectual work associated with the *Looking Backward* task is somewhat different from that involved in the writing assignments mentioned earlier. In their letters of complaint, the eighth graders would need to (1) explain what they expected or hoped; (2) show that their experience fell short of what they had expected; and (3) explain a specific sequence of actions that would resolve the conflict between experience and expectations. In describing their system for organizing laboratory equipment, high school chemistry students would have to classify items on the basis of their use in various experiments. My first point, then, is that different writing tasks make different intellectual demands of writers. My second point is that teachers can show students how to meet those demands. For example, the history teacher who assigned the *Looking Backward* paper might make a practice of having students examine short texts, trying to date those texts by determining, say, what inventions the author does mention and what inventions, known today, the author does not mention. The advantage of this teaching procedure is that it accomplishes two goals at once: it enables the teacher to focus on materials of his or her discipline and at the same time to teach students a discovery procedure which they can use in writing their essays.

None of these suggestions, of course, will solve all the problems of teaching writing in other disciplines. None come with any guarantee of certain success. All entail a good bit of work for us and for our colleagues. That, I think, simply acknowledges reality. Improving student writing is a difficult, time-consuming task, one that demands the best efforts of all of us. These suggestions do, however, help us focus our energies; my own experience suggests that time spent in these areas is likely to pay off. At the very least, it will preclude our having to check papers for grammar and style while someone else reads them for content.

41 Why We Teach Writing in the First Place

Toby Fulwiler
Department of Humanities, Michigan Technological University

Back to the Basics

Schools exist to teach people to think in some systematic way. At the early grades "reading" and "writing" and "arithmetic" are called basic. What they are basic to, is thinking. Later on, in secondary schools and colleges, these basics become attached to particular disciplines—each characterized by a particular pattern of reasoning—history, biology, literature and so on. Along the way, of course, schools teach other things: citizenship, social manners, athletic skills and the like. And sometimes these collateral skills so dominate the curriculum that original or primary intentions get lost, and we talk about schools which "socialize" or "train" or "bore" rather than "educate."

But the basics the public always wants to "get back to" are really the primary language skills which make systematic articulate thought possible. Reading provides us access to information and ideas. Writing and arithmetic provide general tools for manipulating and expressing ideas and information. Unlike speaking, which children learn on their own, long before kindergarten, these more abstract language skills are formally introduced in first grade and developed progressively during the next twelve or twenty years. This rather simple-minded formulation about why we go to school is meant to introduce "writing" as one of the truly elemental—basic—studies for serious students from the earliest through the latest grades.

But, of the three Rs, the role of writing in learning—and in the school curriculum—is perhaps least understood. Everyone believes that reading is *the* basic skill (the *most* basic?); without it few avenues to civilized culture or higher knowledge exist. Everyone also knows that mathematical languages are the foundation on which scientific and technical knowledge—and hence our civilization—is built. Everyone does *not* know that writing is basic to thinking about, and learning, knowledge in all fields as well as to communicating that knowledge. Elementary teachers teach penmanship and believe they are teaching writing; secondary teachers often teach grammar and believe they are teaching writing; while many college professors teach literary criticism and expect that their students already have been taught writing. In other words, many different activities are taught in the name of teaching writing. Furthermore, as Don Graves indicates, courses which do, in fact, teach writing sometimes do so in a harmful manner by suggesting that the "eradication of error is more important than the encouragement of expression" (1978, p. 18).

The emphasis on teaching reading in the elementary school curriculum may actually contribute to the neglect of writing. Many American educators believe that reading must precede writing as people develop their language-using skills; this hierarchical model actually separates reading from writing—which may be a fundamental mistake (Stock and Wixson, p. 00). Schools which subscribe to such an artificial instructional hierarchy are also likely to subscribe to a set of basal readers accompanied by fill-in-the-blank workbooks; these workbooks both help sell the reading series and diminish the amount of writing a teacher is likely to assign in connection with the reading lesson. Graves even suggests that the dominance of reading in the curriculum discourages active self-sponsored learning: "Writing is the basic stuff of education. It has been sorely neglected in our schools. We have substituted the passive reception of information for the active expression of facts, ideas and feelings. We now need to right the balance between sending and receiving. We need to let them write" (1978, p. 27).

Graves' position presents reading as the passive receiving of knowledge and writing as the more active generation of knowledge. We know, of course, that this polarity is too severe. Frank Smith (1971), Kenneth Goodman (1968), and David Bleich (1978), among others, have demonstrated that reading is a highly subjective and active process—hardly the passive activity which Graves describes. Each of us "reads" information differently because we have experienced the world differently. However, there remains enough truth in Graves' observation to consider it further. In a sense, reading is the corollary opposite of writing: readers (and—for that matter—listeners too) take in language from "outside" and process it through an internal mechanism colored by personal knowledge and experience to arrive at meaning. Writers, on the contrary, produce language from some internal mechanism which, as it happens, is also shaped by personal knowledge and experience from "outside," to create meaning. So, just as no reader reads texts exactly the same way as other readers, no writer generates texts which are totally unique or original.

The importance in these qualified comparisons between reading and writing is this: they are interdependent, mutually supportive skills, both of which are "basic" to an individual's capacity to generate critical, independent thinking. Few courses of study, however, in the secondary schools or colleges, seem to recognize explicitly this relationship. Whereas reading is assigned in virtually every academic area as the best way to impart information, introduce ideas, and teach concepts, no such imperative exists with regard to writing. In many subject areas, teachers are more likely to assign machine-scored short answer, multiple choice, and true-false tests than significant written compositions. In fact, in a recent study of the kind of writing required across the curriculum in American secondary schools, Arthur Applebee (1981) discovered that only 3% of assigned writing tasks required students to compose anything longer than one sentence; most of their so-called writing was "mechanical"—filling in blanks, copying, and doing homework exercises. Other courses may assign periodic essay tests, term papers, or laboratory reports but use them to measure—rather than promote—learning.

A recent publication by the American Association for the Advancement of the Humanities reports findings similar to the Applebee study. The report says in part:

> Plainly, schooling as usual won't work. Most schools have a powerful hidden curriculum that precludes the development of higher-order skills in reading, thinking, and writing. The elements of this pernicious curriculum include the following:
>
> No writing in the testing program, only short-answer, true-false, and multiple-choice tests;
> Writing relegated only to English courses;
> Writing viewed as an end, not as a means, of learning;
> No systematic instruction in solving problems, thinking critically, and examining evidence;
> No opportunities for disciplined discussion in small groups;
> No regular practice in writing at length (1982, p. 9).

Not only is the curriculum "pernicious," but teachers are seldom trained to understand fully the degree to which language skills are involved in the development of higher thought:

> Moreover, most teachers are unprepared by their education or professional training to teach and foster the needed skills, just as most schools offer no in-service training for teachers and no small classes, released time, or teacher aides to help evaluate student writing (1982, p. 9).

These studies, together with my personal experience as both student and teacher, suggest that writing has an ill-defined and haphazard role in the curriculum. And where writing has an established role, that role is likely to be superficial or limited in scope. If we are interested in helping schools do better what we believe they are primarily intended to do—teach people to reason systematically, logically, and critically—then we need, as Graves suggests, to balance the curriculum as carefully with regard to writing activities as we currently do with reading activities. Moreover, the curriculum should not include merely *more* writing, but more of certain *kinds* of writing. Let me explain.

Thought and Language

Thirty years ago George Gusdorf (1953) stated clearly the double and often contradictory role language plays in the development of individuals. On the one hand, humans use language to communicate ideas and information to other people; on the other hand, humans use language to express themselves and to develop their own articulate thought. These two functions, the "communicative" and the "expressive," often work in opposition to each other; as Gusdorf puts it: "The more I communicate, the less I express myself; the more I express myself, the less I communicate" (*Language as a Way of Knowing,* 1977, p. 128).

Whereas Gusdorf's formulation of the double role of language may seem obvious and common-sensical, it is surprising to see the degree to which schools promote the one, the "communicative," and neglect the other, the "expressive." Most writing assigned in most curricula asks students to write in order to communicate learned information to teachers—through which writing the students will be evaluated, judged, and graded. Few curricula recognize, implicitly or explicitly, that writing can have an equally important role in generating knowledge (the expressive function) as in communicating knowledge. In other words, an individual's language is crucial in discovering, creating, and formulating ideas as well as in communicating to others what has been discovered, created, and formulated.

Why am I making such an issue about the different functions of writing? Because I believe with James Britton that "knowledge is a process of knowing rather than a storehouse of the known." Much of the "process of knowing" takes place through language. Not only is it the symbol system through which we receive and transmit most information, it is the necessary medium in which we process or assimilate that information. We see and hear language, we explain experience and sensation through language, and we use language to identify the world. Gusdorf says "To name is to call into existence, to draw out of nothingness. That which is not named cannot exist in any possible way" (*Language as a Way of Knowing,* 1977, p. 48). By naming objects and experience we represent our world through symbols. Susanne Langer describes sense data—the stuff we take in from outside—as "constantly wrought into symbols, which are our elementary ideas" (1960, p. 42). In order to think in the first place, human beings need to symbolize, for in using language they represent, come to know and understand the world. We actually do much of our learning through *making* language; or, another way of saying the same thing: language makes thinking and learning, as we know them, possible.

For our concerns here, the process by which we think and learn is most important: What happens to sense data, information, ideas and images when we receive them? How do we manipulate them in our minds, make them our own or do something with them? Psychologist Lev Vygotsky describes "inner speech" as the mediator between thought and language, portraying it as "a dynamic, shifting, unstable thing, fluttering between word and thought" (1962, p. 149). He argues that "thought is born through words . . . thought unembodied in words remains a shadow" (1962, p. 153). Other sensory experience— sights, sounds, smells, tastes, touches—contributes to, but does not in itself constitute, formal thought. We often think things through by talking to ourselves, carrying on "inner" conversations in which we consider, accept, reject, debate, and rationalize. The key to knowing and understanding lies in our ability to internally manipulate information and ideas received whole from external sources and give them verbal shape or *articulation,* which Richard Bailey defines as forming "sensory impressions and inchoate ideas into linguistic form" (p. 27). We think by processing; we process by talking to ourselves and others.

This last point is most important: we often inform ourselves by speaking out loud to others. Drawing on the work of Gusdorf, Langer, and Vygotsky, James Britton argues that the "primary task for speech is to symbolize reality: we symbolize reality in order to handle it" (1970, p. 20). Considered this way, speech serves the needs of the speaker as much as the listener. Britton argues that human beings use "expressive" speech—or talk—more to shape their own experience than to communicate to others: the words give concrete form to thought and so make it more real. This "shaping at the point of utterance" (Britton, 1972, p. 53) helps us discover the meaning (our own meaning) of our everyday experience. As Martin Nystrand summarizes it in *Language as a Way of Knowing:* language "facilitates discovery by crystallizing experience" (1977, p. 101).

We carry on conversations with others to explain things to ourselves. I explain out loud to a friend the symbolism in a Bergman film to better understand it myself. I discuss with my wife the gossip from a recent dinner party to give that party a shape and identity. And so on. The intersection between articulate speech and internal symbolization produces comprehensible meaning. This same intersection helps explain the role of writing in learning.

Many teachers identify writing simply as a technical communication skill necessary for the clear transmission of knowledge. This limited understanding of writing takes no account of the process we call "composing," the mental activity which may be said to characterize our very species. Ann Berthoff describes composing as the essense of thinking: "The work of the active mind is seeing relationships, finding forms, making meanings: when we write, we are doing in a particular way what we are already doing when we make sense of the world. We are composers by virtue of being human" (1978, p. 12). Janet Emig believes that writing "represents a unique mode of learning—not merely valuable, not merely special, but unique" (1977, p. 122). The act of writing, according to Emig, allows the writer to manipulate thought in unique ways because writing makes our thoughts visible and concrete and allows us to interact with and modify them. Writing one word, one sentence, one paragraph suggests still other words, sentences, and paragraphs. Both Berthoff and Emig point out that writing progresses as an act of discovery—and furthermore, that no other thinking process helps us develop a line of inquiry or a mode of thought as completely. Scientists, artists, mathematicians, lawyers, engineers—all "think" with pen to paper, chalk to blackboard, hands on terminal keys. Developed thinking is seldom possible, for most of us, any other way. We can hold only so many thoughts in our heads at one time; when we talk out loud and have dialogues with friends—or with ourselves—we lose much of what we say because it isn't written down. More importantly, we can't extend, expand, or develop our ideas fully because we cannot *see* them. Sheridan Baker writes: "only on paper, by writing and rewriting, can we get the fit, make the thought visible . . . where it will bear inspection both from ourselves and others" (p. 227). Sartre quit writing when he lost his sight because he couldn't see words, the symbols of thought; he needed to visualize thought in order to compose, manipulate, and develop it (Emig, 1977).

School Writing

In 1975, James Britton and a team of researchers published a study of the kind of writing assigned to students, 11–18 years old, in British schools. The results of the study are not surprising: "transactional writing" (writing to communicate information) accounted for 64% of the total writing assigned students between the ages of 11 and 18. "Poetic writing" (writing as creative art) accounted for 18%—exclusively in English classes—while "expressive writing" (thoughts written to oneself) barely shows up at all, accounting for just 6% of the total sample (Britton, 1975). Miscellaneous writing, including copying and note taking, accounted for the rest. The figures are more extreme when the research team looked at the writing assigned to eighteen year olds: transactional, 84%; poetic, 7%, and expressive, 4%.

The fact that students were seldom required to write in the expressive mode suggested to Britton that writing was taught almost exclusively as a means to communicate information rather than as a means to gain insight, develop ideas, or solve problems. This complete neglect of expressive writing across the curriculum is a clue to the value of writing in schools. According to Britton's classification, which closely parallels Gusdorf's identification of the dual function of language, expressive writing is the most personal, the closest to "inner speech" and the thinking process itself. The absence of assigned expressive writing in school curricula suggests that many teachers have a limited understanding of the way language works. As Britton's coresearcher Nancy Martin explains: "The expressive is basic. Expressive speech is how we communicate with each other most of the time and expressive writing, being the form of writing nearest speech, is crucial for trying out and coming to terms with new ideas" (1976, p. 26). According to the research team, personal or expressive writing is the matrix from which both transactional and poetic writing evolve. Serious writers who undertake significant writing tasks almost naturally put their writing through "expressive stages as they go about finding out exactly what they believe and what they want to write." Donald Murray explains: "I believe increasingly that the process of discovery, of using language to *find out what you're going to say,* is a key part of the writing process" (*Research on Composing,* 1978, p. 91, italics mine).

Preliminary findings in Applebee's study of writing in American schools (1981) indicate a pattern similar to the 1967–70 British study; "informational" (transactional) writing dominated the composing tasks in all disciplines; "imaginative" (poetic) writing was limited largely to English classes; "personal" (expressive) writing was virtually non-existent in the sample. Applebee examines one additional category, "mechanical writing," which the Britton study did not consider in detail; Applebee describes mechanical writing as any writing activity which did not involve significant composing on the part of the writer—filling in blanks, translating, computing, copying, taking notes, etc. This category, it turns out, was by far the most frequently assigned writing in American class-rooms and actually accounted for 24% of total classroom activity (Applebee, p. 30).

These studies suggest the kind of writing currently assigned by most teachers and written by most students in the junior and senior high school years. Trans-actional (or informational or communicative) writing dominates the curriculum while there is little or no evidence of expressive (or personal) writing. The pat-tern is a disturbing one, for it suggests that across the curriculum, from subject to subject, writing serves a narrow function. In fact, mechanical writing, in which students do not have to originate or develop thought to any significant extent, is the most frequently assigned form of writing. Transactional writing, the only writing of paragraph or more length assigned in most disciplines, com-municates information, but usually to an audience already familiar with that information, who will evaluate or grade the writing—hardly an authentic act of communication. Expressive writing, which serves the thinking process of the writer directly is generally ignored throughout the curriculum. As Richard Bailey concludes: "the emphasis on writing as a tool for inquiry, a stage in the articulation of knowledge, seems so rare in American schools that it plays a negligible role in the educational system, at least at the secondary level" (p. 31).

Visible Language

When we speak we compose. When we write we compose even better—usually—because we can manipulate our compositions on paper, in addition to holding them in our heads. We can re-view them, re-vise them and re-write them because they are now visible and concrete. Consider, for example, the following piece of writing produced by Anne, a sixth-grade girl, who was faced with giving her first formal speech—a two-minute explanation of how to do something. She had a topic, "stenciling," but was not at all sure how to create a "speech" about it. To make Anne's task manageable, her teacher asked her two questions: first, what do you want to say about stenciling? To which she wrote:

> Stenciling speech
> where you can buy supplies
> What stenciling used for
> ~~question?~~
> Orogin of Stenciling
> Dictionary Definition
> show sample
> Make one

Pleased with her list, but wondering what, exactly, to do next, Anne again asked her teacher for more help. The teacher asked a second question: In what order do you want to tell this? In another two minutes the speech was essentially organized and looked like this:

1. Dictionary Definition
2. Orogin of stenciling
3. show sample
4. Make one
   What stenciling used for
5. Where you can buy supplie

The stenciling speech example is meant to make a simple point: by writing out the list "in the first place," the student was able to move to "the second place"—the organization of the speech—and so solve a difficult problem of communication. Writing the words on paper objectified the thought in the world. Peter Elbow reminds us that it helps "to think of writing as input or as movement of information from the world to the writer" (p. 234). The same "movement" even happens when I write out a grocery list—when I write down "eggs" I quickly see that I also need "bacon." And so on.

Consider another example: Doug, a high school senior, needs to write a paper on the topic "Energy Efficient Transportation," but is not sure what to say about it. He has dozens of scattered impressions, but no developed thought, organizational theme, or focus. His teacher suggests a simple mapping exercise to pull his thoughts together and make them visible. This student produced the following conceptual "map":

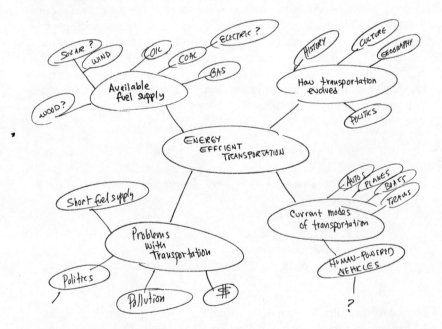

Again, this is not a profound example; it is, however, clear testimony to the power of visible language to suggest, define, organize, and create relationships.

The visual map is really an elaboration of the bacon and eggs principle. In this case, Doug started with a general subject, "Energy Efficient Transportation" and generated as many related subtopics as possible. At some point he can stop and number the clusters according to importance or sequence—or delete irrelevant ones, develop existing ones and add others. For example, one idea, "Alternative Energy" may become the focus for the entire paper. Doug may then decide that "Current Modes of Transport" should introduce his topic while "Evolution of Transportation" is really the subject of another paper. A visual diagram such as this spreads out the options before the writer's eyes and allows him to make carefully reasoned choices about where to go and what to include. While the power of such exploratory writing may seem obvious to many readers, there is little evidence that such writing is valued by, taught, or encouraged by teachers in many school curricula.

A third example of the power of visible language is provided by a philosophy student's journal. Joan, a senior enrolled in her first philosophy course in summer school, was required by her instructor to keep a journal and record her reactions to the class and to new ideas she encountered during this 5-week course. An entry early in her first week of class read like this:

6/10

This philosophy stuff is weird! Hard to conceptualize. You try to explain it to someone and just can't. Like taking 3 pages of the book to decide whether or not a bookcase is there. Someone asked me if you really learn anything from it. I didn't think so but I finally had to say yes. I really never realized how we speak without really knowing (??!) what we are saying. Like I told her, the class is interesting and time goes by fast in it but you have to concentrate and sort of "shift" your mind when you are in class. You have to really think and work hard at keeping everything tied in together—it's like a chain where you have to retain one thing to get the next. I also told her that if you really do think and concentrate you begin to argue with this guy on skepticism, etc. and that's *really* scary—you think at the end of that book will be this little paragraph saying how everything really does exist as we see it and we really do "know" things, they were just kidding!

Here at the beginning of a summer school course (6/10) she is wondering about the nature of her new course of study. "Weird." She encounters Descartes for the first time and openly explores her thoughts on paper, hoping that his ideas are essentially a joke and that Descartes is "just kidding."

Near the end of course, a month later (7/4), after much debate in her journal about her religious beliefs, she writes:

7/4

You know, as the term is coming to a close I am tempted to sit back and think if I really mastered any skills in philosophy. Sometimes when I come up with arguments for something I feel like I am just talking in circles. Or "begging the question" as it's been put. One thing I can say is that Philosophy has made somewhat of a skeptic out of me. We are presented with so many things that we take for granted as being there and being right—we were shown evidence and proofs that may be they really aren't there and aren't true. You know, I still feel like I did the first entry I put in this journal—maybe the last day of class you will say—"I was just kidding about all this stuff—the world really is as you imagine it—there are material things, God does exist with evil, etc." But I realize these arguments are valid and do have their points—they are just points we never considered. I can see I will not take much more for granted anymore—I will try to form an argument in my mind (not brain!).

At this point we see her reflecting on her course of study, on her journal, and on how she has possibly changed. Joan remains a Christian—a belief she has asserted several times in other parts of her journal—but she now also calls herself "somewhat of a skeptic," as she writes about her own changing perceptions. Again, this is informal writing, not meant to be graded—or necessarily ever read by someone else. But the journal writing assignment encourages her to explore and develop her ideas by forcing her still-liquid thought into concrete language.

Joan's final entry, a few days later (7/9) reflects on the value of this expressive assignment:

7/9

Before I hand this in, I have to write a short blurb on what I thought of this journal idea. I have to admit, at first I wasn't too fired up about it—I thought "what am I going to find to write about?" The first few entries were hard to write. But, as time went on I grew to enjoy it more and more. I actually found out some things about myself too. Anyway I did enjoy this and feel I like would be giving up a good friend if I quit writing in it!

The
End
(for now!)

Personal writing, in other words, can help students individualize and expand their learning by encouraging them to force the shadows in their mind—as Vygotsky says—into articulate thought. Art Young, in studying both expressive and poetic writing, argues that such writing not only encourages students to learn about certain subjects and express themselves, but that it gives them the time "to assess values in relation to the material they are studying" (p. 240). Certainly we witness our philosophy student using her journal to mediate between her personal values when she enrolled in class and the somewhat different ones presented by the professor during the course.

Teaching Thinking: Two Solutions

My original premise contends that schools exist to teach people basic literacy skills which, in turn, are prerequisites for people to learn basic thinking skills—which in turn are prerequisites for civilized cultural existence as we know it. If we want schools to do more than teach the "basics" of thinking, if, in addition, we want schools to teach *critical, independent* thinking, then we must question the ill-defined role of writing throughout the curriculum. Brazilian educator Paulo Freire contends that "liberating education" only occurs when people develop their critical reasoning skills, including self-knowledge and self-awareness.

This ability to think critically separates the autonomous, independent people, who are capable of making free choices, from the passive receivers of information. In Freire's terms, liberating education consists of "acts of cognition, not transferrals in information" (1970, p. 67).

While it may be true that schools exist essentially to teach thinking, it is also true that many schools teach conformity and good manners and help justify the reigning political, social, and economic system. As a consequence, liberating education, as Freire describes it, is dangerous insofar as it aims to teach individuals to think autonomously, independently, and critically. Could it be that the lack of expressive writing in the curriculum reflects a lack of interest in critical thought? Or, worse still, are teachers afraid to teach their students to be free?

The Britton research team certainly entertained that possibility: "The small amount of speculative writing certainly suggests that, for whatever reason, curricular aims did not include the fostering of writing that reflects independent thinking; rather, attention was directed towards classificatory writing which reflects information in the form in which both teacher and textbook traditionally present it" (1975, p. 197). And my colleague, Randall Freisinger, gloomily insists that: "Excessive reliance on the transactional function of language may be substantially responsible for our students' inability to think critically and independently . . . Product-oriented, transactional language promotes closure" (*The Language Connection,* p. 9).

But I don't believe that most of my colleagues *want* to promote "closure." I believe they truly want to teach students to be free, autonomous thinkers. They simply do not realize the role writing can play in effecting this. At the same time, however, when I ask teachers from different disciplines to identify the student writing problems which bother them most, a few mention spelling, punctuation, or grammar, while the majority talk about problems related to thinking ability: inability to focus, organize, write a thesis statement, develop a paragraph, use supporting evidence, cite references, etc. When Jack Meiland asked his colleagues the same question he reports similar answers: "The most frequent complaints were that students did not know how to develop their ideas and organize their ideas. They did not know how to formulate their ideas clearly, argue for their ideas, develop replies to possible objections, uncover hidden assumptions, discover the implications and consequences of a position, and so on" (p. 252).

In other words, most teachers recognize that a fundamental writing-thinking connection exists, yet they seldom examine exactly what that connection is, how it works, and how it might inform their pedagogical practice. Meiland, who is aware of that connection, actually created a specific, specialized course in critical thinking, where students were "taught intellectual skills directly and explicitly" (p. 253). He suggests that the best way to teach such skills is to teach "the associated forms of writing. For example, I teach skills of argumentation by teaching students to write argumentative papers" (p. 254).

A more common variation of this "thinking skills course," which will improve writing along the way, is the writing course which means to teach thinking along the way. One such course is offered by Peter Elbow, who teaches his students to freewrite, brainstorm, and keep journals in order to explore and develop their thought through personal, private language (p. 234). A much different approach to accomplish a similar end would be that of Frank D'Angelo, who teaches a highly structured writing course which emphasizes classical imitation. Here students first analyze, then imitate pieces of good writing to emulate "the best features of a writer's style." Such an exercise "mirrors the writer's cognitive processes, leading the student writer to a discovery of new effects" (p. 188). Finally, we might look at the approach advocated by William Coles who argues that writing must be taught as an avenue to power. "To become alive to the implications of language using is not, of course, to become free, but it is to have choices that one cannot have without such an awareness" (p. 23). Coles's approach stresses the value of language-using for writers—enabling them "to run orders through chaos, shape whatever worlds [they] live in, and as a consequence gain the identities [they] have" (p. 23). In other words, writing becomes synonymous with growing—the necessary precondition for autonomy and freedom.

But no matter how successful such skill-specific courses are, I believe the lessons they teach must be reinforced regularly, across the curriculum, in order to have a lasting, purposeful impact. Such courses work best with well-prepared, dedicated, motivated students who are willing to treat seriously what are obviously "practice exercises"—a term used by both Meiland and D'Angelo. Many other students, still groping for a foothold in the academic or social world simply may not be "ready" when such a course comes their way (or is required in their schedule). While good teachers such as Meiland, Elbow, D'Angelo, and Coles can help generate motivation where little existed before, these courses will not reach all students in all curricula.

A second approach, meant to have an impact on *all* students, asks students to learn writing and thinking skills in the context of their own career interests. Richard Ohmann writes: "People have concerns, needs, impulses to celebrate or condemn, to compact with others or to draw battle lines against them, to explain, appeal, exhort, justify, criticize. Such concerns, needs, and impulses are what lead people to write (and to speak), when they are not writing to measure" (1976, p. 153). Students assigned to write "exercise" prose on academic topics to teachers who will "measure" them often do so in prose which Ken Macrorie describes as "Engfish"—the stilted, evasive prose common to school and bureaucratic writing alike. Much poor writing—and poor thinking—according to Macrorie stems from students who "spent too many hours in school mastering English and reading cues from teachers and textbooks that suggested it is the official language of the school. In it the student cannot express truths that count for him" (1976, p. 4). Both Ohmann and Macrorie seek to develop intellectual skills within the context of the individual student's life and work. In other words, if we want writing (and thinking) skills to become useful, powerful tools among our students we must ask them to write (and think) in a context which demands some measure of *personal commitment*—which, in schools, is more likely in their major discipline than in specialized composition classes. Such assignments "nurture the individual voice" (Fader) by asking that voice to engage, through writing, with real, immediate issues.

My colleague, Terry Kent, for example, teaches philosophy and requires his students to explore philosophical issues through expressive writing in their journals—Joan's journal entries (cited earlier) came from Terry's class. Another example of a teacher using writing to promote—rather than test—learning can be found in Helen Isaacson, who teaches folklore at the University of Michigan; she asks her students to generate notes and drafts and speculations about local folklore "to become folklorists, to conduct original research in the field" (p. 246). In other words, *doing* real research, and writing about it, has more meaning to most students than inventing a research project to practice writing research *papers* in English classes. Placing such instruction in a real—rather than imagined—quest for knowledge asks students to both reason and write well—skills they can learn by doing more easily than we can teach by telling.

We know, of course, that the whole school environment influences how students learn to read, write, and think about the world. While individual teachers and particular classes may be the most memorable and visible aspects of education, the more covert structure of the curriculum also "teaches." Schools that offer most of their instruction through large classes, lectures, rote drills, and multiple-choice examinations obviously do little to nurture each student's individual voice. Schools that offer small classes, encourage student discussion, and assign frequent and serious compositions do nurture that voice.

Recently, numerous institutions of higher learning have instituted "comprehensive writing programs" aimed at improving both writing and learning skills *across the curriculum.* At Yale and the University of Michigan, for example, such programs are controlled by boards composed of interdisciplinary faculty concerned with school-wide policies on writing; at Beaver College and Michigan Tech faculty members attend "writing workshops" and learn to assign and evaluate writing more effectively in any academic discipline (*The Forum for Liberal Education*).

Secondary and elementary school programs have also begun more writing across the curriculum programs, influenced nationwide by the work of the National Writing Project and, more locally, by outreach efforts like the University of Michigan's English Composition Board—which, among other activities, distributes *fforum* free to interested teachers.

I mention these programs to emphasize a particular point: While the programs vary widely in size and scope, all assert that writing is a complex intellectual process central to both creative learning and proficient communication. They argue collectively that writing deserves serious reconsideration, increased attention, and ever more thoughtful practice—across the whole school curriculum.

The degree to which the curriculum promotes (demands?) comprehensive language activities on the part of students may be the degree to which it creates a genuinely liberating education. It is apparent to me that we need both pedagogical approaches described here: intensive writing/reasoning courses on the one hand and extensive reasoning/writing activities in all courses on the other. For this to happen consistently, more teachers in all disciplines need to study the several dimensions of language which most actively promote clear writing and critical reasoning. With Lee Odell, I believe teachers might ask questions about their course requirements: Do we ask students to write and talk as much as read and listen? Does each assignment ask students to exercise a particular intellectual skill? (Odell, p. 269). With John Reiff and James Middleton, I hope teachers will view assignments as acts of communication between teachers and students and will question: "To what extent do students fail at writing assignments because we . . . fail to communicate our expectations effectively? Are there criteria we can use both to evaluate our assignments and to revise them for greater effectiveness?" (Reiff and Middleton, p. 263). With Don Murray, I believe that the "need to write in the first place comes from the need to reveal, name, describe, order, and attempt to understand what is deepest and darkest in the human experience" (p. 231): Do our assignments reflect that need? Do they invite such investigation? Do they encourage such expressions? And do our responses to that writing show that we, too, care about the deep and the dark?

When we teachers ask these questions, we will not find quick and dirty formulas or single, simple solutions. Learning to write, like learning to learn, defies prescription. But both writing and learning interlock when teachers ask students to create, contemplate, and act through language as well as drill, copy, and test. As James Moffett puts it: "Instead of using writing to test other subjects, we can elevate it to where it will *teach* other subjects, for in *making sense* the writer is *making knowledge*" (*Coming on Center*, 1981, p. 148). That writing makes sense and knowledge is unquestionable; the real question is, why don't we use it that way?

5.

On Writing and Rhetoric

In this chapter, theorists and teachers tell us that all writing is composed on a particular occasion by an individual or individuals for some audience and purpose. The first five essays trace the origins of this theory of writing to classical rhetoric and relate the legacy of the classical tradition to contemporary conceptions of rhetoric and the teaching of composition. Corbett insists that the fundamentals of the writing situation and process do not change from age to age or culture to culture: Someone writes something to somebody for a purpose. Lauer directs our attention to some of the currents of thought that contributed to the reawakening of interest in rhetorical theory in the United States in the 1960s. Robinson recognizes the influence of scholarship on our thinking about the relationship between thought and language but reminds us that the focus of our teaching has to be on the communicative act. Knoblauch examines the ethical charges that have been leveled at rhetoric and the teaching of rhetoric over the ages and in so doing presents a full and revealing analysis of the relevance, or lack of it, of classical rhetoric for today's classrooms. And Bartholomae describes how teachers can create writing assignments which ask students to draw upon their own cultural and linguistic experiences to develop the discourse and rhetoric of a discipline of their own creation.

The next two essays describe pedagogical practices which ask students to write for specific audiences, purposes, and occasions: Redish advices teachers to ask students to write documents such as those they will compose later on the job; and Shook urges teachers to teach writing by providing students *scenarios* which create situations that require written responses. Morris follows, illustrating how teachers can use students' experience with television to demonstrate that effective speakers and writers adjust their language not only for different audiences, purposes, and occasions but also for the medium in which it will be used.

In the last essay in the collection, Bernhardt reflects upon the common theme that gives it integrity and explores the theme's implications for teachers.

42 My Work in Rhetoric

Edward P. J. Corbett
Department of English, The Ohio State University

I feel like a con man whenever I catch myself talking about "my work in rhetoric." All "my work" is really somebody else's work. I have stolen all of it from wiser heads than mine will ever be. In the argot of the con man, I am a "fence," a purveyor of stolen goods.

What I have appropriated from others is indeed "goods." In fact, it is good goods. This much at least can be said for me: I was shrewd enough to recognize valuable property when I saw it. Others of my contemporaries had gone to the fountainheads before me. Apparently, many of them did not realize the value of what they found there. Even before I had sluiced the streams, I detected the golden grains suspended there in solution.

I came to Aristotle and eventually to Cicero and Quintilian via the eighteenth-century Scottish rhetorician, Hugh Blair. I discovered Hugh Blair, quite by accident, one day in a college library while I was searching for something else. My eye was attracted by a calfskin-covered book on the shelves. It was one of the more than 150 editions of Blair's *Lectures on Rhetoric and Belles Lettres* that were published in England and America after the book was first issued in 1783. I took the book down from the shelf, broke it open, and began reading. An hour later, I left the library, with the book tucked under my arm. Little did I know it then, but that was the beginning of "my work in rhetoric."

I was then in my first teaching job. My graduate work for the M.A. degree had given me a marvelous preparation to teach literature. But in that first job, I was assigned to teach only one literature course (a sophomore survey of English literature) and four sections of freshman composition. In those composition courses, I just thrashed around futilely, because my graduate work had not trained me to be a teacher of writing. My poor students were the victims of my trials and errors. But Hugh Blair's book gave me hope—and something of a method. When I read Blair's book carefully at home, I saw that he was dealing with written discourse, not only the aesthetic kind that I was analyzing with my students in my literature course but also the utilitarian kind that I was struggling with in my composition classes. And I also saw that Blair was operating in a tradition, the tradition of rhetoric, which had its roots in ancient Greece.

I should have known about Aristotle's *Rhetoric*. For my master's degree, I had gone to the University of Chicago, which, under the aegis of Robert M. Hutchins and Mortimer Adler, had become a hotbed of Aristotelianism. Largely because of the influence of Ronald S. Crane, the bible for one of the factions in Chicago's English department was Aristotle's *Poetics*. Hardly any graduate student in the English department there in those years escaped without some exposure to the so-called "Chicago school of criticism." I recall having read Aristotle's *Rhetoric*, but that text did not particularly impress me at the time, maybe because it was overshadowed in that atmosphere by the *Poetics*.

But Blair made me aware that if I wanted some help as a teacher of writing, I had to go back to Aristotle's *Rhetoric* and the dozens of other rhetoric texts that were spawned by that seminal work. Eventually, I got steeped in the rhetorical tradition. Having chosen to do my doctoral dissertation on Blair, I had to spend a couple of years acquainting myself with the history of rhetoric and reading the influential primary texts in rhetoric from the classical, medieval, Renaissance, and eighteenth-century periods.

One of the things that this review of the tradition did for me was make me aware that many of the approaches and techniques that I had used quite instinctively in my composition classes were sound. I also learned, of course, that many of the things I had been doing in my writing classes were idiotic and unproductive. I should have been sued by my students for malpractice.

What Aristotle, Cicero, Quintilian, and dozens of other derivative rhetoricians made me aware of is that there are certain rock-bottom fundamentals about the writing situation and the writing process that do not change from age to age or from culture to culture. Writing was, and still is, a transaction involving a writer, a reader, and a message—someone saying something to somebody else for a purpose. You can't get any more rock-bottom than that.

Rhetoric: The Practical Art

Rhetoric gave a "local habitation and a name" to many of the strategies that I had deliberately or instinctively used myself when I was trying to communicate with others through either the spoken or the written medium. It was reassuring to learn that there was, after all, a method to my muddlings. And if there was a method, there had to be an art that codified all the means to an end. Rhetoric was that art. Aristotle classified rhetoric as one of the practical arts, an art of "doing," a behavior, a skill. The ancients maintained that we acquired a skill by some combination of *ars* (a set of precepts), *imitatio* (observation of the practice of others), and *exercitatio* (repeated practice of the skill). That triad sets up the whole rationale of the pedagogy of composition. If one studies the history of the teaching of writing in the schools or contemplates just the various philosophies of composition that prevail in the schools today, one sees that the various approaches to the teaching of writing are shaped by the particular element in that triad which receives the greatest emphasis.

Because the principles of classical rhetoric were so elementary and universal, I found that they were readily adaptable to the modern classroom. In fact, much of what is touted in modern writing texts as being "new" often turns out to be something old in a new guise with a new name. Some teachers claim that the system of classical rhetoric is too limited for the modern classroom because it deals primarily, if not exclusively, with persuasive discourse. One response to that charge is that all discourse is, in some ultimate sense, persuasive; even if our objective is to inform or enlighten or entertain our readers, we ultimately have to win acceptance of our presentation from our readers. If there is a persuasive thrust in all discourse, classical rhetoric is still the best system of persuasive strategies. It touches all the bases: the three kinds of appeal—logical, emotional, and ethical; the two basic strands of logical appeal—the deductive (the enthymeme) and the inductive (the example); the three kinds of persuasive discourse—the judicial (arguing about things that have already occurred), the deliberative (arguing about things that will or should take place), the ceremonial (arguing about things that are occurring in the present).

Another answer to the charge that classical rhetoric is too limited to be of use in the modern classroom is that even though classical rhetoric was concerned mainly with persuasive discourse, many of the strategies laid out by the classical rhetoricians are applicable also to expository, descriptive, and narrative discourses. Much of the heuristic system (especially the topics), much of the doctrine about the effective arrangement of the parts of a discourse, almost all of the immensely rich collection of instructions about style and rhythm and figures of speech are just as applicable to the expository, descriptive, and narrative modes of discourse as to the persuasive mode.

It should be interesting for readers of this collection of essays to discover just how much other systems of rhetoric and composition represent variations, extensions, refinements, or modifications of the classical system. I can promise quite confidently that readers will not find much that is wholly new in these other systems. The classical rhetoricians did not say it all once and for all, but what they said they said very well.

43 Metatheories of Rhetoric: Past Pipers

Janice Lauer
Department of English, Purdue University

In 1964, when Dudley Bailey published his essay, "A Plea for a Modern Set of Topoi," (Bailey, 1964) he cried to a discipline of English that had little interest in composition research and theory. Only a small minority of English scholars had begun to investigate the tacit assumptions underlying composition pedagogy and to develop alternative theories. But now, only two decades later, the situation has radically changed. Books and journals abound with theoretical and empirical research on composition; new graduate programs in rhetorical theory emerge each year. This richness of rhetoric within the province of English is nothing short of remarkable. But it may puzzle those who have recently entered the profession or who have suddenly become aware of this phenomenon. They may wonder how such interest awakened or why composition studies have taken the direction they have.

I have often asked myself these questions as I have looked back to the period in the sixties when I became interested in composition problems and discovered others so inclined. What drew us to research which was then so professionally unrewarded? The answer to that question is interwoven with the circuitous history of rhetoric itself and with the development of the discipline of English, a story already well-chronicled. (Kitzhaber, 1953 and 1963; Applebee, 1974) This essay will not duplicate that history but will identify some major influences that I will label "metatheoretical" because they pointed out, directly or indirectly, what an adequate rhetorical or composition theory ought to include, ought to explain. These metatheories acted as pathfinders, as pipers whose voices drew composition theory down certain paths.

Although some of the earliest voices we heard came from different fields, a number of them merged to propose a conception of composition broader than that of writing as the creation of a well-wrought urn. Wayne Booth called for his now-well-known rhetorical stance, a balance among the available arguments about a subject, the voice of the writer, and the interests and peculiarities of the audience. (Booth, 1963) Such a conception was revolutionary in those days when textbooks rarely treated any aspect of situational context. Another spokesman for a broad conception of rhetoric was Kenneth Burke who en-visioned a universe of language as symbolic action in which rhetoric functioned as an art of identification, "rooted in an essential function of language itself . . . the use of language as a symbolic means of inducing cooperation in beings that by nature respond to symbols." (Burke, 1969, p. 43) Burke deemed rhetoric essential for social cohesion, a broader and nobler view than the prevalent ones that considered rhetoric was verbal embroidery or as masked deception.

This was more extensive conception of rhetoric was bolstered indirectly by the work of Kenneth Pike who argued that language could only be adequately understood in relation to a unified theory of the structure of human behavior. (Pike, 1967) His idea of interlocking hierarchies influenced the development of tagmemic rhetoric which argued that intelligent syntactic or rhetorical choices could only be made in relation to larger contexts such as whole discourse, im-mediate rhetorical situation, and cultural contexts. (Young, Becker, and Pike, 1970) During this period, Charles Morris's semiotics influenced the develop-ment of another theory of discourse by James Kinneavy (Morris, 1946; Kin-neavy, 1971), a theory that extended composition beyond a preoccupation with exposition to other forms of writing. Moffett and Britton also developed new classifications of discourse (Moffett, 1968; Britton, 1975) with similarities that Kinneavy has identified. (Kinneavy, 1980) These reclassifications of discourse, stemming from semiotics, Piagetian psychology, or inductive research, not only challenged the reigning emphasis on expository writing, asserting the importance of expressive, persuasive, and literary discourse, but they also argued against the pervasive confusion of aims and modes represented in the quartet—descrip-tion, narration, exposition, and argumentation.

In harmony with these voices describing a broader province for rhetoric and composition, a number of scholars spoke of new epistemological ends. Booth advised a restoration of respect for probability, a *sine qua non* for meaningful writing in which good reasons support probable judgments. He explained that our modern culture's excessive reverence for facts and its relegation of every-thing else to mere opinion had created a climate inimical to teaching writing. (Booth, 1974) A more radical treatment of probability was being developed at this time by Michael Polanyi who challenged the bastion of certainty itself, the sciences. Polanyi rejected the objectivist ideal of knowledge that insisted on complete exactitude, objectivity, and explicitness, advocating instead a passion-ate active commitment that involved risk and required choices, that led to judg-ments informed by grounds less compelling, judgments arrived at cooperatively by the enquirer and his accredited audience. (Polyani, 1962) Sam Watson would later characterize Polanyi's work as inherently rhetorical. (Watson, 1981) During this same period, scholars like Scott, McKeon, and Perelman began to describe rhetoric as epistemic, arguing that the act of acquiring knowledge was a rhetorical process of intersubjective choice-making and symbol-using. (Scott, 1967; McKeon, 1971; Perelman and Olbrechts-Tyteca, 1969) These voices blended to draw composition theorists toward the view of writing as essentially an investigative process, a tool for human inquiry, rather than as merely an act of reporting, of providing supportive facts for preconceived judgments. This conception also turned attention to the need for arts of inquiry, for accounts of how good writers discover, support, and communicate probable judgments and new understandings (Emig, 1971).

This view of writing as a way of learning and discovery was supported by an emerging interest in invention. Harrington reminded the profession that rhetoric had always lost life and respect to the degree that invention had not had a significant and meaningful role. (Harrington, 1962) Bailey urged the development of new sets of topoi. Studies of creativity and problem solving stimulated interest in the genesis of creativity, in the processes of discovery, and especially in the role of heuristics as aids to effective inquiry. Torrence and Guilford studied the abilities operative in learning and creating. Wallas, Newell, Simon, and Shaw examined the stages and processes of inquiry and problem solving. (Lauer, 1967 and 1970) Lonergan analyzed the movement toward insight, speaking of its genesis as the "known unknown." (Lonergan, 1957) Parnes and Gordon experimented with methods of enhancing creativity. (Parnes, 1967; Gordon, 1961) These studies contributed to the development of new exploratory models for writers and eventually to revised notions about the genesis of composing as well as about pedagogies for teaching the composing process. More specifically influential on new theories of invention were Pike's tagmemic model and Burke's pentad which composition theorists and textbook writers adapted to create new sets of topoi. These new exploratory guides as well as the entire emphasis upon invention that began in the sixties developed, therefore, in large measure in response to a variety of multidisciplinary voices that not only called for a reinstatement of invention but also investigated the nature of inquiry, offering a basis for new sets of topoi.

Another path opened in the sixties led to a view of writing as a collaborative activity. Philosophers advocated that rhetoric be viewed as a situation of risk in which both writer and reader change, rather than as a one-way exercise of control or manipulation of a reader. (Natanson and Johnstone, 1965) Kenneth Burke saw the goal of rhetoric as a consubstantiality and identification achieved through a dialectical process of naming. (Burke, 1969 and 1962) Polanyi insisted on the importance of the community in the tacit component of inquiry and its necessity for original advances in knowledge. (Polanyi, 1958) Carl Rogers posited threat reduction as a basis for successful communication. (Rogers, 1961) All of these interactive views of rhetoric began to assail the prevailing conception of writing as the creation of a product whose inherent meaning was unaffected by readers. Although deconstructionists would later refine this view, composition theorists had already begun to work in the sixties with a collaborative conception of writing.

A final influence I want to mention here was the work of scholars like Walter Ong whose studies of literacy exercised a more subtle influence on the development of composition theory and pedagogy. (Ong, 1967, 1968, 1971) Those who listened to him began to realize that any adequate theory must reckon with such complex cultural influences as changing technologies, shifting conceptions of education, and primary and secondary orality.

Composition research that began in the sixties, therefore, harkened to a variety of voices that suggested new ways of viewing writing theory and pedagogy. These pipers led to a reconception of the province of composition as more extensive than exposition or persuasion, as more meaningful and complex than isolated treatments of words, sentences, and paragraphs. They stimulated a view of writing as a process of inquiry, as a way of learning, capable of being facilitated by arts of invention. They opened up a perspective of writing as an interactive search for meaning rather than as the delivery of preconceived judgments, as the conquest of an audience, or as the creation of a well-wrought urn. They fostered the development of the inventional arts of beginning and exploring. And finally they prompted the investigation of multiple influences on the development and enhancement of literacy. Some of these paths brought theorists to forks in the road from which they took new directions; but many paths still offer important avenues for investigation. What remains characteristic of composition theory and pedagogy is its continued openness to multidisciplinary studies as a source of leads in its investigation of the complex human activity of writing.

44 A Rhetorical Conception of Writing

Jay L. Robinson
Department of English, The University of Michigan

Thought and language are so closely interrelated that many theorists have considered language as nothing other and no less than the external realization of thought. Although some forms of social discourse—greetings, cocktail party chit chat—have been seen as more closely analogous to the gesture systems of birds and non-human mammals than to processes of human conceptualization, our more serious uses of language are taken to reflect the ways our minds organize the world into conceptual categories and the ways we fuse our perceptions, thoughts and feelings into assertions about ourselves and our world.

Traditional grammar, and the schoolroom tradition based on it, assumed almost an identity between thought and language. Goold Brown, an influential grammarian of the 19th century and a New England Quaker schoolmaster, defined language this way: " . . . language is an attribute of reason, and differs essentially not only from all brute voices, but even from all the chattering, jabbering, and babbling of our own species, in which there is not an intelligible meaning, with division of thought, and distinction of words."

When Goold Brown and other traditional grammarians speak of language in this way, they have in mind writing, not speech: speech, except in its carefully planned uses for argumentation and oratory, is too ephemeral to be taken seriously—too like, in its everyday uses, chattering, jabbering, babbling. Modern theorists are less quick to dismiss speech, or to see it as something utterly different from writing; and they are more cautious in asserting an identity between thought and language—certainly between language and reason. Yet modern theorists still see closer relations between thinking and writing than between thinking and speaking. Lev Vygotsky, the Russian cognitive psychologist, views writing as the expression of what he calls "inner speech": a language-like and language-derived system of generalized concepts and relationships that permits a human being to make expressible sense of his world. Writing, for Vygotsky, is the act of making inner speech intelligible and communicable to others by converting it from private to public forms.

Two differing pedagogies have emerged in response to traditional and more modern conceptions of the relation between thinking and writing. Traditionalists customarily focus their attention on the written language students have produced, or on the linguistic forms they want students to produce. They mark errors in student papers and have students correct them; they use a variety of linguistic drills (sentence combining, for example) to encourage fluency, accuracy, and maturity of expression; the more tradition-bound of them even teach grammar, or those portions of grammar that treat "division of thought"—subjects, predicates, and sentence types—and "distinction of words"—parts of speech. The assumption motivating such work, though not always recognized, is that careful, conscious attention to expression of thought will lead inevitably to clearer thinking: to sharpen language is to sharpen thought.

An alternative and to some extent more modern pedagogy focuses on the processes of thinking themselves, and is founded on the assumption that students will write more effectively as they can be helped to think more clearly. Teachers who make this assumption emphasize pre-writing activities, things done before a student puts pen to paper. These activities include reading or viewing and class or small-group discussion of stimulating materials; study of logical strategies and fallacies; freewriting, brainstorming, and other stimuli to invention; exercises in perceptual acuity. Inventionists would agree with this assertion: to sharpen thought is to sharpen language.

There is yet a third general approach to the teaching of composition now attracting more followers—an approach that might be termed "rhetorical." As the name suggests, this pedagogy has ties with a rich tradition which originated in classical Greece and held currency in the West until the 19th century. But the new approach has been much influenced by current findings in psychology, in linguistics and sociolinguistics, and in philosophy.

The rhetorical approach acknowledges that a relationship exists between thought and language, thinking and writing, but focuses on neither. Instead, its center of concern is the communicative act itself. Its intent is to identify the participants in the act and the factors that influence it, then to explain the relation of these participants and factors as they give shape to a final written product. Teachers who employ this approach assume that students have language, that they can think, and that they can use language to express their thoughts if they can be helped to see clearly their purpose in writing, their stance or relation to the topic they are addressing, the special demands imposed by the medium they are using, and the particular needs of their audience. The argument for a rhetorical approach might be put in this oversimplified way:

Students use language in purposeful ways every day of their lives to make meaning of their world, to communicate and cooperate with others: They are familiar, in other words, with the rhetorical demands of everyday life. A canny teacher can make use of what students already know about their language and its uses. But writing, and the uses of writing for academic or professional purposes, imposes new demands that differ from those of everyday interaction through language. Written texts have their own conventions of organization and style; a writer stands in a more removed relation to his topic than does a speaker; the writer's audience must be imagined and its needs projected (nobody questions or talks back to a writer). New rhetoricians claim that students will write better as they come to understand the nature of the communicative acts they engage in; that students will write better if they are given purposeful tasks and real audiences to write to.

Let me close with two contentious contentions, and then a qualification (a familiar rhetorical strategy for an academic). Contention one: Most of us who teach composition have failed to acknowledge that writing is an exceedingly complex act; our failure to recognize its complexity has hampered our efforts to help students. Contention two: We have not often questioned the validity of our methods for teaching composition by measuring them against a set of coherent and self-consistent assumptions about what the act of writing is and how the ability to perform that act develops. The qualification is this: There is no single, universally accepted theory that explains the act of writing nor is there such a theory that explains how the ability to write develops. As a result, our methods must be eclectic, and one test of their validity must be whether or not they work. But our methods must not be ungrounded: they must be tested against the best statements we can make about what writing is and how it is learned.

Because what we know about the act of writing is as limited as what we know of its acquisition, we might do well as teachers to follow the rhetoricians—at least for the time being—as we wait for surer knowledge about the relations of language and thought. Most uses of language are transactive; that much we do know. And assignments that require students to say something to somebody for some purpose in some one or another form are likely to engage their thinking and to show them that language is as variable as the human contexts in which it is used. That lesson can be conveyed in any classroom; and it is likely to be an enduring one.

45 Rhetoric and the Teaching of Writing

C. H. Knoblauch
Department of English, SUNY, Albany

In Plato's *Gorgias* Socrates takes the rhetorician sternly to task for having mastered, not a true art like medicine or politics, which is grounded in learning and moral commitment, but a mere "knack," like food preparation or personal adornment, where flattering appearances are valued over substance (465A). The rhetorician, he claims, deals only with strategies of persuasion, and with the prescribed formulas of suasory discourse, regardless of the content of a given argument or the justification for seeking to persuade in the first place. Neither learning nor moral commitment is essential to the rhetor as such, but only a technical virtuosity in composing. Potentially, then, the rhetorician is little better than a charlatan, seeming, for example, more knowledgeable about medicine than the doctor merely by sounding more convincing. For the orator, Socrates asserts, "there is no need to know the truth of the actual matters, but one merely needs to have discovered some device of persuasion which will make one appear to those who do not know to know better than those who know" (459C).

For centuries rhetoricians have struggled to defend themselves from Plato's attacks by arguing, with Aristotle, that an orator must also be a philosopher, literally a lover of wisdom, and by insisting, with Quintilian, that the good orator must first be a good person who joins learning with ethical awareness in the service of responsible conduct. But always these defenses have had about them the odor of rationalized self-interest—like the NRA's insistence that guns don't kill people ("only people kill people"). It isn't rhetoric that deceives, but only the evil orator. . . . Maybe so, but still, we think, an instrument that begs so conspicuously to be abused is hardly well defended on the basis of its ostensible moral neutrality. Plato's arguments do not disappear so easily: indeed, they have proven resilient for more than 2000 years. In my opinion, they are unanswerable as long as we are willing to accept their basis, Plato's assumptions about the nature of rhetoric: that it defines nothing more than a set of optional communicative vehicles for ideas that are somehow preconceived; that it offers a collection of empty forms available to good and evil alike for conveying truths—or errors or falsehoods—to a variety of audiences on a variety of (ceremonial) occasions.

Herein lies a problem for contemporary writing teachers. It seems to me that we often do accept Plato's views about the difference between knowledge and articulation, intellectual "content" and verbal "form." And having granted his assumptions, we are vulnerable to his charges. When we speak these days of "the rhetorical approach" to teaching writing, we typically mean a concern for modes and forms of discourse: description, narration, exposition; five-paragraph themes, "comparison/contrast essays," topic-sentence paragraphs; plain versus elevated, or correct versus incorrect, style. A so-called "rhetoric" textbook talks about these forms, labelling and taxonomizing them as though they really existed out there in Plato's Ideal Space, as though writers selected them in advance from some inventory that the rhetorician is responsible for stocking. A "rhetoric reader" offers presumably typical samples of these modes and forms, though with a revealing cautionary note that—awkwardly—the models seldom demonstrate a single option but instead merge several in peculiar hybrids. Teachers who use "the rhetorical approach" tend to believe, whether they say it out loud or not, that what students write matters less than how they write it, that learning to manipulate public and professional formulas (the term paper, the business letter) is more important than thinking well in language or discovering personal stances and values, that technical decorum is the focus of a writing course, not the intellectual and moral growth of writers. In "the rhetorical approach" writing tends to be conventionalized and ceremonial, like the famous abortion essay, where the pros and cons have been rehearsed until the subject is now conveniently moribund so that the advantages of comparing-and-contrast-ing can shine forth without the troubling interference of a live, recalcitrant human issue.

As long as we writing teachers accept Plato's divorce of knowledge from articulation, or teach as though we accepted it, I say Plato was right to call us an unscrupulous lot, engaged in low, dishonest business. How can we at once concede his premises and escape his conclusions? Teaching by "the rhetorical approach" we often demonstrate to our more sophisticated students the trivial, ritualistic nature of classroom writing. We watch them, bored but tolerant, suppressing their intelligence in order to jump through our hoops. Fortunately, that intelligence enables them to survive us and learn to value their writing—as soon as they find readers who also value it. At the same time, though, we also offer weaker minds an art of dissembling, the knack of saying nothing or of recapitulating a party line in polite, decorous prose. The moral lesson for these students is that playing the game and withholding commitment will take you far. Strategic timidity can be worth at least B—. Finally, in the worst cases, usually involving unpracticed writers, we retard the capacity to write while simultaneously extinguishing the desire to try. That is, we make writing superficially difficult by asking students to do it *this* way instead of that while also making it irrelevant through our insistence on following the rules first and saying something meaningful only afterwards (if at all). To the extent that we can all recollect these cases, Plato was surely right: our preoccupation with formal propriety can do as much harm as good, and we might be well advised to find a more respectable line of work. Better, perhaps, to do away with writing courses and emphasize composing in the disciplines, where at least it might go on in the context of directed intellectual dialogue and in the interest of new learning. One can find some motivation in history writing or psychology writing, but what is the earthly good of comparison/contrast writing?

Having said all this, however, I am no less enthusiastic about the importance of rhetoric and the value of teaching writing, even in writing courses. What sustains me is not some ingenious answer to Plato's objections (I can't think of any), but rather my unwillingness to accept his assumptions about rhetoric, especially his sense of its restricted role in learning and communicating. Let me offer some alternative assumptions, closer to a modern philosophic temper. As I see it, rhetoric is not brought optionally to the service of some subject, medicine, or law, or history, as an all-purpose, hand-me-down system of forms for anyone's content. Rather, any subject is the very thing it is by virtue of the peculiar cast of its rhetoric: hence, we may speak of the rhetoric of law or the rhetoric of history, meaning those particular language-acts which define a discipline by representing an epistemological as well as methodological context for its practitioners. Apart from discourse, there is no "history"; and apart from rhetoric there is no historical discourse. If we view rhetoric as an art, a practice, a way of doing something, it is the process of using language to organize our experience and communicate it to others. If we view it as a science, in the classical sense, a field of study, its concern is with the multiple ways in which language makes experience intelligible and communicable. As a science, I would locate it in semiotics, the study of how any sign or sign-system organizes experience. And I would locate within rhetoric the study of speech (oral discourse), "composition" (in the sense of written discourse), and poetics, the study of discourses claiming distinctive cultural value. From this vantagepoint, rhetoric is clearly not an "approach" to teaching writing at all: it is, instead, a context for that teaching, a set of attitudes, assumptions, and concepts which together make the teaching of writing a coherent activity. "Techniques" for composition instruction may differ from those useful in teaching oral argument, but a "rhetorical approach" cannot be distinguished from some presumed alternative: rhetoric is generic; composition is specific.

The definitions I have offered evidently alter the classical view of rhetoric. In particular, they acknowledge a much closer connection between knowing and articulating. We use discourse to organize experience—and "ordered experience" is another name for knowledge. Acts of language have heuristic value, as numerous contemporary linguists and composition theorists have argued. Discourse *makes* knowledge, rather than merely dressing it up for public display. The process of making connections which lies at the heart of learning lies also at the heart of composing, so that verbal composition is a mode of learning, a manifestation of the process of discovering coherence. Discourse also communicates, to be sure, but communicating is neither more nor less important than learning: indeed, the two motives interanimate, to use I. A. Richards's term. In writing we learn about things through the effort to make communicative sense out of them; and we communicate by making the track of our learning visible and in some way meaningful to readers. The harder we work to learn, the richer our communication; the harder we work to communicate, the richer our learning. Given this modern view, Plato's belief that knowledge somehow exists independently of articulation, and the subsequent differentiation of learning from the forms of discourse, is erroneous and unproductive. The process of writing makes form: we do not start from a perception of some formal absolute, filling in a structural shell as we would pour the ingredients of a pie into its prefabricated crust. The mental effort to make assertions and to connect them as a coherent pattern over time causes form to emerge gradually, unpredictably, contingently, the ultimate achievement of an effort to make meaning in a temporally linear medium. The modern rhetorician's concern, and it should be the writing teacher's concern as well, is not to taxonomize formulas for discourse, but to study and to nurture the capacities by which we make coherence out of the chaos of experience, a coherence which verbal action distinctively enables us to shape.

I would point out in passing that these views are not original to the twentieth century. The revolution in rhetorical theory that they represent has been in progress for some 350 years, since Descartes and Locke challenged the ancient supposition that language was merely the dress of thought. Writing teachers can profit from studying the history of rhetoric in order to discover a more reliable and productive underpinning for their instruction than that offered by Plato and the classical, formalist tradition. But a more important point for now is that, if Plato's theory of discourse is limited, then contemporary teaching based on it is similarly limited. At the same time, since we are slowly elaborating a richer theory, we need not accept ancient assumptions, nor need we suffer the abuse that Socrates directed at Gorgias. Consider an alternative frame of reference for the writing class. I would say that a teacher who accepts the context of modern rhetoric first of all values writers over writing, the unending search for new meaning over the artifacts that are its residue. Texts are not monoliths, incapable of change or growth, but only moments in a lifelong learning experience, a succession of inherently unstable coherences, freely altered and abandoned with the evolution of insight. The teacher is less concerned, then, with formal or technical evaluation, as though The Text were primary, than with the quality of a writer's understanding, his or her developing capacity to make statements that matter. The point of writing is to learn by taking imaginative risks; it is to make, test, and reformulate coherences, not to master rubrics for the ceremonial display of trivial thinking. The teacher-reader's role in nurturing writers is to convert their premature conclusions about their experience into new problems for solution through facilitative responses aimed at stimulating more writing, not labelling errors or insisting on the reader's personal notion of an Ideal Text. The writer strives repeatedly to create order from chaos; the reader monitors the striving through dialogue about the meaningfulness of the (always) emerging discourse. Learning and communicating go on in the context of shared intellectual inquiry, just as they go on in the world we are supposed to be preparing our students to inhabit as thoughtful and responsible human beings.

Can there be a more profoundly ethical activity than the striving to make new meaning through discourse? The matured ability to order experience enables moral choice and responsible action, so that our teaching of writing, which aims at this matured ordering capacity, is intimately connected to the growth of ethical awareness. To view writing as thinking and not just an exercise in formal display is to refute Plato's argument about the superficiality, the ethical indifference of rhetoric. It also sensitizes us to our preeminent obligation of making students accountable for what they think and say. There is no true literacy, I suggest, apart from judgment and moral commitment: and the only way to encourage that literacy is to take students' meanings seriously. The writing class is well suited to engaged intellectual inquiry because it need not follow the teacher-based agenda of a "content" course given to introducing a particular subject in a predetermined way. We can allow students to examine their experience, their values and commitments, through reading and writing in directions they find personally significant. The consequence need not be diffuseness or relaxation of academic rigor; on the contrary, it should be an intensified awareness, a deeper penetration of issues arising from the freedom to dwell at length on substantial human questions and to experiment with stances toward them in the presence of a discerning reader. This seems to me our strongest argument for the role of a writing course in the liberal arts curriculum. Importantly, it is an argument based on our recognition that rhetoric is not a "knack" as Plato thought but a fundamental manifesting of the capability for symbolic action that defines our humanity.

46 Writing Assignments: Where Writing Begins

David Bartholomae
Department of English, University of Pittsburgh

To begin to write is to "know" what at the outset cannot be known except by inventing it, exactly, intentionally, autodidactically. (Edward Said, *Beginnings*)

I want to use this occasion* to work on the paradox at the center of this passage from *Beginnings:* to begin to write is to "know" what cannot be known. It has become commonplace for English teachers to talk of writing as a "mode of learning," or of writing as "discovery." And it has become common to represent the writer's struggle as a struggle for realization: "How can I know what I mean until I see what I've said?" This representation of writing is conventionally in service of a pedagogy whose primary aim is to enable students to work *out* something that is inside them: insight, vision, ideas, connections, wisdom.

If, however, we take knowledge to be something that is outside the writer, something inscribed in a discourse—the commonplaces, the texts, the gestures and jargon, the interpretive schemes—of a group from which the writer is excluded, then the paradox must be read differently. To discover or to learn, the student must, by writing, become like us—English teachers, adults, intellectuals, academics. He must become someone he is not. He must know what we know, talk like we talk; he must locate himself convincingly in a language that is not his own. He must invent the university when he sits down to write.

This is what I take Burke to be talking about when he talks about persuasion as "identification":

> The individual person, striving to form himself in accordance with the communicative norms that match the cooperative ways of his society, is then, concerned with the rhetoric of identification. To act upon himself persuasively, he must variously resort to images and ideas that are formative. Education ("indoctrination") exerts such pressure upon him from without; he completes the process from within. (1969, p. 39)

The struggle of the student writer is not the struggle to bring out that which is within; it is the struggle to carry out those ritual activities that grant one entrance into a closed society. Or, as Foucault would have it, "The discourse of struggle does not oppose what is unconscious, it opposes what is secret."

Teachers as priests of mystery, teaching as indoctrination, writing as identification—these are not popular definitions. They do, however, provide a way of talking about the business of assigning writing to students. For me it is a necessary way of talking. Let me work this out by telling some stories.

When I was first a Director of Composition, and before I was tenured (this is to add spice to the story), at about the tenth week of classes, a bunch of students came into my office to register a complaint about one of their teachers, a senior colleague of mine, a full professor and a distinguished scholar. It seemed that he had assigned one paper in the first week of the term but hadn't assigned

*This paper was presented as the keynote address at the Delaware Valley Writing Council Conference, March 1982.

any writing since. His students, rather, had been listening to lectures on the paragraph and the sentence, on style and organization, and they had, as well, been given the task of copying out longhand essays by Lamb, Macaulay, Ruskin and Carlyle. The students were wondering how in the world he was ever going to grade them, since he seemed to be collecting such unusual artifacts to judge.

I mustered up my courage and went to visit this professor, told him of the complaints, and mentioned as gently as I could that the rest of us were assigning one—and in some cases two—papers a week. Here is his response: "I assigned a paper early in the term and they wrote miserably. If I assign more writing, they'll only make more mistakes." When I asked whether this meant, then, that the best writing course is the one in which students never wrote, where potential never had to be compromised by execution, he said, "No. When they are ready to write, I'll set them to writing again."

Let me call this the Big Bang theory of writing instruction. Students are given instruction in writing as a subject—sometimes through lectures, sometimes through textbooks, sometimes through classroom analyses of prose models—and then, when they are ready, they write. The assignment, then, serves as a test. It is the students' opportunity to show that they have mastered the subject. There are Little Bang versions of this available everywhere: in most textbooks, for example, where writing is broken up into sub-skills—description, narration, exposition, argumentation.

Now if writing is conceived of as *technique*—as a means for communicating what is known and not as a way of knowing itself—and if the techniques being taught are simple enough—the 5 sentence paragraph, ABAB comparisons—then it is not unreasonable to suppose that students can pass the weekly test. If, however, the students are also to learn to write like Lamb or Macaulay, to represent themselves within those peculiar gestures and patterns—and I am not willing to quickly condemn the copying out of essays in that course—then that copying will have to be accompanied by assigned writing of quite another kind. The ability to write like Macaulay, in other words, will not come in a big bang. The indoctrination will have to be "completed," in Burke's terms, by acts of writing that complete the shaping of a writer. "If he does not somehow *act* to tell himself (as his own audience) what the various brands of rhetoricians have told him, his persuasion is not complete." (1969, p. 39)

Perhaps this leads to our first principle of assignment making. If assignments invite students to enter into a discourse which is not their own, and if their representations will only approximate that discourse (if they don't come in a big bang), then assignments must lead students through successive approximations. The movement through successive approximations is a cycle of expectation and disappointment. There is no clear-cut developmental sequence here; students do not move easily from one level of mastery to the next. This is what it means to be going after secrets. As Kermode says,

> Hot for secrets, our only conversation may be with guardians who know less and see less than we can; and our sole hope and pleasure is in the perception of a momentary radiance, before the door of disappointment is finally shut on us. (1979, p. 145)

Here is my second story. A teacher at a school I recently visited gave what I thought was a wonderful assignment—and she gave it knowing that her students, at least most of them, would have to write their papers over again, perhaps several times, since in many ways it was an impossible assignment. She asked students to read through the journals they had been keeping over the semester and to write about what they had learned about themselves from *reading* the journal. What I admired in this assignment, and what makes it such a difficult assignment, is that students were asked to write about what they had learned by reading the journal and not what they learned by writing in the journal. This is a nice stroke, since it defines the journal as a text and not an experience, and it defines the person writing as a composite of several people and not as a moment of feeling or thought. The assignment defines the student as, simultaneously, a textual presence—the "I" in a passage dated September 3rd and the "I" in a passage dated October 5th—and as an interpreter of texts, someone who defines patterns and imposes order, form, on previous acts of ordering. Who is to say quickly what *that* person might learn? The subject of this assignment, then, is language and language using. Students are not invited to believe that a subject can be something else—experience, truth, data—something that exists outside language, something language can record. This is often the trap of journal writing; students are led to believe that the journal is a true record of true feelings— a rare occasion for self-expression. As Bruner says (and I've taken this passage from a fine article by Ken Dowst describing the kind of composition course that depends most heavily on carefully crafted and carefully conceived assignments):

> A student does not respond to a world that exists for direct touching. Nor is he locked in a prison of subjectivity. Rather, he *represents* the world to himself and acts in behalf of or in reaction to his representations. . . . A change in one's conception of the world involves not simply a change in what one encounters but also in how one translates it. (Dowst, 1980, p. 68)

A change in one's conception of the world by means of a change in how one translates it—perhaps here we have the beginnings of a second principle for assignment-making. We shouldn't provide a subject only; we should provide the occasion for translation. To put it more simply, the journal assignment undercuts students' impulses to write about journal writing without writing about the writing in the journal. It allows them to translate (or to "read") those moments of "feeling" as moments of artifice or representation, as evidence of the roles defined as a writer shaped experience, history, the "stuff" of his or her life.

My next story comes again from my own school. A group of us were asked to put together an experimental course, not just a reading course or a writing course, but a course to, as we later said, introduce students to the language and methods of university study. We decided that this should be a course in which students didn't learn a subject—something already prepared by one of the traditional academic disciplines—but it should be a course in which students invented a subject by inventing a discipline, one with its own specialized vocabulary and its own peculiar interpretive schemes.

Now this course would need a nominal subject—a subject that would provide the occasion for a discourse. And the subject we chose was "Growth and Change in Adolescence." It seemed to provide, in Freire's terms, a "generative" theme, one that students could write on with care and energy. The first assignment, then, had to be an impossible one. Students could write about adolescence, but not as we would write about it. They would use the language, and the commonplaces, immediately available to them, but these would not be the language or commonplaces of a small, professional, closed, interpretive community. The sequence of assignments would have them writing about the same subject over and over again, with each act of writing complicating and qualifying the previous act of writing, each paper drawing on the language developed by the group. The papers were regularly duplicated and used as the basis of class discussion. The instructors would outline, highlight and push on class discussion; they would not provide theories or terms of their own. The last assignment in the course, then, would be a record of this new discipline—the study of the process of change in adolescence developed by the group.

The assignments went something like this. There was a group of assignments that asked students to develop a theory on the basis of their own experience.

- Think of a time in the last 2 or 3 years when something significant happened to you, something that caused you to change or to change your mind. Then do what you can to help the rest of us understand the process of change.
- Think of another time. . . . What now can you say to help us understand the process of change?
- Think of a time when, by all popular expectation, you went through an experience that should have caused you to change, but it didn't. What now . . .?
- Think of a time when you decided to make a change in yourself. What happened? What now . . . ?

Students began to develop a process of interpretation, one that dealt more with the dynamics of change (family, school, friends, enemies, goals, self-images) than with the mechanism of change. And they developed a shared set of terms: the Jones dilemma (competition with an older, successful brother); the Smith syndrome (anger directed at a parent who had left home); the Kowalski problem (wanting to be good but wanting, as well, to be cool).

These papers served as the basis for a longer paper, one we called, "A Section of Your Autobiography," dealing with the sorts of changes the students went through in the last three years. We took the class's autobiographies to central printing, had them bound, and sold them back to the class as a text. They became, then, "case studies." And we led students through a series of papers that asked them to read the autobiographies, locate patterns of themes and experiences, invent names for those patterns and develop theories to account for them.

The final set of assignments directed the students to rework those papers in the context of three standard, academic accounts of adolescence—one by a psychologist, one by a sociologist, and one by an anthropologist.

This became an enormously popular and successful course. In fact, when my college began its own version of "writing across the curriculum," it was offered as a model for courses in departments other than the English department. One psychologist was quite interested until he realized, as he said,

> You know, the problem is, that at the end of the course they're likely to get it
> all wrong. After all—what about Piaget and Erikson. They're not going to get
> that stuff on their own.

Of course not, that's the point. They can only approximate the conventional
methods of academic psychologists, only pretend to be psychologists or sociologists or anthropologists, and they will not *get* the canonical interpretations
preserved by the disciplines. But they will learn something about what it means
to study a subject, to carry out a project. And they will begin to learn what a
subject is—how it is constituted, how it is defended, how it finds its examples
and champions, how it changes and preserves itself. There is, then, a way of
studying psychology by learning to report on textbook accounts or classroom
lectures on the works of psychologists. But there is also a way of learning psychology by learning to write and, thereby, learning to compose the world *as* a
psychologist. In his four years of college education, a student gets plenty of the
former but precious little of the latter. He writes many reports but carries out
few projects. And this leads me to my next principle of assignment making.
Individual assignments should be part of a larger, group project. I'll have more to
say in defense of this.

My last story comes from Tolstoy; although to be honest, it came to me
from Ann Berthoff and is available in her wise and eloquent book, *The Making
of Meaning* (1981, pp. 61-94; pp. 140-147). Tolstoy set out to teach the children of his newly emancipated serfs to read and write. He began, he said, by
asking his students to write about what seemed easiest—the most simple and
general subject.

> In the first class we tried compositions on given themes. The first themes that
> must have naturally occurred to us were descriptions of simple objects, such
> as grain, the house, the wood, and so forth; but, to our great surprise, these
> demands on our students almost made them weep, and, in spite of the aid
> afforded them by the teacher, who divided the description of its growth, its
> change into bread, its use, they emphatically refused to write upon such
> themes, or, if they did write, they made the most incomprehensible and
> senseless mistakes in orthography, in the language and in the meaning.

Now Tolstoy was not a Big Banger. He tried again; in fact, he tried, as he says,
different assignments. "I gave them, according to their inclinations, exact,
artistic, touching, funny, epic themes—and nothing worked."

By chance, however, he hit upon a method (and "method" is his term) that
did. He happened one day to be reading proverbs ("a favorite occupation") and
carried the book with him to school. "Well," he said to his students, "write
something on a proverb." The best students pricked up their ears. "What do you
mean by on a proverb? What is it. Tell us!" the questions ran. Tolstoy goes on:

> I happened to open to the proverb: "He feeds with the spoon, and pricks the
> eye with the handle." "Now imagine," I said, "that a peasant has taken a
> beggar to his house, and then begins to rebuke him for the good he has done

him, and you will get that 'He feeds with the spoon, and pricks the eye with the handle.' "

"But how are you going to write it up?" said Fedka and all the rest who had pricked up their ears. They retreated, having convinced themselves that this matter was above their strength, and betook themselves to the work which they had begun. "Write it yourself," one of them said to me. Everyone was busy with his work; I took a pen and inkstand, and began to write. "Well," said I, "who will write it best? I am with you."

Tolstoy began to write the story to accompany the proverb and wrote a page. He says, and you'll now begin to see the point this story, the story of this assignment, makes for Tolstoy:

> Every unbiased man, who has artistic sense and feels with the people, will, upon reading the first page, written by me, and the following pages of the story, written by the pupils themselves, separate this page from the rest as he will take a fly out of the milk: it is so false, so artificial and written in such bad language. I must remark that in the original form it was even more monstrous, since much has been corrected, thanks to the indications of the pupils.

The sight of the teacher writing caused a flurry in the classroom. One student said, "Write, write or I'll give it to you!" Others crowded around his chair and read over his shoulder. The commotion was such that Tolstoy stopped and read his first page to them. They did not like it. Nobody praised it. In defense of himself, Tolstoy began to explain the "plan" of what was to follow. They butted in, "No, no, that won't do," he made corrections, and they began helping him out. All, Tolstoy says,

> were exceedingly interested. It was evidently new and absorbing to be in on the process of creation, to take part in it. Their judgments were all, for the most part, of the same kind, and they were just, both as to the structure of the story and to the details and characterizations of the persons. Nearly all of them took part in the composition: . . .

Two, however, stayed on and worked late into the night, annoyed when Tolstoy wanted a break. One of those who remained asked, "Are we going to print it?" When Tolstoy said yes, he replied, "Then we shall have to print it: Work by Mákarov, Morózov, and Tolstoy."

There are many ways of reading this story. It could be said that Tolstoy was lucky enough to find the right assignment: a theme on a proverb. It's as though you could go to the exercise exchange and find the assignment whose subject is just right for your students—sports for the athletes, drugs for the heads, movies for the rest, proverbs for the children of Russian peasants. I don't choose to read the story this way. While I believe it is important for teachers to consider carefully the subjects they present to students, and while I believe students write best about subjects that interest them—subjects they believe in, subjects they know something about, subjects they believe there is reason to write about and for which they can imagine an occasion for writing (witness Booth's story about his frustrated graduate student in "The Rhetorical Stance")—the very notion of motive is misunderstood if a motive is taken to reside in a subject. The question, rather, is one of how students can be taught to imagine a subject as a subject, not as a thing they like or don't like, but as a discourse, as a set of conventional, available utterances within which they can locate utterances of their own. The question is not one of which subject will work, but of how students can learn to work on a subject and of why such work is worth the effort.

Tolstoy's students didn't leap to the proverb assignment; they told *him* to write the theme, convinced the subject was "beyond their strength," and went back to their own work. Their first question, you remember, to Tolstoy's assignment, "write something on a proverb," was, "What do you mean '*on* a proverb'? What is it? Tell us?" Tolstoy read them a proverb, but they never started writing until he answered the *first* question and showed them what it meant to write *on* a proverb. He did this by writing with them, by showing them not a subject, but the subject as a potential discourse, a story about a beggar and a peasant who abuses him while offering charity. It was at that point that the students had a subject, and the subject was not the story and not the proverb, but the act of amplification. A subject is not a thing but an action—thinking, describing, analyzing, elaborating, naming. All subjects, and this is what I take to be the burden of the post-structuralists, are as Richards says, "characteristic uses of language." Tolstoy, then, gave his students not just a language but a discourse, a conventional procedure for elaborating a subject.

How else might we read the story of Tolstoy and the proverb? It could be read as support of the notion that teachers should write papers along with their students. I'm not very keen on this, either as a reading or a practice. Writing teachers should be writers, this I believe deeply. But they should be too busy with their own projects, and with the exacting task of writing assignments and writing to students about their writing, to have time for weekly papers in concert with a class. Besides, the presence of Tolstoy writing in the classroom had only shock value. The students became writers only when they participated in his writing. They began to learn when they began assisting him in a project he had begun, and a project can be begun by the text of a well-crafted and self-conscious assignment, one that presents not just a subject but a way of imagining a subject *as* a subject, a discourse one can enter, and not as a thing that carries with it experiences or ideas that can be communicated.

One could read the story as evidence that students should begin with narrative, with storytelling, since this draws upon patterns of organization closest to the pattern of experience. I don't believe that this is a true statement about narrative, and the evidence Tolstoy provides shows the children choosing detail and projecting narrative as an interpretation of a concept (another interpretation) coded in the proverb.

Tolstoy does argue, however, for a form of "natural" expression that is only impeded or thwarted by education. Here is his interpretation of the event:

> It is impossible and absurd to teach and educate a child, for the simple reason that the child stands nearer than I do, than any grown man does, to that ideal of harmony, truth, beauty, and goodness, to which I, in my pride, wish to raise him. The consciousness of this ideal is more powerful in him than in me. All he needs of one is the material [and we have to wonder what "material" means in this sentence], in order to develop harmoniously. The

moment I gave him full liberty and stopped teaching him, he wrote a poetical production, the like of which cannot be found in Russian literature. Therefore, it is my conviction that we cannot teach children in general, and peasant children in particular, to write and compose. All that we can do is to teach them how to go about writing.

We cannot teach children to compose; all we can do is to teach them how to go about writing. This is another paradox, and I'd like to try to make sense out of it.

Now in working on the Tolstoy Paradox, I do not choose to read these passages as celebrations of natural innocence, where a good assignment replaces "teacher-sponsored writing" with "student-sponsored" writing, freeing a student from the fetters of an oppressive culture.

Tolstoy's own accounts of his "method" show him getting in his students' way more than his narrative would lead one to believe. The prime consideration, he says, in designing a sequence of "themes" should not be length or content but "the working out of the matter." And this, the working out of the matter, was the occasion for teaching.

At first I chose from the ideas and images that presented themselves to them such as I considered best, and retained them, and pointed out the place, and consulted with what had already been written, keeping them from repetitions, and myself wrote, leaving to them only the clothing of the images and ideas in words; then I allowed them to make their own choice, and later to consult that which had been written down, until, at last, . . . they took the whole matter into their own hands. (Tolstoy, 1967, p. 224)

When Tolstoy talks about choosing, selecting, preserving and remembering, he is not talking about "natural" acts but a system that is imposed. He, and the text he has in mind, *allow* for certain choices. The procedure must be learned.

Derrida has taught us that the Rousseauesque notions of a "natural" language are all symptoms of a longing for a perfect relation between the word and the thing it is meant to signify for a language that gives us direct access to the truth, without the mediation of the stuff and baggage of a culture, for a form of understanding that represents data raw and not cooked, for a mode of composition in which thinking and writing do not interfere with each other. What comes before speech, he argues, is writing, that conventional system, discourse, that inscribes us as we inscribe it. There is, then, no natural or pure language because the language we use always precedes us, belongs to others, and it, and not the writer, determines what is written. The writer does not write but is rather, written, composed by systems he did not invent and he cannot escape. Our language is derived, "stolen," never original. The celebration of innocence, Derrida argues, is not a denial of teaching but a denial of writing.

But Tolstoy, in his rejection of education, does not reject writing, even though he feels the burden of the role of the teacher. In fact, in a telling passage, he says that after the episode with the proverb he felt not just joy, but dread—

Dread, because this art made new demands, a whole new world of desires, which stood in no relation to the surroundings of these pupils, as I thought first.

This is the Tolstoy that gives his student "material." All they need of me, he says, is material—not pencils and paper, not subjects, but the material (as in fabric) that is woven with the habits, discriminations, preconceptions—the "stuff" of his material, that is, textual, culture. It is exclusive. It privileges some statements at the expense of others. It is driven by a law of exclusion—this then fits, that, "the world of his pupils," does not. At one point, one child in a "fatigued, calmly serious and habitual" voice comments on his text. Tolstoy says, "The chief quality of any art, the feeling of limit, was developed in him to an extraordinary degree. He writhed at the suggestion of any superfluous feature, made by some one of the boys."

Let me put my cards on the table, and explain why I want to read Tolstoy this way. I think a good assignment teaches by interfering. It interferes with a student and his writing.

Tolstoy's "method"—the method that does not teach composing but how to go about writing—could be seen to be in service of what we now comfortably call the "Process" approach to composition instruction. If the act of composing is beyond a teacher's art, if it is a natural or mysterious facility, then a teacher can at least attend to the behavior of composing—to the business of prewriting, revising and editing. This is how I take the pedagogies of the "new rhetoric." The tagmemics, the pentads, the class-room heuristics—all these are devices that precede writing. They are not part of a project. The nine-fold grid may give a new perspective on, say, a tree (and the metaphor of vision is telling) but it does not give a language. What happens to the student when he begins to write, when he locates himself in a discourse, is that he is caught up in all those available phrases about nature, and ecology and the pastoral world that turn his "vision" into an occasion for cliché.

Don't get me wrong. Writing is a behavior and a good set of assignments teaches a student to understand this—to experiment with varieties of planning activities, to take time with his writing, to (often for the first time) revise by re-working and not just re-copying a text, and to edit, to make corrections. I'll confess, however, that I think most of the attention to pre-writing is a waste of time, unless pre-writing is, in fact, the first act of writing—in Tolstoy's terms—the first "working out of the matter." Most pre-writing activities, however, treat "ideas" as though they existed independently of language, of the sentences that enact them. And, in my experience, students treat these exercises the way they used to treat outlining; they either do them after they have written the paper, or they do them and then go about writing the paper the same damn way they have always written—starting at the top, working to the bottom and then handing it in for a grade.

Let me go back to Ann Berthoff. Here is what she says about Tolstoy and his teaching:

Nothing is needed more urgently in the current reassessment of what we think we have been doing in teaching composition than a critical inquiry into this concept of the simultaneity of thinking and writing, of the role of consciousness in composing. Tolstoy's description here is a useful point of departure for that inquiry because it reminds us that composing is both creative and critical and that it is an act of mind; it doesn't just happen; it is conscious. (1981, p. 89)

This consciousness is critical consciousness, not consciousness as it is represented by classroom heuristics. It is rooted in an act of reading. She says, elsewhere in her book, that "writing can't teach writing unless it is understood as a nonlinear, dialectical process in which the writer continually circles back, reviewing and re-writing: certainly the way to learn to do that is to practice *doing* just that." (1981, p. 3). The key words here are "reviewing" and "dialectical," and they are difficult words to understand. Let me try to put them into the context of assignment making.

I'm concerned now with that version of "thinking" which is textual, not mental, since it involves reading and interpretation ("reviewing") and a use of language in service of dialectic. Here's an assignment: It was given to me by a teacher at a school I visited as a consultant.

Pick a poem that you like. Discuss why you like it by analyzing its features rather than defending your response. Think before you write so that you produce a coherent and well-organized essay.

This is the sort of assignment that most likely will prove the law of reciprocity—what you ask for is what you'll get. It's poorly written and demonstrates, more than anything else, a teacher's boredom and inattention, and it would be the exceptional student who would make anything of it other than the occasion for poor writing and inattention. There is no indication of how or why the fact that one likes a poem is dependent on an "analysis of its features." Nor is there any clue as to what it means to "discuss" while at the same time not "defending a response." The final sentence, "Think before you write so that you produce a coherent and well-organized essay," is not-quite-so-polite way of saying, "Please do a decent job of this" and it finesses the whole question of how "thinking before writing" (making an outline? getting one's thoughts together?) leads to a "coherent, well-organized essay." There is, however, a rhetoric at work here—the rhetoric of the controlling idea in service of what seems to be an act of new criticism—but the demonstration that Tolstoy provided, the way he assisted students in a project he had begun—and it was *his* project, belonging to his culture—this assistance is missing. The word "analyze," for instance, exists as an invocation, a magic word calling up powers to possess the student. It does not belong to the vocabulary shared between teachers and students; it does not, in fact, belong to the vocabulary shared between teachers in different academic departments. It presumes to tell students to do what they cannot know how to do—and that is to carry out an act of analysis as it is represented by the conventions of the discourse of a certain form of literary criticism.

Our assignments are often studded with such words—think, analyze, define, describe, argue. These words, however, are located in a very specialized dis-course. Analysis, for example, is a very different activity—its textual forms, that is, vary greatly—in an English course, a history course, a sociology course or a chemistry course. When we use such words, we are asking students to invent our disciplines, to take on the burden of the mindset of our peculiar pocket of the academic community. This is not a bad thing to do, even though it is cause for dread as well as joy. It is why, for me, a good set of assignments leads a class to invent a discipline, a set of specialized terms (a jargon) and a subject with its own privileged materials and interpretative scheme.

Because writing—or writing that is not report or debate—is the invention of such a project, writing is also, as we are fond of saying, a mode of learning, where learning is a matter of learning to use the specialized vocabulary and interpretative schemes of the various disciplines. To learn sociology—and to learn it as an activity, as something other than a set of names and canonical interpre-tations—is to learn to write like a sociologist, for better or for worse. Students cannot do this, however, without assistance, since the conventions that govern a rhetoric do not "naturally" belong to the mind, the heart, reason, or the soul. Reason, in fact, is not an operative term if one begins with a conception of rhetoric. It is a metaphor, a way of authorizing one discourse over another, but it is not a descriptive term.

Here is a sequence of assignments that offers more by way of assistance in the "working out of the matter." It comes from a source in 19th century fiction.

Bleak House

I. In order to prepare a paper on the narrative in *Bleak House,* I'd like you to do the following:
   1. Locate two passages that, as you read them, best characterize the voice and perspective of Esther Summerson as she tells the story. Write them out.
   2. Locate two passages that, as you read them, best characterize the voice and perspective of the other, the unnamed narrator. Write them out. Working primarily from one passage for each narrator, write a paper that compares the way they see the world of *Bleak House* and the way they tell a story. Be sure to look at sentences as well as sentiments; that is, pay attention to language each uses to locate a perspective and a world.

   Then, when you've done this, go on to speculate about how the pres-ence of two narrators controls your reading of the story.

II. I'd like you to look, now, at the first and last chapters. Who gets the first word and who gets the last word and the difference it makes. What differ-ence does it make, that is, to you and your attempt to make sense out of the novel?

III. Here is a passage from an essay by J. Hillis Miller. In it, he offers one ac-count for the effect on a reader of the presence of the two narrators. I'd like you to write a paper that talks about the way his reading is differ-ent from yours, and about what difference the difference makes to you.

Be sure, again, to talk about sentences as well as sentiments. What, for example, does Miller notice that you didn't? And what did you notice that he leaves out? What special terms does he use that you don't. What difference do they make?

IV. On the basis of these 3 papers, write an essay to help us better understand narrative technique in *Bleak House*. Don't feel you have to settle the question once and for all. Remember, that is, that the rest of us are working on this problem too, and that we're looking for your help. We're not beginners and we have a lot invested in our own projects.

Often any such assistance is at odds with the peculiar rhetoric of the composition class, with its obsessive concern for the thesis, the controlling idea. When, for example, we ask students to write about texts, the tyranny of the thesis often invalidates the very act of analysis we hope to invoke. Hence, in assignment after assignment, we find students asked to reduce a novel, a poem or their own experience into a single sentence, and then to use the act of writing in order to defend or "support" that single sentence. Writing is used to close a subject down rather than to open it up, to put an end to discourse rather than to open up a project. This, I think, is the rhetoric that is "natural" to our students. If English teachers can have any effect on students' writing, it should be to counter this tendency. To interfere with it.

The term "interference" comes to me from Kenneth Burke, whose writing I admire for the way it enacts a constant dissatisfaction with the thesis. Burke's rhetoric is in service of a form of knowledge that is not equated with certainty. His sense of a dialectical use of language is a use of language that allows the writer not only to translate "reality"—the subject that is only a *thing* to be written about—but also to transcend the conventional and often oppressive gestures built into the history of our language, to transcend, then, the inevitable reduction caused by writing. Burke says

> We would only say that, over and above all, there is implicit in language itself the act of persuasion [that domination or closing down of a subject] ; and implicit in the perpetuating of persuasion, there is the need for interference. For persuasion that succeeds, dies.

Burke, then, brings me to my last principle of assignment making. A good set of assignments assists students toward a subject by interfering with their immediate procedures for dominating a subject by reducing it to a closed set. Edward Said, whose words stood at the beginning of this essay, said that writing requires the writer to maintain an "obligation" to "practical reality" and a "sympathetic imagination" in equally strong parts. By obligation, he means

> the precision with which the concrete circumstances of any undertaking oblige the mind to take them into account—the obligation not just passively to continue, but the obligation to begin by learning, first, that there is no schematic method that makes all things simple, then second, whatever with reference to one's circumstances is necessary in order to begin, given one's field of study.

And by "sympathetic imagination," he means

> that to begin to write is to "know" what at the outset cannot be known except by inventing it, exactly, intentionally, autodidactically. (1978, p. 349)

I have been offering a defense of a sequence of related and redundant assignments, assignments that define both a project and a way of working on a project, assignments that are designed to enact for students that there is no schematic method to make all things simple. And I have been arguing that an intellectual project requires indoctrination, assistance, interference and trust.

Let me conclude with a passage from the poet, William Stafford.

> A writer is not so much someone who has something to say as he is someone who has found a process that will bring about new things he would not have thought of if he had not started to say them. That is, he does not draw upon a reservoir; instead he engages in an activity that brings to him a whole succession of unforeseen stories, poems, essays, plays, laws, philosophies, religions, or—but wait!
>
> Back in school, from the first when I began to try to write things, I felt this richness. One thing would lead to another; the world would give and give. Now, after twenty years or so of trying, I live by that certain richness, an idea hard to pin, difficult to say, and perhaps offensive to some.

A sequence of assignments is repetitive. It asks students to write, again, about something they wrote about before. But such a project allows for richness; it allows for the imagination that one thing can lead to another, that the world can give and give. This is an idea hard to pin, difficult to say, and, perhaps, offensive to some.

Our students have come to us, however, to learn. It is not enough to say to them that knowledge is whatever comes to mind. If we have them write one week on Democracy, and the next on Pollution and the week later on My Most Memorable Character, that is what we are saying to them. Tell me what comes to mind. The writing that I value, that demands something of me as a reader, that turns back on whatever comes quickly to mind, requires repeated and on-going effort. Students need to work at finding something to say. They have to spend time with a subject. That, to me, is what it means to be a writer at a university.

47   Preparing Students to Write on the Job

Janice C. Redish
Document Design Center, American Institutes for Research, Washington, DC

Students as Future Employees

Think of the work and living situations in which the students you are now teaching will find themselves five or ten years from now. Both as consumers (for example, as renters, home owners, or bank customers) and as employees, they will have to deal with written documents almost every day. As readers of these documents, they may fuss and fume at the inaccessibility of the information, the gobbledygook in the sentences, or the unattractive design of these documents—just as you and I do now. But how will they do when *they* are asked to *write* these documents—memos for their bosses, reports to clients, or notices for the public?

Perhaps if we spend more time teaching students how to write the types of documents that they will be asked to write on the job, we will someday see more clearly-written and well-organized public documents. I am not belittling the importance of teaching literary criticism or creative writing. I am arguing in favor of *also* giving a critical place in the secondary school and college curriculum to expository writing of the kind one finds in offices, social service agencies, school administrations—in almost any field you can imagine your students entering.

It isn't fair to our students to assume that they will get good job-related writing skills later on. By the time they get to an advanced college or postgraduate level, most students think that they have learned how to write. A few students, notably engineering majors, take specially designed technical writing courses, but most students are never trained to write for the different rhetorical situations they will face on the job.

Inaccurate Perceptions of Writing on the Job

In working with hundreds of professionals in more than 20 government agencies during the past three years, my colleagues and I have found that many of our clients had been unprepared for the role that expository writing would play in their lives. I think that, like our clients, students misunderstand the need for writing skills:

1. Students don't realize how much time they will spend writing on the job. They see themselves in the future as lawyers or nurses or research associates or social service workers, not as writers. Yet, in any of these occupations, our students are going to spend a good part of each day putting words on paper. And as they climb career ladders into administration or management, the time they spend writing is likely to increase, not decrease.

2. Students don't realize the variety of writing that most people do on the job. Asked to name the type of writing a college professor does, most students would reply "research articles for journals." But a typical college professor also writes memos to colleagues, secretaries, and administrators; committee reports; proposals for funding; reviews of other people's work; reference letters for students; letters to prospective students; etc. Just think of *all* the writing you do for your job in the course of a week or month and the variety of audiences and purposes you must attend to. Do your students realize how many tasks a typical teacher has to handle?

3. Students don't realize how much review and revision goes into writing on the job. We seldom ask students to complete more than one draft; but, in work settings, most writing (particularly of junior staff) is reviewed before it goes out to the client or the public. Often the writer must negotiate with several reviewers to reach consensus on the wording of a letter, memo, or report.

Having students do collaborative writing and setting up review procedures
that require revision would better prepare students for on-the-job writing.
4. Students think that good writers can just plunge in and write. They don't
   realize that expert writers often spend *more* time *planning* than writing.

Planning Is One Key to Successful On-the-Job Writing

With our professional clients we stress the importance of the planning stage in
any writing task. By asking our clients to articulate plans for the written product,
we help them to become more aware of what they are already doing as well as to
think about what should be done. When clients first begin to use our multi-
step process model, they often complain that they don't have the time to devote
to planning. The five planning questions we pose, however, only take a lot of
time to answer when writers are learning how to use the model. Over time, the
planning process becomes semiautomatic and can be accomplished very quickly.
   To help writers plan, we pose these five questions:

1. What is the *scope* of the document? Writers must understand the question to
   be addressed or the message to be presented. If you have ever turned back a
   paper with the comment, "You didn't understand the assignment," you know
   that students sometimes do not clarify the scope of the writing task before
   they begin.
2. Who are the *audiences* for the document? Most writing in offices or agencies
   has multiple audiences. Some are inside the agency (reviewers or supervisors);
   others are outside (the client or the public). It is our experience that writers
   in bureaucratic organizations are highly attuned to the wishes of their internal
   audiences, but they are often isolated from their external audiences. Similarly,
   students write to impress their teachers; they seldom have to deal with
   realistic external audiences. If they were given assignments that had both
   internal audiences (the teachers) and external audiences (roles played by
   peers or people outside of school who react to the writing), they might become more sensitive to multiple audiences.
3. What is the *purpose* of the writing? In the world of work, each piece of writing has at least one purpose, perhaps several. A memo may need a different
   organization and tone if the writer's goal is to persuade someone to act than
   if that goal is to set forth alternative actions in a neutral fashion, or if it is to
   preserve a record of a meeting for the files. Unless writers can articulate what
   they are trying to achieve, they may make inappropriate choices of language
   or organization and then wonder why the writing didn't succeed.

To be successful communicators, writers have to understand the audiences and
purposes of the document, and also have to tell the readers what the document
is, whom it is for, and why the readers should deal with it. One of the major
causes of obscurity in business and government writing is that writers never
address readers and do not provide any context-setting statements to tell the
readers what the document is about.

4. What is the *readers' task*? In order to make a document useful to the audience, writers must consider how readers will use the document. Many business and government documents are used primarily for reference, but students who are used to writing narratives often continue to use the storytelling approach even when they are writing in work settings. Reference documents require explicit titles, informative tables of contents, headings that pose or answer questions, and a design that allows easy access to different sections of the document. To be prepared to be on-the-job writers, students should have broader experiences than only writing essays that are read like stories.

5. What *constraints* will limit what writers can do? Learning how to balance research time and writing time, how to meet deadlines, and how to keep to page limitations are important skills for students who would be successful employees. Writers who articulate their constraints at the beginning of a writing task can develop plans for handling the constraints rather than allowing the constraints to interfere with final production.

Writing down the answers to the five questions about scope, audience, purpose, readers' task, and constraints at the beginning of a writing assignment makes students think about the *process* of writing. To show students how planning can affect writing, we can present assignments in which students have to prepare the same content material for different purposes and different audiences and discuss the differences in organization, tone, and choice of language called for by different plans. These different assignments would help to prepare better writers who might someday produce business and government writing that is a pleasure to read.

48 A Case for Cases

Ronald Shook
Department of English, University of Idaho

It is unfortunate that our new-found awareness of writing as process hasn't yet extended to a parallel awareness that any act of communication is a response to a situation—a situation which may, in fact, have other possible responses. For example, faced with a large and angry man who wants to rearrange my face, I might fight, run, or talk him out of it. It is this principle—language use as a response to a situation—which should govern our lives as teachers of writing. A failure to recognize and use this principle as we teach writing has a number of unfortunate consequences: First, it forces us to unusual lengths to provide methods of invention and audience analysis for our students; second, it leads to a tendency to speak of *An Essay or A Theme,* as if they were artifacts unearthed by a team of archeologists, and to giving writing assignments which are themselves artifacts (*A Narration, A Cause and Effect Essay*); third, it gives much of our writing a sterile, cut-off-from-it-all feeling.

Consider a typical writing assignment from a typical rhetoric:

Think of a place that is important to you and describe it to a friend who
might be interested.

The steps the students go through before they can even begin to communicate
about this topic are tortuous. First, the students must find a subject to write
about. This is *invention* in the current sense of the word, often involving complicated heuristics and discovery procedures—freewriting, brainstorming, conceptual
blockbusting, or whatever. Second, once students have discovered what they are
to write about, students must marshal arguments, data, facts, suppositions, lies,
generalities, and specifics, all to develop an idea which has, as often as not, been
made up out of whole cloth—invented. Third, the poor students must visualize,
make up, create, imagine an audience for this information. Finally, students are
ready to begin communicating. When students have completed this long process,
they are graded on (1) how well the invention went, (2) how real the details
were, (3) how well developed the structure was, (4) how well the sentences
flowed, (5) how well the words were spelled, and (6) how neat the punctuation
was, as if these six processes existed discretely, like motes of dust in a sunbeam.

On the other hand, consider how we normally communicate in writing. It
usually is a two-step process. First, a situation arises which needs a written reply
to resolve it: The bank sends us a note telling us we're overdrawn; our kid's
teacher wants to test her for a speech impediment we know she doesn't have;
a pastoral scene sets words dancing in our minds; a group of us decide to declare
our independence from Great Britain. Second, we create texts *which will answer
the demands of the situations.* An over-simplification, of course, but organizing
communication in terms of situation and response will help us to understand it,
and perhaps indicate where we have gone wrong in the assignments we create
for students.

Consider the elements of the situation as I have described it above. First,
there is no need for elaborate heuristics and discovery mechanisms in order to
uncover a subject; the subject, indeed the substance of the communication, is
inherent in the situation. Writers don't have to figure out what to write about or
even what to say; most of the time that's already apparent: They tell the bank,
"I am not overdrawn"; they tell the teacher, "My child speaks very well."
Second, because the audience is part of the situation, it does not need to be
created or defined but addressed. With subject matter, content, and audience
inherent in the situation, writers need only turn their minds to the meat of the
problem: Finding and arranging arguments. Success in such a situation is determined by how the bank or teacher (or King George III) reacts—how well the
writer has accomplished the rhetorical purpose generated by the situation.

One way out of the dilemma caused by disembodied assignments is to make
them real. Ideally, teachers would put students in situations in which their success at writing is measured by success or failure in important tasks: Staving off
financial ruin, keeping out of jail, getting or keeping a job, fomenting an
insurrection. However, since these are not practical classroom activities, the
second best approach is to use *cases* as the basis for assignments.

A *case* is a scenario which creates a situation requiring writing as a response to that situation. The situation is typically as real as possible, with sometimes several pages of supporting information. In it the audience, the problem, the data, are all carefully laid out as they would be if the students were actually involved. The students study the material, and then produce the document called for by the events outlined in the case. The students' grade on the assignment is based on the effectiveness of the response to it. That is, the controlling question in grading is, "How well have the students met the rhetorical demands of the situation?" Since purpose, subject matter, and audience are inherent in the assignment, the discussion in class becomes not how to invent an audience, but how to address the one that is there; not what to say but how to say what is there to be said. The discussion also centers around what information is crucial, what can be summarized, and what can be left out—around strategies of presentation rather than modes of discourse. In other words, writers can quit spending time on material unique to composition classes and can get to the heart of composition— arranging information in the best possible order for a particular purpose as they would in a normal, real world, rhetorical situation.

A natural consequence of a case approach is that assignments can neither be casually created nor casually given to a class. Since a case may have fifteen pages of supporting data and comprehensive directions for responding, some time must be spent on presenting the assignment to the class. The students must receive the information in enough time to assimilate and understand it—to become familiar with the situation and the problem. After students have a good grasp of the case, they need to walk through it with the teacher, making sure that they understand the sorts of things that need to be said and possible approaches to saying them. It is not at all unusual for consideration of a case, its background, and approaches to it, to take two or three class periods. Making up such assignments can be difficult; however there are texts (more and more of them now) available on the market that present cases ranging from two to seventeen pages long.

Teachers who have used the approach like cases because they make heuristic and discovery procedures part of the writing process, not an antecedent to it. For basic writing classes it is especially helpful because it eliminates the "finding a subject, audience, and purpose," trap that often simply stops writers cold. Students, on the other hand, appreciate a case approach because they can see sense in it. A well-constructed case has a probability to it; it reflects a situation in which students could well find themselves. Students also like it because cases are "easy to get into," which I interpret as meaning that students would rather spend time working with the message to be delivered than wrestling a blank sheet of paper two falls out of three.

49 The Language Environment of Student Writers

Barbra S. Morris
English Composition Board, The University of Michigan

Since April of 1978 faculty of the English Composition Board (ECB) have been reading essays written by undergraduates as they enter the University of Michigan for the first time. During the past four years we have evaluated approximately 20,000 samples of students' writing; we have, over time, come to recognize certain styles of writing that many of these entering college students have in common.

One style of writing, readers say, creates a "strobe light effect"; an essay contains a sufficient number of ideas but the ideas are not in an order that allows a reader to follow the writer's line of thought easily nor are the ideas connected by transitions. Because ideas are not differentiated from each other in importance nor linked well to one another, they read more like rapid-fire individual observations than thoughts that have been integrated into a unified theme governed by a consistent point-of-view. Readers refer to this style of presentation in expository writing as "chaotic" writing.[1]

One example is the following paragraph taken from an essay written by an entering freshman on the subject of smoking (the seriousness of the problem was to be discussed and possible solutions suggested). The writer concludes with the following four sentences (reproduced as they appeared, though I have numbered each sentence for discussion):

> [1] More propaganda about stopping or baning cigarettes should be used. [2] If the younger generation was more aware of the potency of cigarettes, there would be a large decrease in the percentag of smokers. [3] Cigarette smoking is an unimagenative way to combat anxiety or nervousness. [4] Once one makes a decision to stop smoking, don't procrastinate, the delayance will only prolong the way back to achieving a healthy mind and sound body.

Here, sentences 1 and 2 combined together make a single argument: increasing the number of advertisements and testimonials about the harmful effects of cigarettes will persuade many young people to break their smoking habit. Then, however, the writer introduces a new idea, one that does not follow from the previous argument; no connection between the increased use of propaganda to prevent smoking and finding imaginative alternatives to smoking is established. Moreover, no connection between anxiety or nervousness and individuals' smoking habits is made. Finally, the writer concludes the essay by putting together two different types of sentences which have contrasting tones and intentions: first, a warning to stop smoking and, secondly, a speculation about the harmful effects of delaying to do so.

Despite the problems of coherence in this paragraph, the writer demonstrates an awareness of several sentence structures and different sorts of rhetorical strategies. When these sentences are read together, however, the reader experiences jarring shifts in content and emphasis. Taken together, the sentences lack the collective, coherent power of a sustained argument; considered individually, they are understandable. Where have our students learned this chaotic style of communication? Why does disconnected discourse *sound* all right to them?

One of the answers offered to these questions about students' difficulties with written composition originates from a recognition of the differences between informal conversation and formal academic writing. Those who argue for this explanation of the problem hold that inexperienced writers lack substitutions for inflections of voice and other signals speakers use to communicate meanings face-to-face; writing is extremely difficult because, they claim, the act of writing is different from the act of speaking. Novice writers have not yet learned the appropriate, and very different, vocabulary of cues experienced writers use to signal transitions between ideas, or to indicate the degree of emphasis being placed upon an idea. It is true, of course, that parallels between informal speech and formal academic writing are so few that making a transfer from speech to writing required in school is exceptionally difficult. Nevertheless, I no longer believe that by itself the difficulty of transferring the spoken word to the page accounts for many patterns of writing ECB readers find; I believe that chaotic writing, for instance, is a particular style of communication which students have learned from the language environment most teachers of writing would rather forget while they are in the classroom: television.

We must keep in mind that the language environment of our students has changed during the past several decades. In 1980 the *New York Times* calculated that "by the time the typical American schoolchild graduates from high school he or she will have spent 11,000 hours in school and 15,000 in front of the television tube. Another way of saying this is that American students confront two 'curriculums'—two sets of ideas and impressions that are, in some fundamental ways, diametrically opposed."[2]

Researchers tell us as well that sustained, well-developed conversations occur less frequently in homes now because families spend so much of their time watching television. It can be argued, then, that television now provides a predominant and much-reinforced source of language learning for many in our society; the experience of watching and *listening to* television is certainly far different from that of engaging in sustained conversations (or reading or even spending time thinking one's own thoughts). In addition, since we cannot respond to individuals shown on television as we do to those with whom we talk, we do not listen to oral communication in the same way we once did.

I believe we must pay more attention to the oral language environment television creates. To refer to Mina Shaughnessy, "if our students are to have the ability to make maps of where [they are] going," they must have an idea of "where [they have] been" (p. 249). Therefore, we must help our students understand "what it is the language of television is saying to us."[3]

Let's examine some differences between the messages we receive daily from television and the language we hear elsewhere; differences between language learning from television and ways in which we experience language otherwise are worth specific consideration.

One very familiar form of television language occurs in commercials; as many as twenty commercials are likely to be broadcast in an hour of prime television time. Because these commercial "spots" are so expensive for advertisers to broadcast and generally last only thirty seconds, television producers and writers have developed conventions of communication which eliminate both the need for transitions between units of spoken discourse as well as between the pictures we see. As viewers, therefore, we have learned, because we have been forced to do so, automatically and intuitively to supply an immense amount of information. Because we are so familiar with the genre, we *fill in the blanks*; consider, for instance, the following transcript of a 30-second commercial as it was broadcast this year by CBS:

Illustration I

Kitchen scene: A mother, father, and young son are in a kitchen eating breakfast.

Father: Big game tonight, huh?
Son: Dad, gonna be there?
Father: I'll be there.

Office scene: The father is at his desk now with his supervisor standing nearby.

Supervisor: Frank, I need this analysis before you leave.

We see alternating quick cuts of scenes showing son looking distressed during play of game and father absorbed in work at his desk. At the conclusion of the scenes, father arrives at the game and son is overjoyed.

Unseen Narrator (speaks during these scenes):
When you've got an important deadline, you need a Honeywell Office Automation System. Using a desk-top terminal, executives can organize data, analyze statistics, and get their work done. At Honeywell, we know how important it can be to meet a deadline.

(sound of musical scale ascending in the background)

Narrator: Honeywell.
You should see what we do with computers.

The dialogue between these characters conveys only enough information to re-inforce the message we receive visually. The "story" is a device; it rapidly appears and then disappears from the screen. So accustomed are we as viewers to process-ing such rapidly-paced dramatic vignettes whose issues are quickly resolved that we ignore "unanswered" questions we would ask if this story appeared in print: Why can't Frank return after the game to finish his work at the office? Why can't the son be told that his father will be late arriving at the basketball court? In fact, we have no time to question the problem as it is given nor the solution offered. And the advertiser hopes we come to believe that somehow Honeywell improves the life of a family as well as the efficiency of an office. The viewer is "taught" a great deal by Honeywell, but much that is "learned" results from our being willing to make *unspoken* connections between ideas.

Commercials, carefully scripted with underdeveloped plots, provide only one kind of familiar television language experience. A similar kind of language ex-perience requiring the television viewer to create bridges between ideas is required of listeners during televised broadcasts of spontaneous live events.

Nielsen ratings inform us that approximately one-fourth of the vast amount of viewing time of the American public is spent looking at sports events of various kinds.[4] An exact transcript of approximately 20 seconds of reportage from the 1982 NCAA championship basketball game between North Carolina and Georgetown serves as an illustration of what popular television sports commentary has accustomed viewers to hearing:

Illustration II

But you can hear the big guy comin' behind ya and Jimmy Black tries to get it up on the short hop.

It's not there and here comes Jordan again. We said a very dangerous offensive rebounder. What an awful feeling that's gotta be, Billy, to know that Ewing is coming down your back. He is one of the best runners for a big man I have ever seen in basketball and I think that's one of the assets he has and a lot of people don't rate it.

There's Ewing.

Perkins a short hook.

He got it off quickly.[5]

As in the case of the Honeywell commercial, this language of television, also accompanied by an informing picture, lacks transitions between observations—those links we expect to find in print. And, unlike the commentary of a radio broadcast, which supplies listeners with a rich context of description while a contest proceeds, the commentary of television is predominantly a mixture of objective details and subjective elaborations. We "see" the information that connects whatever statements we hear. The point is, finally, that though there is not *one* kind of television broadcast that has dominated the verbal world of our students, by and large, the majority of television's languages have one thing in common: they have accustomed viewers to verbal comments without verbal transitions.

My students are surprised to discover that television has acclimated them to this particular style of communication which is vastly different from the highly informative, carefully sequenced writing I know they must learn to produce for academic audiences. They are also pleased to discover that, to some extent, they have mastered the language of television. What they must do, I point out, is learn to move from one language to the other. I introduce them to the differences between television language and reading and writing by distributing the schema reproduced in Figure 1 (p. 322).

In some of my classes a discussion of this issue is sufficient. Introducing the idea to students that a special language environment (actually, a cluster of similar but differing languages) has influenced their own patterns of discourse is helpful in and of itself. In most of my classes, however, I pair this schema with one or more assignments that either require students to study and report upon the features of their favorite television language to the class or I ask them to analyze a "chunk" of television language I have audiotaped and transcribed into a printed text.

INTERLANGUAGE LEARNING SCHEMA

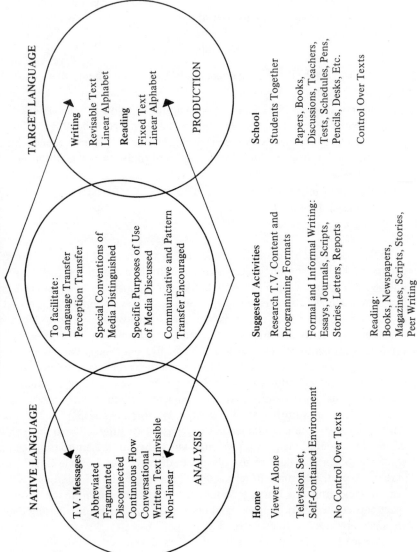

NATIVE LANGUAGE

T.V. Messages

Abbreviated
Fragmented
Disconnected
Continuous Flow
Conversational
Written Text Invisible
Non-linear

ANALYSIS

To facilitate:
Language Transfer
Perception Transfer

Special Conventions of
Media Distinguished

Specific Purposes of Use
of Media Discussed

Communicative and Pattern
Transfer Encouraged

TARGET LANGUAGE

Writing

Revisable Text
Linear Alphabet

Reading

Fixed Text
Linear Alphabet

PRODUCTION

Home

Viewer Alone

Television Set,
Self-Contained Environment

No Control Over Texts

Suggested Activities

Research T.V. Content and
Programming Formats

Formal and Informal Writing:
Essays, Journals, Scripts,
Stories, Letters, Reports

Reading:
Books, Newspapers,
Magazines, Scripts, Stories,
Peer Writing

School

Students Together

Papers, Books,
Discussions, Teachers,
Tests, Schedules, Pens,
Pencils, Desks, Etc.

Control Over Texts

Figure 1

The bridge between the world of television and the world of written and spoken communication is a better understanding of television itself; the words we hear from television are "rather like the language we speak; taken for granted, but both complex and vital to an understanding of the way human beings have created their world.[6] The teacher of writing *can use television* to help students escape from, or transcend, the language limits of the television medium alone.

Notes

[1] Judith Kirscht and Emily Golson, unpublished paper, "Empty and Chaotic Essays: Are They the Products of Our Own as Well as Our Students' Errors and Expectations?" 1982, p. 1.

[2] "The Schools and TV: Two Kinds of Teachers," *New York Times,* (20 April 1980), p. 29.

[3] Fiske, John and John Hartley, *Reading Television,* (New York: Methuen 1978), p. 20.

[4] Cole, Barry, Ed., *Television Today,* (New York: Oxford University Press, 1981), p. 74.

[5] Barbra Morris and Joel Nydahl, "Sports Spectacle as Drama: Image, Language, and Technology," *The Second International Conference on Television Drama,* 25 June 1982 (East Lansing, Michigan: Michigan State University), p. 16.

[6] Fiske and Hartley, p. 16.

50 Contexts in Which Students Make Meanings

Stephen A. Bernhardt
Department of English, Southern Illinois University, Carbondale

A common theme, which really has two parts, emerges in this collection: that we need to see the language activity of our students as a process of making meanings, and that these meanings must be embedded in situations of use. In largest terms, our efforts must be directed toward helping students discover and respond to meaningful contexts of language use. This is, of course, easy to say but difficult to achieve.

In its nobler manifestations, the art of rhetoric embraces both aspects of the above theme: it suggests how students might go about discovering what they have to say about a given topic and then planning how to say it with a certain purpose and audience in mind. There is nothing base in such a program, and Corbett, among others, finds sustenance in the practice of traditional rhetoric and the advice it offers for making meaning in context (p. 288). But a constant tendency throughout the history of rhetoric is to debase the practice of rhetoric, to reduce it to mere rehearsal of empty forms or to pat advice on what good writing is, without respect for the meanings which the writer might need to make, nor regard for the necessary adaptation of any piece of language to its context of use. Throughout its history, attempts have repeatedly been made to eviscerate rhetoric—by reducing it to a set of tricks, as some of the lesser sophists of the third, fourth, and fifth centuries were prone to do; by employing rhetoric in endless and empty scholastic debates in the Middle Ages; or by aligning the traditional components of invention and logic with philosophy or science and leaving only style and delivery to the province of rhetoric, as in the Ramistic rhetoric of the sixteenth century or the eloqutionist and stylistic rhetorics of the last two centuries. When rhetorical practice succumbs to such tendencies, it deserves the criticisms described by Knoblauch (pp. 295-99) and our scorn as well, for the teacher becomes a purveyor of technical skills without concern for how rhetorical skills might affect the making of meaning in the lives of the writer or reader, or influence the progress of society at large.

Rhetoric is also debased by those who would argue for the sanctity of truth without regard for the contexts which shape truths. The argument is based on the essential rationality of people, so that where truth is, there is no need for rhetoric, but rather a simple, straightforward presentation of a proposition. This second sort of debasement has surfaced repeatedly: in the Platonic criticism of Sophistic rhetoric, in early Christian homiletics, in the insistence on the sanctity of facts in scientific logic, and in the practice of those rhetoricians who urge us to give our full energy to allowing our students to free their honest voices, to pay no attention to how something is said but only to what the student is trying to articulate. Both tendencies—elevating either what is said or how it is said to a position of exclusive respect—exacerbate the age old tension between form and content; obviously, one must strive toward a harmony between what one is saying and the way one is saying it. To elevate either form or content at the expense of the other is to insure a lopsided, failed rhetoric.

Too often, our classroom practice demonstrates the same tendencies toward the debasement of rhetoric which characterize its history. Far too often, students find themselves rehearsing the same dull, deadly prose essays, for little purpose other than to offer something to a teacher for evaluation, with little investment of thought or feeling. They write these essays knowing they are telling the teacher what the teacher already knows, with the full knowledge that such things are written in school as part of the grade exchange economy. Some students become good at such exercises; some do not and never will. All know that such writing is something which goes on in English classes and in very few other places, and that what counts in an English class frequently does not in other places. The question is, how can this practice be broken; how can we help students come to know writing as something which can help them create meaning in their lives, as well as serve them as they engage themselves with the tasks which confront them?

That is a good question. Students come to us unequipped to see into their futures and envision the sorts of writing which might lie ahead. The contexts of language use in their lives would seem to be primarily oral, for they are immersed in what Ong describes as secondary orality, in which the constant media of exchange are either face-to-face verbal or electronic (See especially Ong, "The Literate Orality of Popular Culture Today," in *Rhetoric, Romance, and Technology*, pp. 284-303). Many do not write in the ways which schools value, and they do not foresee a need to do so. They see parents who are not primarily oriented toward print and who write infrequently, at least in the home environment. If students work, it is likely to be in positions which place very little emphasis on the skills of literacy—the jobs available to teens simply do not demand nor reward literate behavior. A few students may arrive in our classes with a predisposition toward print: we recognize those students who are readers and writers and who will continue to be if only we manage to stay out of their way. A few others may be persuaded by our courses that an advanced literacy will serve them well in the present and in the future. But many students do not seem to care about print in their lives inside or outside the school.

This is not meant to suggest that all is hopeless, that we ought simply to abandon print culture in the face of what appears to be an uphill battle. Signs of an increasingly literate society have already made the pages of our cultural barometer, *Time* (August 23, 1982:65-66), where it is reported that high school students are buying serious reading materials in greater volume than ever before. Granted, by serious I do not mean *Silas Marner* or *Moby Dick*, but books by such young adult authors as Judy Blume, Robert Cormier, or S. E. Hinton. According to *Time*, one major publisher reports an increase of 400% in sales of teen paperbacks since 1980. The status these authors have achieved is attested to by their works being made into films by major studios, a process certain to lead to ever greater sales. A second indication that we may be moving toward an increasingly literate general populace can be found in an article by John Bormuth, "The Value and Volume of Literacy." All volume indicators of literacy are up, as they have been every year over the past ten years, almost without exception. We consume ever increasing amounts of everything that is associated with literacy and which might be measured: from paper clips and pencils, to magazine subscriptions, to library holdings and lendings, to sales of paperbacks (pp. 118-161). Further evidence of an upturn in literacy among our youth is seen in the leveling off of aptitude test scores, reversing a long-term downward trend. And it may be true that we have been looking in the wrong places when we attempt to assess student literacy in terms of formal school writing. We know very little about what sorts of literate behavior serve the students outside the school environment. Shirley Brice Heath's ethnographic work shows that reading and writing do play functional roles in American communities, even those characterized by low incomes, low status jobs, and low educational levels (pp. 123-133). We may not be quite at the point where we can say that Americans, whether teenage or adult, take their minds as seriously as their bodies, but the market is certainly ripe for a series of bestsellers on the euphoria which attends mental jogging: We will soon be hitting the wall of advanced literacy and pushing on.

Signs are also there for those who would see them that teachers are attempting to help students make increasingly meaningful use of language in classroom contexts. Those who attend state or national meetings of teacher organizations such as those of the National Council of Teachers of English know the sort of careful attention being given to writing and reading by ever-increasing numbers of teachers. Some teachers have begun to wonder whether too much attention has been given to writing at the expense of other English teaching concerns. Whatever the case, teachers at every level are participating in greater numbers than ever before in their professional organizations, and the publications of these organizations bulge with articles describing enlightened theory, research, and method in teaching toward all levels of literacy.

One result of the attention to the teaching of language activity is increased concern about the contexts in which students make meaning before they enter our classrooms: a desire to understand what competencies students possess by virtue of being members of our culture. Morris, writing in this chapter on students' familiarity with television discourse (p. 318), is one striking example of a teacher who helps students make sense of their worlds. Instead of expressing dismay at the insistent presence of TV, its impoverished language, or its debilitating cognitive influences, Morris chooses to see what use might be made of it. Without scorn for those who would choose to watch TV instead of reading a book or writing a letter, Morris shows how this world can become a source of learning for the teacher, shaping her classroom behaviors. She shows in fine detail how to make use of the generalization which Robinson offers earlier in this chapter (p. 295), that our students come to us with highly evolved rhetorical insights upon which we should build. Some of these insights are derived from electronic media. Watch, for example, how quickly any teen can channel-check, spinning the dial at breakneck pace, immediately identifying programs by genre, by historical period, by any number of formal conventions. They know and can mimic the language of TV; they know the structures of dialogue, plot, transition, closure, and other narrative devices. The general populace can even come to appreciate new genre which explode traditional conventions of plot and character: The success of *Hill Street Blues* is one example of the public's eagerness to work at understanding new forms of narration. Other rhetorical/linguistic competencies are developed through work with computers, through the networks of social communication, and through the simple business of getting things done on a daily basis. What we need to do is appreciate and tap these understandings, to come to know and use the discourse worlds of our students rather than to label and reject the students as semi-literates because they do not know the rules of our particular modes of written classroom discourse. Morris's insight extends to other realms of discourse: to the rules of discourse in insider groups, to the rules for discourse with parents or adults, to the rules which govern the intense, important adolescent courtship strategies. In this chapter, Bartholomae gives us insight into how we might devise assignments which do not presume that students know our sorts of discourse; he shows how we might make constructive use of what they do control (p. 302). Like Morris and Bartholomae, we need to summon a genuine interest in the worlds of our students and learn to marvel at what they are capable of doing. We cannot simply use the language of students as a point of departure, desiring to forget it as soon as possible as we socialize them into our world and our values. This would be like saying that all dialects are of equal value, then suggesting by word and deed that standard English is the only dialect sufficiently valuable to have currency in the school setting. As Stock suggests (p. 332), we want to give students an appropriate language so we can talk together about what is important to us as writers, but we also need to show students that we participate in meaningful ways in the contexts in which they make meanings.

We are fortunate in that many of the writers in this volume have offered alternatives to the traditional contexts of classroom writing: alternative roles for teachers and students, roles which seek to escape the meaningless bind in which students find themselves always and only writing for an audience of one, who already knows what is to be said, in forms that are predictable and pre-established, for purposes which suggest that writing is meant to be judged for its approximation to the standards of schoolroom English. From the British experience, represented in this volume by Britton (p. 221), Fulwiler (p. 273), and Bailey (p. 24), we can learn a way of thinking about English instruction which stresses writing across the curriculum. Others, too, are attempting to reintegrate the experiences of reading and writing in various subject areas. Hansen shows how powerfully reading and writing can be integrated in the early grades, with a large measure of respect for learners governing their own learning (p. 155). Meiland suggests that writing can be a mode of open ethical inquiry wherein students struggle with truth instead of presenting a prepackaged argument (p. 251). It is remarkable how similar are the lessons of this volume for all situations, from elementary, to secondary, to university and beyond: Students need to develop their uses of language not for simple editorial correctness, but because of the powerful role writing plays in making meaning.

Other contributors suggest that while writing can serve the teacher as a check over learning or give the students practice in essay writing, it needn't always serve these purposes. Young offers a useful description for moving students through various realms of discourse, with the aim of demonstrating the powerful role writing can play in discovering and giving voice to important ideas

(p. 240). Sometimes, at least, writing can be for the students, to help them realize what they think, to discover what they believe. At other times, the writing can be directed in meaningful ways to other students in the class, or to audiences beyond the confines of the classroom. These practitioners all converge on a single point, that writing can liberate personal meaning by playing a heuristic role. Writing becomes a means not simply of putting in words prepackaged meaning, but of construing, in Berthoff's terms, of actually discovering and making a world of meaning (p. 166). In this process, teachers must reconceive their roles, becoming facilitative and nurturing, setting a context in which such learning can come about.

Once again, however, the corollary to this point must not be overlooked, for our students are too complex, their language too varied, their meanings too multitudinous to expect that one sort of meaning making will satisfy all. Some programs of rhetoric have based their recovery of meaning in student writing on the suggestion that all writing should be intensely personal, on the assumption that the only sort of meaningful writing is that which rehearses events in one's own life which were intensely emotional. This sort of writing attempts to free the "real person" through utter honesty about deeply personal experience. Such pieces go for the emotional jugular vein: the death of grandfather, the first stirrings of love in an adolescent breast, a moment of supreme embarrassment. Eventually, such writing becomes no less distressingly recognizable than the sort of dry, committee-composed academic English which so many of us find odious. Clearly the antidote to dry, boring classroom prose is not simply freedom from one conditioned sort of prose and license to compose in another clichéd style. What students need to learn is to be effective composers in a variety of registers. Couture says it well: "Teachers trying to get students to write with conviction would be more successful if they helped students discover the multiple 'voices' they must employ when addressing different audiences for different purposes" (p. 144). There is nothing ignominious in this. We continually adapt our spoken language not only to the meanings we wish to express, but in accordance with our purposes, our audiences, and the surrounding context of the utterance. The infinite variability of language, shaped by the effects we intend our utterances to have, calls for constant creativity and adaptability. To gain the ability to adapt language to suit our purposes in writing is not to give up the essential self, but to learn to create the many selves which each of us is. It is not the one true self that we find and present in our writing; rather we recreate ourselves in each instance of language use. Like Peer Gynt, we may wish we could peel our way layer by layer to find out what the onion really is at heart, but the onion is really only a series of layers. So language is one of the phenomena by which we make ourselves by construing layers of meaning.

If we reject the idea of one true self and one clear truth, we enter into a subjective world which contains many truths, in which the important notion is perspective. If we look at an issue from one vantage point, from one observer's perspective, we are likely to see things differently than if we had another vantage. Those contemporary rhetoricians whom Lauer (pp. 290-93) describes as being so influential over our current practice, such as Pike with his tagmemic matrix or Burke with his pentad, show us that we can be enriched by multiple perspectives, that the radical indeterminacy of experience is something to rejoice in, for as we learn to look at life from various angles we deepen our understanding. Language reflects the same indeterminacy: It is not set, locked, single dimensional, but variable, suggestive, multi-faceted. The same experience can be reflected in many language forms, and learning to find meaning by shifting situational perspective should be a central focus of our teaching.

Learning to use the many voices that each of us possesses can be aided by the sorts of writing assignments suggested in the latter half of this chapter. The use of cases begins to simulate the way the world imposes writing on us. Instead of assuming that writing is internally motivated by the need to express meanings welling up from within, a contextual approach assumes that writing often is functionally motivated; in Bitzer's terms, the world imposes a situation which demands that some exigence be remedied through writing (pp. 21-38). That language development might be functionally motivated can and has been cogently argued (see, for instance, M. A. K. Halliday, *Learning How to Mean: Explorations in the Development of Language.*) From this viewpoint, language is from the start not an egocentric activity, but a social one, a tool for getting people to behave in certain ways. From such a perspective, learning to use language is less a matter of increasing one's capacity to convey the full range and complexity of one's thoughts and more a matter of pragmatic efficiency. The question of effectiveness changes, then, from "Did I fully express my ideas?" to "Did my words accomplish their intended effect?"

With the sorts of writing suggested by Redish (p. 312), and Shook (p. 315) in this chapter, students are put into a situation which presents some of the richness and complexity which characterize actual writing situations. Much of the necessary information is supplied, and the student's task is to move from a situation toward a written response which is part of that situation. These methods of case study attempt to simulate the conditions for writing in situations outside the classroom, beginning with the assumption that writing is not typically an isolated activity pursued for its own sake, but is embedded in a larger context of ongoing activity. The attempt is to change the ground rules of classroom discourse from students writing in very predictable patterns for teacher approval to students adapting their writing to various audiences and purposes.

The underlying model of language use in contextual approaches emphasizes individual control of variation in response to the varying constraints which the world presents. Working within such a framework demands that the teacher be able to engage the students with the task. The case approach has a puzzle-like quality that requires students to solve the problem of an appropriate response to a given situation. The approach risks rejection by students who have been conditioned to think they need to learn to produce a certain type of academic text. The goal of the case method is moving students toward a rhetorical consciousness which will undergird all writing tasks, in class and out, rather than encouraging competence within a single, restricted register. Shook finds that students are willing and able to "get into" cases, but many teachers will find that much work will have to be done to get students to accept the challenge of the task. Here, White's strategies for locating important places within the students' lives may help motivation (p. 46). If it is possible to locate meaningful loci within the students' lives which involve legal reasoning and writing, then it might also be possible to locate those aspects of our students' lives which are affected by job-related tasks as described by Redish. The hard trick in a contextual approach is to get the students to willingly engage with the task in a spirit of gamelike enthusiasm. This can be particularly difficult when the several agendas of the classroom clash: when the making of meaning or the discovery of appropriate language runs up against the teacherly role of evaluator and assigner of grades. The teacher needs to openly air the difficulties of simulating worklike or outside-of-schoolroom situations for writing, and then work out a satisfactory means of evaluating while still encouraging risky prose which stretches the limits of student language use. Without engagement, the pursuit of writing, whether cast in cases, altered for various audiences, or approached under job-like conditions, will simply assume the status of one more schoolroom exercise which demands little more than the filling in of a form.

An advantage of situationally defined rhetorical tasks is that they give the students something to work with, information to manipulate, and language to shape, in addition to whatever previous knowledge and experience is brought to the task. Some students will find it easier to work within the constraints of such assignments than to attempt to create a text totally from within. We often assume that writing which is close to the self is easiest and most accessible, but it is easier for some to imagine a situation in which the writing is directed toward a clear goal—a request for information, a justification of one's actions, an act of praise or blame. Non-situationally motivated forms of discourse—description, narration, personal reflection—may be difficult because they lack a defining context. Setting out assignments which are situationally defined also gives the teacher a means of developing criteria for assessment. Does the piece of writing accomplish its stated purpose? Is it well adapted to the audience as stipulated? Instead of fostering a belief in "good writing" abstracted from any context, with qualities such as clarity, economy, or good organization, a situational approach sets its own criteria for evaluation. What Clark says so well about institutional methods of evaluation applies equally to classroom assessment of language (p. 59). Before judgment is rendered on any execution of language, we must understand the writer's intention. Where possible, the writing and assessment could actually involve the intended audience. In the best rhetorical world, our students would be writing not within contrived situations but real ones, and the effectiveness of their prose could be judged by the audience or by whether or not the piece accomplished what it set out to do. Writing would count, it would matter, it would change the world.

Our ability to contextualize the writing in our classrooms is limited only by our willingness to learn through participation in other worlds of discourse. Many of us are comfortable with only a narrowly confined range of texts: personal or factual essays, literary works, and responses to literature. Valuable as these texts are, as committed as we are to our students being able to read and interpret such texts, they represent only a small fraction of what gets written or read in our society on a daily basis. To contextualize our teaching demands that we step outside our comfort zones and embrace worlds of the sort described by the writers in this collection. To Redish, it means making a place in the classroom for the language of government, of business, of law, including texts as diverse as documents explaining regulations to an affected public, contractual language, or the ubiquitous forms which continually present themselves for us to squeeze our answers into. For White, too, the classroom would be a place for consideration of legal literacy, as it would be a place to encourage scientific literacy for Dunn and Rueter (p. 32). The classroom would be an arena for considering the problems of language specialization and the implications for society of there being large areas of discourse which affect the general public, but which are largely not understood and often avoided by those who are affected. The classroom would consider the particular difficulties of the specialist who recognizes the need to communicate with a non-specialist audience, and so become a workshop for the reworking of information for special purposes or audiences. As teachers in context, we would need to welcome the languages of the world into our classes, finding our ways as best we could through the unfamiliar thickets of strange discourses.

Luckily, we would have our students for guides. We would learn alongside them, sharing in the demands for literacy placed upon them by their worlds. We would be reaching out beyond the confines of the class, investigating the way language works, coming to know its variety, gaining power over its forms. Our preoccupation with expressive discourse might still assert itself, insofar as everything to which we give value can find expression in language which assigns value, whether the field be science, law, medicine, history, or literary studies. We would operate within an enriched context, in which all discourse was recognized as shaped by situations of use. The ideas a writer put forth would continue to be stressed and we would value thoughtfulness as much as we always have. At the same time, every act of discourse would be seen to·involve human participants, people working together through the medium of language, negotiating meanings in ways which have the potential to contribute in honest, ethical, important ways to the general welfare or to our individual development as thinkers and doers. And these socially motivated ideas would seek expression in the most appropriate, creative texts which might be constructed, based upon an appreciation of the past and present practice of written English. Because of their continual emphasis on students making meanings in context, the real value of the essays in this collection is the promise of liberating writing as a powerful tool for making meaning, for our students and ourselves, in the contexts in which we find ourselves now and in those contexts in which we anticipate finding ourselves in the future.

Afterword

For some time, I have self-consciously avoided the language currently used by some theorists and teachers of writing to describe the processes of composition to themselves and their students. I have done so because their metaphors strike me as inappropriate to the act of writing. I believe that to write is to engage in a particularly human and potentially humane enterprise. Therefore, it is uncomfortable for me to conceive of writing in martial language—with such labels as tactics, strategies, and attack skills; or in the lexicon of computer technology—input, or feedback, and "chunks" of meaning; or even in the contractual bottom lines and product-labelling terms of business and industry.

I am particularly unsettled by these metaphors of our time because as a student and teacher of language and literacy, I know the power of the symbol system which constitutes language. The words we use to describe writing to our students suggest to them the kind of activity we believe writing to be. Our words are not merely audible or visible signs. Unlike the smoke which represents fire, or the marker which indicates the contour of the road, or the name "Patches" which is herself to my cat, words are not substitutes for concrete objects or events or procedures. They are not terms associated in one-to-one correspondence with what they concretely signify. Rather, the words we use are what Susanne Langer calls "proxies for their objects." They are the "vehicles for the conception of objects" (Langer, p. 45), and with them we communicate our concept of writing to others. The language with which we describe the acts of writing is rich in latent meanings; therefore, if we suggest to our students that they develop writing strategies or attack writing problems, we lead them to regard acts of writing as competitive and adversarial: The writing itself is the enemy to be defeated. If we suggest that they seek feedback and react to input to their drafts, we suggest that they should strive for products much like computer print-outs, the result of orderly, programmed procedures. If we refer to their products, we imply that their work is the result of a series of assembly-line procedures calling for fulfillment of the *specs*. Similarly, if we speak to one another about diagnosing our students' writings in order that we may treat the deficiencies they demonstrate or remediate the weaknesses they suffer, we imply that our students' writings—if not our students themselves—are ill. If we say they are suffering from writer's block, anxiety, or frustration, we suggest that their maladies are psycho-

somatic. Finally, if we describe to one another how we provide enriching therapeutic experiences for our underdeveloped writers, who are functioning at
immature stages of growth in writing, we imply that our students' ability to
write has been stunted, and, too often, we assume that their ability to think has
been stunted as well.

I am much more comfortable when I describe writing in self-consciously
human metaphors—in terms of voice and vision and thought. I understand that I
speak metaphorically when I suggest that to write is to commit one of our
several voices to the page and thereby to see our words held in place for careful
scrutiny and reflection, to give our ideas form which can preserve them for
others' examination and reflection. I also understand that I speak in a chorus
with teachers whom I admire: teachers like Dan Fader, who insists that students
write in the language of their own voices rather than in borrowed language that
is foreign enough to them to permit them to speak it or write it without possess-
ing it and, therefore, without being responsible for it; teachers like Don Murray,
who describes what happens when he satisfies the itch, the need to speculate in
writing like this: "I give it words in my head and on my notebook page, it begins
to become a vision. I see a shadowy outline of a mountain range I may choose
to map" (p. 230); and teachers like Ann Berthoff, who describes the process of
interpretation that underlies both reading and writing as "a matter of seeing
what goes with what . . . [of making] sense of the world [in language]" (p. 168).

When I talk to my students about writing, I say obvious things to them in
language that is hardly noteworthy or memorable. Things like: No one else has
the same mind that you have. No one else has had the same experiences, has
read with quite the same understandings. No one else sees the world, or hears
it, or tastes, feels, smells it just the way you do. Only you have your unique
understandings to explore and to communicate to others. Writing is one way to
explore, and it is one way to share your explorations and understandings with
others. I do not know any formulas which will enable you to write effectively.
The writing you will compose here will be more the result of your accumulated
experiences with reading and writing than with anything you may learn in this
course; your growth in writing ability will be more the result of your willingness
to observe the writing of others carefully, to think about what you observe, and
to practice and practice and practice your own writing, than learning the lessons
of any textbook or handbook I can recommend. To become effective writers
you will have to give your writing the time and attention it requires and to
assume responsibility for it. I assure my students that even though I cannot
give each of them years of experience with reading and writing or simple
formulas for writing effectively, as a reader interested in their writing—in their
thinking—I can do much to help them become better writers.

When I noted earlier that I have no memorable language for talking about
writing to my students, I was not being completely honest. In fact, I know some
wonderfully memorable words and phrases that speak effectively to my students and for that matter, to my colleagues as well. I teach all my students the
heuristic acronym *MAPS* created by Bernard Van't Hul at the University of
Michigan to remind all of us that effective language use depends upon the

*M*edium in which it is delivered, the *A*udience, and *P*urpose for which it is shaped, and the *S*ituation in which it takes place. In Van't Hul's words, I give my students an easily recalled, powerful guide to composition.

I use some equally memorable words for talking about my practice with my colleagues, words I've learned from teachers who have written essays for this book. I frequently borrow the term *Writing Across the Curriculum* which James Britton and his colleagues coined in the 1970's to describe their work—hoping it would "sound American" and thereby gain currency in Britain. Or I speak of *English in Every Classroom,* a slogan Dan Fader used when he began to ask teachers in all disciplines to be teachers of reading and writing in the 1960's. I use these terms because I know the heuristic acronym *MAPS* and slogans like *Writing Across the Curriculum* and *English in Every Classroom* are meant to capture the imagination and to challenge me, my students, and my colleagues to do more than mouth slogans. They challenge us to live up to our language, to make real differences, to apply the human sense that the ideas behind our language imply. In fact, they invite us—as does all the language in this book—to become teachers of literacy.

Patricia L. Stock

Bibliography

Robert Root
Department of English, Central Michigan University

American Association for the Advancement of Humanities. *Humanities Report,* Vol. IV, No. 2 (February, 1982).

Anderson, Richard C. "The Notion of Schemata and the Educational Enterprise," *Schooling and the Acquisition of Knowledge.* (Eds.) R. C. Anderson, R. J. Spiro, and W. E. Montague. Hillsdale, NJ: Lawrence Erlbaum, 1977.

_____ . "Role of the Reader's Schema in Comprehension, Learning and Memory," *Learning to Read in American Schools.* (Eds.) R. Anderson, J. Osborn, and R. Tierney. Hillsdale, NJ: Lawrence Erlbaum (in press).

_____ , Ralph E. Reynolds, Diane L. Schallert, and Ernest J. Goetz. "Frameworks for Comprehending Discourse," *American Education Research Journal,* 14 (1977), pp. 367–382.

Applebee, Arthur N. *Writing in the Secondary School: English and the Content Areas.* NCTE Research Report No. 21. Urbana, IL: NCTE, 1982.

Describes a study of the writing secondary school students are asked to do in six major subject areas and includes a good annotated bibliography of sources which provide strategies for incorporating writing into content area instruction.

Arnheim, Rudolf, W. H. Auden, Karl Shapiro, and Donald A. Stauffer. *Poets at Work: Essays.* NY: Harcourt, Brace, 1948.

Four essays on the creative process gleaned from analysis of manuscripts, worksheets, and completed poems.

Atwell, M. *The Evolution of Text: The Interrelationship of Reading and Writing in the Composing Process.* Unpublished dissertation, Indiana University, 1980.

Reports a study in which writers were asked to produce a narrative essay, half of which was visible to them as they wrote, half not visibly available; and discusses how writers act as readers as they develop discourse.

Aulls, Mark W. "Relating Reading Comprehension and Writing Competency," *Language Arts,* 52 (September, 1975), pp. 808–812.

Children's identity as writers helped create interest in reading among elementary students.

Ausubel, David P. "The Use of Advance Organizers in the Learning and Retention of Meaningful Verbal Material," *Journal of Educational Psychology,* 51 (1960), pp. 267–272.

*Where the titles of the entries in this bibliography are not self-explanatory, the entries have been annotated briefly.

Reports on a study in which students presented with background material learned and retained the information in a text significantly better than those who were not presented with advance organizers.

Bailey, Dudley, "A Plea for a Modern Set of Topoi," *College English* 26:2 (November, 1964), pp. 111–117.
Proposes the contents of a rhetoric textbook for the modern college English class.

Bailey, Richard W. "This Teaching Works." Report to the Faculty of the College of Literature, Science, and the Arts of the University of Michigan, 1981.

Baker, Sheridan. "Are You Communicating?" *AAUP Bulletin*, 39 (Autumn, 1953), pp. 432–437.
Argues against teaching communication skills in Freshman English and for the use of argumentative essays on ethical bases to lead students to "ponder the grand and terrifying questions."

——————— . "Writing as Discovery." *ADE Bulletin*, 43 (November, 1974), pp. 34–37.
Argues that "writing is our chief means of discovering knowledge and values and what is valid" and that creative writing should not supplant expository writing in composition classes.

Barnes, Douglas. *Language in the Classroom*. Bletchley, England: The Open University Press, 1973.
One of ten study guides prepared for the Open University course "Language and Learning"; reports on the uses of language in learning.

——————— , James Britton, and Harold Rosen. *Language, the Learner and the School*. Revised ed. Harmondsworth, England: Penguin Books, 1971. (Available from Boynton/Cook)
Provides essays on language in the classroom; stresses the value of talking in students' learning and writing; and gives recommendations for a language policy across the curriculum.

Barritt, Loren, "Writing/Speaking: A Descriptive Phenomenological View," *Exploring Speaking-Writing Relationships: Connections and Contrasts*, (Eds.) Barry M. Kroll and Roberta J. Vann, Urbana: NCTE, 1981, pp. 124–133.

Basic Writing: Essays for Teachers, Researchers, and Administrators. (Eds.) Lawrence N. Kasden and Daniel R. Hoeber. Urbana, IL: NCTE, 1980.
Ten essays on basic writing, describing the field, summarizing current and needed research, and providing insights into the basic writer, program design and evaluation, and teacher-training in this area.

Beach, Richard. *Writing About Ourselves and Others*. Urbana, IL: ERIC/NCTE, 1977.
A synthesis of theory concerning autobiography, memoir, and portrait writing, theory concerning different characteristics of self, and composing process theory, followed by a thorough practice section.

Beck, I. L. "Developing Comprehension: The Impact of the Directed Reading Lesson," *Learning to Read in American Schools*. (Eds.) R. Anderson, J. Osborn, and R. Tierney. Hillsdale, NJ: Lawrence Erlbaum (in press).

Belanger, Joseph. "Reading Skill as an Influence on Writing Skill," Unpublished Dissertation, University of Alberta, 1978. ERIC ED 163 409.
Contains comprehensive reviews of the literature on the interrelationships of the four language processes, as well as a very useful bibliography.

Berman, Ronald, "Stamping Out Illiteracy," *The Chronicle of Higher Education*. October 2, 1978, p. 72.
Argues against remedial education and for disciplines of intellectual activity and knowledge.

Bernstein, Basil. *Class, Codes, and Control.* Vol. 1: *Theoretical Studies Toward a Sociology of Language.* London: Routledge and Kegan Paul, 1970.

A collection of essays on the relationship between the various features of spoken and written language and the social contexts in which they function, including an essay by Bernstein on his distinction between "restrictive" and "elaborative" codes and their relation to the social class.

Berthoff, Ann E. *Forming/Thinking/Writing: The Composing Imagination.* Montclair, NJ: Boynton/Cook, 1981.

Describes the "dialectical notebook" and other activities Berthoff uses to teach writing.

_____ . *The Making of Meaning: Metaphors, Models, and Maxims for Writing Teachers.* Montclair, NJ: Boynton/Cook, 1981.

Presents the philosophical argument for the centrality of interpretation in the processes of writing.

_____ . *Reclaiming the Imagination.* Montclair, NJ: Boynton/Cook (forthcoming).

Essays by artists, philosophers, and scientists concerning the processes involved in making sense of experience.

Bitzer, Lloyd F. "Functional Communication: A Situational Perspective," *Rhetoric in Transition.* (Ed.) Eugene E. White. University Park: Pennsylvania State University Press, 1980, pp. 21–38.

Black English and the Education of Black Children and Youth. (Ed.) Geneva Smitherman. Detroit: Center for Black Studies, Wayne State University, 1981.

Collection of documents emerging from the King "Black English" case, including an essay by James Baldwin on Black English and interpretations of the issues in the litigation by specialists in reading, testing, and curriculum.

Bleich, David. *Readings and Feelings: An Introduction to Subjective Criticism.* Urbana, IL: NCTE, 1975.

Bloom, Lois. *Language Development: Form and Function in Emerging Grammars.* Research Monograph No. 59. Cambridge, MA: MIT Press, 1970.

Blumenthal, Arthur. *Language and Psychology.* NY: John Wiley, 1970.

Presents a useful historical account of theories of language and their relationship to thinking and learning.

Booth, Wayne C. *Modern Dogma and the Rhetoric of Assent.* Chicago: University of Chicago Press, 1974.

Examines assumptions about rhetoric and belief in the late sixties.

_____ . "The Rhetorical Stance," *College Composition and Communication,* 14 (October, 1963), pp. 139–145.

Argues that effective writing is produced when writers assume a balanced rhetorical stance which gives weight to the subject matter, audience, and voice.

Bormuth, John. "The Value and Volume of Literacy." *Visible Language,* 12 (Spring, 1978), pp. 118–161.

Bower, G. H., J. B. Black, and T. J. Turner. "Scripts in Memory for Text." *Cognitive Psychology,* 11 (1979), pp. 177–220.

Bransford, J. D. *Human Cognition: Learning, Understanding, and Remembering.* Belmont, CA: Wadsworth, 1979.

Reports on current work in cognitive psychology, indicating applications of basic research, and emphasizing the active nature of learning, understanding, and remembering.

_____ , J. R. Barclay, and J. J. Franks. "Sentence Memory: A Constructive versus Interpretive Approach," *Cognitive Psychology,* 3 (1972), pp. 193–209.

_____ and M. K. Johnson. "Contextual Prerequisites for Understanding: Some Investigations of Comprehension and Recall," *Journal of Verbal Learning and Verbal Behavior,* 11 (1972), pp. 717–726.

_____ and N. S. McCarrell. "A Sketch of a Cognitive Approach to Comprehension," *Perceiving, Acting, and Knowing: Toward an Ecological Psychology.* (Eds.) W. Weimer and D. S. Palermo. Hillsdale, NJ: Lawrence Erlbaum, 1974.

_____ , B. S. Stein, T. S. Shelton, and R. A. Owings. "Cognition and Adaptation: The Importance of Learning to Learn," *Cognition, Social Behavior, and the Environment.* (Ed.) J. Harvey. Hillsdale, NJ: Lawrence Erlbaum, 1980.

_____ , B. S. Stein, and N. J. Vye. "Helping Students Learn to Learn from Written Texts," *Competent Reader, Disabled Reader: Research and Application.* (Ed.) M. Singer. Hillsdale, NJ: Lawrence Erlbaum, 1982.

Britton, James. "The Composing Processes and the Functions of Writing," *Research on Composing: Points of Departure.* (Eds.) Charles R. Cooper and Lee Odell. Urbana, IL: NCTE, 1978.

Distills the discourse theory expounded in Britton's two major works and offers recommendations for further research.

_____ . *Language and Learning.* Harmondsworth, England: Penguin Books, 1970. (Available from Boynton/Cook)

Provides the basis for theories underlying the work of the Schools Council Project. Examines the participatory and speculative nature of language usage and the development of the cognitive processes as well as language development in the pre-school, primary, and secondary periods of a child's education.

_____ . *Prospect and Retrospect: Selected Essays of James Britton.* (Ed.) Gordon M. Pradl. Montclair, NJ: Boynton/Cook, 1982.

_____ . "The Student's Writing," *Explorations in Children's Writing.* (Ed.) Eldonna L. Evertts. Urbana, IL: NCTE, 1970.

One of a series of short articles on speech and the function of writing as an equivalent to speech; the stages of youthful writing; the ways children and adults "represent their worlds in language"; and appropriate places for attention to form.

_____ , Tony Burgess, Nancy Martin, Alex McLeod, and Harold Rosen. *The Development of Writing Abilities (11-18).* Schools Council Research Studies. London: Macmillan Education, 1975 (Available from NCTE)

An explanation and report of the Schools Council Project. Important for the sense of range it gives us in student writing and for theoretical background on discourse and the composing process.

Bruce, B. "A New Point of View on Children's Stories," *Learning to Read in American Schools.* (Eds.) R. Anderson, J. Osborn, and R. Tierney. Hillsdale, NJ: Lawrence Erlbaum (in press).

Bruner, Jerome S. *The Process of Education.* Cambridge, MA: Harvard University Press, 1965.

Develops four themes: the role of structure in learning, the necessity of responding to learning readiness, the nature of intuition, and the desire to learn, all with an interest in classroom application.

_____ . *Toward a Theory of Instruction.* Cambridge, MA: Harvard University Press, 1966.

A series of essays including discussion of patterns of growth, teaching a native language, and the will to learn, drawing on cognitive psychology.

_____ , R. Oliver, and P. Greenfield. *Studies in Cognitive Growth.* NY: John Wiley, 1966.

Reports important experimental studies on the interrelationship of thought and language and the influence of formal schooling on their development.

Brunetti, Gerald J. "The Bullock Report: Some Implications for American Teachers and Parents," *English Journal,* 67:8 (November, 1978), pp. 58-64.

_____ . "A Language for Life: A Review," *Research in the Teaching of English,* 11 (1977): pp. 61–67.

A sympathetic review of the Bullock Report with particular commendation of the idea that "language development occurs in all phases of the school curriculum and that all teachers, however they might feel about it, are necessarily language teachers" (p. 65).

Bullock, Sir Alan. *A Language for Life.* London: H. M. Stationery Office, 1975.

A summary of a national investigation of the state of British education and the role of language in learning, presuming an "organic relationship between the various aspects of English and . . . the need for continuity in their development throughout school life."

Burgess, Carol, *et al. Understanding Children Writing.* Harmondsworth, England: Penguin Books, 1973. (Available from Boynton/Cook)

Collects and comments on writing of children. Useful for its insights into the developmental aspect of writing and the value of expressive discourse.

Burke, Kenneth. *A Grammar of Motives,* NY: Prentice-Hall, 1952.

Explains "dramatism" and applies its analyses of various philosophies. An accessible study of semantics.

_____ . *A Rhetoric of Motives.* Berkeley: University of California Press, 1969.

Posits that identification is the ultimate goal of rhetoric.

Chafe, Wallace L. "The Deployment of Consciousness in the Production of a Narrative," *The Pear Stories: Cognitive, Cultural, and Linguistic Aspects of Narrative Production.* (Ed.) Wallace L. Chafe. Norwood, NJ: Ablex, 1980.

Chomsky, Carol. "Reading, Writing, and Phonology," *Psycholinguistics and Reading.* (Ed.) Frank Smith. NY: Holt, Rinehart and Winston, 1973, pp. 91–104.

Explores the relation of orthography to sound structure and the motivation behind nonphonetic aspects of spelling.

Children and Writing in the Elementary School: Theories and Techniques. (Ed.) Richard L. Larson. New York: Oxford University Press, 1975.

A collection of articles and excerpts reinforces findings of Britton and Moffett and offers readings in theories of written discourse and teaching techniques, and responding to student writing.

Christensen, Francis. *Notes Towards A New Rhetoric: Six Essays for Teachers,* NY: Harper & Row, 1967.

Christensen's explanation of his generative rhetoric, and demonstration of the use of the cumulative sentence in modern and contemporary prose.

Clark, Michael. "Contests and Contexts: Writing and Testing in School," *College English,* 42 (1980) pp. 217–27.

Analyzes various writing tests to demonstrate the implicit social and political contexts that surround the production and evaluation of writing, especially as writing functions within institutional contexts and for purposes of placement and evaluation.

_____ . "There Is No Such Thing as Good Writing (So What Are We Looking For?)," *"Reinventing the Rhetorical Tradition.* (Eds.) Aviva Freedmen and Ian Pringle. Canadian Council of Teachers of English. Conway, AR: L & S Books, 1980. (Available from NCTE)

Describes the theoretical bases for the more concrete argument of "Contests and Contexts," drawing on work done by Bernstein and Labov.

Classical Rhetoric and Modern Discourse: Essays in Honor of Edward P. J. Corbett. (Eds.) Robert Connors, Lisa Erde, and Andrea Lunsford. Carbondale: Southern Illinois University Press (forthcoming).

Cognitive Processes in Writing. (Eds.) Lee W. Gregg and Erwin R. Steinberg. Hillsdale, NJ: Lawrence Erlbaum, 1980.

Coles, William E., Jr. *Teaching Composing: A Guide to Teaching Writing as a Self-Creating Process.* Rochelle Park, NJ: Hayden, 1974.

A description of how a sequence of thirty writing assignments is designed to increase students' abilities with the English language by increasing their understanding of the nature of language in general: what language is, how it functions, why it is important.

_____ . "Teaching the Teaching of Composition: Evolving a Style," *College Composition and Communication,* 28 (October, 1977) pp. 268–270.

_____ . *The Plural I: The Teaching of Writing.* NY: Holt, Rinehart and Winston, 1978.

A novelistic class-by-class account of a writing course in which one teacher performs his style with a group of students in such a way as to enable other teachers to make styles of their own.

Collins, James L. "Speaking, Writing, and Teaching for Meaning," *Exploring Speaking-Writing Relationships: Connections and Contrasts.* (Eds.) Barry M. Kroll and Roberta J. Vann. Urbana, IL: NCTE, 1981, pp. 198–214.

Composition and Its Teaching: Articles from College Composition and Communication During the Editorship of Edward P. J. Corbett. (Ed.) Richard C. Gebhardt. Urbana, IL: NCTE, 1980.

Contemporary Rhetoric: A Conceptual Background with Readings. (Ed.) W. Ross Winterowd. NY: Harcourt Brace Jovanovich, 1975.

Provides a lengthy introduction to contemporary rhetoric and a variety of essays and excerpts by major figures on invention, arrangement, and style.

Corbett, Edward P. J. *Classical Rhetoric for the Modern Student.* 2nd Ed. New York: Oxford, 1971.

An extensive and thorough introduction to classical rhetoric and its applicability in the modern world. Includes a number of carefully analyzed examples from ancient and modern writers.

_____ . "The Rhetoric of the Open Hand and the Rhetoric of the Closed Fist," *College Composition and Communication,* 20 (December, 1969), pp. 288–296.

Analyzes the new forms of rhetoric that appeared in the 1960's and compares them to the traditions of classical rhetoric, arguing for the relevance of classical rhetoric today.

_____ . "The Status of Writing in Our Society," *Writing: The Nature, Development, and Teaching of Written Communication.* Vol. 1. *Variation in Writing: Functional and Linguistic-Cultural Differences.* (Ed.) Marcia Farr Whiteman. Hillsdale, NJ: Lawrence Erlbaum, 1981.

Demonstrates that, in spite of a demand for writing, schools do not teach the kind of writing needed.

_____ . "The Theory and Practice of Imitation in Classical Rhetoric," *College Composition and Communication,* 22 (October, 1971), pp. 243–250.

_____ . "The Usefulness of Classical Rhetoric," *College Composition and Communication,* 14 (October, 1963), pp. 162–164.

Coulthard, Malcolm. *An Introduction to Discourse Analysis.* London: Longman, 1977.

Defines discourse analysis, summarizes a range of research analyzing spoken and written texts, and describes implications for teaching.

Crystal, David and Derek Davy. *Investigating English Style.* Bloomington, IN: Indiana University Press, 1969.

Describes and applies a method for making descriptive comparisons of the features of spoken and written texts.

D'Angelo, Frank. *A Conceptual Theory of Rhetoric.* Cambridge, MA: Winthrop, 1975.
Argues for a holistic composing process dependent on underlying thought processes.

D'Arcy, Pat. "Going Back Inside," *The London Times Educational Supplement,* January 28, 1977, p. 19.
A former member of the Schools Council "Language Across the Curriculum" project explains the difficulties of implementing such a policy in an actual school setting.

Dawe, Charles W. and Edward A. Dornan. *One to One: Resources for Conference-Centered Writing.* Boston: Little, Brown, 1981.

de Villiers, Jill G., and Peter A. de Villiers. *Language Acquisition.* Cambridge, MA: Harvard University Press, 1978.
Provides a review of research as well as an overview of current language theory.

Diederich, Paul B. *Measuring Growth in English.* Urbana, IL: NCTE, 1974.

Dixon, John. *Growth Through English.* Reading, England: National Association for the Teaching of English, 1967.
A report based on the Anglo-American Dartmouth Conference, 1966.

Dooling, D. James and R. Lachman. "Effects of Comprehension on Retention of Prose," *Journal of Experimental Psychology,* 88 (1971), pp. 216–222.

Dow, Ronald H. "The Writer's Laboratory—One Approach to Composition," *Arizona English Bulletin,* 16 (February, 1974), pp. 55–66.

Dowst, Kenneth. "The Epistemic Approach: Writing, Knowing, and Learning," *Eight Approaches to Teaching Composition.* (Eds.) Timothy R. Donovan and Ben W. McClelland, Urbana, IL: NCTE, 1980.
Demonstrates the epistemic approach to teaching writing, viewing language as a way of knowing and writing as a way of composing reality.

Edwards, V. K. *The West Indian Language Issue in British Schools: Challenges and Responses.* London: Routledge and Kegan Paul, 1979.

Eight Approaches to Teaching Composition. (Eds.) Timothy R. Donovan and Ben W. McClelland. Urbana, IL: NCTE, 1980.

Elbow, Peter. *Writing with Power: Techinques for Mastering the Writing Process.* NY: Oxford, 1981.
Directed at the writing process, including dealing with an audience, getting feedback, and thinking both creatively and critically.

_____ . *Writing Without Teachers.* NY: Oxford, 1973.
Describes a developmental process for writing and a method of learning to write without a teacher in which groups of interested writers work together, critiquing each other's work.

Emig, Janet. *The Composing Processes of Twelfth Graders.* NCTE Research Report No. 13. Urbana, IL: NCTE, 1971.
Emig based her understanding of how children write upon an observed process rather than a prescribed procedure grounded upon analysis of a finished product.

_____ . Writing as a Mode of Learning," *College Composition and Communication,* 28 (1977), pp. 122–128.
Suggests that writing enables interaction between thinking and language which promotes discovery of new knowledge.

_____ . *The Web of Meaning: Essays on Writing, Teaching, Learning, and Thinking.* Montclair, NJ: Boynton/Cook, 1983.
A collection of the author's essays written over the past twenty years.

English in the Eighties. Papers Given at the Third International Conference on The Teaching of English, Sydney, Australia, 1980. (Ed.) Robert D. Eagleson. Norwood: South Australia: The Australian Association for the Teaching of English, 1982. (Available from Boynton/Cook)

Exploring Speaking-Writing Relationships: Connections and Contrasts. (Eds.)
Barry Kroll and Roberta J. Vann. Urbana, IL: NCTE, 1981.
  A collection of essays exploring the relationship between speaking and writing from a variety of perspectives including business, media, EFL, hemispheric function, linguistics, reading, phenomenology, and development.

Evaluating Writing: Describing, Measuring, Judging. (Eds.) Charles R. Cooper
and Lee Odell. Urbana, IL: NCTE, 1977.
  An important collection of articles on evaluation of writing, including Richard Lloyd-Jones's influential explanation of primary trait scoring plus Cooper on holistic evaluation, Kellogg Hunt on syntactic structures, and Mary Beaven on "Individualized Goal Setting, Self-Evaluation, and Peer Evaluation."

Fader, Daniel. *The Naked Children.* NY: Macmillan, 1971.
  An account of Fader's attempt to continue the "English in Every Classroom" approach described in *Hooked on Books* in a Washington, DC ghetto school; it is also a telling recreation of the experience of education.

——————— , with James Duggins, Tom Finn, and Elton McNeil. *The New
  Hooked on Books.* NY: Berkeley, 1976.
  An expanded version of *Hooked on Books,* offering a context for teaching the program, expanding the section on writing, and adding essays on the practical environment and an updated reading list.

——————— . "On Nurturing the Individual Voice," *fforum* vol. 2, no. 1
  (Winter, 1981), pp. 53–54.
  Describes today's students and the importance of teaching them reading and writing at all levels of instruction.

Fawcett, Robin P. *Cognitive Linguistics and Social Interaction: Towards an
  Integrated Model of a Systemic Functional Grammar and the Other Components of a Communicating Mind.* Heidelberg: Julius Groos Verlag, 1980.

Flavell, J. H. *Cognitive Development.* Englewood Cliffs, NJ: Prentice-Hall, 1977.
  Flavell summarizes the Piagetian and information-processing views of the development of cognitive skills in children.

——————— . "Metacognitive Development," *Structural/Process Theories of
  Complex Human Behavior.* (Eds.) J. M. Scandura and C. J. Brainerd. The
  Netherlands: Sijhoff and Noordoff, 1978.

Flower, Linda and John R. Hayes. "The Cognition of Discovery: Defining a
  Rhetorical Problem," *College Composition and Communication,* 31 (1980),
  pp. 22–32.
  Views writing as a means of making, rather than discovering, meaning, and offers a model of the rhetorical problem in which the writing is an attempt to "solve" the problem.

——————— . "A Cognitive Process Theory of Writing," *College Composition
  and Communication,* 32 (December, 1981), pp. 365–387.

——————— . "Problem-Solving Strategies and the Writing Process," *College
  English,* 39 (1977), pp. 449–461.

Foucault, Michel. "Language to Infinity," *Language, Counter-memory Practice.*
  (Ed.) Donald F. Bouchard. Ithaca: Cornell University Press, 1977, pp. 53–67.
  Posits that each work of literature is a defense against the death of language, a continuous contribution to an endless work, the Library.

Freire, Paulo. *Education for Critical Consciousness.* Seabury Press, 1973.
  A radical conception of language in which "decoding" (construing letters) and "decodification" (interpreting meanings) are kept together from the start.

——————— . *Pedagogy of the Oppressed.* NY: Herder and Herder, 1970.
  Describes Freire's theories of teaching and learning.

The Future of Literacy. (Ed.) Robert Disch. Englewood Cliffs, NJ: Prentice-
Hall, 1973.

A useful collection of articles on four broad topics: the impact of literacy on nonliterate peoples and nations, the relationship between literacy and politics, literature and literacy, and literacy and the media.

Gerrard, Michael S. "Literacy, Testing, and the Core Curriculums in England," *The College Board Review,* 115 (Spring, 1980), pp. 24–27, 36.

General impressions of changes in education in England since the Bullock Report, including a report on the British approach to competency testing.

Goodman, Kenneth S., "Behind the Eye: What Happens in Reading," *Reading: Process and Program.* Urbana, IL: NCTE, 1970, pp. 3–30.

Presents a psycholinguistic view of language and reading: definitions, descriptions of processes, a model of reading, techniques and strategies, critical reading.

Gordon, William. *Synetics: The Development of Creative Capacity.* New York: Harper & Row, 1961.

Argues that "creative efficiency" can be increased by an understanding of psychological processes.

Graesser, Arthur C., Sallie E. Gordon, and John D. Sawyer. "Recognition Memory for Typical and Atypical Actions in Scripted Activities: Tests of a Script Pointer & Tag Hypothesis," *Journal of Verbal Learning and Verbal Behavior.* 18 (1979), pp. 319–332.

Graff, Harvey J. *The Literacy Myth: Literacy and Social Structure in the Nineteenth-Century City.* NY: Academic Press, 1979.

An important historical study of rates and usages of literacy in three 19th century Canadian cities: Hamilton, London, and Kingston, relating literacy to political and social trends.

Graves, Donald. *Balance the Basics: Let Them Write.* NY: The Ford Foundation, 1978.

Argues for teaching reading and writing together in the elementary school.

Gregory, Michael, and Susanne Carroll. *Language and Situation.* London: Routledge and Kegan Paul, 1978.

Gremmo, M. J. *Reading as Communication.* ERIC Ed 149 628.

Argues that language in scientific discourse tells what the writer is going to do or has done without disclosing intent.

Groff, Patrick. "The Effects of Talking on Writing," *English in Education,* 13 (1979), pp. 33–37.

Review of research on effects of oral language activities on writing improvement; concludes that writing is not improved by speech activities.

Guilford, J. P. "Creativity: Yesterday, Today, and Tomorrow," *Journal of Creative Behavior,* (1967), pp. 3–8.

Halliday, M. A. K., *Learning How to Mean: Explorations in the Development of Language.* London: Edward Arnold, 1975.

Adopts a functional view of language and explains language as "a system for making meanings" rather than for "generating structures."

_____ and Rugaiya Hasan. *Cohesion in English.* London: Longman, 1976.

A standard text on the analysis of specific features of written texts that are associated with organization patterns larger than the sentence.

Hargreaves, Davie. *Adult Literacy and Broadcasting: The BBC's Experience.* New York: Nichols, 1980.

Harpin, William. *The Second 'R': Writing Development in the Junior School.* London: George Allen and Unwin, 1976.

Explains research into the development of language abilities in children at three ages and attempts to understand differences; discusses implications of research results.

Harrington, Elbert. "A Modern Approach to Invention," *Quarterly Journal of Speech,* 48 (1962), p. 373–78.
   Attempts to ally invention and rhetoric to liberal education in general.
Heath, Shirley Brice. "The Function and Uses of Literacy," *Journal of Communication* 30:1 (Winter, 1980), pp. 123–133.
   Reports on a five year study of one community's reading and writing behavior and draws conclusions about the functions of literacy in society and the ways it may be obtained.
Hendrix, Richard. "The Status and Politics of Writing Instruction," *Writing: The Nature, Development, and Teaching of Written Communication.* Vol. 1. *Variation in Writing: Functional and Linguistic-Cultural Differences.* (Ed.) Marcia Farr Whiteman. Hillsdale, NJ: Lawrence Erlbaum, 1981.
   Argues that writing must be viewed in a social context before questions of improvement, testing, and quality can be answered and that educational policy as well as research and pedagogy will have to answer these questions.
The Humanities in American Life. Report of the Rockefeller Commission on the Humanities. Berkeley: University of California Press, 1980.
Hunt, Kellogg W. "A Synopsis of Clause-to-Sentence Length Factors," *English Journal,* (1965), pp. 300–309.
   Describes indexes of maturity in writing and defends the T-unit as a measure of syntactic fluency.
Iser, Wolfgang. *The Act of Reading: A Theory of Aesthetic Response.* Baltimore: The Johns Hopkins University Press, 1978.
Johnson, Marcia K., John D. Bransford, and Susan K. Solomon. "Memory for Tacit Implications of Sentences," *Journal of Experimental Psychology,* 98:1 (1973), pp. 203–205.
Judy, Stephen. *The ABCs of Literacy: A Guide for Parents and Educators.* NY: Oxford, 1980.
   An accessible book for both educators and members of the community. Argues that change in literacy instruction needs an overhaul of aims and an alteration of teaching conditions which must begin in the schools and the communities, and involve other disciplines.
Kermode, Frank. *The Genesis of Secrecy: On the Interpretation of Narrative.* Cambridge: Harvard University Press, 1979.
   Expanded versions of six lectures on approaches to general problems of interpretation, centering on Biblical narrative.
Kinneavy, James. "A Pluralistic Synthesis of Four Contemporary Models for Teaching Composition," *Reinventing the Rhetorical Tradition.* (Eds.) Aviva Freedman and Ian Pringle. Conway, AR: L & S Books, 1980.
   A review of the theories of Kinneavy, D'Angelo, Moffett, and Britton, and an attempt to synthesize them.
——————. *A Theory of Discourse.* Englewood Cliffs, NJ: Prentice-Hall, 1971.
   Draws on classical rhetoric, logic, linguistics, and literary theory to explore the aims of discourse and develops four types of discourse: expressive, literary, referential, and persuasive.
Kirby, Dan and Tom Liner. *Inside Out: Developmental Strategies for Teaching Writing.* Montclair, NJ: Boynton/Cook, 1981.
   "A book for teachers in middle school through college" showing how they can "nurture the rich linguistic resources their students bring to class."
Kitzhaber, Albert R. "Teaching English Composition in College," *Teaching Freshman Composition.* (Eds.) Gary Tate and Edward P. J. Corbett. NY: Oxford, 1967, pp. 3–24.

Koch, Carl and James M. Brazil. *Strategies for Teaching the Composition Process.*
Urbana, IL: NCTE, 1978.
Kroll, Barbara. "Learning and Acquisition: Two Paths to Writing," *English Education,* 11 (1979), pp. 83–90.
Demonstrates that good student writers make use of a writing "monitor" to help them assess the appropriateness of writing at "micro" and "macro" levels.
Kuhn, Thomas. *The Structure of Scientific Revolutions.* 2nd Edition. Chicago: University of Chicago Press, 1970.
Discusses the role of widely-accepted models or "paradigms" in preventing alternative perception and evaluation of data and ideas, with each shift in perspective causing a shift in the description of the paradigm.
Labov, William. "The Logic of Nonstandard English," *Linguistics and the Teaching of Standard English to Speakers of Other Languages or Dialects.* Monograph Series on Language and Linguistics No. 22, 1969.
A classic statement of the hidden yet crucial political forces that influence the way people speak and write.
_____ . "Objectivity and Commitment in Linguistic Science: The Case of the Black English Trial in Ann Arbor," *Language in Society,* 11:2 (1982).
Discussion of the King case in the context of studies of Black English and the emergence of influential blacks trained in anthropology and linguistics.
_____ . "The Transformation of Experience in Narrative Syntax," *Language in the Inner City.* (Ed.) William Labov. Philadelphia: University of Pennsylvania Press, 1972.
Describes similarities in structures of narratives told by a variety of people.
Langer, Susanne K. *Philosophy in a New Key: A Study in the Symbolism of Reason, Rite, and Art.* Cambridge, MA: Harvard University Press, 1942.
Argues that the brain constantly engages in a "process of symbolic transformation"; examines the logic of signs and symbols and "the significance of language, ritual, myth and music," and mentality itself.
Language and Literacy in Our Schools: Some Appraisals of the Bullock Report. (Ed.) Harold Rosen. London: University of London Institute Studies in Education, 1975.
Language and Social Context. (Ed.) Pier Giglioli. Harmondsworth, England: Penguin Books, 1972.
Essays by Bernstein, Labov, and others related to sociolinguistics and to cultural anthropology as it involves the function of language and speech in society.
Language as a Way of Knowing: A Book of Readings. (Ed.) Martin Nystrand. Toronto: Ontario Institute for Studies in Education, 1977.
Excellent collection of essays which illustrate the heuristic function of language.
The Language Connection: Writing and Reading Across the Curriculum. (Eds.) Toby Fulwiler and Art Young. Urbana, IL: NCTE, 1982.
Emphasizes writing as a means of learning and balances theory and practice directed at writing and reading across the curriculum.
A Language for Life: N. U. T's Commentary on the Bullock Report. London: National Union of Teachers, 1976.
Language Policies in Action. (Ed.) Mike Torbe. London: Ward Lock Educational, 1979
Reviews work of teachers to implement the policies formulated by the Bullock Commission.
Larson, Richard. "Discovery Through Questioning: A Plan for Teaching Rhetorical Invention," *Contemporary Rhetoric.* (Ed.) W. Ross Winterowd. NY: Harcourt Brace Jovanovich, 1975.

Attempts to create an accessible list of modern "topoi" in imitation of the classical model; Winterowd's introduction to the article provides a useful context.

Lauer, Janice. *Invention in Contemporary Rhetoric: Heuristic Procedures.* Unpublished doctoral dissertation, University of Michigan, 1967.

――――――. "Heuristics and Composition," *College Composition and Communication,* 21 (1970), pp. 397–404.

Argues for the study of heuristics in the teaching and research of composition; provides a lengthy "psychological bibliography" on the subject.

Lerner, J. W. *Children with Learning Disabilities.* Boston: Houghton Mifflin, 1981.

Lewis, C. S. *An Experiment in Criticism.* Cambridge, England: University Press, 1961.

This exploration of how we read (and misread) is suggestive of ways writing might be used in the literature classroom.

Literacy and Social Development in the West. (Ed.) Harvey J. Graff. Cambridge, England: University Press, 1981.

A collection of seminal historical researches into the relationship between literacy and social development.

Literacy for Life: The Demand for Reading and Writing. (Eds.) Richard W. Bailey and Robin Melanie Fosheim. NY: The Modern Language Association (forthcoming).

A collection of essays treating world literacy, the relationship of literacy to politics, the uses of literacy in vocations and professions, the problems of literacy in various educational settings, and the teaching of literacy.

Lockridge, Kenneth. *Literacy in Colonial New England.* NY: W. W. Norton, 1974.

An important historical study of the development of literacy in New England to 1800, with discussions about literacy and social development, literacy and education, and literacy and economic status.

Lonergan, Bernard J. F., S. J. *Insight: A Study of Human Understanding.* London: Longman, 1957.

Describes insight as the "supervening act of understanding" and deals with it as a heuristic activity and as knowledge.

Luria, A., "Speech Development and the Formation of Mental Processes," *A Handbook of Contemporary Soviet Psychology.* (Eds.) M. Cole and I. Maltzman. NY: Basic Books, 1969.

Marland, Michael. *Language Across the Curriculum: The Implementation of the Bullock Report in the Secondary School.* London: Heinemann Educational, 1977.

A book with chapters by various authors designed to be "a practical help to those in secondary schools developing their own 'language policy across the curriculum.' "

Macrorie, Ken. "The Circle of Implication," *College English,* 28 (March, 1967); reprinted in *Ideas for English 101: Teaching Writing in College.* (Eds.) Richard Ohmann and W. B. Coley. Urbana, IL: NCTE, 1975.

Describes how to be a sympathetic teacher-judge of student writing.

――――――. *Searching Writing.* Rochelle Park, NJ: Hayden, 1980.

Martin, Nancy. *The Martin Report: Case Studies from Government High Schools in Western Australia.* Education Dept. W.A., 1980.

――――――, Pat D'Arcy, Bryan Newton, and Robert Parker. *Writing and Learning Across the Curriculum, 11–16.* London: Ward Lock Educational, 1976.

Examines writing as a means of learning not only in English classes but in all other disciplines as well.

McKeon, Richard. "The Uses of Rhetoric in a Technological Age: Architectonic Productive Arts." *The Prospect of Rhetoric.* (Eds.) Lloyd Bitzer and Edwin Black. Englewood Cliffs, NJ: Prentice-Hall, 1971, pp. 44–63.
Provides an overview of classical and modern rhetoric with an emphasis on rhetoric as an art of doing.

Mehan, J. R. "TALE-SPIN, An Interactive Program That Writes Stories," *Proceedings from the Fifth International Joint Conference on Artificial Intelligence,* 1977, pp. 91–98.

Mellon, John. *Transformational Sentence-Combining: A Method for Enhancing the Development of Syntactic Fluency in English.* Champaign, IL: NCTE, 1969.

Miller, Carolyn R. "A Humanistic Rationale for Technical Writing," *College English,* 40 (1979), pp. 610–617.

Moffett, James. *Active Voice: A Writing Program Across the Curriculum.* Montclair, NJ: Boynton/Cook, 1981.
A program extending from elementary through college levels, emphasizing use of primary sources and the projects in subject areas. Rich in ideas for writing assignments and flexible for adaptation to different levels of student ability and maturity.

_____ . *Coming on Center: English Education in Evolution.* Montclair, NJ: Boynton/Cook, 1981.
A collection of Moffett's writings in the 1970's with connecting headnotes, analyzing forces at work on education and offering recommendations for teaching reading and writing after an assessment of current theories.

_____ . "Integrity in the Teaching of Writing," *Phi Delta Kappan,* 61 (December, 1979), pp. 276–279.
A theoretical statement including a taxonomy of writing activities from handwriting through revising inner speech.

_____ . *Teaching the Universe of Discourse.* Boston: Houghton Mifflin, 1968.
Suggests an outline of the student's intellectual growth, insists that the student be the center of the curriculum, and argues *against* teaching parts *as* parts and *for* a holistic approach.

_____ and Betty Jane Wagner. *Student-Centered Language Arts and Reading, K-13.* 2nd Edition. Boston: Houghton Mifflin, 1976.
A comprehensive account of Moffett's theories and a wealth of curricular activities organized according to his hierarchy of discourse and levels of abstraction.

Morris, C. W. *Signs, Language, and Behavior.* Englewood Cliffs, NJ: Prentice-Hall, 1946.
An early study of the significance of signs, applying semiotics to discourse, language, and behavior.

Murray, Donald M. *A Writer Teaches Writing: A Practical Method of Teaching Composition.* Boston: Houghton Mifflin, 1968.
A humane and sensible analysis of the relationship between student and teacher in a writing class, with very down-to-earth sections on techniques.

_____ . *Learning by Teaching: Selected Articles on Writing and Teaching.* Montclair, NJ: Boynton/Cook, 1982.

_____ and Donald Graves. "Revision: In the Writer's Workshop and in the Classroom," *Journal of Education,* Boston University School of Education, 162 (1980), pp. 38–56.

The Nature and Measurement of Competency in English. (Ed.) Charles R. Cooper, Urbana, IL: NCTE, 1981.
A collection of essays ranging broadly over the issues of measurement and assessment in English, including articles on competence in reading, media

competency, and the politics of minimum competency as well as an overview of the issues and articles on language competence and competence in writing.

New Essays in the Teaching of Literature. Proceedings of the Literature Commission, Third International Conference on the Teaching of English, Sydney, Australia, 1980. (Eds.) David Mallick, Peter Moss, and Ian Hansen. Norwood, South Australia: The Australian Association for the Teaching of English, 1982. (Available from Boynton/Cook)

Odell, Lee. "Piaget, Problem-Solving, and Composition," *College Composition and Communication,* 24 (1973), pp. 36–42.

——————. "The Process of Writing and the Process of Learning," *College Composition and Communication,* 31 (1980), pp. 42–50.

Argues that the conceptual activities students must go through vary with assignments across the curriculum and that teachers need to understand the process of learning as it relates to the process of writing.

Ohmann, Richard. "The Decline in Literacy Is a Fiction, If Not a Hoax," *The Chronicle of Higher Education,* October 25, 1976, p. 32.

Analyzes the evidence used to indicate a "literacy crisis" and suggests that the real literacy crisis is being ignored by the media while misleading data generate a false crisis.

——————. *English in America: A Radical View of the Profession.* NY: Oxford, 1976.

A broad description and condemnation of the complicity between academic institutions, particularly English departments in colleges and universities, and repressive mechanisms of capitalist society. It analyzes the general paradigms that govern the organization and content of composition texts that are frequently used in college courses.

Olson, David R. "Oral and Written Language and the Cognitive Processes of Children," *Journal of Communication,* 27 (Summer, 1977), pp. 10–26.

Claims that the ability to draw conclusions from stated premises is unique to "literate" thinking.

Ong, Walter J., S. J. *The Barbarian Within and Other Fugitive Essays and Studies.* NY: Macmillan, 1962.

A collection of essays on words, teaching and communication, and culture.

——————. "Beyond Objectivity: The Reader-Writer Transaction as an Altered State of Consciousness," *The CEA Critic,* 40 (November, 1977), pp. 6–13.

Claims that there is no one-way human communication. Text is merely an object until a human mind interacts with it.

——————. *Interfaces of the Word,* Ithaca: Cornell University Press, 1977.

A series of essays extending the thesis Father Ong posits in *Presence of the Word.*

——————. "Literacy and Orality in Our Times," *Profession '79.* NY: Modern Language Association, 1979.

Provides an overview of the relationship between literacy and orality in contemporary times.

——————. *Rhetoric, Romance, and Technology: Studies in the Interaction of Expression and Culture.* Ithaca, NY: Cornell University Press, 1971.

A history of rhetoric through the romantic period and into the age of technology.

——————. *Presence of the Word.* Minneapolis: University of Minnesota Press, 1967.

A cultural history of the West in terms of the organization of the human sensory system as it responds to the predominant media of each age.

——————. "The Writer's Audience is Always a Fiction," *Interfaces of the Word.* Ithaca, NY: Cornell University Press, 1977.

Discusses the differences between the concept of audience in speaking and that in writing and the kinds of masks or identities that speakers and writers wear.

Osgood, Charles, and Thomas Sebeok. *Psycholinguistics.* Bloomington, IN: Indiana University Press, 1969.
Explains how psycholinguistic theory accounts for the understanding of natural language and describes research that supports that model.

Oxenham, John. *Literacy: Writing, Reading, and Social Organization.* London: Routledge and Kegan Paul, 1980.
Concisely discusses contemporary problems of literacy in the world, the future of literacy, and its relationship to social and technological change.

Paris, S. G., and B. K. Lindauer. "The Development of Cognitive Skills During Childhood," *Handbook of Developmental Psychology.* (Ed.) B. Wolman. Englewood Cliffs, NJ: Prentice-Hall (forthcoming).

Parnes, Sidney J., Ruth B. Moller, Angelo M. Biondi. *Guide to Creative Action.* NY: Scribners, 1977.
Offers ways of "cultivating creative behavior" and readings on the subject.

Perelman, Chaim, and L. Olbrechts-Tyteca. *The New Rhetoric: A Treatise on Argumentation.* Notre Dame, IN: University of Notre Dame Press, 1969.
An attempt to revive the art of rhetoric with a thorough discussion of the framework, starting point, and techniques of argumentation.

Perl, Sondra, "Understanding Composing," *College Communication and Composition,* 31:4 (December, 1980), pp. 363–369.
Explains recursive features of composing, including retrospective structuring and argues against a linear model of the writing process.

_____ and Arthur Egendorf. "The Process of Creative Discovery: Theory, Research, and Implications for Teaching," *Linguistics, Stylistics, and the Teaching of Composition.* (Ed.) Donald McQuade. Akron: University of Akron, 1979, pp. 118–134.
Explains revision as a two-phase sequence in which the writer reviews a draft first, to clarify ideas, and second, to adjust writing for readers.

Petrosky, Anthony, "From Story to Essay: Reading and Writing," *College Composition and Communication,* 33 (February, 1982), pp. 19–37.
Posits the theory that comprehension is an act of composition.

Philosophy, Rhetoric, and Argumentation. (Eds.) Maurice Nathanson and Henry W. Johnstone, Jr. University Park: Pennsylvania State University Press, 1965.
A collection of essays intended to argue that philosophy, rhetoric, and argumentation are interdependent.

Piaget, Jean. *Language and Thought of the Child.* Trans. M. Gabain. London: Routledge and Kegan Paul, 1959.
Analysis of research into the cognitive processes underlying the acquisition of language. Introduces the substance of Piaget's theory of learning and his research method.

_____. *Psychology and Epistemology: Towards a Theory of Knowing.* NY: Viking, 1971.
Attempts to link theories of cognition with psychoanalytic thought, and argues for a recognition of the personal psychological bases of thought.

Piaget in the Classroom. (Eds.) Milton Schwebel and Jane Raph. NY: Basic Books, 1973.
A collection of essays explaining and applying Piaget's theories of development, including a section on implications for open classrooms.

Pike, Kenneth L. *Language in Relation to a Unified Theory of the Structure of Human Behavior.* 2nd Ed. The Hague: Mouton, 1971.

A technical, updated elaboration of Pike's tagmemic theory.

Plato. "Phaedrus," *The Collected Dialogues.* (Eds.) Edith Hamilton and Huntington Cairns. Princeton, NJ: Princeton University Press, 1961, pp. 229–308.

Plato criticizes "handbook" and "sophistic" rhetoric; calls for the formulation of a philosophical rhetoric, and worries about the effects of literacy on the fabric of society.

Polanyi, Michael. *Knowing and Being.* (Ed.) Marjorie Grene. London: Routledge and Kegan Paul, 1969.

This collection of Polanyi's essays includes four chapters on tacit knowing; the introduction by the editor ties the essays to Polanyi's other works.

——————. *Personal Knowledge: Towards a Post-Critical Philosophy.* Chicago: University of Chicago Press, 1958.

An inquiry "into the nature and justification of scientific knowledge" ranging into larger questions of knowing and arguing for "personal participation" of the knower in all acts of understanding. Describes "personal knowledge" as a fusion of the personal and the objective.

Postman, Neil. *Teaching as a Conserving Activity.* NY: Delacorte, 1979.

Argues that education must conserve tradition in an age of innovation and innovate in an age of tradition, and argues against the changes in schools in the last decade.

Psycholinguistics and Reading. (Ed.) Frank Smith. NY: Holt, Rinehart and Winston, 1973.

Articles include: "Psycholinguistic Universals in the Reading Process," "Analysis of Oral Reading Miscues," "Illiteracy in the Ghetto," "Learning to Read Without a Teacher," and "Reading, Writing, and Phonology."

Reactions to Ann Arbor: Vernacular Black English and Education. (Ed.) Marcia Farr Whiteman. Arlington: Center for Applied Linguistics, 1980.

Reinventing the Rhetorical Tradition. (Eds.) Aviva Freedman and Ian Pringle. Canadian Council of Teachers of English. Conway, AR: L & S Books, 1980. (Available from NCTE)

Evolving from the 1979 CCTE Conference on "Learning to Write," this collection gathers together papers by nineteen participants, including articles by Emig, Britton, Kinneavy, Murray, Berthoff, Corbett, Winterowd, Butturff, Sommers, and others.

Research on Composing: Points of Departure. (Eds.) Charles R. Cooper and Lee Odell. Urbana, IL: NCTE, 1978.

An anthology on developments in composition theory and pedagogy and related fields with essays on discourse theory, the functions of writing, revision, the writing of young children, "Hand, Eye, and Brain," cognitive-developmental psychology, and invention.

Richards, I. A. *Interpretation in Teaching.* London: Routledge and Kegan Paul, 1938.

Theorizes on the nature of rhetoric, grammar, and logic, and argues that the aim of education and learning is "an increasing organic interanimation of meanings" and "the biologic growth of the mind."

——————. *Practical Criticism: A Study of Literary Judgment.* NY: Harcourt, Brace, 1929.

Extended criticism of thirteen poems and a lengthy discussion of its implications.

——————. *The Philosophy of Rhetoric.* London: Oxford University Press, 1936.

An analysis of the interaction of words in context and the ways in which a "continual synthesis of meaning" produces misunderstanding as well as complexity of meaning in discussion and texts.

Rogers, Carl R. *On Becoming A Person: A Therapist's View of Psychotherapy.* Boston: Houghton Mifflin, 1961.

A collection of Rogers' articles arranged around a theme moving "from the highly personal to the larger social significance."

Rose, Michael Anthony. *The Cognitive Dimension of Writer's Block: An Examination of University Students.* Unpublished doctoral dissertation, University of California at Los Angeles, 1980.

Rosenblatt, Louise. "Towards a Transactional Theory of Reading," *Journal of Reading Behaviours,* Vol. 1, 1969.

Argues that the reader's experience of literature, far from being a passive process, is a form of intense personal activity.

Rouse, John. *The Completed Gesture.* NY: Skyline Books, 1978. (Available from NCTE)

Essays on "myth, character, and education" suggestive of ways in which storytelling allows students to reclaim imagination as a power of mind.

Rumelhart, D. E. and A. Ortony. "A Representation of Knowledge in Memory," *Schooling and the Acquisition of Knowledge.* (Eds.) R. C. Anderson, R. J. Spiro, & W. E. Montague. Hillsdale, NJ: Lawrence Erlbaum, 1977.

Said, Edward. *Beginnings: Intention and Method.* Baltimore: Johns Hopkins University Press, 1978.

Sapir, Edward. *Culture, Language and Personality.* Berkeley: University of California Press, 1961.

Schank, R. and R. Abelson. *Scripts, Plans, Goals, and Understanding: An Inquiry into Human Knowledge Structures.* Hillsdale, NJ: Lawrence Erlbaum, 1977.

Scheffler, Judith A. "Composition with Content: An Interdisciplinary Approach," *College Composition and Communication,* 31 (1980), pp. 51–57.

Explains the Freshman Interdisciplinary Studies Program at Temple University.

Schools Council Project: Writing Across the Curriculum. London: Ward Lock Educational, 1976. (Available from Boynton/Cook)

Six pamphlets dealing with a variety of topics integral to establishing writing-across-the-curriculum projects.

Schor, Sandra. "Style Through Control: The Pleasures of the Beginning Writer," *Linguistics, Stylistics, and the Teaching of Composition.* (Ed.) Donald McQuade. Akron: University of Akron, 1979, pp. 72–80.

Argues that "style" has no place in the composition class; and that teachers must emphasize "control" instead.

Scott, Robert L. "On Viewing Rhetoric as Epistemic," *Central States Speech Journal,* 18:1 (February, 1967), pp. 9–17.

Argues that rhetoric is a way of knowing, not merely argumentation of prior knowledge.

Scribner, Sylvia and Michael Cole. *The Psychology of Literacy.* Cambridge, MA: Harvard University Press, 1981.

Reports on an empirical study of literacy conducted by the authors.

Shaughnessy, Mina. *Errors and Expectations: A Guide for the Teacher of Basic Writing.* NY: Osford, 1977.

An indispensable book for the teacher of basic writing and a valuable resource for all writing teachers.

Simon, Sidney B., Leland W. Howe, and Howard Kirschenbaum. *Values Clarification: A Handbook of Practical Strategies for Teachers and Students.* NY: Hart, 1972.

Sledd, James. "Review of Black English and the Education of Black Children and Youth and Reactions to Ann Arbor," *English World-Wide: A Journal of Varieties of English* (forthcoming).

Critical review of the King case as argued in court and as subsequently interpreted, concluding that it is "at best an inconclusive skirmish and at worst
confused defeat."

Smith, Frank. *Comprehension and Learning: A Conceptual Framework for
Teachers.* NY: Holt, Rinehart and Winston, 1975.
Draws on information-processing theory and psycholinguistics to discuss
the differences and relationship between comprehension and learning and the
ways children in the classroom learn and are discouraged from learning.
—————— . "The Relations Between Spoken and Written Language,"
Foundations of Language Development: A Multidisciplinary Approach.
Vol. 2. (Eds.) Lenneberg and Lenneberg. NY: Academic Press, 1975.
An essay discussing selected key points in his application of psycholinguistic
theory and information processing theory to the understanding of written lan-
guage.
—————— . *Understanding Reading.* NY: Holt, Rinehart and Winston, 1971.
Smith's application of psycholinguistic theory and information processing
theory to the understanding of written language.

Snell, Bruno. "The Forging of a Language for Science in Ancient Greece,"
Classical Journal, 56:2 (November 1960), pp. 50–60.
Discusses the effect on language of the development of scientific terminology
in Ancient Greece.

Sokolov, A. "Studies of the Speech Mechanisms of Thinking," *A Handbook of
Contemporary Soviet Psychology.* (Eds.) M. Cole and I. Maltzman. NY:
Basic Books, 1969.

Stalker, James C. "Written Language as a Dialect of English," *College Composition and Communication,* 24 (1974), pp. 46–49.

Sternglass, Marilyn. "Composition Teacher as Reading Teacher," *College Composition and Communication,* 27 (December, 1976), pp. 378–382.
Discusses the need to teach students how to read the sentences that sentence
combining and generative rhetoric would have them write.

Stibbs, Andrew. *Assessing Children's Language: Guidelines for Teachers.* London:
Ward Lock Educational, 1979. (Available from Boynton/Cook)
Discusses the principles of assessing language and evaluates the testing and
examining now being practiced in England with case histories of children's
language use.

Stotsky, Sandra. "A Review of Research on the Relationship Between Reading
and Writing: Directions for Further Research." Paper Presented at the Annual
Meeting of the National Council of Teachers of English, November, 1981, and
at the Annual Meeting of the International Reading Association, April, 1982.
—————— . "Types of Lexical Cohesion in Expository Essay Writing: Implications for Teaching the Vocabulary of Academic Discourse," *College Composition and Communication* (forthcoming).
A critique and revision of Halliday and Hasan's scheme for analyzing lexical
cohesion, together with a lengthy discussion of the implications for teaching
reading and assessing growth in writing.

Studies in Discourse Analysis. (Eds.) Malcolm Coulthard and Martin Montgomery,
London: Routledge and Kegan Paul, 1981.
A theoretical introduction to verbal interaction.

Teaching Composition: Ten Bibliographic Essays. (Ed.) Gary Tate. Fort Worth:
Texas Christian University Press, 1976.
An indispensable research tool, including essays by top scholars on research.

Teaching for Literacy: Reflections on the Bullock Report. (Eds.) Frances R. A.
Davis and Robert P. Parker, Jr. London: Ward Lock Educational, 1978.
Sixteen essays by British and American educators on the recommendations
of the Bullock report.

The Teaching of Technical Writing. (Eds.) Donald A. Cunningham and Herman A. Estrin. Urbana, NCTE, 1975.

A collection of articles, divided in sub-categories which define technical writing, discuss curriculum and students needs, offer a wealth of teaching ideas, and even treat technical writing as an art.

"The Teaching of Writing in Great Britain," *English Journal,* 67.8 (November, 1978) pp. 49–67.

A collection of four articles explaining some of the ideas of the British Writing Across the Curriculum Project and their implications for American teachers.

Tierney, Robert J., J. LaZansky, T. Raphael, and P. Cohen. "Authors' Intentions and Readers' Interpretations," *Understanding Readers' Understanding: Bridging Theory and Practice.* (Eds.) R. J. Tierney, P. Anders, and J. Mitchell. Hillsdale, NJ: Lawrence Erlbaum (forthcoming).

Torrance, E. Paul. *Guiding Creative Talent.* Englewood Cliffs, NJ: Prentice-Hall, 1962.

Torbe, Mike. *Language Across the Curriculum: Guidelines for Schools.* London: Ward Lock Educational, 1976.

This brief pamphlet suggests ways in which schools may choose to implement the recommendation of the Bullock Report that "every secondary school should develop a policy for language across the curriculum."

_____ and R. Protherough. *Classroom Encounters: Language and English Teaching.* London: Ward Lock Educational, 1976.

Vygotsky, Lev. *Mind in Society: The Development of Higher Psychological Processes.* Cambridge, MA: Harvard University Press, 1978.

A collection of Vygotsky's writings on the development of perception, attention, memory, language, and play, and some implications for education.

_____. *Thought and Language.* Cambridge: MIT Press, 1962.

Vygotsky explores the intersection of thought and language by analyzing the dynamic nature of children's understanding of word meaning.

Watson, Sam. "Breakfast in the Tacit Tradition," *Pretext,* 2 (1981), pp. 9–31.

White, James B. *The Legal Imagination.* Boston: Little, Brown, 1973.

Williams, Raymond. *Marxism and Literature.* Oxford: University Press, 1971.

Williams, J. T. *Learning to Write or Writing to Learn?* London: The National Foundation for Educational Research, 1977.

A sharply worded attack on the Bullock Report and on the recommendations of the Schools Council for a program of writing across the curriculum.

Young, Richard E., Alton L. Becker, and Kenneth L. Pike. *Rhetoric: Discovery and Change.* NY: Harcourt Brace and World, 1970.

Draws on tagmemic theory to interpret rhetoric as a process of discovery and of choosing options to effect audience change; emphasizes a heuristic to promote discovery as well as a series of chapters on the relationship between writer and reader.

Zorn, Jeffrey L. "Black English and the King Decision," *College English,* 44 (1982), pp. 314–320.

Review of Smitherman's volume on the King case, calling it "a sprawling, uneven, tremendously valuable document, worthy of very wide dissemination and very close scrutiny."